D0099298

# HOW

# JUDAISM

# BECAME AN

# AMERICAN

# RELIGION

# THE

# CHOSEN

# WARS

## STEVEN R. WEISMAN

SIMON & SCHUSTER

New York   London   Toronto   Sydney   New Delhi

Simon & Schuster
1230 Avenue of the Americas
New York, NY 10020

First Simon & Schuster hardcover edition August 2018

SIMON & SCHUSTER and colophon are registered trademarks of Simon & Schuster, Inc.

For information about special discounts for bulk purchases,
please contact Simon & Schuster Special Sales at 1-866-506-1949
or business@simonandschuster.com.

The Simon & Schuster Speakers Bureau can bring authors to your live event.
For more information or to book an event, contact the
Simon & Schuster Speakers Bureau at 1-866-248-3049
or visit our website at www.simonspeakers.com.

*Interior design by Ruth Lee-Mui*
*Illustration by Tom McKeveny*

Manufactured in the United States of America

1   3   5   7   9   10   8   6   4   2

Library of Congress Cataloging-in-Publication Data

Names: Weisman, Steven R., author.
Title: The chosen wars : how Judaism became an American religion / Steven R. Weisman.
Description: New York : Simon & Schuster, [2018] | Includes bibliographical references and index.
Identifiers: LCCN 2017059402 (print) | LCCN 2017058478 (ebook) | ISBN 9781416573265
(hardcover : alk. paper) | ISBN 9781416573272 (trade pbk. : alk. paper) |
ISBN 9781416578994 (ebook)
Subjects: LCSH: Judaism—United States—History—18th century. | Judaism—United States—
History—19th century.
Classification: LCC BM205 .W45 2018 (ebook) | LCC BM205 (print) | DDC 296.0973—dc23

LC record available at https://lccn.loc.gov/2017059402

ISBN 978-1-4165-7326-5
ISBN 978-1-4165-7899-4 (ebook)

*For Elisabeth*

# Contents

# Timeline

**Twelfth century:** Maimonides writes "Guide for the Perplexed."

**1492:** Spanish Inquisition, Jews expelled from Spain and later Portugal; Columbus "discovers" America, probably with Jews aboard.

**1517:** Martin Luther posts 95 Theses, starts Protestant revolution.

**1543:** Copernicus publishes heliocentric model of Earth revolving around sun.

**1563:** Joseph Caro organizes rabbinical teachings into *Shulchan Aruch* (The Set Table).

**1654:** First Jews arrive as a group on American shores (New Amsterdam) aboard the *Ste. Catherine*, establish Shearith Israel in New York.

**1656:** Spinoza excommunicated in Netherlands.

**1664:** British seize New York from Dutch.

**1679:** Synagogue in Prague installs an organ.

**1695:** First Jews in South Carolina.

**1720:** Ashkenazim become majority of Jews in New York.

**1730s–40s:** First Great Awakening, pressure on Jews to convert.

**1740:** Jews granted naturalization rights in colonies.

**1749:** Kahal Kadosh Beth Elohim established in Charleston.

**1768:** Gershom Mendes Seixas elected spiritual leader of Shearith Israel in New York.

**1776:** American Revolution, British capture New York; Seixas flees the city.

**1783:** Moses Mendelssohn publishes *Jerusalem* in Berlin.

**1790:** Washington's letter to the Jews of Newport, Rhode Island.

**1790:** Shearith Israel establishes "bill of rights" for Congregation.

**1791:** Jews granted citizenship in France.

**1795:** First Ashkenazi synagogue in America (Rodeph Shalom) in Philadelphia.

**1800:** Charleston has largest Jewish community in the United States: five hundred people.

**1800 and after:** The Second Great Awakening.

**1810:** Seesen Temple in Germany becomes first "Reform" synagogue.

**1818:** Hamburg Temple installs an organ.

**1819:** Society for the Culture and Science of Judaism established in Germany.

**1819:** Rebecca Gratz establishes Female Hebrew Benevolent Society in Philadelphia.

**1819:** Hep-hep riots in Germany.

**1824:** Isaac Leeser emigrates to America at age 18.

**1824:** Dissenters at Beth Elohim create "Reformed Society" in Charleston, declaring "this country is our Palestine."

**1825:** B'nai Jeshurun (Ashkenazi) breaks away from Shearith Israel, second synagogue in New York City.

**1825:** Mixed choir introduced in Mikveh Israel in Philadelphia, Mordecai Manuel Noah seeks Jewish "refuge" on Niagara River.

**1826:** Maryland "Jew Bill" adopted and grants Jews full rights.

**1830:** German migration to the United States surges.

**1830:** *Principles of Geology* by Charles Lyell posits that earth is hundreds of millions of years old; Leeser delivers first sermon in English at Mikveh Israel in Philadelphia.

**1836:** Benjamin Silliman says six-thousand-year-old Earth should not be taken literally.

**1837:** Joseph Seligman arrives in the United States.

**1838:** K. K. Beth Elohim synagogue destroyed by fire in Charleston; the first Jewish Sunday school established in Philadelphia.

**1840:** There are fifteen thousand Jews in the United States, up from three thousand a decade earlier.

**1840:** Abraham Rice first ordained rabbi to settle in the United States.

**1840:** Damascus affair; thirteen Jews accused of murdering a priest.

**1840s:** The first rabbis (at least eleven) come to America from Germany. There are eighteen formally organized congregations in the United States and a proliferation of synagogues in major cities.

**1841:** Beth Elohim in Charleston reopens with organ.

**1843:** The lawsuit over an organ goes to court in Charleston.

**1842:** New York City forbids religious instruction in schools.

**1842:** Har Sinai Verein in Baltimore, first Reform congregation in America, adopts Hamburg prayer book.

**1843:** B'nai B'rith established; *The Occident* started by Leeser.

**1846:** Isaac Mayer Wise arrives in America, settles later in Albany; Rabbi Max Lilienthal tries to launch beit din.

**1846:** Court of Appeals in South Carolina upholds Beth Elohim's right to install an organ.

**1847:** Wise and Leeser meet in Albany; Wise first proposes *Minhag America* as prayer book.

**1848:** German and French uprisings, Jews flee in larger numbers.

**1849:** *The Asmonean* is founded by Robert Lyon; Rabbi Morris Raphall arrives in America; Wise renews his contract in Albany; Wise's daughter dies.

**1850:** Wise attends debate in South Carolina, later dismissed at Beth El in Albany.

**1851:** Wise establishes mixed seating in Albany.

**1851:** Edward Hitchcock's *The Religion of Geology and Its Related Science* is published.

**1852:** Jews from Lithuania and Poland establish first Eastern European Orthodox synagogue in New York.

**1853:** Heinrich Graetz publishes the first volume of *History of the Jews*; Oheb Shalom conservative synagogue is founded in Baltimore.

**1854:** The Young Men's Hebrew Association (YMHA) started in Baltimore; there are seven religious schools in the United States.

**1854:** Wise joins B'nai Yeshurun as rabbi, starts the *Israelite*.

**1854:** Wise moves to Cincinnati; mixed seating at Temple Emanu-El in New York; Wise publishes *A History of Israelitish Nation*.

**1855:** There are now seventy-six congregations in the United States.

**1855:** Merzbacher prayer book at Temple Emanu-El; family pews at Emanu-El.

**1855:** Cleveland rabbinical conference adopts the Talmud as legally binding; both Wise and Leeser are criticized from opposite ends of spectrum.

**1855:** David Einhorn becomes rabbi at Har Sinai in Baltimore.

**1857:** Wise introduces *Minhag America* prayer book; Samuel Adler succeeds at Temple Emanu-El.

**1858:** Mortara affair; seizure of "baptized" Jew in Bologna provokes controversy.

**1858:** Sinai "Temple" in Chicago.

**1859:** Charles Darwin's *On the Origin of Species* is published.

**1860:** There are 160 organized Jewish communities in thirty-one states; a quarter of those communities are in New York City.

**1861:** Jewish Reform Society established in Chicago.

**1861:** President Abraham Lincoln takes office; Civil War begins; 150,000 Jews in America, 25,000 in the South. Rabbi Raphall's speech on National Fast Day defends slavery, is rebutted by Heilprin and Einhorn.

**1863:** Ulysses S. Grant's General Order No. 11 bars Jews from certain occupied areas.

**1865:** Lincoln's assassination is mourned by Jews.

**1866:** Friday evening services at a fixed time started by Wise in Cincinnati; dedication of Plum Street Temple.

**1867:** Free Religious Association is founded with Wise and Lilienthal in attendance.

**1868:** Death of Isaac Leeser.

**1869:** Philadelphia conference, disagreement between Wise and Einhorn.

**1870:** Of 152 synagogues in America, more than thirty have organs.

**1871:** Cincinnati rabbinical conference; Wise proposes changes in Yom Kippur.

**1873:** The Union of American Hebrew Congregations is established.

**1875:** Hebrew Union College opens.

**1876:** Adas Israel splits from Washington Hebrew over organ installation; Felix Adler starts the Society for Ethical Culture in New York City.

**1877:** There are 277 congregations and 250,000 Jews in the United States.

**1877:** Rutherford B. Hayes elected president; Reconstruction ends. Joseph Seligman excluded from Grand Union Hotel in Saratoga Springs, New York.

**1879:** Traditionalists meet in Philadelphia, revive Hanukkah; *The American Hebrew* starts publishing.

**1881:** Czar Alexander II of Russia is murdered, unleashing pogroms; two million Jews immigrate to the United States in the ensuing decades.

**1883:** Trefa Banquet.

**1885:** Competing sermons between Rabbis Kaufmann Kohler and Alexander Kohut.

**1885:** The Pittsburgh Platform adopted, watershed for "Classical Reform."

**1886:** Jewish Theological Seminary founded by dissenting traditionalist New York rabbis.

**1888:** The Jewish Publication Society is reestablished.

**1889:** The Central Conference of American Rabbis is founded.

**1892:** The *Union Prayer Book* is published.

**1897:** The First Zionist Congress meets in Basel, Switzerland; the Central Conference of American Rabbis (CCAR) opposes establishing a Jewish state.

**1902:** The Union of Orthodox Rabbis is founded; Solomon Schechter becomes chancellor of Jewish Theological Seminary.

**1903:** Rabbi Kohler takes over Hebrew Union College.

# Glossary

**Adjunta:** synagogue trustees.

**Adonai:** a Hebrew name for God, spoken in place of YHWH, often translated as "the Lord."

**Ashkenazi (plural Ashkenazim):** Jews with roots in German-speaking areas of Europe.

**BCE:** Before the Common Era, used widely in place of BC (Before Christ). CE (Common Era) refers to the period after the birth of Jesus.

**Bar and Bat Mitzvah (Son/Daughter of the Commandments):** the ceremony of admitting a Jewish boy or girl into adulthood, signaled by reading the Torah.

**Beit Din:** rabbinical court.

**Bima:** the raised stage from which the Torah is read during services.

**B'nai B'rith (Sons of the Covenant):** the leading Jewish fraternal and service organization in the United States in the nineteenth century, established in 1843.

**Common Era (CE):** alternate term referring to the period after Jesus Christ, or AD (Anno Domini). BCE (Before the Common Era) is the equivalent of BC (Before Christ).

**Converso:** a Jew forced to convert, or converted voluntarily to Christianity, in the era of the Spanish Inquisition. Jews who practiced their religion covertly were called by the despised name *marranos,* or pigs.

**Diaspora:** Jews living outside the land of Israel. (*See also* Galut.)

**Elohim:** Hebrew name for God, plural of El.

**Galut:** Hebrew word for forced exile of Jews.

**Haftarah:** reading from the Prophets, following the reading from the Torah, during Sabbath services.

**Halakhah:** The body of ancient traditional Jewish law. *See also* Oral Law.

**Hanukkah:** Jewish holiday celebrating the rededication of the Temple in Jerusalem in 165 BCE, marked by lighting eight candles on successive days.

**Hasidism:** the fervently pietistic and mystical movement among Jews of Eastern Europe that spread in the eighteenth century.

**Haskalah:** the Jewish enlightenment movement in eighteenth- and nineteenth-century Germany.

**Hazan:** the leader who chants prayers at religious services; also called cantor.

**Herem:** excommunication or censure for violation of Jewish laws.

**Israel:** biblical name for the Jewish people as descendants of the patriarch Jacob, whose name was changed to reflect his having wrestled with God.

**Kaddish:** the prayer mourning the dead.

**Kahal Kadosh (Holy Community):** often abbreviated as KK before the name of a synagogue congregation.

**Kippah:** Hebrew word for head covering, often a skullcap. *See* yarmulke.

**Kol Nidre (All Vows):** the prayer recited or sung at Yom Kippur (the Day of Atonement) annulling vows made before God.

**Kosher:** the term for what is acceptable to eat under strict Jewish dietary laws.

**Landsmannshëftn:** hometown immigrant association.

**Maskilim:** adherents of Haskalah, the Jewish enlightenment movement in Germany.

**Mehitzah:** partition separating men and women in the synagogue.

**Messiah:** the term referring to a future Jewish king from the Davidic line whose arrival would usher in a period of redemption for the Jews.

**Mezuzah:** small handwritten scroll containing passages from Deuteronomy affixed in an amulet to the doorpost of one's house.

**Mikveh:** ritual bath.

**Minhag:** Hebrew for custom or rite.

**Minyan:** quorum of males required for prayer service.

**Mitzvah (plural:** mitzvot): Hebrew for "commandment," as in the 613 positive and negative commandments of ancient Jewish reckoning, also commonly used to refer to a good deed.

**Mohel:** person who performs a ritual circumcision.

**Oral Law:** laws, rules, interpretations, and commentaries not written in the Torah but expounded by ancient rabbis and regarded by traditionalists as having divine authority because they are based in commandments from God to Moses and transmitted orally from generation to generation until finally written down before the Common Era and in the centuries afterward.

**Parnas:** president of a congregation.

**Pharisees:** a sect or school of thought in the period before and after the Common Era defending the divine status of the Oral Law and the Talmud. Pharisees gained eventual dominance over the Sadducees, who questioned the authority of these laws. *See also* rabbinic Judaism.

**Piyyutim (singular:** piyyut): Jewish liturgical poems.

**Rabbi:** teacher, spiritual leader of a congregation.

**Rabbinic Judaism:** the term for traditional Judaism following the rules of the Talmud as codified and written down by rabbis in the years before the Common Era and the centuries afterward. *See also* Oral Law, Pharisees.

**Rebbe:** Hasidic term for grand rabbi.

**Rosh Hashanah:** Jewish New Year.

**Sadducees:** the ancient sect that opposed the authority of the corpus of Oral Laws embraced by the rival sect known as Pharisees.

**Sephardi (plural:** Sephardim; adjective: Sephardic): Jews tracing their roots to Spain and Portugal but also the places to which they fled from these areas, including France, the Netherlands, North Africa, and the Middle East.

**Shammash:** the person who carries out largely secular duties at a synagogue, i.e., sexton.

**Shema:** the central expression of Jewish belief in one God, from a verse in Deuteronomy.

**Shivah:** mourning period following the death of a family member.

**Shofar:** ram's horn sounded in the season of the New Year.

**Shohet:** ritual slaughterer of kosher meat.

**Shul:** Yiddish word for synagogue congregation.

**Siddur:** prayer book.

**Tallith:** prayer shawl.

**Talmud:** the basic text of traditional Jewish law, custom, and practice compiled by rabbis just before the Common Era and in the five centuries afterward. It consists of the Mishnah, a compendium of laws that believers say were given orally by God to Moses, and the Gemara, or commentaries on and interpretations of these laws. *See also* Oral Law.

**Tefillin:** translated as "phylacteries," consisting of two boxes containing Scripture and leather straps bound to the forehead and left arm during prayer.

**Torah:** the five books of Moses, or the first five books of the Hebrew Bible, also called the Pentateuch.

**Trefa:** forbidden food under Jewish dietary law.

**Wissenschaft des Judentums (Scientific Study of Judaism):** Movement among Jewish intellectuals and scholars in the nineteenth century, applying modern methods of research, analysis, and criticism to Judaism and its texts.

**Yarmulke:** Yiddish word for skullcap. In Hebrew: kippah.

**YHWH:** the name of the God of the Israelites, represented by four Hebrew consonants (i.e., the tetragrammaton), pronounced by some as Yahweh or Jehovah. Because of its sanctity, the name ceased to be pronounced by Jews in early post-biblical times. *See also* Adonai

**Yom Kippur:** the Day of Atonement that concludes the ten days of repentance following Rosh Hashanah.

*Introduction*

# JEWS IN AMERICA:
# A PART BUT APART

Hundreds of guests gathered at the magnificent Plum Street Synagogue in downtown Cincinnati for a joyful celebration on a warm and rainy afternoon on July 11, 1883. The occasion was the graduation of four American-trained rabbis at the new Hebrew Union College, the first ordination of Jewish clergy on American soil. Participants from across the country came to salute an event they felt certain was marking another significant step in the arrival of American Jews as equals to Christians in the Gilded Age. From the afternoon ceremony at the temple, a grand edifice of Moorish design crowned by minarets and illuminated inside by chandeliers and candelabras, the guests repaired to a funicular railway ascending Mount Adams, two miles away. They then crowded into Highland House, a banquet hall near the Cincinnati Observatory, overlooking the Ohio River, for a gala dinner and more festivities.

It was there that an extraordinary debacle took place.

The furor was provoked by the menu. For reasons that remain unclear, the caterer decided to serve crabs, shrimp, clams, and frogs legs to the guests, an egregious violation of kosher laws. Traditionalist rabbis for whom shellfish and amphibians were considered *trefa*, or forbidden by the Torah's laws, were insulted by the mere sight of such a sacrilege at a Jewish occasion. Some of the rabbis stormed out, according to an eyewitness, and the event turned into a faux pas heard round the Jewish world. The controversy marked another step toward the unraveling of Jewish unity in the United States. And it would be known historically in Jewish circles as the Trefa Banquet.

The gossipy outrage was later ridiculed as overwrought by Rabbi Isaac Mayer Wise, founder of Hebrew Union College. He called it much ado about "stomach Judaism." But the star-crossed banquet sounded a call to battle among traditionalists and helped drive American Jews apart into disputing (and disputatious) factions. Two years after the banquet, a convocation of rabbis declared a new set of principles for American Judaism in Pittsburgh, effectively establishing the Reform movement. In the following decades, the opposing factions coalesced into Reform, Conservative, and Orthodox Judaism.

These developments, in turn, marked the emergence of an American Judaism, more than 200 years after the first Jews landed on American shores. Even the splitting of American Judaism into three main branches was a singularly American phenomenon. In the 1830s, Alexis de Tocqueville had observed the religious character of the American people, but also their propensity—so different from his native country's Catholicism—to find their fragmented way through a diverse variety of practices and beliefs. "There is no country in the whole world in which the Christian religion retains a greater influence over the souls of men than in America," Tocqueville wrote, while noting the innumerable Christian denominations defining morality as a religious and not just a social tenet.[1] In the late nineteenth century, the Jews were showing that their fissiparous tendencies were no different from those of many Christian believers. Like the proliferating Baptists, Southern Baptists, Episcopalians, Unitarians, Presbyterians, Methodists, Quakers, Lutherans, Mennonites, Millenarians, Second Adventists, the Church of Jesus Christ of Latter-Day Saints, Evangelicals, among others, Jews of traditional and nontraditional leanings were seeking their own distinct paths to God.

In 1880, the Jewish community in America was still small, though far-flung, barely more than a quarter of a million souls. Soon after that year, a flood of more than two million Jews, many of them Yiddish speaking, would be washing up on American shores over the next four decades. The new immigrants were escaping a wave of savage pogroms in Russia and Eastern Europe. They made a decisive impact on Jewish culture and belief, engulfing an established population that responded with mixed feelings about their arrival, especially in New York and other large population centers. They were also to become the forebears of most American Jews today. But when these new Jews arrived, they inherited and over time largely accepted the legacy of Americanized Judaism created over the previous two centuries. That legacy had altered Jewish doctrines, teachings, and daily customs as they had been passed on to succeeding generations, and it continues to largely define Judaism in America today. The historian of American religion Sydney E. Ahlstrom has called this period of change "a most remarkable accommodation to the American scene" and the institutionalization of "a new and distinct stage in the history of Judaism."[2]

How American Judaism emerged out of turmoil and tradition to redefine itself in its distinctive forms at the close of the nineteenth century is the subject of this book.

The chronicle begins with the landing of twenty-three beleaguered Sephardic Jews who had escaped by sailing ship from Brazil to Nieuw Amsterdam (New York City) in 1654. In short order, there arose fierce divisions in the New World between traditionalists and those who wished or needed to adjust and even discard Jewish practices and doctrines. Disputes unfolded in many places, and Jews of all sorts joined the fray—rabbis, intellectuals, businessmen, educators, civic leaders, and congregants themselves. As communities were ripped apart by disagreements and challenges, a new generation of émigré rabbis and their followers codified American Jewish innovations in the early and mid-nineteenth century, influenced by reformist initiatives taking place in German-speaking lands of Central Europe. Many American Jews and their spiritual leaders increasingly feared that acceptance by non-Jews might come at the cost of their religious identity. They wanted Judaism to survive. They believed it could do so only by adapting to the modern world.

Traditionalist foes of many of these adjustments waged a counterreformation of sorts in Europe, calling themselves adherents of orthodoxy. In America, these traditionalists failed to stem the tide of change for most of the nineteenth century, but their arguments lived on. They led to the establishment toward the end of the century of Orthodox Judaism and later in the twentieth century to the denomination known as Conservative Judaism, which embodied an attempt by traditionalists to Americanize Orthodoxy. Conservative Judaism, which held fast to an updated form of tradition, attracted many of the newly arrived Yiddish-speaking Jews in the 1880s who feared that the reforming rabbis and leaders were destroying Judaism in order to save it.

The rabbis and leaders who modified Jewish practices and doctrines did not see themselves as revolutionaries. Far from it. Rather, they argued that their modifications were themselves in the solid tradition of Jewish intellectuals and sages, over thousands of years. They certainly saw themselves as liberating Judaism from the legalistic explanations accumulated over the centuries, which they felt had become unreasonable and illogical. But they contended that the body of laws emanating from the ancient texts of the Talmud had themselves contained updated explications of biblical laws and narratives in response to contemporary demands and sensibilities. In a well-known example of such adjustments, the Torah commands "an eye for an eye" and "a tooth for a tooth." The rabbinic interpreters had long ago agreed that such a definition of punishment was not to be taken literally, but rather to be interpreted as calling for the guilty party to pay an appropriate compensation to the victim. Still another example of Jewish sages adjusting practice to contemporary needs, perhaps one of the most important, occurred in the closing centuries before the Common Era (i.e., BC)—their effort to elevate regular prayer and the reading of Scripture to a central place in everyday piety, replacing the offering of animal sacrifices at the Jerusalem Temple as the main act of worship in Judaism.

The thesis of this book is that the Judaism of America today—even as practiced by many in the traditionalist Orthodox branch—bears witness to a spirit of dynamism and change similar to what had existed among the rabbis and Jewish scholars throughout Jewish history. That spirit infused the rulings and actions of German reformers of the nineteenth century. The impact was different in the United States, however, where it produced a particularly *American* response, influenced inevitably by the culture of a country that disdained religious hierarchies while allowing and even encouraging citizens of all faiths to create institutions reflecting their own, distinctive understanding God.

This book is a work of storytelling. It is derived from the historical record that these contending rabbis and congregations left behind, and from research by scholars delving into the debates and those who shaped American Jewish history. Its focus is on the drama and personalities that make up a narrative that is unfamiliar to most Americans and even most American Jews. From the narrative in this volume, one can experience the early disagreements over mixing men and women in worship services, the use of English, the introduction of sermons, the elimination of many obscure poems and prayers, and the inclusion of live organ music and choirs of men and women. The story of American Jews seeking to make their services more decorous, and in some cases consciously like services at church, has a contemporary feel. In South Carolina, the fight over an organ was settled by a precedent-setting court case.

But a major focus of the disputes of this earlier era was more theological and existential in nature. It centered in America on whether Jews should pray for an altogether human messiah to deliver them back to the Holy Land, there to worship at the rebuilt Temple in Jerusalem destroyed by Titus's Roman legions in 70 CE. For as long as Jews have seen themselves as exiles—which they have done since that temple's destruction—they have prayed for a return to Zion. But in early nineteenth-century America, where Jews were emancipated and accepted as equal American citizens, they

xxvi                        INTRODUCTION

instead embraced the United States as their Zion. There was no longer a need in their view to pray for a messiah or for the prophet Elijah to come back to life and lead them away from the land to which they now happily extended their loyalty. The dispute over the Messiah grew so emotional that it provoked a fistfight and riot on Rosh Hashanah in 1850 on the pulpit of Isaac Mayer Wise's synagogue in Albany, New York, and the sheriff's police were called in to clear the sanctuary.

During the Civil War, loyalty tested the Jews in a different way. They divided over their fealty to the Union and the Confederacy but also over whether Jewish law permitted slavery. Many Jews, even in the North, noted that the Bible condoned slavery. But abolitionists invoked the biblical prohibition of returning a runaway slave to the master (Deuteronomy 23:16) and similar passages as evidence that slavery was morally unacceptable. In the eyes of many Jews, advocates of slavery who cited Jewish teachings legitimizing it did much to discredit the exercise of interpreting Scripture literally and yielding unquestioningly to its authority.

For all religious adherents, the nineteenth century was also a time of deep divisions over the difficulties of adjusting to a culmination in the influence of science, including Darwinism and recent discoveries in geology and paleontology. The divine authority of Scripture was also challenged by a growing realization, based on the work of biblical scholars following the practice of modern literary criticism, that biblical stories came from different authors and could no longer be taken literally. Many religious academics, Jewish and Christian, thought the Bible was to be understood as a collection of Bronze Age parables and legends, in which various personalities struggled over their own bad behavior, providing moral teachings for the ages. Thus, American Jews in the nineteenth century learned to seek the truth within the stories while not necessarily embracing their literal veracity. They found solace in the idea that some Talmudic scholars, at least, understood that the moral teachings were the point of the stories, irrespective of whether the events in the Bible occurred. Here again their search for deeper ethical meanings of ancient texts has a modern relevance.

Nothing less than an evolving mission of Jews in contemporary society rose to prominence in the nineteenth century, redefined by reformers in a way that influenced Jewish beliefs among traditionalists as well. As Jews relegated to the sidelines the requirement to carry out hundreds of practices in clothing, diet, work, and prayer, they revised a fundamental tenet of the role of Jews in history. Instead of expressing belief in a messiah to reestablish the Kingdom of David in Zion, the reformers and Americanizers came to see the Jews *themselves* as a messianic people, a priestly tribe designated by God to bring the belief in one God to the rest of the world, not to bring about conversions but to set an example as created in God's image to seek justice and charity on behalf of God.

The idea of a Jewish "mission" to spread morality in the world, including the non-Jewish world, had been incubated in Germany. But the concept of this mission was brought to full flower by American Jews, who aligned it with a patriotism shared by their fellow Americans. Today it dominates Reform Judaism, but it echoes through Conservative Judaism and some Orthodox circles as well. The history recounted here helps to explain why a majority of American Jews say that they regard social justice for all peoples, not just Jews, as a central tenet of their *religious* beliefs.

Idealism and commitment to exemplary works is built into the DNA of a great many Americans as well as American Jews. It can be traced to the audacious pilgrims aboard the *Arbella* who escaped persecution in England and organized themselves in the Massachusetts Bay Colony in 1630 around John Winthrop's vision: "We shall be as a city upon a hill, the eyes of all people are upon us." American Jews have come to define a similar universalist mission from the divine message conveyed by the prophet Isaiah, translated as: "I the Lord have called you . . . and set you for a covenant of the people, for a light unto the nations . . ." (Isaiah 42:1–7). Some modern theologians say the distinctive Jewish mission has been to survive genocide, persecution, and dispersal because they were true to the mysterious and uplifting spirit of texts of disputed provenance from the mists of antiquity. But one insight becomes obvious. The struggles among Jews of today to define their special status and mission—to serve as the custodians but not sole proprietors of universally applicable ethical precepts—are rooted in the debates and skirmishes of the past.

## BECOMING AN AMERICAN RELIGION

Three factors contributed to the transformation of Judaism into an American religion.

First came the practical exigencies of living, and earning a living, for Jewish immigrants in America—the fact that they traveled, often alone and isolated, from community to community. Jewish peddlers had to travel and establish roots in places that lacked kosher butchers or effective means to carry out other dietary restrictions, such as separating meat and dairy consumption, using different sets of dishes. Many Jews journeyed while subsisting on bread and butter to avoid eating forbidden foods, but others succumbed to pressures or simply hunger and abandoned their longstanding dietary laws. As they set up stores, they found it difficult to close them during the Sabbath holiday, especially in communities that required stores to be closed on Sunday, the Christian Sabbath.

To survive and prosper, many felt they had to adapt. Revising doctrine to justify such adaptations came later. It was only after changing their customs that Jews sought religious leaders to provide the rationale for the changes in practice dictated by circumstance. Yet for all these adaptations, Jews strove to retain their identity with prayer, liturgy, Sabbath observance, circumcision for males, and display of Jewish symbols, such as mezuzahs on their front doors, the Star of David, the Ten Commandments, and passages from the Bible featured on their sanctuary walls.

A second factor was the determination of Jews to conform to American culture. Accepted as equals in their adopted nation, they followed in the path of some Jews in Europe and rejected their identities as a separate nation following a rigid code of behavior governing diet, clothing, relationships between husbands and wives, how and when one prayed, and how one marked the Sabbath and other holidays. These practices were enforced by rabbinical authorities that ran Jewish affairs in Jewish communities, apart from the secular governments in which Jews resided. In many cases, the alien governing authorities in Europe were happy to cede their writ over social customs to rabbis empowered to set the rules, reinforcing Jewish communities as a segregated and second-class or third-class grouping in ghettos. Jews could leave those communities to do business with non-Jews, always fearful of persecution and violence, but no one doubted their authority to govern themselves, until modern times.

In America, however, Jews lived in a secularly neutral state, with guarantees of being treated as equal citizens considerably beyond the rights obtained in parts of Europe. As the historian Jonathan Sarna has noted, they felt liberated in their new land, and confident enough to effectively reinvent their faith with new roots in America. Influenced by Jewish "reformers" in Germany, they embraced American culture on an equal footing with adherents of other religions and beliefs, each allowed to operate irrespective of the state. Exercising the right to govern their own practices in each community, American Jews could be Jews in an American way. They wanted no "chief rabbis" to dictate rules for a disparate Jewish population. They could, and did, elevate the role of women in Judaism, bringing them down from behind barriers and authorizing them to establish religious schools to educate children. They allowed men and women to sit together in family pews, a step that did nothing less than transform the relationship between the synagogue and its congregants, now participating in services as families. Even the traditionalist Jews instituted rules of decorum to reduce the mumbling cacophony of individuals chanting at their own speed, and make the service more like those at churches, with recitations and standing and sitting down in unison.

After a long history of following the teachings of the Talmud, American Jews wrested the leadership of their religion from rabbinical authorities. They did so in part because there were no rabbis in America until the 1840s, although there were learned lay leaders and hazans, or cantors. Even after rabbis arrived, it remained common for congregations, not rabbis, to assert the democratic spirit of their new country and dictate what went on at synagogues. It was believed that if democracy was good enough for American citizens, it was good enough for American members of Jewish congregations. Disputes between rabbis and lay leaders of their congregations became the norm. "We have no ecclesiastical authorities in America, other than the congregations themselves," lamented Isaac Leeser, a prominent exponent of Jewish orthodoxy. "Each congregation makes its own rules for its government, and elects its own minister, who is appointed without any ordination, induction in office being made through his election."[3]

The terminology for what to call a house of worship also evolved. Following the practice of some Jews in France and Germany, American Jews adopted the word *temple* for their synagogues. Though *temple* was a universal term, it bore ideological significance especially for reformist Jews, who employed it to show that Jews did not need to pray for the restoration of the Temple in Jerusalem because they had temples of their own in America. Jews also established myriad civic, charitable, and secular organizations like B'nai B'rith (Children of the Covenant) to establish their identity outside the practice of religion, adjusting to American cultural norms even as they felt excluded from some clubs in their communities. These secular organizations emboldened lay leadership to take control of how their synagogues would be governed.[4]

A third and perhaps most American factor in how Judaism became an American religion was intellectual. Jews in America were educated in matters outside their religion. They had little choice but to come to grips with modern thought and the evolving revolutionary concepts of science, citizenship, anthropology, history, and literary analysis in an egalitarian democracy.

Scientific discoveries since Galileo had long rendered obsolete the religious cosmology of the sun revolving around the Earth. Galileo was condemned by the Roman Catholic Church in 1633, but change in religious thinking was inevitable. Jews who were accomplished in medicine, the arts, and physical sciences had begun to thirst for secular knowledge in this same era. Shortly after Galileo, the philosopher Baruch Spinoza was excommunicated in Amsterdam in 1656, for unspecified "heretical" views. Spinoza later made clear that he could not believe in a god that designated Jews alone as his "chosen people." Going further, like some of the founders of America who were enlightened Christians, many American Jews felt they could no longer believe in a god who intervened daily in world affairs. They saw that stories of the Bible sometimes contradict each other or plain common sense. Whereas the prophets decreed that Jews were punished for their sins and rewarded for their virtue, the books of Ecclesiastes and Job teach the opposite, that reward and punishment are beyond human understanding. But it was discoveries in geology, paleontology, and archeology that shattered the literal foundation of the Bible beyond repair, just as Jewish populations proliferated in the United States. Although many Jews had always harbored skepticism toward biblical stories, it became impossible in the modern era for educated and uneducated alike to think that the Earth was six thousand years old or created in six days. Darwin's works challenged to the core the story of humanity's creation in Genesis.

Along with the widening of physical and life sciences came changes in the science of history—the birth of historical relativism, or what is known as "historicism," following the philosophy of Hegel that social norms are best understood as a product of a society's historical context. In the late nineteenth century, the study of other religions in the ancient Near East—many of them with legends, rituals, and beliefs so similar to those of Judaism—led to the view of Judaism as a body of beliefs of a particular tribe in the region with its own God rivaling the gods of other tribes. Of course, the Bible itself makes clear that although "God is one," other peoples of the region had rival gods that Jews were implored to reject. But scholarly explorations of these other sects, based on recovered artifacts, helped to ignite a passion for seeing Jewish history as a product of its time and place as well as an inspiration for universal truths.

The study of religious traditions from other cultures, including Asia, also contributed to an intellectual awakening to the universal impulse toward faith. The Torah (or Pentateuch, i.e., the first five books of the Bible), was clearly written by several authors, according to the work of German scholars. How, after all, could the Torah have been handed down to Moses on Sinai if Deuteronomy vividly describes Moses's own death and burial? Many of the founding accounts of Judaism, even the Exodus story, came to be seen as etiological myths, written to explain and justify the origins and uniqueness of Jewish claims to the land of Canaan, or Palestine. Scholars

believed a history of the Jewish people that could be told without the legends and miracles of the Bible made it easier intellectually for Jews to adapt
to modern cultures and demands.

## A PART BUT APART

The historian Arnold Eisen, chancellor of the Jewish Theological Seminary,
recounts a story of an itinerant peddler, Joseph Jonas, one of the first Jews
to travel west of the Alleghenies, in 1817. A Quaker woman was excited to
meet him. "Art thou a Jew?" she asked with wonder. "Thou art one of God's
chosen people." But then upon inspection she expressed disappointment.
"Well, thou art no different to other people."[5]

For American Jews, the idea of "chosenness" has always presented problems of how to identify themselves as a people "apart" but also a people
as "a part" of America, accepted by Americans, like all other people. The
Bible, Eisen notes, refers at least 175 times to the Jews as chosen by God to
fulfill certain roles in their redemption. Jews are identified as a "special treasure" of God at Mount Sinai, for example. But it is not until the chapters of
Isaiah—which scholars believe were written much later than the period of
the prophet himself—that Jews are described as chosen to be what is often
translated as "a light unto the nations." The special status of Jews in these
passages has evolved, especially among American adherents in the nineteenth century, but also among many others, into "an explicit mission" for
Jews to become "the servant of mankind"—and even that Jewish suffering
is proclaimed as evidence of "the mark of election" to carry out this task.[6]
As Judaism came to flourish in the United States, American Jews struggled
with this paradox: that Jews saw themselves as commanded to dwell separately from humanity to serve a divine purpose, as a beacon to humankind,
but also to be grateful that they could belong in their new land as equal to
others.

The growing acceptance of Jews by non-Jewish fellow citizens thus
posed both a challenge and opportunity to integrate themselves in American society—while cherishing their separateness as a sacred mission. Many

American Jews reconciled these two imperatives by redefining the nature of their history of Diaspora, or exile. They saw these punishments less as retribution for misdeeds committed in antiquity and more as a sacred assignment to disperse, proclaim justice, and set an example for a world in need of repair.

For many Jews today, the embrace of a distinctively Jewish social gospel, akin perhaps to the social gospel of Christianity, is an important part of their faith. But it was through the process of Americanization that the social gospel entered American Judaism. Doing God's work on Earth—a legacy of the Enlightenment, the Transcendental movement, the Second Great Awakening, Reform Judaism, and other intellectual strands in American history—is referred to by some American Jews today as *tikkun olam* ("repairing the world"), a distinctly modern phrase adapted and reinterpreted (indeed misinterpreted) from Jewish mystical writings. Some also use another contemporary term *B'tselem Elohim* ("in the image" of God), to describe the importance of treating all of humanity with compassion. But this task of religious believers tending to the secular world remains a contentious issue for Jews and non-Jews alike.

What is beyond dispute is that Jews are heirs to a long and much-debated history on this and many other issues. How could it be otherwise? The Bible recounts many stories of Jews arguing with God—from Abraham to Jacob wrestling with the angel and changing his name to Israel ("contending with God") to Job to the prophets like Isaiah and Jeremiah. Jews willing to challenge God could not but share a history of challenging each other.

But the story of the journey and all these disputes among American Jews begins with the landing of the first Jews in New York City more than 350 years ago.

# THE
# CHOSEN
# WARS

*One*

# COMING TO AMERICA

The first Jews to arrive in the New World may well have been converts or secret Jews aboard one of Columbus's ships that landed in 1492 on an island in the Bahamas that Columbus named San Salvador. Indeed, Columbus could have been one of these "hidden" Jews himself.[1]

The year 1492 is also associated with a more catastrophic event for Jews, and Muslims as well: the horrific eradication of their life in Spain carried out under the decree of Ferdinand of Aragon and Isabella of Castile, who had united as king and queen to create a unified Spain in 1474. The Spanish Inquisition was a holocaust of torture and executions inspired by the Catholic Church and driven by the conviction that the Jews were infidels responsible for killing Christ. It was accompanied by spectacles of mass murder to entertain the populace, and it wiped out a community that had prospered peacefully, materially, culturally, and intellectually in Spain for hundreds of years. Portugal followed Spain and expelled its Jews or forcibly baptized them in following years. Those who converted or secretly maintained Jewish rituals—the so-called *conversos* (sometimes called "New Christians") or *marranos* ("pigs")—were hardly spared the church's cruel persecution.[2]

The Spanish Inquisition also produced a vital new chapter in Jewish survival. From Iberia, Jews fled to France, England, Germany, North Africa, Egypt, Turkey, Palestine, eastward as far as what is today Iraq and Iran. A primary haven was the Netherlands, where the Jews' capabilities at business and trade helped turn Holland into a world commercial and cultural power in the seventeenth century. The Jews in the Netherlands were not full citizens, but they still enjoyed many civil and economic rights, and they became investors in the Dutch East India and West India Companies and other enterprises that established footholds in North America.

In 1630, Dutch forces took the Brazilian coastal city of Recife from their longtime enemy, the Portuguese. Dutch Jews then settled in Recife, establishing a community that included rabbis, a synagogue, and two Jewish schools. But the Portuguese took Recife back in 1654, and the Jews fled yet again—some to England (where they petitioned to be returned after the expulsion in 1290), some to the Caribbean, some to Amsterdam—and some, probably unintentionally, to New Amsterdam in North America.

It was there that twenty-three Jewish asylum seekers sailed into New York Harbor aboard the French frigate *Ste. Catherine* in September of 1654. Their arrival in New Amsterdam was by some accounts accidental, after a storm-tossed voyage. Individual Jews had settled earlier in the area, but never before had a group come with the intention of seeking collective asylum and protection. Their appearance was hardly auspicious, in any case. Peter Stuyvesant, the despotic Dutch colonial governor, was imposing a series of edicts to accommodate a population growing rapidly from only one thousand at the beginning of the decade. He rerouted streets, established building codes, and banned citizens from throwing trash and dead animals into roads. The Jews had hardly set foot on the city's shores when the captain went to a local court to sue his passengers for a payment he claimed they had not made, implying to Dutch authorities that, like it or not, this would be their last stop. Very quickly, however, the Jews established a synagogue congregation, Shearith Israel (Remnant of Israel), then as now following Spanish and Portuguese Jewish customs. An early task was locating a cemetery for Jews and bringing in the first Torah scroll from Amsterdam. For the next 171 years, Shearith Israel was to serve as the only Jewish congregation in the city. (It is now located at the Spanish & Portuguese Synagogue on Central Park West.) [3]

All religious adherents in America are pilgrims in some sense. So argues Martin Marty in his book *Pilgrims in Their Own Land*, which asserts that no faith has ever felt "truly installed" in the United States. Escaping from imprisonment, slavery, debt, low status, poverty, and persecution, he contends, most immigrants were pilgrims when they arrived in America—"and pilgrims they have remained in their new land."[4]

But more than the followers of any other religion, Jews see themselves as escapees, strangers, as *galut*—the Hebrew term for uprooted and living in exile—or Diaspora, a theme that derives from the long narrative of Jewish history and literature. Yet like Odysseus, Jews in biblical literature always contemplate a return—and a redemption. The theme of exile abounds in the earliest biblical writings: the expulsion of Adam and Eve, God telling Abram (later Abraham) to leave his native land for Canaan, and the escape from famine to Egypt by Abraham's descendants. Always on the move, the Jews took flight from slavery back to the Promised Land, along the way receiving a body of laws from God in Sinai. These historical memories are tattooed into the Jewish psyche. But the escape from persecution to Dutch territory in the New World in the seventeenth century was different. It led eventually to Jews accepting their existence in a new Promised Land, for which their arrival in New York marked the beginning of a struggle to belong.

New York was hardly welcoming at the start. Stuyvesant, famous already for his wooden leg and authoritarian ways, made it clear that inhabitants had to adhere to the Dutch Reformed Church. Stuyvesant regarded the Jews as "a deceitful race" whose "abominable religion" worshipped "the feet of Mammon."[5] He tried to keep the Jews out altogether as "hateful enemies and blasphemers."[6] But to their defense came the West India Company and the Jews of the old country, noting that the refugees from Recife could help bring the prosperity Stuyvesant was trying to foster. Stuyvesant bowed to their wishes. The arrival and forced acceptance of the Jews, in turn, helped open the boundaries of tolerance for others, including Quakers, Lutherans, and Catholics.[7] Still their rights remained limited, and they had to battle for the right to trade and practice religion publicly.

The new clusters of Sephardic Jews in New Amsterdam were a cosmopolitan lot compared to their Ashkenazi counterparts back in Germany and Eastern Europe. They were heirs to a separate tradition of "port Jews," the term for inhabitants of coastal areas of Europe and the Caribbean willing to keep their customs and worship private in order to thrive and be seen as equals to the Protestants and Catholics with whom they lived.

Their accommodations of lifestyle and ancient Jewish practices to the new world in which they sought to do business had been influenced by years of exile, persecution, and the need to travel long distances. Disputes over longstanding Jewish identity, separateness, and traditional beliefs were already flaring in the Netherlands. In 1656, two years after the Recife Jews landed in America, traditional Jewish authorities in Holland excommunicated Baruch Spinoza for "evil opinions and acts," "abominable heresies," and "monstrous deeds." It has never been clear what Spinoza had done by the age of twenty-three, with no published writings to his credit, to have outraged the Jewish establishment. But he later became a well-known rationalist philosopher and acquaintance of Descartes whose ideas continued to challenge the rabbinate. Spinoza not only disputed the Jews' status as God's chosen people, he challenged the veracity of the divine origin of the Jews' sweeping code of behavior that believers understood as given by God on Mount Sinai. It would take two centuries for those ideas to become more mainstream.

In New Amsterdam, the Jews were doing their best to maintain their religious identity and practices when a new challenge arose in 1664. That year a British fleet under the command of Colonel Richard Nicolls set out from Coney Island and seized control of the Dutch colony. He granted its inhabitants the rights of English colonists, including freedom of worship—but

only for anyone who professed Christianity. That barrier did not last. It fell
after 1700, leading to a further influx of Jews. By 1740, Parliament granted
the Jews naturalization rights in the colonies. Still, Jews in all the British territories were encouraged to practice their rites unobtrusively.[8]

In this incubated setting, Jews began to identify themselves as adherents of a unique religious faith, but nonetheless a faith like others in the
New World. Their loyalties beyond their faith were to the larger community in which they lived. As a result, they prospered as merchants, traders,
shopkeepers, artisans, doctors, and landowners, dealing comfortably and
even intimately with non-Jews. In the countries from which they had emigrated, Jews had earlier prospered by employing their broad connections
via cross-border letters of credit, bearer bonds, and other financial instruments. These were elements invented by Jews that contributed to the early
European banking system. Paul Johnson, in his history of the Jews, regards
the evolution of these instruments as a critical building block of modern
capitalism. "For a race without a country, the world was a home," he writes.
"The further the market stretched, the greater were the opportunities."[9]

Bringing that talent to the New World, Jews traded throughout the
colonies—in textiles, spices, jewels, rum, furs, and other goods, including slaves.[10] They also traded with Indians, merchants in the Caribbean
islands, and commercial centers in Europe, often furnishing supplies for
armed forces. Their lives were hardly easy. Dangers arose from hazards on
the roads and high seas, not least from pirates, privateers, and enemy war-
ships.[11] When fortune turned against them, they served time in debtors'
prison, from where they relied on the charity of more prosperous Jews. And
from New York, they spread to Newport, Charleston, Savannah, Philadelphia, and Richmond. Estimates based on a 1790 census are that the American Jewish population numbered 1,300 to 1,500 in this period. The largest
communities were New York and South Carolina, with the rest scattered
in New England, Pennsylvania, Virginia, Maryland, Georgia, New Jersey,
and North Carolina.[12] In all these places, they sought to maintain traditions
while adjusting to lifestyle and business realities. Generally, they did not try
to control what fellow Jews did in their business lives but instead confined

their religious activities to their own spheres, respecting the Sabbath, worshipping in makeshift synagogues, and keeping Jewish dietary laws when possible.

Other practices to which they adhered included circumcising their sons, the ancient sign of the covenant between God and the descendants of Israel, praying with their *tallit* (prayer shawl) and *tefillin* (phylacteries), and their belief in the coming of a messiah to deliver Jews back to Zion. In 1769, the Reverend Ezra Stiles, a founder of Brown and later president of Yale, recounted that he saw Jews frightened by a thunderstorm opening their doors and windows and singing prayers for the Messiah to deliver them.[13]

Stiles figured in another aspect of Jewish integration in colonial era society—the perils of acceptance and even love by non-Jews. As a prolific diarist and genuine philo-Semite, or "lover of Jews," Stiles professed his admiration for the Hebrew race even while echoing the common Christian theme that the Jews did not understand their own Bible correctly. Later as president of Yale, he required instruction of Hebrew for its students. When Stiles's friend, Aaron Lopez, one of the wealthiest Jews in America, died from a carriage accident in 1792, Stiles praised him but with a well-intentioned reservation. "He was my intimate Friend and Acquaintance!" the Yale president said. "Oh, how often have I wished that sincere pious and candid mind could have perceived the Evidence of Christianity, perceived the Truth as it is in Jesus Christ."[14] (It was a confession laden with irony. Lopez had arrived in New York in 1740 as a Catholic named Duarte but later adopted the name Aaron, had himself circumcised, and lived as an observant Jew.)[15]

As Stiles's diary attests, Jews in the colonies generally did interact with Christians, visiting them in their homes and going ahead with intermarriage, by one estimate affecting 15 percent of Jews in the colonial era. Intermarriage was almost always a prelude to falling away from the faith, a frightening prospect to many in the community. Some families disowned their daughters and sons who married non-Jews. Others were more accepting. But the colonial years pointed to intermarriage as one of the first big issues that proved divisive within the community of American Jews.[16]

Congregation of Mikveh Israel of Philadelphia, established in 1740 when Jews applied for a cemetery plot to Thomas Penn, was one of the earliest of its kind in the colonial era. But shortly after its founding, members of the congregation complained to a visiting chief rabbi of Amsterdam that one of their leaders in Philadelphia had performed a marriage ceremony for his niece, though she was married to a non-Jew, and that he gave last rites for another Jew who had married outside the faith. The dissident who performed these rites, Mordecai M. Mordecai, said it was his right to interpret the law as best he could. The congregation members disagreed with his use of "erroneous legalistic loopholes" and sought to bar him from the synagogue.[17]

Another case, that of Jacob Franks, a shipowner, businessman, and merchant who served as an agent of King George III in the French and Indian War, illustrated the stresses on each family. Franks and his wife, the former Abigail Levy, had emigrated from London. Though British, he was a Jew of Ashkenazic or Germanic origin. He had lived as a boarder in the Levy household and married Abigail when she was only sixteen. They had nine children, three of whom died in infancy. Franks served as president, or *parnas*, of Shearith Israel and along with the Levys mingled socially among the city's Protestant elite: the Livingstons, Bayards, De Lanceys, and Van Cortlandts.

Worldly and educated, Abigail wrote letters to her children quoting the novels of Henry Fielding and the works of Dryden, Montesquieu, and Pope. She proudly observed the Sabbath, kept kosher, and worshipped at the synagogue on the High Holidays. Wedded to tradition, she was not above impatience with it, writing her son with complaints about "the many superstitions we are clog'd with."[18]

But the Franks family's stately existence blew up in 1743, when their daughter Phila ran off with Oliver De Lancey, the unruly scion of a wealthy family, one of many who lent their names to streets in Lower Manhattan. Years earlier, Oliver and some friends had been accused of breaking into and ransacking the home of a Dutch Jewish emigrant, swearing, and threatening to rape the wife. Charges were not brought in that episode. Jacob reconciled himself to Phila's marriage, perhaps seeing some advantage to it, but Abigail refused to speak to her or let Oliver in her home. There is no evidence that mother and daughter ever reconciled. In still another instance of difficulties in mingling with the majority population, Judah Monis, the first Jew in America to receive a college degree—from Harvard, where he was an instructor in Hebrew—nonetheless converted two years after graduating, in 1722, motivated perhaps by his need for a job, and his falling in love with a Gentile, Abigail Marret.[19]

## REVOLUTION AND ANOTHER ESCAPE

The American Revolution confronted the few hundred Jews living in New York City, especially the so-called patriots, with something tragically familiar—a forced exodus. A few weeks after July 4, 1776, the British under General William Howe moved swiftly to snuff out the insurrection in the American colonies and take the city from the rebels.

General George Washington, anticipating an attack, had amassed his troops defensively in lower Manhattan. But British ships had surreptitiously ferried Howe's army from New England to Staten Island for their assault. After crossing New York Harbor, General Howe seized control of Brooklyn Heights and then hopscotched across the bay to Lower Manhattan. Washington fled across the Hudson River to New Jersey and then Pennsylvania. The British managed to remain in the city through most of the Revolutionary War.

Like other citizens of the busiest port in North America, Jews faced a dilemma as this drama unfolded. In light of their precarious history, they vacillated between the patriots and their new British military overlords, in some cases pledging allegiance to both sides for as long as it was practical. Most in the city and the colonies generally appear to have lined up with the rebels, however. Many joined the Continental Army and fell in battle. Others contributed funds. For example, in Philadelphia, Haym Salomon, a Polish Jew, raised such large sums that James Madison praised him as "our little friend in Front Street" who, to his astonishment, asked for no recompense.[20]

Not surprisingly, war posed new tests to the ability of Jews to maintain their identity, laws, and traditions. A 1777 diary entry from a Hessian officer fighting for the British, Conrad Doehla, attests to the problem: "The Jews [in America] cannot . . . be told, like those in our country, by their beards and costume, but they are dressed like all other citizens, shave regularly, and also eat pork . . . moreover do not hesitate to intermarry. The Jewish women have their hair dressed and wear French finery like the women of other faiths. They are very much enamored of and attached to Germans."[21]

After Washington fled New York, so did many Jewish patriots. Among them was a young New York–born cleric with piercing eyes and thick dark hair named Gershom Mendes Seixas, who had been elected spiritual leader of Shearith Israel in 1768 at the remarkably young age of twenty-two. Seixas, the son of a Sephardic father and an Ashkenazic (German-speaking European) mother, was a scion of the congregation, which had moved to a modest two-story building on Mill Street, just south of Wall Street.

Seixas (pronounced *Say-shas*) was described by associates as a man of considerable intellect and charm. Though he lacked formal religious training, he had been determined to go into the ministry rather than business trades. In his escape from New York, he took the synagogue's Torah scrolls—partly burned when Hessian soldiers set fire to the sanctuary—along with other paraphernalia, going first to Connecticut, where British forces continued to harass settlements along the coast, and then to Philadelphia. (Jewish refugees in Norwalk, Connecticut, likened the city's destruction by the British to the destruction of the Temple in Jerusalem in the same season, commemorated in the fast of Tisha B'av.) In Philadelphia, Seixas served as *hazan*, or cantor, at Mikveh Israel.

Toward the end of the war, Shearith Israel's president, or *parnas*, Hayman Levy, beseeched Seixas to return to his home synagogue. But Seixas was not so eager. He wrote Levy that he had heard many reports about "divisions among the reputable members of the congregation, by which means a general disunion seems to prevail instead of being united to serve the Deity, consonant to our holy law." In 1757, for example, leaders of the congregation had tried to oust members who did business on the Sabbath, ate nonkosher food, and committed "other Heinious [sic] Crimes." But six months after being expelled, the miscreants were welcomed back, along with their donations and dues.[22]

Despite the turbulent atmosphere, Seixas gently told Levy that if perhaps his starting salary of £80 a year (plus a small bachelor's quarters and free firewood) could somehow be raised, he might consider returning to his old congregation. "Do that what you know to be right, that the Lord may be with thee in all thy ways," Seixas wrote the parnas.

Levy was a tough-minded businessman and storekeeper originally from the Lake Champlain region, where he sold goods to Indians in return for furs. He had once even been fined by his own congregation for using "indecent and abusive language," perhaps another example of what Seixas had been concerned about. Yet Levy gave in to Seixas's demands and offered a salary of £200, asking him to return at once, before Passover. That did not end the controversy. Mikveh Israel in Philadelphia, home synagogue of the famed Haym Salomon, financier of the war, protested Seixas's decision to leave so quickly. Seixas appealed to Levy for a delay, noting that the roads were difficult to travel in the winter in any case. Levy was adamant, and by April 1784, Seixas was back at Mill Street, where he served until his death in 1816. Reflecting the spirit of its role in a new nation, Shearith Israel welcomed Governor George Clinton to its synagogue in 1783 by likening the victory for independence to the Jews' return from exile. A Hebrew prayer at the congregation compared the birth of the thirteen states to the deliverance of the Jews from bondage that would hasten the Jews' own redeemer.[23]

But the saga of Minister Seixas has another revealing component about the important but still precarious role that Jews played at the time of the American revolution and its immediate aftermath. In this period, Jews in America remained small in number—no more than 2,000 to 3,000.[24] They constructed synagogues as the character of their life adjusted to the comforting idea that they could thrive in a brand-new country that was uniquely welcoming to them. Americanization represented an unprecedented chapter of belonging, a complete break from the traditions of their forefathers in the long and tortured history of Jewish experience.

## TO BIGOTRY NO SANCTION . . .

The inauguration of General Washington as the first president in 1789 served as an emotional capstone for Jews living in the newly established United States. Seixas, as a widely renowned figure in the colonies, represented the Jewish community at the festivities, along with fifteen Christian ministers. He also became the first Jew to serve as a trustee of Columbia College, founded by royal charter in 1754 as Kings College and then still a Christian institution. Seixas was a traditionalist on most matters, but he later became the first "rabbi" (however unofficial the term for him) to use English (rather than Portuguese) for some prayers. As an acquaintance of Christian leaders in the community, he sometimes gave sermons to Christian congregations, including St. Paul's Episcopal Church, and invited Christian ministers to his congregation. He went so far as to describe himself as "minister" to the Jews of New York City, a symbol of his acceptance outside his community. In the process, he became what one historian calls "the first Jewish example of a type of religious leadership characteristic of Protestantism in the American setting but new to the Jewish tradition"—a full-fledged member of the new country's pluralistic religious establishment.[25]

But how established were the Jews, actually?

Some old restrictions on Jews remained even after a revolution waged partly in the name of freedom of religion. Seixas, when he was still back in Philadelphia, shortly after American independence, joined with Haym Salomon and other members of their congregation to petition the Pennsylvania authorities against a new requirement that members of the state legislature take an oath containing the phrase "I do acknowledge the Scriptures of the Old and New Testament." They were unsuccessful in their appeal, although a parade in Philadelphia in 1788 attests to the equal status of Jews in that community. To celebrate the new Constitution, Jews marched in the city and conspicuously ate kosher at their own table afterward.[26]

Similar strictures applied to Jews for many decades after the revolution. The right to hold public office remained limited for decades in Maryland, New Hampshire, and elsewhere. A group of Jews petitioned the Maryland

Assembly to adjust the language restricting officeholding to Christians in the 1790s, but it took another couple decades for the small community of Jews in Baltimore to get the state to extend liberties to Jews in 1825.

A close reading of the Jewish community's relationship with George Washington also suggests a certain tentativeness to their acceptance. One of Seixas's brothers, Moses Mendes Seixas—among the organizers of the Bank of Rhode Island and the president of the historic Touro Synagogue in Newport, Rhode Island—presented Washington with a letter on the occasion of his visit in 1790. "Permit the children of the stock of Abraham to approach you with the most cordial affection and esteem for your person and merits, and to join with our fellow citizens in welcoming you to Newport," it declared to the new president. (The congregation, founded in the 1600s, employed a Palladian-style design for the new synagogue, the first in New England, dedicated in 1763. It served as a hospital for the British military during the Revolutionary War and was returned to the Jews after the British evacuated. In the nineteenth century, it became known as the Touro Synagogue, named after one of its early families in honor of their generosity for its upkeep. It remains the oldest surviving synagogue building in the United States.)

Washington's letter to the Jews of Newport in response is justly famous. It suggested that for the Jews, America might prove itself to be the Promised Land for which they yearned, a harbinger perhaps of the debate to come among American Jews over whether their loyalty to the United States should be compromised by prayers for deliverance back to the Holy Land on Judgment Day. But a double-edged meaning could have been inferred as well from one of Washington's equally famous phrases: "For happily the Government of the United States gives to bigotry no sanction, to persecution no assistance, requires only that they who live under its protection should demean themselves as good citizens, in giving it on all occasions their effectual support."

Was there, one might ask, a whiff of conditionality in Washington's suggestion that the Jews should "demean" themselves as a requirement for citizenship? The challenge of comporting themselves, and perhaps conforming themselves, was to be a major recurring theme of the American Jewish experience.

## SEPHARDIM VS. ASHKENAZIM: EARLY SKIRMISHES

The earliest difficulties within the Jewish community derived from customs followed by two traditions, Sephardic and Ashkenazi. Begun as a predominantly Sephardic community, New York had from its earliest days a portion of non-Sephardic Jews. A famous example was Asser Levy, who had immigrated to Amsterdam from Vilnius, or Vilna, then part of Poland, before coming to New Amsterdam, by some accounts as a part of the group of asylum seekers aboard the *Ste. Catherine*. In New York, he successfully demanded the right of Jews to stand guard with Dutch burghers to protect the city. It was not until 1720, however, that Ashkenazi Jews formed a majority of the city's population, and Shearith Israel, established by Sephardim, became an initial battleground over their varying customs and traditions. Ashkenazi arrivals often viewed their Sephardic brethren as elitist, complacent, and more lax in their observances, but many Sephardim argued that the opposite was the case, looking down on Ashkenazi Jews as abrasive and uncouth. Indeed, some Sephardic communities turned inward in America and increased their attachment to orthodox traditions.

The division of Jews into different camps was an old story, going back at least to the time when the Babylonians destroyed the First Temple in Jerusalem in the sixth century BCE and Jews were divided into inhabitants of Babylon and Palestine. More diffusions occurred after the fall of the rebuilt "Second Temple" to the Romans in 70 CE. These scatterings of Jews in the Mediterranean world were sometimes followed by persecution and forced exile. But many if not most Jews no doubt also voluntarily traveled and settled in new homelands to seek opportunities as merchants and adventurers.

Establishing themselves in Spain, they spoke the medieval dialect of Spanish known as Ladino, and this became the language of their subsequent exile in the rest of Europe from the Spanish Inquisition. Meanwhile, probably around the eighth century, Jews began migrating from Italy to the Rhineland, where they became known in Hebrew as Ashkenazim, eventually adopting a combination of German dialects that later evolved into Yiddish, with a healthy dose of loan words from Hebrew and various Slavic languages. (The term *Sephardim* comes from a certain place name, otherwise unknown, in the Biblical Book of Obadiah, one that sounds a bit like Spania, "Spain." The term *Ashkenazi* derives similarly from another place name associated with a European kingdom cited in the book of Jeremiah.)

A visitor to America in 1790 complained that synagogues "have no regular system" and their services were "in a state of fluctuation."[27] Synagogues were generally organized by a president or warden (*parnas*), a standing committee, and a hierarchy of members, usually with the biggest donors attaining higher status. Synagogue governance was thus a radical departure from what many Jews had experienced in large parts of Europe. No government or rabbinical authority existed in the New World to set the rules for Jews. It was the lay leadership, for example, that could wield the power of *herem*, or excommunication (though such actions were more frequently threatened than executed), and establish all sorts of rules governing conduct.

Adopting the spirit of the age, synagogues started writing constitutions. In 1790, Shearith Israel adopted a "bill of rights" enshrining sovereignty and opening membership and authority to more than just traditional elites.[28] Synagogues became places mirroring the civics of the US government, deriving their rules from the "consent of the governed." It was in that context that divisions over ethnic practices, liturgy, and other matters were adjudicated, particularly between various forms of Ashkenazi and Sephardic traditions.

The first Ashkenazi synagogue in America, Rodef Shalom of Philadelphia, was established in 1795 when Germans wanting to pray according to the German and Dutch rules broke away from the Sephardic rituals of Mikveh Israel, founded a half century earlier. The first such synagogue in New York also had a contentious beginning. Shearith Israel, proud of its status as the one and only synagogue in the city, asked the Common Council of New York to be granted exclusive right to slaughter and sell kosher meat in 1813. A faction in the synagogue objected, arguing that the law was "an encroachment on our religious rites," and the council reversed itself.[29] Later an ugly dispute arose over Seixas's widow's pension. These episodes demonstrated that all was not peaceful within the congregation.

Another problem was the chaos of the services themselves—a cacophony of noisy individual prayers and worshippers interrupting the reading of the hazan. The congregation leaders sought to impose some order by introducing what became known as "decorum" in the service. Rules were introduced in 1805 "to promote solemnity and order" that might be presentable to outsiders and inspire congregants.[30]

Despite these changes, several younger Ashkenazi members at Shearith Israel were not satisfied. They asked for more. First, they sought permission to conduct their own Sabbath services under Ashkenazi tradition, though only in the summer. It is not precisely clear which traditions they wanted to change—the two branches of Judaism contained many sub-branches following different rules of when Jewish boys should begin to wear prayer shawls, what foods can be eaten on Passover, and which blessings are called for at what time. Whatever the specifics, the Askhenazi congregations were summarily rebuffed. Later they broke away to form a new organization called Hebra Hinuch Nearim (Society for Youth Education) paving the way for establishment of Congregation B'nai Jeshurun (Children of Israel, *Jeshurun* being a poetic name for Israel) in 1825. The new congregation first rented a place at Pearl Street, closer to where many of them had moved, and then bought and remodeled their own building, converting what had been the First Coloured Presbyterian Church in 1827.

The thirty-two founding members of B'nai Jeshurun devoted themselves to strict keeping of their faith in accordance with German and Polish traditions. They also adapted services used by the Great Synagogue of London, the earliest Ashkenazi congregation established in the British Isles after Jews were permitted to return to England in the seventeenth century, having been expelled in 1290. B'nai Jeshurun leaders also called for less formal worship, accompanied by explanations for young people not versed in Jewish law, and for no permanent leader to dictate norms to others.

In declaring their independence, these Ashkenazi Jews importantly introduced a new willingness to challenge authority in a spirit of anti-elitism and a demand for democratic self-government. Later B'nai Jeshurun broke another barrier: it became the first congregation in New York to conduct services in English.[31] B'nai Jeshurun also focused in its first decades on instituting decorum (omitting obscure prayers and reading prayers like the Kaddish in unison rather than in what was sometimes a cacophonous babble), and reforming the practice of worshippers paying to receive synagogue honors, such as reading from the Torah. In addition, they dropped the requirement for special gowns to be worn by the cantor and rabbi, all of these changes invigorating the service with a new emphasis on performance.

Soon and inevitably, there was a revolt against B'nai Jeshurun for becoming too "Americanized" and perhaps too affluent. Thus, a separate group of newcomer German, Polish, and Dutch immigrants established Congregation Ansche Chesed, a third congregation in New York, in 1829. It was so impoverished that it had to ask for ornaments and building materials from the more affluent Shearith Israel, and it struggled to maintain rituals of meat slaughtering, baking matzo, and building a ritual bath, or *mikveh*. It also experienced personnel struggles. The minutes show that members complained that the hazan was frequently seen gambling and hanging out at billiard parlors and perhaps even houses of prostitution, making him "unfit." By the 1840s the congregation was on a steadier footing and started to enforce rules of decorum designed to avoid "the present confusion" in the service and have only those authorized to read prayers out loud.[32]

These disputes paved the way for a pattern that became typical in American synagogues. As Jacob Rader Marcus, an eminent historian of early American Jewry, has written: "Squabbles in God's house were almost as traditional as the liturgy itself; one sometimes suspects that these quarrels testified to a rugged spiritual health."[33]

## ARARAT AND THE DREAM
## OF INDEPENDENCE

As comfortable as Jews were living as equals in America, there remained a yearning among some for something more—the self-governing status of a different era in Europe, and perhaps the ancient epoch of Jewish kingdoms in antiquity. An important figure in that historical longing was also an early precursor to the modern movement of Zionism. But Mordecai Manuel Noah was as eccentric as he was compelling.

Like Seixas, Noah was not a rabbi even though he welcomed the trappings of one. (There were no rabbis in the United States until the 1840s, but there were some in Jamaica, Surinam, Curaçao, and elsewhere in the Americas.) Noah was in fact a journalist, playwright, and sometime diplomat whose editorials on the War of 1812 led to an appointment by President James Madison as consul to the Kingdom of Tunis before he was removed on the ground that it was inappropriate for a Jew to serve in a Muslim realm. Noah's protests over the ouster were ignored at the State Department, deepening his concerns about the precarious status of Jews in the United States.

In New York City, Noah was active in Tammany Hall politics and rose to the position of high sheriff. In 1825, the same year as the rebellion of Ashkenazim at Shearith Israel, he took up an altogether different cause. With virtually no support from anyone—not even his fellow Jews—he sought to establish a Jewish "refuge" on Grand Island in the Niagara River, just south of Niagara Falls. Noah proposed to call his new community Ararat, after the mythical mountain where his biblical namesake's ark came to rest.

Encouraged in part by a group of German Jewish intellectuals with whom he corresponded, Noah sought permission to set up his community from the New York legislature. Some lawmakers were favorable, but in the absence of a bill, Noah persuaded a friend to purchase a section of Grand Island for his purpose. For the opening of his community, Noah presided at a dedication ceremony on the Niagara riverbank. He turned it into quite a scene. Cannons boomed, and military and Masonic groups marched. Wearing a red ermine-trimmed robe, with a medal around his neck, Noah proclaimed himself "Governor and Judge of Israel." The band played the "Grand March" from Handel's oratorio *Judas Maccabeus* (it had been composed in 1746). Noah read his "Proclamation to the Jews" urging young people the world over to come to his colony, where polygamy would be forbidden and prayers would be offered in Hebrew. Noah also declared that Jews throughout the world ought to defray the costs of establishing Ararat as a farming community and refuge.

For all its crackpot absurdity, Ararat embodied a longstanding aspiration for Jews, the idea of complete self-government as a means to self-preservation. But Ararat never got off the ground. Indeed, Noah seems never to have set foot on the island himself. But Noah's antics, with their historically resonant and prophetic elements, contained the seeds of what he predicted would come true—establishment eventually of a homeland in Palestine. In asserting that such a place would come to be, Noah channeled traditional Jewish prayers that were to be increasingly challenged by Jews living and growing perfectly comfortable in the United States.

In fact, Noah had for years been speaking of the Zionist ideals in concrete terms. As early as 1818, at Shearith Israel, he flatly predicted that the Jews would one day return to Palestine "in triumphant numbers" to "take their rank among the governments of the earth." Years later, in 1837, he wrote a *Discourse on the Evidences of the American Indians Being the Descendants of the Lost Tribes of Israel* but declared once again his belief that with the help of England and France, the Jews would eventually reestablish their homeland in the place of their ancient kingdoms.

"I confidently believe in the restoration of the Jews," Noah declared again in 1844, in New York, adding an appeal to American Christians to help, citing passages in the Bible. These proclamations were seen among some Jews as dangerous, not only because they exposed Jews to accusations of divided loyalties, but also because they fed Christian and anti-Semitic impulses to convert or get rid of Jews in America. Among the worriers was Isaac Leeser, a hazan in Philadelphia who was the most prominent traditional Jewish religious scholar of the era. He declared that the Jews "had better remain as they are now, scattered over all the earth, rather than expose themselves to an extermination by some modern Haman," a reference to the evil persecutor of Jews in the Book of Esther.[34]

Restive as Jews and their leaders were over these sectarian issues, a different storm was brewing in what was then the largest Jewish community in America—Charleston, South Carolina. It started with a fire that nearly destroyed the entire downtown.

*Two*

# LET HARMONY ASCEND

The ocean air that buffeted the busy docks at Charleston Harbor in the years after the American Revolution was suffused with the briny fragrance of world commerce: dried fish from New England, coffee from Brazil, tobacco from Cuba, and pomegranates, bananas, and citrus fruit from the Caribbean. It was a time and place of hard work, sweat, prosperity, and self-assurance.

Charleston, South Carolina, had been a major trading center in the British colonial era, and its success only grew in America's first decades. Fort Sumter, constructed to defend the port in the War of 1812, stood proudly on an island in the bay to guard the city's wealth and strategic importance. Charleston was also a major center in the slave trade. As an export center, the port was a crucial place for shipping cotton, indigo, and rice grown at nearby plantations, some of which were also owned by Jewish families that had immigrated to South Carolina in the previous century.[1]

Accompanying the Jews' good fortune in the early decades after the revolution was a religious revival spreading throughout the United States, known as the Second Great Awakening—and a cultural revival as well. New churches, theaters, societies, and clubs sprang up throughout the cobblestone streets of Charleston's downtown, which was also filled with banks, offices, stores, hotels, warehouses, coffeehouses, and shops, many of which were Jewish owned. Along the waterfront at Broad Street and East Bay Street, elegant Georgian-style mansions of brick, iron filigree, and masonry with balconies, verandas, gardens, and gates stood as symbols to the city's confidence and affluence.

The population of 18,000 people in 1800 was also an extraordinarily cosmopolitan mixture of British colonial descendants, French Huguenots, North and Southern Germans, Creole émigrés from the Caribbean, African slaves—and a handful of increasingly influential Jews. Indeed by 1800, Charleston had the largest Jewish community in the United States—500 people, out of a total population of 1,000 Jews in South Carolina, which in turn constituted something like 40 percent of the entire Jewish population of 2,500 in the United States. By 1811, the estimate of Jews in Charleston, many of them Sephardim who had emigrated from the Netherlands or the Caribbean, climbed to a range of 600 to 700, some of whom owned slaves or engaged in the slave trade.[2]

But in 1838, an unprecedented disaster struck Charleston's complacency and prosperity. After an unusually dry spring left the city's cisterns dangerously low, a fire broke out on the evening of April 27 in a shed in the city's commercial center. By late evening it had roared throughout the downtown's wooden buildings. Overwhelmed by the water shortage, firefighters resorted to demolishing buildings to create firebreaks, blowing them up with gunpowder in some cases. Before being contained, the conflagration swept through nearly 150 acres at the heart of the city's commercial district, destroying more than a thousand buildings, most of them made of wood, including homes, stores, a recently constructed hotel, and stables. Among the ruins were the smoldering remains of three churches—and one synagogue, Congregation Kahal Kadosh Beth Elohim (Holy Congregation House of God) established as the city's first Jewish congregation in 1749.[3] Indeed of the 560 homes and businesses destroyed, Jews owned or rented 69.[4]

Its synagogue in ruins, the Beth Elohim congregation met at the Hebrew Orphan Society building and began raising funds from around the country, the Caribbean, and elsewhere overseas for a new place of worship, although most funds came from fire insurance proceeds. Before long a cornerstone was laid on January 3, 1840, for the new marble building designed by a New York architect, Cyrus L. Warner. The builder was David Lopez, from a prominent family of Sephardic families. (In 1853, he also later built Institute Hall, the Italianate structure where South Carolina's official secession was signed in 1860.)

The new synagogue was designed to replicate a Greek temple, the fashion of the day for churches, banks, and other public buildings. It was of brownstone covered with stucco, 80 feet in length with a domed ceiling, six Doric columns in front, a marble floor, a mahogany ark, and a bronze chandelier. In another distinctive feature, its door did not face the street but was on the left side of the building, so that congregants could face east, toward Jerusalem, as they prayed toward the ark. As was traditional, the reading desk (*bimah*) was in the center, though many years later it was moved to the front of the ark, where it stands today.[5]

On the wall of the synagogue were placed the Ten Commandments and—in an unusual innovation—only ten of the thirteen Articles of Faith enunciated by Maimonides, the preeminent Sephardic scholar who interpreted and codified Talmudic law in twelfth-century Spain. Omitted were the belief in the coming of a messiah who will someday restore Israel's fortunes, the resurrection of the dead, and the restoration of the Jerusalem Temple, where animal sacrifices would be resumed as they had existed before the fall of the Temple in 70 CE.

The new synagogue introduced an even more startling innovation—an organ—on the gallery at the western end of the sanctuary.

On March 19, 1841, as an overflow crowd attended the opening of the new synagogue, and the hazan sounded the shofar four times, and the choir sang the Eighteenth Psalm ("This is the day which the Lord hath made; we will rejoice and be glad in it"). Worshippers carried the Torah scrolls to the ark and lit the eternal flame.

Together they sang a hymn composed by Penina Moïse, daughter of a prominent Charleston family who had earlier helped found a Sunday school at the synagogue (the second one in America, after Philadelphia) and who had already become well known as a poet, educator, and early Jewish woman of letters in America. Clearly patterned after the popular Protestant church hymns of the day, the song culminated with a mixture of Jewish tradition and churchly music. The melody is lost, but it may well have been borrowed from a church hymnal and certainly sounds like one:

> Here, Oh Supreme! Our humble invocation;
> Our country, kindred, and the stranger bless!
> Bless too this sanctuary's consecration,
> Its hallowed purpose of our hearts impress.
> Still, still, let choral harmony,
> Ascend before thy throne;
> While echoing seraphim reply
> The Lord our God is one! [6]

The plea for "choral harmony," perhaps a reference to the angels surrounding the heavenly throne in Isaiah, was heartfelt, especially because it came after the struggles to rebuild the synagogue. But in fact, the history of the congregation at Beth Elohim had been filled with discord—over doctrine, over practices, and over whether the installation of an organ, and playing it on the Sabbath, violated Jewish law. The dispute in the tiny Jewish community of Charleston was an incubator of the forces that tore apart and ultimately transformed Judaism in America in the first century after the American Revolution.

## A COLONIAL ERA BEGINNING

The first Jew of record in South Carolina, probably a *converso,* a Jew who had ostensibly converted to Christianity (though some continued to practice Judaism in secret following the Spanish Inquisition), was an interpreter for some Indians who were apparently Catholic, brought from Florida in 1695. The governor, implementing the colony's ban on Catholics, sent them back. The episode illustrates the crucial role of Protestant religious identity throughout the colonies, but especially in the South. Two years later, for example, the colonial Assembly granted full freedom of worship—to Protestants only. Thus could Jews hold various public offices in Charleston into the era of independence, from police warden to postal officer and registrar. They also served on boards and commissions running schools, the local hospital, and orphanages.[7]

In the early eighteenth century, many Jews who settled in Charleston came from the Caribbean. They ranged from ordinary tradespeople to families of considerable wealth, and most arrived in the 1740s as the city took off as a commercial center. One prominent slaveholder, Mordecai Cohen, one of the wealthiest Jews in the city, had come from Poland and rose to financial success after starting out as an immigrant peddler. He purchased a 1,000-acre estate called Soldier's Retreat, overlooking the Ashley River and operated by his son David, where slaves helped work in the fields and raise the Cohen children. (By 1830, an estimated 83 percent of Jews in Charleston were in families that owned slaves.)[8]

Jews also voted in an election in 1703, which one historian speculates might have been the first such exercise of franchise in the West.[9] Later in the century, they brought steamboats to the Savannah River, ran steamships to Havana, and helped establish the chamber of commerce. There were well-known Jewish writers, artists, teachers, lawyers, physicians, and publishers. Two of the four newspapers in Charleston were edited by Jews at one point. They were founding members of the Supreme Council of Scottish Rite Masonry in Charleston in 1801.[10]

The influx of Jews stirred some resentment in the city. A letter in the *Charleston Gazette* of December 1, 1778, charged that immigrants of "the

Tribe of Israel" arriving from Georgia came "with their ill got wealth." But published letters by Jews assailed such slurs, showing confidence among them that they could speak out on their behalf. "Wealth and culture did not change the fact that some Jews felt uneasy in social situations," writes the historian James William Hagy.

Difficulties arose for Jews, however, out of their need to keep their shops open on Sunday, in violation of the state's blue laws. The Sunday closings, affirmed by the South Carolina legislature in 1685 and again in 1712, were a hardship for Jews obliged by religious doctrine to keep their stores closed on Saturdays as well. (Indeed, their synagogue penalized them if they violated Jewish Sabbath restrictions.)

In 1776 a grand jury in Charleston called for Jews to be "restrained from allowing their negroes to sell goods in shops," presumably because, while Jews could not themselves operate their stores on the Jewish Sabbath, they could delegate non-Jewish employees to do so. In 1801, the city council made it a crime for anyone to "exercise any worldly labor, business or work" on Sunday. The difficulties continued well into the nineteenth century, directed in particular at instances of Jews improperly selling goods to African Americans, which they may have done to create a legal fiction—selling their wares to blacks, who would then resell them, and then settling accounts after the Sabbath. Many arrests of Jews took place for such infractions in the state. Attempts to overturn these laws as unconstitutional were rejected on the ground that closures were within the ambit of police regulations and that, in any case, Christianity was part of "common law." (The South Carolina legislature did not relax the Sunday laws until 1983.)[11]

The Revolutionary War posed a dilemma for Jews in Charleston, dependent as they were on commercial ties with both sides. The first Jew believed to have died in the war of independence was Francis Salvador of South Carolina, scion of an aristocratic merchant Sephardic family tracing its roots to Amsterdam and England. Their property wealth extended to 200,000 acres in Greenwood County in the Piedmont Plateau, where some evidence suggests the Salvador family may have been planning to establish a haven for Jews. Salvador—who the records show had dealings with such Carolina patriots as William Henry Drayton, Charles Cotesworth (C. C.) Pinckney, and Edward Rutledge—was at his upcountry plantation when Cherokee Indians attacked, apparently encouraged by British sympathizers as the colonies headed toward revolt.

Under siege, Salvador rode his horse twenty-eight miles through hostile territory to alert local patriot militias, thus becoming known in local lore as a Jewish Paul Revere figure in South Carolina. Salvador and Major Andrew Williamson made a surprise early-morning counterattack on the Indians but were ambushed, and Salvador was shot and scalped. In his final minutes of life, he asked Williamson if they had won the day. "I told him yes," Williamson later recalled. "He said he was glad of it and shook me by the hand, and bade me farewell and said he would die in a few minutes." Salvador was twenty-nine years old and very likely perished before hearing of the Declaration of Independence.[12]

## A "HOLY CONGREGATION" CHAFES UNDER TRADITION

Charleston's most prominent Jewish congregation, Kahal Kadosh Beth Elohim, was the fifth Jewish congregation in the colonies, following others that had been formed in New York, Newport, Savannah, and Philadelphia.[13] Its first chief rabbi was Moses Cohen, though no proof exists that he was ordained. Worshippers met initially at a wooden house on Union (now State) Street near Queen Street, and kept to strict Orthodox traditions. Anyone violating the Sabbath or other holidays was subject to "severe penalties and forfeiture of the honors of the Synagogue," according to the congregation's earliest historian, Nathaniel Levin. They used the Minhag Sepharad (Sephardic Custom), adopted by Portuguese congregations in London and Amsterdam, and power was vested in an *adjunta*, or board, of eighteen members. Isaac DaCosta was elected hazan. Joseph Tobias was parnas, and Philip Hart was mohel, performing circumcisions.[14]

Beth Elohim "numbered among its members the most intellectual men among the Jews of America; many, too, whose fathers had lived here before them, and who by their industry and by their integrity had made the name Jew respected," wrote an early historian of the community, Barnett A. Elzas. "The Jew was a man here." But Elzas also described the original bylaws as "severely autocratic," exercising great control over the conduct of Jews within the synagogue and outside it, in a manner that perhaps paved the way for difficulties.[15]

Indeed, this early period was not without internal divisions, but details are sketchy. In 1775, a group of five congregants (including Isaac DaCosta) claimed that two other congregants, Emanuel Abrahams and Myer Moses, had acted "contrary to the original institution & rules" of the synagogue. No specifics exist. But the five dissidents appear to have defected to another place of worship with plans to build another synagogue. Their defection occurred just as a group of new arrivals, some from Germany, came to Charleston, splitting it into the same two ethnic factions that were driving Sephardim and Ashkenazim apart in New York, Philadelphia, and elsewhere.

With British forces occupying Charleston, at least some Jewish patriots fled. Isaac DaCosta, like Seixas in New York, escaped to Philadelphia, where he also joined the Sephardic congregation, Mikveh Israel, in 1782. But his return after the war reignited the synagogue's ethnic divide, just as in Shearith Israel. It was kindled by DaCosta's family wanting him to be buried in a separate Sephardic cemetery.[16]

After sending its own congratulatory letter to Washington in 1790, Beth Elohim petitioned South Carolina the next year to incorporate officially, pledging that its members would "be conducive to the decent and regular exercise of their religion and public worship of the Almighty God, ruler of the universe, to the proper maintenance of the poor, and to the support and education of the orphans of their society. . . ." The South Carolina legislature authorized its incorporation the same year.[17]

By 1820, Charleston continued to be the home of the largest Jewish community in the United States, with a population that had grown to 700,

compared to only 550 in New York City, 450 in Philadelphia, 200 in Richmond, 150 in Baltimore, 100 in Savannah, and 500 to 600 others in the rest
of the country. (In all, Jews constituted less than a tenth of a percent of the
total US population of 4 million.)[18]

Internal disagreements at Beth Elohim spilled into a struggle to find
a suitable hazan after the death of the incumbent in 1805. One candidate
was brought in from London and sent back immediately. The arrival of
the Reverend Abraham Azuby as the hazan and rabbi of Beth Elohim
in the 1790s repaired the breach between the Sephardic and Ashkenazi
branches, but Azuby died in 1805, whereupon the congregation appealed
to Bevis Marks Synagogue, the oldest in London, for help in filling the va-
cancy. But the rabbi they sent from London, Benjamin Cohen D'Azevedo,
arrived with his family only to be rejected as "sickly" and for other reasons
not qualified.

The synagogue then turned to its own members to fill the job. In 1811
they recruited Emanuel Nunes Carvalho, a London-born rabbi who had
served in Barbados and then New York. But he too ran into controversy
and trouble with the board, according to the writings of Mordecai Manuel
Noah, who lived for a time in the city. According to Noah's writings, Carvalho's offense was teaching the children of the synagogue to sing a concluding
psalm in the morning service in a "handsome manner" that did away with
the "discordance" everyone was accustomed to. Noah had a gift for exaggeration, but he reported that a dispute over the singing led to a "rabble" of
"vagrant Jews" fighting one another at the synagogue.[19]

Increasingly, however, the Jews of Charleston were chafing under the
liturgy and order of service they found alien and restrictive. Congregation
members were growing uneasy about the practice of allowing members to
bid on various honors, such as taking the Torah from the ark or reading
from it. The Sabbath service was too long for many. It took three hours or
more and was entirely in Hebrew, of a kind chanted or mumbled hurriedly
and indistinctly by congregants, robbing the prayers of any religious significance, in view of the critics. "Almost no one understood the language," one
early dissenter, Abraham Moïse, later wrote. "Substance has yielded to form,

the religion of the heart to the observance of unmeaning forms and ceremonies, while we are forced to witness the impious exchange of the honours of the synagogue for a consideration in pounds, shillings, and pence." In a biography of his grandfather, the writer L. C. Moïse described that service as imbued by "cabalistic and Talmudic writings, and the erroneous doctrines of the imperious rabbis." [20]

But decisions on making changes in the service belonged to a select category of leaders called yahidim—people who had resided in the city for two years. Only they could vote for members of a twenty-five-member "General Adjunta" and also a smaller "Private Adjunta," which in turn elected the parnas, and the rules also banned anyone from forming a second synagogue congregation in Charleston.

On December 23, 1824, increasingly frustrated by what they felt were obsolete and obscure practices at Beth Elohim, forty-seven members of the congregation signed a petition, or "memorial," to call for changes in the service. The "memorial" instructed Aaron Phillips, their chairman, to deliver it to the synagogue board. "The memorial of the undersigned, showeth unto your honourable body, that they have witnessed with deep regret, the apathy and neglect which have been manifested towards our holy religion," it began. "As inheritors of the *true faith*, and always proud to be considered by the world as a portion of 'God's chosen people,' they have been pained to perceive the gradual decay of that system of worship, which, for ages past, *peculiarly* distinguished us from among the nations of the earth." Elaborating, they noted that they had become "seriously impressed" with the belief that "certain defects" in the system of worship were the source of the problem. These defects, they argued, would "darken the mind" of future generations, preventing them from a "more rational means of worshipping the true God." The manifesto called first for at least some prayers to be repeated in English by the reader in order to achieve "more decency and decorum." Not everyone, it noted, had the time to learn Hebrew and thus understand the service. Next, the manifesto called for "the absolute necessity of abridging the service generally." The length, it was argued, meant that the prayer readers, rushing to finish before noon, raced so fast through the Hebrew that the words were nearly incomprehensible. Expressing disdain for the bidding wars over honors, such as the honor of reciting the blessings before and after each section of the weekly Torah portion, the petitioners argued that such auctions gave an unfortunate impression to children and strangers, perhaps reinforcing the unwanted stereotype of Jewish crassness. And they called for sermons or lessons to be delivered as ministers in churches had done. Finally, they warned, that actions must be taken to protect Jews in the face of Christian missionary activity, and they cited examples of reforms under way in Holland, Germany, and Prussia.

"We wish not to *overthrow*, but to *rebuild*," the manifesto concluded. "We wish not to *destroy*, but to *reform* and *revise* the evils complained of; we wish not to *abandon* the Institutions of Moses, but to *understand and observe* them; in fine, we wish to worship God, not as *slaves of bigotry and priestcraft*, but as the enlightened descendants of that chosen race whose blessings have been scattered throughout our land of Abraham, Isaac and Jacob."[21]

Who were these petitioners?

First, they tended to be younger and less wealthy members of the congregation. Many had gotten to know each other through outside social and charity groups, such as the Hebrew Orphan Society and the Freemasons, or through private academies for the young, such as one established by a local writer and educator, Isaac Harby. As a group, the petitioners "were young, civically involved, and philanthropically oriented individuals," writes the scholar Gary P. Zola. In effect they represented what Zola calls "the first formalized effort to reform Judaism in North America."[22]

As radical as the dissenters were, they gave no suggestion that they wanted to withdraw from Beth Elohim. Rather they wanted to reform it from within. But their wishes for change in the system were not to be fulfilled.

## THE SCHISM DEEPENS

It did not take long for the reformers' plea to be spurned. On January 20, 1825, the adjunta noted that such fundamental changes in the synagogue required a revision of its 1820 constitution, which could only be adopted by the executive officers or by two thirds of the congregation's members. In other words, the petitioners were told they needed signatures of two thirds of the synagogue congregation even to have a debate.[23]

In response, the dissenters decided to create the "Reformed Society of Israelites for Promoting True Principles of Judaism According to Its Purity and Spirit," adopting their own constitution on February 15, 1825. The reforms constituted an agenda far more radical than anything seen so far in the United States. In 1826, the Society made a clean break from Beth Elohim and began soliciting funds. They maintained that far from seeking radical changes, they wanted to make it more possible to adhere to fundamental principles of Judaism. But the leadership of Beth Elohim disagreed, and for the time being, their ruling was law.

Initially, the Reformed Society met in a Masonic hall in 1824. Two years later it was incorporated by an act of the state legislature and appealed for subscriptions in a circular calling for more English to be used in prayers. The society's credo substituted the immortality of the soul, an emerging idea among some Jewish scholars, for the traditional Jewish belief in a resurrection of the dead. They further declared that only the Ten Commandments, not the entire Torah, were revealed by God to the Jewish people—and that the 613 commandments that by ancient reckoning governed daily practices of Jews were also not revealed orally by God to Moses, as traditional Judaism asserted. The society also introduced a newly explicit concept of "good faith towards all mankind" as a Jewish tenet and discarded the belief in a personal messiah, replacing it with the idea that God was the "only true Redeemer" for humanity. This latter declaration was an implicit message of rejection of Christianity as well. In keeping with a custom that started in Europe, the synagogue that the Reformers had in mind would also be called a "temple," intended partly to suggest that worship would be conducted in a place supplanting the ancient Temple in Jerusalem, which Jews supposedly no longer needed to mourn and for which restoration was no longer seen as necessary.[24]

These bold steps were taken in the shadow of the doctrine as enunciated in the twelfth century by Maimonides, whose thirteen articles that Jews were to embrace "with perfect faith" had served as a lasting legacy for many Jews for many hundreds of years. Scholars note that Maimonides's tenets were intended less as dogma than as a pedagogical tool. But they were taken as important by Jews because of their help in understanding how to relate to God. Maimonides was a pathfinder for Jews in many other respects by helping to define the identity of God for a modern world. Scholars note, for example, that in the early parts of the Bible, God could be encountered on Earth as an angel, or present inside a burning bush, or as an actual, human-shaped God with a body that could be observed by Moses and others on Mount Sinai. Toward the end of biblical times, God was unseen, residing in highest heaven, surrounded by angels but accessible to ordinary humans only through prayer.[25] Maimonides took the existence of God further into the realm of an incorporeal, unknowable, and eternal entity, though Maimonides also continued to maintain that the laws of Moses—transmitted from God in "written" and "oral" form—were true and divine, as were the interpretations applied by the rabbinic sages. His contention that God's identity was essentially incomprehensible to ordinary mortals has stood the test of time for Jews throughout the world.

Besides omitting the concept of a personal messiah, the Reformed Society proposed a number of more down-to-earth changes. Believing that covering men's heads during services was never intended to be a legal requirement, some members prayed bareheaded. A confirmation service was proposed, calling for young adults to come forward and confirm their devotion to Judaism, mirroring a practice in churches. The reformers also laid plans for their own prayer book, or *siddur*, in which original prayers in English accompanied translations into English of Hebrew prayers, along with the Hebrew originals. Overseen by David N. Carvalho, Isaac Harby, and Abraham Moïse and published in 1830, it became the first published reform prayer book in North America. Many experts view *The Sabbath Service and Miscellaneous Prayers, Adopted by the Reformed Society of Israelites,* as one of the most radical liturgical innovations in Judaism introduced up until that time.

The articles of faith embraced by the Reformed Society were certainly part of Jewish tradition. They acknowledged God to be the creator of the universe, that there was only one God and that God's identity was all-knowing but not "corporeal" or comprehensible, as Maimonides had suggested. They held that God rewards those who observe his commandments as delivered to Moses, but that an all-encompassing humanism, directed at all peoples and not just the Jews, "is among the most acceptable offerings to the Deity" and that "the pure and upright heart is the chosen temple of Jehovah," an alternative pronunciation of the name of God in the Bible. (The name "Jehovah" was thought at the time to be the original pronunciation of the sacred name of God in the Bible, YHWH, which had ceased to be pronounced out loud by Jews in early post-biblical times.) But references to the Messiah, the resurrection of the dead, and return of Jews to Zion, along with the rebuilding of the Temple in Jerusalem, were conspicuous by their absence, borderline heretical, and precedent setting.[26]

Gary P. Zola summarizes the dominant themes of the society as anti-rabbinical, based on the belief that Judaism had long been manipulated by the laws of the ancient Jewish sages. The Charleston reformers accused the Talmudic rabbis of "priestcraft," a disparaging term used in early modern Europe to condemn the obscurantism and corruption of the Christian priesthood. In addition to their disdain for the negative influence of Talmudic sages, the members of the Society professed a patriotism toward America rooted in Jewish tenets. Of equal importance, Zola notes, was its effective codification of the idea that because God does not intervene in daily affairs, it is up to humans to execute his moral code through good deeds. The issue of whether or not God rewards and punishes humans for their individual or collective behavior has been debated by scholars citing texts for and against through the millennia. But the South Carolina Jews gave strong new impetus to the idea that people are responsible for their own actions. As Harby put it, the beauty and splendors of Nature reflected the existence of God, even if the notion of God's intervention to punish those who sinned was "preposterous and unjust."[27]

The God of these South Carolina Jews was best understood by reason and not blind faith in revelation from ancient times—again, a concept as old as Maimonides. But in revising the service and prayers for Jews, the reformers were not just adjusting doctrines. They were clearly emulating parts of church worship, such as the use of choirs, hymns, and an emphasis on restraint and dignity. No less important was their stress on religious tolerance and liberal universalism. These tenets embodied an attempt to universalize Judaism, as Zola puts it—to "Americanize" it—while taking pride in Judaism as a principal source of universal civilization and morality.[28]

## THE LEGACY OF ISAAC HARBY (1788–1828)

The revolt of reformers can be usefully understood through Harby's unorthodox but idealistic career as educator, journalist, playwright, literary critic, newspaper publisher, and editor. For Harby, as he put it, "the great cause of IMPROVEMENT in government, in religion, in morals, in literature, is the great cause of mankind."[29] Of major importance, however, was Harby's concern—hardly without foundation—that an increasingly organized effort among Protestant evangelicals was under way to convert American Jews and that steps had to be taken to strengthen Judaism against such an assault.

While defending Judaism, however, he conceded that he and other Jews actually knew little about their traditions, including Hebrew, and that the Spanish and Portuguese rituals at Beth Elohim were a barrier rather than a vehicle to achieving a new understanding of his own faith. Harby was also candid about his yearning for status and fame as a literary figure in the community at large. "Is there more praise in disgracing my forefathers than in becoming illustrious myself?" he once wrote.[30]

Like many Sephardic Jews in America, Harby was originally descended from a family tracing its history to Spain and Portugal before the Inquisition. From there the family fled to Morocco and then to England, where Isaac's grandfather worked as a jeweler and had six children, including Solomon, Isaac's father. Solomon Harby arrived in Charleston in 1781 as the British faced defeat in the Revolutionary War and earned a reasonably secure living as a butcher and later an auctioneer. He was apparently not a particularly observant member of the Jewish community, having once been fined for not attending a general meeting of the synagogue. But he appears to have been involved in the Masonic lodge movement, where Jews and others developed values of public service and other civic virtues.

Isaac was only seventeen when his father died and he became head of a family in straitened circumstances. But he continued to pursue a classic education, learning Latin, Greek, and French and other works of literature. He studied at an academy operated by the Reverend William Best, where he devoured Herodotus, Plutarch, Homer, Milton, and Sir Walter Scott, while also learning to draw. He also studied Protestant and Methodist religious treatises. Untrained in Talmudic studies, he nonetheless developed pride in his Jewish heritage and even claimed that the name Harby derived from the Hebrew word for sword, an inspiration for his creating a family crest featuring the image of a sword and shield. Enjoying the civic life of debate and public service, he wrote an ambitious twenty-page composition at a young age entitled an "Essay on Truth," rejecting notions of supernatural revelation and divine intervention in the world. He decided early to pursue a career in law, teaching, and writing. He published essays and articles for newspapers under various pseudonyms and tried his hand at writing plays, with little success. After a local theater manager rebuffed him, evidently regarding Harby's work as pretentious and academic, Harby started a literary magazine called the *Quiver*, possibly the first literary journal published by a Jew in the United States. Its purpose, Harby grandiloquently declared, was to offer the people of South Carolina "a species of DIVERSION, rather of a more refined, and we hope, of a more agreeable nature, than drinking punch or playing billiards." It ran poetry, humorous anecdotes, letters seeking romantic advice, essays about local theater, and theater reviews before it folded after less than a year.

These failures led Harby to move briefly to an island southwest of Charleston where he took up a kind of quest for spiritual meaning and a need to educate the world about Judaism, a subject that he knew little about except from Christian scholars. Moving back to Charleston in 1809, Harby took up playwriting again, again without success, so he turned to teaching, establishing an "academy" in 1810 modeled after English Latin grammar schools, where he oversaw the teaching of reading, writing, grammar, rhetoric, arithmetic, history, geography, Latin, and Greek. At last, he achieved success. The academy appealed to Charleston's emerging Jewish elite families, providing Harby with what Zola, his biographer, describes as "emotional and financial stability." He married Rachael Mordecai in 1810. A few years later, he grew restless again. This time he purchased a newspaper, a not unusual occupation for successful Jews in the South.

The newspaper business was booming, in fact. His paper, called the *Investigator*, changed its name to the *Southern Patriot and Commercial Advertiser* in 1814, containing original pieces and reproducing articles from other papers in the United States and London. Working through local politicians, including up-and-coming Representative John C. Calhoun, he got a contract from the government to print the text of laws passed by the legislature in 1816.

Still, Harby rarely dealt with Jewish topics, except to oppose attempts to convert Jews and to praise Napoleon for his efforts to emancipate French Jews. Eventually the paper failed, and Harby went back to teaching at his reopened academy, though by now he had become a person of prominence in Charleston and able to enroll nearly ninety students, most of them Jewish, some from the Hebrew Orphan Society. Tuition payments to the school kept Harby reasonably comfortable, at least for a time. While keeping up with his literary writings about Byron, Sir Walter Scott, and Shakespeare, Harby then wrote his third (and last) play, *Alberti*, which debuted in 1819—a success at last. The play was set in Florence at the time of the Medicis, dealing with a complicated romance of two feuding brothers over a love interest against a backdrop of the struggle for political freedom. It was so popular that President James Monroe came to see it while in Charleston.

The play brought him some financial success, but it was not enough to reverse the declining fortunes of his academy, forcing him to borrow money from the Hebrew Orphan Society, with which he became enmeshed in a legal dispute. To make ends meet, Harby turned back to journalism and became a contributing editor for the *Charleston Gazette*, where he advocated road improvements, warned of fire hazards, dispensed advice on nosebleeds, and emphasized the importance of female modesty.

As the debates over free states versus slave states heated up in the 1820s, Harby defended the rights of slave states and, like many of his cohorts, feared the radicalism of those advocating abolition, especially by violence. A trial in 1822 over a revolt led by a former slave who had purchased his freedom stirred fears of spreading rebellion. Harby declared the insurrection "a scheme of wildness and of wickedness, enough to make us . . . shudder at the indiscriminate mischief of the plan and its objects." After serving briefly as editor of the *Gazette*, Harby started a new afternoon paper called the *Examiner*. He backed the fiery antiestablishment war hero Andrew Jackson in the fateful 1824 election won by John Quincy Adams, and supported him again in 1828, when Jackson defeated Adams and went to the White House.

Yet Harby's financial troubles deepened. He had to close his academy and teach at another school for economically disadvantaged students. It was in this period of economic frustration and disappointment that he turned to a new cause—reforming Judaism. He spoke out on behalf of the Reformed Society of Israelites, defending the society's stance on reform in speeches and a pamphlet, and served as its president in 1827. His purpose was clear: to alter and revise those parts of Judaism's "prevailing system of worship, as are inconsistent with the present enlightened state of society, and [are] not in accordance with the Five Books of Moses and the Prophets."[31]

*Three*

# REBELLION IN CHARLESTON

A troublesome specter haunted American Judaism in its early decades, despite the sense of belonging felt by most Jews. It was the specter of conversion. The first Jewish periodical in the United States, *The Jew,* published by Solomon Henry Jackson in New York City in the 1820s, was essentially an anti-missionary journal, for example. But it took some time for Harby and others to come to grips with the phenomenon. Initially, when the Reformed Society was getting started in 1824, Harby was sympathetic but not yet fully engaged in its commitment to adapt Judaism to contemporary demands. As the movement gathered steam, however, he was motivated to join the cause in large part to combat efforts by Protestant evangelical groups to persuade Jews to come to Jesus. The concerns had a basis in real events. In 1816, an organization called the "American Society for Evangelizing the Jews" was established in New York, followed by similar groups in Boston and other cities, all determined to make Jewish assimilation in

America into a stepping-stone to a full embrace of Jesus Christ. The activities of these groups were reported in the Charleston press, and publicity was given to the activities of those Jews who had decided to convert.

Harby appears to have grown obsessed with these developments. He dipped into various publications favoring conversion and other descriptions against them. He made clear that he was not opposed to Bible societies per se, only to these societies targeting Jews. In 1823, responding to a famous proselytizer's plan to deliver lectures in Charleston, Harby assailed "those fond preachers who are vainly toiling to convert the Jews, by the very scripture which the Jews have taught them."[1] His sensitivity extended to deploring the Jewish stereotype of Shylock in *The Merchant of Venice*.

Also of concern was publicity over what was known as the "Maryland Jew Bill," a measure debated in the 1820s aimed at granting Jews in Maryland total political equality there. The bill was enacted in 1826, but many Jews were alarmed over the noisy resistance to it. It did not help that anti-Semitism came in the guise of romanticizing Jews as exotic and even virtuous and worthy of conversion. To refute such writings, Harby realized he had to counter the ignorance among Jews of their own religion, so he embarked on writings about Jewish matters and invited readers to come see the Torah at Beth Elohim.

Harby's comrades in arms were David N. Carvalho, who was to play a major role in revising the prayer book, and Abraham Moïse, the most fervent organizer and a close friend. At the society's first-anniversary meeting on November 21, 1825, at a Masonic Hall, Harby delivered the keynote, notable for its articulation of the desire for change in Jewish self-identity. "Your principles are rapidly pervading the whole mass of Hebrews throughout the United States," he declared. "What is it that we seek? The establishment of a new sect? No. Never. . . . What is it then that we ask of Hebrew Vestry? The abolition of the ancient language and form of Jewish worship? Far from it."

He opposed establishing a new synagogue and instead called on the leaders of Beth Elohim to "open the door to reason—to welcome, with the welcome of brethren, those who desire to add dignity to their religion."

The objective, he said, was to respect the feelings of the pious but to re-move those parts of the service that "excite the disgust of the well-informed Israelite"—what he called rabbinical "interpolations" and repetitions. He pro-posed inclusion of English translations of prayers chanted in Hebrew, efforts to institute some solemnity in the service, and a "lecture or discourse upon the law" that would instruct worshippers and elevate their understanding.

Three important justifications figured in Harby's message: prayer, to come from the heart, must be uttered in languages that people could un-derstand, namely English. Though Harby was a major advocate of students learning Greek and Latin, he argued it was absurd to use Hebrew exclusively for communicating with the divine. Second, Harby buttressed his proposal to set aside "rabbinical interpolations" by his reading of Jewish history, which came not simply from the Bible but from non-Jewish sources describing the suffering and dignity of Jews throughout history. He did not specify what he meant by these "interpolations," but the general efforts to interpret Jewish law—what the biblical scholar James L. Kugel calls "the great Interpretive Revolution"—occurred in the centuries before and after the fall of the Tem-ple in 70 CE. These interpretations produced the rules that were to govern Judaism until modern times. For example, Deuteronomy's most famous exhortation—the "Shema," or "Hear, O Israel"—contains a series of com-mands for Jews to love God "with all your heart and with all your soul and with all your might." It tells Jews to teach God's commands to their children and bind them on their hands, between their eyes, and on their doorposts. It was the sages who converted this generalized and perhaps metaphorical commandment into a series of specific acts of piety and prayer. "It is no exaggeration to say that nearly every page of the Torah included at least one verse that had been radically recast by ancient interpreters," writes Kugel.[2]

Harby did not doubt that Jews since antiquity had preserved their iden-tity and their religion by following this array of strictures on human con-duct: eating kosher food, binding the commandments on their foreheads, and observing the Sabbath. But now that Jews were ready to contribute to civil society in Europe and America, he said, the "follies" and "vices" pro-duced by rabbinical interpreters should be seen as the work, not of God, but of men, "retired within their closets, and shut up over their useless volumes" rather than their surroundings—men "who substituted shadow for substance, and form for reality," as he put it. He attacked the rabbis whose interpretations bore the force of law down through the millennia as "fabulists and sophists, who, caught in the net of platonic subtlety, mingled Grecian metaphysics with Phariseean materialism; ceremonial and verbal refiners, who tortured the plainest precepts of the Law into monstrous and unexpected inferences." And not least, Harby noted, these interpretations had drawn derision from non-Jews with whom Jews increasingly were interacting in America.[3]

The "fabulists" of which Harby spoke were the interpreters of what is called the Oral Law, which the rabbis since ancient times have regarded as spoken directly from God to Moses. For Harby, however, "The only Law is the written one, found in the books of Moses." Harby deplored the fact that even in America, Jews believed that "rabbinical doctrine or ceremony" had divine status and did not understand the necessity of adopting Judaism "to the circumstances of the times in which we enjoy our liberties." He singled out exceptional men of letters he said had risen above the obscurantist interpolations of the rabbis, listing Maimonides, Spinoza, and Moses Mendelssohn, the eighteenth-century German scholar associated with Haskalah, the "Jewish enlightenment." He also cited Isaac D'Israeli, a British contemporary and man of letters who later became best known as the father of Benjamin Disraeli, the Victorian-era British prime minister.

For the most part, he went on, rabbinic doctrine accepted by the majority of rabbis had become oppressive, foisted on the multitudes who then succumbed to the "bigotry of intellect and credulity of belief." Harby did not blame the many centuries of Talmudic rabbis themselves. Indeed, he maintained that mistreatment of Jews throughout the ages had forced them to retreat into their own communities and ghettos, while adhering strictly to tradition as a survival mechanism. But now it was time to realize, he said, that the days of rejection and humiliation were over, and that Jews in America had been free from this subjugation. It was time, he said, for the Jews of America to adapt the institutions handed down to them "to

the circumstances of the times in which we live." They were not abandoning their tenets or practices, he went on. Rather they were abandoning the
"rubbish" of the ages.[4]

In conclusion, Harby delivered a distinctly religious and Jewish inter-
pretation of the United States as "God's new Israel." He cited Malachi and
Psalms to claim that the Bible had even referenced places outside the land
of Israel that would shelter the people of Israel. And he argued that perhaps
Jews had been dispersed for a reason—a mission—to spread the name of
God among the Gentiles. And he concluded with an exhortation from the
Psalm 131:

> Behold how good and how pleasant it is
> For brethren to dwell together in unity!

Harby's address was so well-received he distributed it as a pamphlet
a few weeks later, and it succeeded in bringing attention for his views to
non-Jews, including Edward Livingston, former US representative of New
York and later President Jackson's secretary of state. Another notable commentator was former president Thomas Jefferson, then in his eighties,
who said that while he was "little acquainted with the liturgy of the Jews or
their mode of worship," he found Harby's approach "entirely reasonable."
(Jefferson, after his retirement from the White House, had become increasingly outspoken as a skeptic of the Bible, asserting that Jesus never intended
to declare himself the son of God.)

The *Christian Examiner and Theological Review,* an historically important journal of liberal Christianity with followers among Unitarians and also
such figures as Ralph Waldo Emerson of the Transcendental movement,
praised the Harby address for holding "just and noble views of civil and
religious liberty." Harby's peroration was noticed in Europe as well. A Brus-
sels journal compared it to the Protestant Reformation and hailed Harby as
someone who overcame the prejudices of his own religious heritage.[5]

Another figure in the liberal Christian movement, the Reverend Samuel Gilman, Unitarian minister of the Second Independent Church of

Charleston—later the Unitarian Church of Charleston—praised Harby's "discourse" and also recounted his experience of attending services at Beth Elohim in an article in 1826 in the *North American Review* of Boston, perhaps the leading literary journal of its day.

Gilman (1791–1858) was a major figure in establishing Unitarianism in the antebellum South, and became a beloved figure in Charleston's social and intellectual scene—though he is perhaps best known today as the author of his alma mater's hymn, "Fair Harvard." The Sabbath service he attended, Gilman wrote, was difficult for an outsider to follow, marked by incessant murmuring of Hebrew and occasional Spanish, people standing up and down and walking in and out, while chanting "with great indistinctness and volubility, now sinking into a low murmur, now in violent vociferation."[6] Gilman's record is one of the few that describes what it was like to be in a service at Beth Elohim at the time that reformers wanted to break away.

These were the qualities that "reformers" in Charleston were trying to tame. Gilman praised Harby, declaring in a backhanded compliment that he previously had no idea that so many Jews had "surmounted the proverbial prejudices of their race" to embrace the liberal spirit of the age. In a possible indication that Gilman and Harby had communicated—although there is not necessarily evidence that they even knew each other—Gilman cited Harby's declaration that he had no intention of establishing a new sect of Jews, and that his purpose was only to align Judaism with the "enlightened" practices of Jews in France and Germany. Gilman erroneously suggested that the Jews might even shift Sabbath worship from Saturday to Sunday but later was corrected by Harby.

Not all the reaction was positive, of course. Harby's nemeses in this period included Mordecai Manuel Noah, who ridiculed the reform initiative as ignorant and antithetical to his own cause of trying to establish a colony for Jews in North America. A more serious and sustained criticism came from a prominent Jew in Richmond, Virginia, Jacob Mordecai, an observant Jewish educator and leader of Congregation Kahal Kadosh Beth Shalome, who charged that the Reformed Society would "destroy the ancient fabric of Israelite worship" and "gradually undermine all confidence in their religion under the pretext of divesting it of Rabbinical impurities and interpretations."

Mordecai, descended from a family that had emigrated from Germany, had served in the Continental Army under General George Washington. Like Harby, he had struggled to make a living (as a tobacco merchant) but gave up business to establish an "academy" where he could impart the knowledge he had gained from studying the Bible and Jewish law. The Warrenton Female Academy became one of the leading institutions for women in the country. Harby, he said from Richmond, obviously knew too little of Jewish law to suggest changing it. He then backed up that assertion with his own knowledge of history, arguing that Harby misunderstood the Protestant Reformation (which Harby cited as a model), in that Martin Luther's teachings resulted in "atrocious persecution and spiritual intolerance" of Jews.

Introducing lectures in English, abolishing offerings, translating prayer books, and setting forth more uniform and orderly chanting of prayers could be considered acceptable, Mordecai conceded. But he charged that these changes seemed a subterfuge aimed at getting Jews to "cease to exist" as a separate people. Nor was it a blessing that the Jews were integrating themselves into the American fabric, Mordecai argued, because in places like Turkey and Arabia they enjoyed a "sovereign authority" over their own affairs that was preferable to falling under civil laws in the United States. American Jews, Mordecai reminded Harby, still suffered exclusion from certain political rights in America, including the military.

As for Harby's study of history, Mordecai ridiculed his reliance on modern Christian scholars of Hebrew and on such ancients as Josephus (the first-century Roman Jewish scholar he labeled a "half traitor"), Saint Jerome, Gibbon, the writings of Deists, Spinoza ("an atheist of the first order"), and other "calumniators of Jews." He pointed out that Moses Mendelssohn, the great founder of enlightened Judaism and acquaintance of Immanuel Kant, was, for all his revolutionary thinking, an adherent to the Talmud that Harby was rejecting. Harby was clearly incapable, Mordecai declared, of understanding the writings of the rabbinic sages whom he dismissed as ignorant and bigoted. But what infuriated Mordecai the most was Harby's embrace of the anathema that the United States was somehow the "new Jerusalem" that could replace the Jewish people's object of yearning to return to the Holy Land. "The Scriptures speak of no other 'spot as the future country of the Israelites'" than the land of Israel. "There is no enigma to solve, no room for 'fanciful conjecture' to justify a 'belief that America truly is the land of promise spoken in our ancient Scripture.'"

Mordecai appealed to Jewish youth not to be misled by Harby's delusion that they could abandon tradition and still be Jews. He beseeched young Jews not to "take the fatal leap that is to separate you for ever from the religion of your fathers. . . . We wish to caution [you] in the language of our law giver: 'take heed to thyself that you be not snared.'"[7]

## REFORMED SOCIETY: ATROPHY AND REVIVAL

The arguments that tore the Jewish community apart in South Carolina have been likened by some traditionalists to the internal conflicts among Jews that contributed to the destruction of the Second Temple, as Jews descended into "a disjointed tribe, rent asunder by fierce party strife, and arrayed in hostile position against each other."[8]

But for all the sound and fury of the 1820s, the Reformed Society atrophied rapidly after its initial few successful years. One reason was that Harby dropped out of the battle. Devastated by the death of his wife in 1827, Harby was left to care for their six young children. He continued to teach and write, but Charleston's own economy suffered, losing business to northern ports. Despite his efforts, Charleston became caught up in evangelical fervor among Christians, and Harby's appeals for tolerance and universalism seemed increasingly out of favor in the Gentile community, as Baptists, Methodists, and Presbyterians held revival meetings filled with sermons and themes of repentance, damnation, and salvation.

Disillusioned by Charleston and attracted by the cultural life of New York, Harby moved there in 1828. He became editor of the *New York*

*Mirror, And Ladies' Literary Gazette,* which featured writers such as James Fenimore Cooper, Washington Irving, and John Greenleaf Whittier. He was also drama critic for the *New York Evening Post,* established as a Federalist newspaper years earlier by Alexander Hamilton and John Jay but later evolving toward the antiestablishment Jacksonian view under the influence of a new associate editor, William Cullen Bryant. Struggling to make a living, Harby started a "classical & English Academy" for instruction of youth in New York, and advertised that it would accept women in June 1828. But it was not to be. Within months he succumbed to typhoid fever and died by the end of the year, leaving his children to be raised by his sister.

Back in Charleston, the Reformed Society faced relentless hostility of the old guard at Beth Elohim, and angry divisions even among families, with dissenters turning against their own siblings and parents. Other issues divided them as well. A prominent member who was expelled, for reasons that are not clear, although it could have been because he kept a shop open on the Sabbath, was Philip Benjamin. He was the father of Judah P. Benjamin, later senator from Louisiana and the Confederate secretary of state.

In 1833 the society formally abandoned the idea of starting its own synagogue and resolved to return the money raised for it. The society continued to exist on paper, but not as a congregation. It effectively ceased to exist by the late 1830s.

Yet the failure of the dissidents sowed the seeds of success when Beth Elohim reached out for a new hazan. By this time, the American Jewish population was increasingly dominated by Ashkenazim. Still bruised by their fights with Reformed Society dissidents, the traditionalists at Beth Elohim were determined to find a compatible replacement. They turned to the Reverend Gustavus Poznanski (his Hebrew name was Gedalia; it was common in this period to refer to rabbis as "the Reverend"), who was with Shearith Israel in New York City, serving as *shohet* (kosher butcher), shofar blower, and assistant hazan on the High Holidays.

Arriving in 1837 in Charleston, Poznanski made an immediate, favorable impression among those hoping he would restore order to a divided and unruly community. But he turned out to be something less than what the hidebound conservatives expected. Born in what was then called Storchnest, in western Poland but then part of Prussia, Poznanski (1805–1879) quickly learned that he had to navigate the lingering ill feelings at the synagogue, where traditionalists remained concerned about lapses in Jewish practices. His biographers say, however, that he was a master at bridging differences and imposing what he called "a more earnest respect for our religion." Only one year after his arrival at the age of thirty-four, he was elected for life. In the same year, he also married Esther (Hetty) Barrett, the eighteen-year-old daughter of a prominent family in town, which "certainly made Poznanski's position in Charleston more secure and relieved him of financial worries," writes one of his biographers, Solomon Breitbart.[9]

It should have been obvious that Poznanski had liberal and even anti-establishment leanings, however. He had received some education in Hamburg, a center of the Reform movement in Europe, making it likely he benefited from a secular German education and would be receptive to demands for change in rituals and practices. The way was paved for a confrontation because Poznanski's arrival coincided with a new constitution at Beth Elohim, consolidating the two boards (adjuntas) into a single board of trustees and a single president (parnas). In a gesture to the reformers, the hazan was to be qualified in English and required to give a "suitable address" on the Sabbath in English—and the congregation was given more authority over synagogue affairs.

The charter fired a warning shot by declaring that no "innovations" in the service be approved by the parnas or the administration unless approved by three-quarters of the members. Evidently, with the ill-fated Reform Society in mind, the constitution also barred members from joining any independent body that adopted innovations or alterations "in the Mosaical or Rabbinical Laws."

But the constitution also implied that the reforms already adopted at Beth Elohim, such as barring the practice of letting members bid for privileges with public offerings, could not easily be rescinded either. These limited reforms had given Beth Elohim the distinction of being one of the first American synagogues to ban such sales of privileges. Among these congregations were Har Sinai in Baltimore, which adopted a reform-oriented prayer book in use at the Hamburg Temple in Germany; Temple Emanu-El in New York; and Congregation Ansche Emeth in Albany, New York.

In addition, the Charleston fire one year after Poznanski's arrival changed the equilibrium of forces keeping the Beth Elohim congregation together. To pay for the rebuilding of the synagogue, the congregation needed new members, including disaffiliated reformers. The expanded body of members now contained more of those who favored changes. As plans for a new synagogue proceeded, thirty-eight members of the congregation petitioned the board to consider installing an organ in the new synagogue, noting that playing or listening to organ music constituted "nothing incompatible" with Jewish doctrine. They noted that organs had been installed in Prague a century earlier and that organs had been introduced elsewhere in Germany and in France.

The request ushered in a historic turning point at the synagogue—and in the relationship between Judaism and the American judicial system.

## A BRIEF HISTORY OF THE ORGAN

The use of an organ in a synagogue had gone through a stormy history in Europe well before its installation provoked a furor in Charleston. The complex arguments surrounding such an innovation illustrates the extent to which modern Jews were growing uncomfortable with Talmudic hair-splitting applied to contemporary life. A principal argument against the organ in Europe started with the importance of the Sabbath ban on work. Traditional rabbis said playing an organ or perhaps any musical instrument violated that injunction. An organ, after all, functions as a kind of giant whistle through which compressed air is forced, constituting a mechanism that strict adherents of Jewish law maintained should not be permitted during the day of rest, just as operating almost any piece of equipment or turning on a light switch is considered a violation of Sabbath rules in traditional Judaism.

"Debate over the employment of an organ in Jewish worship remained the single most significant marker of the boundary between Liberal and Orthodox Judaism in Germany throughout the nineteenth century," writes the religious scholar David Ellenson.[10] The German Orthodox establishment, for example, directed that any student serving in a community employing an organ during the Sabbath or any other time should have his ordination certificate canceled.

The organ controversies also illustrate the care that advocates of change took to argue that they were not trying to discard Jewish law but rather to reinterpret it in light of modern developments and practices for Jews wishing to retain their traditional identity. The German "reformers" insisted that they were applying interpretations in the tradition of the sages of old. Their contention that they were merely interpreting the law, and not abrogating it, incensed traditionalists with its additional brazenness, however. Orthodox scholars regarded the heretical views of reformers in Germany as "evil" on two counts: inherently wicked and even more so because reformers were allegedly arrogating unto themselves the right to reinterpret Jewish law to conform to their desired practices.

How directly the European furor over organs in synagogues influenced South Carolina is not clear from the record, although contemporaneous accounts show that the Jews of South Carolina were more than aware of these controversies. The most historically important early furor over an organ in Europe flared at the Hamburg Reform temple in Germany, one of the first major "Reform temples" recorded in Jewish history. (The very first Reform synagogue is generally considered to be the one in Seesen, built in 1810.) The Hamburg temple's installation of an organ in 1818 ignited furious protests among the Orthodox rabbinate throughout the city. The rabbinic court of the city then issued a pamphlet in 1819 (*Eileh Divre ha-Brit*, "These Are the Words of the Covenant") containing twenty-two opinions signed by forty rabbis declaring that the organ and other practices were "outside the pale of Judaism."

An important corollary of the basic argument against playing an organ on the Sabbath was that, even if doing so were acceptable, there might be a temptation to repair a broken organ during the day of rest, which would be an even more egregious violation of the ban on work. To engage in a practice that might invite a transgression of Jewish law could thus be seen as forbidden on its face. This variant was offered by Rabbi Leopold Stein of the Rabbinical Commission to the Frankfurt Assembly, who said it was acceptable to play an organ on the Sabbath, but not to repair one. Stein gave his approval to playing an organ in theory, noting that the Talmud had alluded to an instrument in the ancient Temple of Jerusalem as having many pipes, bringing forth many sounds. But still he warned against installing one as a temptation to the violation of having to repair it.

Some opponents of the organ conceded that there were references to musical instruments being played in the Temple of Jerusalem before its destruction, but they deemed this fact to be irrelevant. They argued that rabbinic law held that after the Temple's destruction, Jews must mourn its loss and that an organ was thus inappropriate as an expression of joy counter to that spirit of lamentation. But other rabbis replied that although Jews were not allowed to be joyous in their secular lives, they could praise God with joy, even on the Sabbath.

A number of other rationales were cited by the opponents of the organ in Hamburg. Perhaps the best key to understanding the spirit of that disapproval could be found in the generalized biblical command "Thou shalt not walk in their ways." This phrase comes from Leviticus 18:3, and it refers to the injunction against "pagan" practices of others in Canaan or Egypt. The passage had been interpreted by traditionalists throughout the ages to say that whatever the goyim did in their practices, Jews must not follow suit, even if there was no other reason not to do it. Rabbi Isaak Noah Mannheimer of Vienna, declared, for example: "I admit that the sound of the organ, like the sound of bells, has become too much a characteristic of the Christian Church, and it is therefore offensive to the Jew."[11]

But just because something is accepted by Christians, does that mean it can't be accepted by Jews? Were Jews not even allowed to wear clothes worn by "pagans"? Reformers and organ proponents argued that such logic was absurd on its face, except in cases of outright idolatry. Thus, Rabbi Aaron Chorin of Arad, Hungary, observed that Christians were not idolaters and that the organ was a "sweet practice" that uplifted the soul. He and others cited texts noting that Jews could honor God with song and "every musical instrument."

Although the Hamburg organ stirred the most famous uproar over the issue in Europe until that time, the actual precedent setting the controversy had occurred in Prague. The Prague records show that an organ was in use going back to 1679 in the Maisel Synagogue of the Holy Community there. It was that precedent that Reformers cited as justification nearly 150 years later in Hamburg and that Orthodox rabbis disputed, saying that the authorities in Prague were simply mistaken. In any case, rabbis of the Orthodox Rabbinical Court in Prague said that records showing the use of the organ a century earlier were effectively a lie and that the practice now "sickens and pains the heart of the listener," irrespective of any such precedent. Rabbi Moses Sofer Schreiber of Pressburg added that the organ was associated with idol worship. He asserted that evidence that it was played during Sabbath was contrived, and that in any case, because the Prague organ was not repaired after it broke down, the Jews of Prague must have recognized that it had been a violation of Jewish law.

## "THIS SYNAGOGUE IS OUR TEMPLE"

Whatever the role of precedent in Prague and Hamburg, it was only a matter of time before reform-minded Jews in America became less interested in invoking rabbinic interpretations of the past and determined to abandon the authority of such interpretations altogether. That was the case in Charleston, where there were few precedents at the time of the organ controversy. (In Savannah, Congregation Mickve Israel dedicated a synagogue in 1820 at a ceremony that included an organ played by the musical director of the city's Independent Presbyterian Church as the Torah scrolls were carried into the new building. But it was not clear how continuously the practice was kept up. A fire destroyed the synagogue in 1829, and it was rebuilt in 1838, but no mention of an organ was recorded again. Mickve Israel's Torah scrolls, both dating from the fifteenth century, are thought to be the oldest in the United States. One was brought from England in 1733 by the original group of 42 Jews that came to Savannah and the other was sent later from London's Bevis Marks Synagogue in 1737.) [12]

The petitioners in favor of an organ at Beth Elohim, many of them former members of the Reform Society, said they merely wanted to use every "laudable and sacred mode by which the rising generation may be made to conform to, and attend our holy worship." But to traditionalists, the request marked a recrudescence of the demands from the Reformed Society. The board ruled against the idea four to one in 1840. But Poznanski's sentiments in favor of the organ were becoming increasingly clear, as were the sentiments of the broader membership of the congregation itself, especially at a congregation meeting in July 1840, when a congregant, Jacob Simon Jacobs, was censured for using "improper & unbecoming language" toward the hazan. So contentious was that session that it opened with a dispute over whether Poznanski should even be allowed to speak. The vote was fifty-six to thirty-one in favor.

Abraham Moïse, a respected elder, proposed that voluntary funds be raised for the organ, declaring that music was "the universal language of the soul." Nathan Hart, the president, at first declared the resolution out of order, but his ruling was overturned, and the members approved the motion by a close vote. A separate resolution thanked Hart for the "dignified manner and impartial conduct" of the meeting. But the die was cast for a fight that would be anything but dignified.

Traditionalists at the congregation, incensed over their defeat, quit the synagogue and organized a new congregation, Shearith Israel, sometime after the vote. Then, following the death in 1840 of two traditionalist leaders at Beth Elohim, Hart and H. M. Hertz, the tide turned more decisively there. A new reform-oriented congregation president, Abraham Ottolengui, a businessman born in Charleston and educated in England, took office, speeding the eclipse of traditionalist rule. Since many traditionalists had quit, the new and younger rump congregation amended the 1836 constitution, increasing the board to seven to make it easier to ram through changes. There would be even more English in the service, and the decision was made to place the Ten Commandments and Articles of Faith on synagogue walls, eliminating—with Poznanski's approval—the part of Maimonides regarding the coming of a messiah, the resurrection of the dead, and the restoration of the Temple under the "House of David."

The organ finally arrived at the synagogue and was placed on the gallery at the western end. On March 19, 1841, as an overflow crowd attended, the hazan sounded the shofar four times, and Penina Moïse's hymn was sung. A speech by Poznanski made it clear, as the dissidents had earlier feared, that the organ was only the start of a campaign of liberalization of Jewish law and practice that might be even more intolerable to the dissidents.

Poznanski, for example, praised "the restoration of instrumental music" in the synagogue, declaring that it "was beautiful and salutary as well as scripturally proper in praising God with strong instruments and an organ." He further praised the expansion of English "instead of a tongue unintelligible" to most members. His speech won plaudits from the *Charleston Courier* newspaper, which declared that "the dark clouds of sectarian prejudice and religious intolerance seem every where to be fast fading away, before the widely spreading lights of right, reason and philosophy." The paper praised "the introduction of instrumental music in a Jewish synagogue, contributing much by its sweet and majestic harmony to hallow the ceremonies of the occasion."[13]

Finally, standing thousands of years of doctrine on its head, Poznanski proudly and boldly embraced the concept that Jewish worshippers were meeting in a temple, making it clear that it was a substitute for the destroyed Temple of Jerusalem, discarding by implication the prayers for restoration of the old structure. "This synagogue is our *temple*," Poznanski declared, "this city our *Jerusalem*, this happy land our *Palestine*, and as our fathers defended with their lives *that* temple, *that* city, and *that* land, so will their sons defend *this* temple, *this* city, and *this* land."

These quotations came from an account in a local newspaper, because Poznanski declined to publish his talk, perhaps realizing how heretical it would appear.[14] Whether his motive was to abandon an ancient tenet of Judaism or simply to win acceptance by the many Christians in the audience, his comments no doubt reflected the sentiments of most Beth Elohim members. But subsequently the congregation met again and, while endorsing the organ, decreed that future changes in the service, including more use of English, required its approval. They were effectively warning the board not to go further with radical change.

Beth Elohim's changes, meanwhile, were being noticed elsewhere. Isaac Leeser, the leading traditionalist who was based in Philadelphia, called on Jewish leaders throughout the United States to create a national organization of synagogues, presumably to enforce a traditionalist line. Leeser's call was rebuffed, inevitably, by Beth Elohim's trustees, for important reasons. The board charged that any effort to create such an authority, with its implied coercive tendencies, was "alien to the spirit and genius of the age in which we live" and "wholly inconsistent with the spirit of American Liberty." The congregation followed suit, informing Leeser through Abraham Moïse, a trustee, that he regarded his invitation as hostile to reformers in Charleston and indeed the rest of the South. Moïse added for good measure that Leeser was behaving like the Catholic Church in its efforts to oppose Martin Luther. Some historians see Beth Elohim's defiance of Leeser as a precursor to South Carolina's growing disenchantment with dictates from the North.

Dissident traditionalist Jews were not about to let the matter rest. Several resorted to a scurrilous charge: a challenge to the legitimacy of Poznanski's birth. This early South Carolinian "birther" movement directed the hazan to petition his ancestral town of Storchnest for his birth certificate. Word came back a few months later with the reassurance that Poznanski's father had indeed married "a virtuous Jewish virgin" and that all the children were indeed legitimate.[15] Not surprisingly, their efforts only emboldened Poznanski. He now became a well-known leader of the reform movement. On the other hand, to save money, Beth Elohim and Shearith Israel agreed to cooperate on the appointment of a kosher butcher.

Yet less than a year after the new Beth Elohim synagogue reopened, the balance of authority on its board began to shift. With changes in the membership, a majority now formed to oppose the reforms championed by Poznanski and the president, Abraham Ottolengui. Tellingly, an early dispute flared over a tradition at the synagogue to hold a remembrance ceremony to mourn the destruction of the temple in Jerusalem and call for its restoration. Despite Poznanski's earlier admonition about Beth Elohim being "our temple," the ceremony was retained, perhaps because alcoholic drinks were part of the tradition. Other debates erupted over a request for an English-only Sabbath service on Saturday afternoons.

Into this combustible atmosphere Poznanski moved to light another fuse. In a Passover sermon in 1843, he proposed that Beth Elohim celebrate holy days like Passover for only one day, not the traditional two days. Two-day celebrations, he said, were a relic of the ancient past, when calendars were uncertain, a concern he said was made obsolete by "the progress of astronomical science." The board, now dominated by conservatives, revolted and denounced Poznanski's proposal as "calculated to create discord & anarchy in a religious body when there should always be peace & harmony."

Poznanski responded at first in conciliatory fashion. He worried that he had underestimated the alarm he would cause, and he asked permission to stop delivering sermons in English if that was what the board wanted. It was a passive-aggressive approach, and it worked. The board backed down and resolved to continue the use of English. But a question arose: who should decide such grave matters of reinterpretation—the congregation or the new board? At the next general meeting, attended by only fifty-one members, a motion to adhere to rabbinic traditions was narrowly defeated.

Suddenly realizing that they could turn the tide if they could recruit more members, the traditionalists began a campaign to bring some of the secessionist members back from Shearith Israel into the Beth Elohim fold. If they succeeded, they could restore the rule of rabbinic law, install a ritual bath, and effectively fire Poznanski, who by now had reaped the enmity of traditionalists even as he inspired the reformers on to increasingly progressive steps.

To bring the traditionalists back to the congregation, the four conservative members of the board moved to vote them in. They called on Ottolengui to convene a board meeting to do so. Seeing the threat, Ottolengui called a meeting of the entire congregation rather than the board to block the dissidents' membership campaign. Meeting soon thereafter, the congregation asserted that it—not the board—had the right to determine service procedures. But the congregants continued to worry that the board would try to pack the membership with secessionist conservatives. The members then amended the constitution to require that any new *voting* members would have to be approved by the congregation, not the board.

Escalating the fight and refusing to admit defeat, the four traditionalists on the board defiantly convened their own meeting and promptly admitted forty-two Shearith Israel members to the congregation. Now the congregation, newly packed with traditionalists, voted to "adhere rigidly to our sacred and ancient forms and customs" and to stop the "great and growing evil" of reformers. And with little sense of irony, they also declared that their purpose was "to restore concord and harmony."

These actions cleared the way for the traditionalists to rescind the earlier changes in the constitution and ban instrumental music as "obnoxious to the consciences of many Israelites." They then ordered Poznanski to return certain materials in his possession. He refused and resigned. The board resolved to meet again, but when its members arrived at the synagogue, the gates were locked. The traditionalists broke in and selected a new hazan. When the organist refused to stop playing at services they fired him too, or tried to.

The records of this later period of turmoil are scant, but it appears that the two sides established a modus vivendi in which it was acknowledged that Beth Elohim consisted of an "Organ Congregation" and the "Remnants," alternating the use of the sanctuary each week.

Even so, the two sides went to court. The Reform faction filed suit against the Orthodox holdouts in 1843 in a case destined to become a landmark in the annals of the relationship between Jews and the government.[16]

## I'LL SEE YOU IN COURT

Officially, the dispute over the organ at Beth Elohim in Charleston came to be known as *The State of South Carolina ex relatione Abraham Ottolengui et al., vs. G. V. Ancker et al.* Each side enlisted teams of prominent, talented, and expensive lawyers whose roles in the case attested to the connections enjoyed by the Jewish community. The reformist plaintiffs, for example, employed Henry Bailey, South Carolina's attorney general, and the traditionalist defendants brought in Christopher G. Memminger, who was many years later to become the hapless Treasury secretary of the Confederacy as it spiraled into insolvency.

The traditionalists first advanced a wide argument, offering testimony that the organ and Poznanski's teachings about the Messiah were contrary to Jewish practice and law. The judge quickly found that approach irrelevant.[17] After a four-day trial, the jury ruled in favor of the "organ congregation," holding that the anti-organ faction had resigned as members and not been legally readmitted. Rejecting the outcome, the anti-organ dissidents appealed, claiming that they had not *actually* resigned from Beth Elohim in the first place, despite the fact that they had stopped paying dues and going to meetings. They took their case to the South Carolina Court of Appeals, the state's highest appellate court, where Judge A. P. Butler upheld the lower court decision in 1846.

The Butler ruling was historic, not because of its attitudes toward reform, or even an organ. Its significance lay in its making clear that religious laws were not enforceable by civil courts in the United States, as they had been in Europe. "There should be great caution observed in cases like the present," Butler said, noting that judges must avoid "questions of theological doctrine, depending on speculative faith, or ecclesiastical rites." Were a synagogue to decide to become a mosque, the issue of its public charter as a corporation might arise, he said, but that was not the case here.

But Judge Butler's decision is also interesting because it revealed a bias toward reform animating the congregation members at Beth Elohim. It noted, for example, that religious institutions "cannot withstand the agitations of free, active and progressive opinion." Religious laws are products of human beings, he said, and "cannot be subjected to Procrustean limitations." Going further, and showing that he had become quite educated over obscure aspects of Judaism, he noted that the prayer book at Beth Elohim was of Spanish origin and was different from a prayer book from Poland, and that "religious rituals" would inevitably be "modified to some extent, by the influence of the political institutions of the countries in which they are practiced." He was thus accurately describing, perhaps without realizing it, the evolving condition of the Jewish experience as it adjusted to American culture.

As for the contention that the organ's introduction violated the synagogue charter, the judge said that no charter could be written to outlaw changes in ritual and society over time. Turning to matters of faith and heresy, he noted that the pro-organ faction was not disavowing its faith in Judaism, and that it was impossible for the court to rule on their sincerity. Suppose that the court had even tried to ascertain whose faith was authentic? Would he have taken testimony from them, or from Jews in other parts of the world—in Palestine, Germany, England, or other parts of the United States? To do so would be entering into "the labyrinth of curious and recondite learning, without a clue by which he could escape from its bewildering perplexities."

Why did such a pathbreaking rebellion occur in South Carolina, of all places? No consensus prevails among scholars on the social and other factors that led the Jews of Charleston, many of their leaders following Sephardic tradition, to foment a revolution in American Judaism. (The majority of Jews in Charleston and the United States in this period were Ashkenazim, however.) A fascinating debate among the experts over the role of local factors, as opposed to influences from abroad, continues to enliven Jewish journals and publications.

The most obvious explanation for the Charleston rebellion was that it was inspired by the spirit of the American Revolution. In their history of Charleston Jews published in 1950, Charles Reznikoff and Uriah Z. Engelman wrote that the city's Jews were "intellectuals, cultured and worldly-wise," and influenced by the Declaration of Independence.[18] The problem with this "spirit of the age" argument is that it does not explain why it happened in Charleston and not in Philadelphia or New York. Jacob Rader Marcus argues that it was a case of leadership in Charleston, who he said were unusually radical for their time. "Change was the spirit of the times," writes James Hagy, endorsing Marcus's point of view. "Individuals in Charleston had been affected by the ideas of John Locke, the Enlightenment, the American Revolution, the United States Constitution, the French Revolution, Thomas Jefferson, Andrew Jackson (who ran for president in 1824), Romanticism, the Protestants, and the residents of Charleston." Charleston's Jews were "Americans first and Jews second," he writes. They wrote books, read newspapers, went to see plays, practiced law, and engaged in other secular pursuits. And they also "wanted to look good in the eyes of their Protestant neighbors."[19] South Carolina, of course, would go on to champion the doctrine of nullification against laws enacted by Congress, and later its seizure of Fort Sumter became the spark that started the Civil War. These disparate events attested to the spirit of rebelliousness among its people generally.

Still another factor in the evolution of Reform is the one cited in part by Isaac Harby—fear of Jews being delegitimized as reflected in the battle over the Maryland "Jew Bill," which allowed Jews to hold public office in the 1820s but only after overcoming fierce opposition. The Jews of South Carolina also plainly feared that an overly zealous adherence to ancient ceremonies and laws made them more vulnerable to discrimination.[20]

The Charleston congregation split on generational lines, with the younger worshippers rebelling against foreign-born elders still wedded to tradition. The elders were more prosperous in jobs as accountants, storekeepers, merchants, and brokers. A couple were plantation owners. Most were comfortable with their status—and with the status quo. By contrast, the reformers were in their thirties, American-born, with more modest occupations, such as clerk, jailer, deputy marshal, printer, blacksmith, author, teacher, and painter.

Some insight into the restless spirit of the younger members of the congregation can be gleaned from the diary of Joseph Lyons, who graduated from South Carolina College in 1832 and apparently at some point entertained the ambition of becoming hazan. He dutifully fasted on Yom Kippur and observed the Sabbath but was put off by the chanting in a "guttural

harsh barbarous tongue." Deciding that life as a chanter of Hebrew was not
for him, he moved to Paris, where he died at the age of twenty-four of "consumption."[21]

Many scholars have explored the conundrum that similar reforms of
Judaism—such as introducing "decorum" and banning the auction of honors—had been spreading in Europe in the previous two decades, but that
many of the Jews of South Carolina were of Sephardic heritage and unlikely
to be guided by these trends. An early historian of Charleston's Jewish community, Rabbi Barnett A. Elzas (1867–1936), who served many years at
Beth Elohim, has noted the number of times that reform proponents cited
changes under way in Holland, Germany, and Prussia as their inspiration.
But other experts suggest that Sephardic Jews had their own impetus to discard many Talmudic doctrines.

For example, Rabbi Allan Tarshish, another historian of South Carolina
Jews, speculates that the Sephardic Jews of Charleston were influenced by a
spirit of challenging the Talmud that dated from the "converted" Jews who
practiced their religion in secret to escape persecution in Spain.[22] In addition, research by Jakob J. Petuchowski, a scholar at Hebrew Union College
in Cincinnati, has shown that Jews who escaped from Spain for Holland and
Italy were taken aback by the dominance of rabbis in other parts of Europe
who hewed rigorously to Talmudic rules of conduct. As Sephardim grew in
status in Europe, they started to feel that the Messiah delivering Jews back
to Palestine may have been a worthy goal for the destitute Jewish flotsam
and jetsam of Europe, but not for the wealthy business classes emerging in
the seventeenth century of northern Europe. They interpreted the words of
Jeremiah—"And seek the peace of the city whither I have caused you to be
carried away captive, and pray unto the Lord for it; for in the peace thereof
shall ye have peace" (Jeremiah 29:7)—as meaning that it was in fact a Jewish obligation to remain and flourish in the Diaspora.[23]

Those historians who argue that the *marranos*, while living secret lives,
relied only on the Bible (most likely in Latin) to remind them of their Jewish heritage, and not the copious rabbinic teachings it spawned, cite the
example of Uriel Da Costa (1585–1640?), a Jew from Portugal of parents

who had converted from Judaism to Catholicism to escape persecution. As a youth, Da Costa fled to Amsterdam, reexamined his Jewish heritage, and became disenchanted with rabbinic Judaism consumed by legalisms and doctrines. His book *An Examination of the Traditions of the Pharisees* outlined his case. Unfortunately, Da Costa's skepticism did not turn out well. Ostracized, he wandered back and forth between Amsterdam and Hamburg, and was eventually excommunicated. He ended up killing himself. Da Costa's writings may have influenced Spinoza, and Spinoza's so-called heresies were also well known to Jews around the world.[24]

Whatever the factors that led to Judge Butler's ruling, it was significant that while he grounded his reasoning in process, he was seen to have largely legitimized the cause of reform, change, and adjustment to new patterns in society and artistic expression. He also used dramatic language that evokes the spirit of the times: "The granite promontory in the deep may stand firm and unchanged amidst the waves and storms that beat upon it, but human institutions cannot withstand the agitations of free, active and progressive opinion." The judge praised all sides for making their case "with uncommon learning and ability." But his ruling was decisive.[25]

The reformers had won. They not only established the right to interpret Jewish law their own way. They also consolidated the principle that each Jewish community could determine its own practices, based on a democratic process and without interference by a minority citing traditional Jewish law as enforced by the state. Their cause of transforming Jewish practice was soon to be buttressed by a major demographic shift in American Judaism.

*Four*

# THE GERMAN IMMIGRANTS

The South Carolina organ controversy raged through Charleston in what had been, as much as anyplace, a center of Jewish life in America. But in the 1840s, the demographics of the American Jewish population were changing because of a new factor: the influx of German Jewish immigrants. These immigrants would have a decisive impact on practices and beliefs in the decades before and after the Civil War.

They were part of a large flood of immigrants from Central Europe, including the German states, the Austrian empire, Alsace-Lorraine, and the Baltic states. From 1820 to the Civil War, 1.7 million Irish and 1.3 million Germans came to the United States, unleashing an anti-immigration backlash in a country of 31 million people in 1860. That hostile response was epitomized by the establishment of the Native American Party, or "Know-Nothings," in 1854. Jews were only a small portion of this wave, and for that reason, perhaps, Jews were not singled out in the nativist antipathy of the era.¹ At the opening of the 1840s, the United States sheltered only 18 formally organized Jewish congregations. By 1855, the number exploded to 76 congregations. That number grew to 277 by 1877. The first "official" census of Jews, in 1878, measured their population at 250,000, which meant that the Jewish population had grown at nearly fifteen times the rate of the nation as a whole.² Although many of these Jewish newcomers were single men looking for opportunities who had left their families behind, nearly a third of the new immigrants came with wives and children.³

An irony was that the German states had encompassed a region where some Jews prospered and became part of the commercial, cultural, and intellectual class. It was thus, at one level, an improbable place from which the major portion of American Jews would flee. But a new wave of violence and hatred also flared in Germany in the post-Napoleonic era, erasing any possibility of complacency among prospering Jewish families, not to mention the many more such families subsisting as subjugated and impoverished citizens on farms and in villages and cities.

Northern Europe had not become a home for Jews until the closing days of the Roman Empire, and probably later. Their movement north was hastened after the empire adopted Christianity and split apart. Through the Middle Ages, Jews lived through occasional periods of tolerance disrupted by bouts of persecution and punitive regulations, including requirements that they live isolated in ghettos. In these separated communities, they developed a communal existence underscored by loyalty to rabbinic tradition. These factors led Ashkenazic Jewry to become more inward and insular, more attached to Jewish law, and perhaps less cosmopolitan than Sephardic Jews, whose elite scholars were influenced by outside cultures, particularly Muslim intellectuals. But over time, elite educated Jews who had managed to prosper because of their business abilities as traders, bankers, and travelers became more worldly and successful, while the non-Jewish world came to depend on their financial skills. A handful of successful banking families like the Wertheimers helped to finance various wars among Europe's imperial families.

The rise of nation states following the Reformation and the Thirty Years' War, which ended in the Peace of Westphalia in 1648, unleashed a new round of tyranny and violent intimidation in German-speaking lands, scattering Jews eastward into Poland, Russia, and Slavic parts of the old Holy Roman Empire. There they embraced an increasingly fervent piety, later evolving into Hasidism. These pietistic Jews did not influence the Jewish experience in America until they immigrated at the very end of the nineteenth century.

Following the breakup of Napoleon's empire at the Congress of Vienna in 1815, Germany remained a collection of states and principalities. (It was not to become fully unified until after the Franco-Prussian War in 1871.) Jews in these lands faced a series of calamities in that period, including failed harvests, unemployment among peasants who had fled to the cities, and savage anti-Semitism. The "hep-hep" riots of 1819 were so called because the rioters shouted "Hep! Hep!" at Jews, mimicking a foul command of shepherds, although some experts say the cry stood for the Latin *Hierosolyma est Perdita* ("Jerusalem is lost"). The violence erupted in Würzburg and spread throughout the German confederation, with rioters murdering Jews and destroying their property. A virulent recrudescence of anti-Semitic propaganda focused on repealing the rights granted Jews by Napoleon after the French Revolution.

In the stressed German economy, Jews became an easy object of fear. German governments imposed new restrictions on Jewish rights, including the right to marry, rescinding those granted by the French. The turbulent failed political uprisings of 1830 and 1848 exacerbated these hatreds in places such as Bavaria and Posen, where Jews following Polish customs were dubbed "Poles" by other Germans. These conditions, along with the fear of military conscription, drove thousands of German Jews to immigrate to America as well as to the east. Many immigrants were men, but many also were women who had worked as domestic servants, seamstresses, or shopkeepers in family businesses that had fallen on hard times.

The Jews' migration was a small but significant part of a larger flood of what eventually totaled five million Central Europeans to the United States in the nineteenth century. Along with millions of Irish fleeing famine conditions in their native land, they formed the first mass migration to American shores. Upon arriving, they wrote to family and friends to join them. German newspapers and books also spread the word and promise of freedom. "Here we are all the same, all the religions are honored and respected and have the same rights," an early German Jewish immigrant, Aaron Phillips, wrote to his parents in Bavaria. "An Israelite with talent who does well, can like many others achieve the highest honors."[4] In some cases, whole communities in Central Europe decamped, often settling in proximity with Catholic or Lutheran communities from Germany and continuing to speak German or Yiddish in their adopted country. Jewish records show that in the 1840s and 1850s, Abraham Lincoln encountered many immigrant Jewish shopkeepers and businesspeople in his travels in Illinois and throughout the country, some of whom later became political allies and supporters in the presidential campaign of 1860 and in the White House.[5]

The new influx changed the nature of the Jewish identity and experience in several ways. First was economic, as Jews sought livelihoods in far-flung parts of the country as peddlers, where they confronted challenges to maintaining Jewish practices. Second was their interest in setting up secular institutions such as hospitals, orphanages, news publications, social clubs (including Masonic lodges), and various types of charities. These organizations often commanded loyalty far greater than their synagogues did and supplanted them in setting rules for Jewish identity. Third was the fact that an emigration of rabbis from Germany brought more concrete influences from changes in doctrine and practice under way in the old country, while lay leaders of congregations continued to hold sway in setting standards of conduct.

Economic opportunities and difficulties were probably paramount in transforming Jewish identity, however. The early decades of the century brought a construction of new canals, roads, and railroads, helping to transform an agrarian American economy based on barter and exchange to a new system of markets in which farm goods and manufactured products could be transported over long distances. An indispensable feature of the new economy was a remnant of the old—peddling, an occupation, along with moneylending and small shopkeeping, that Jews had filled for centuries in Europe and took to by the thousands in America.

A successful peddler could purchase a wagon and a horse or two for the sale of stoves, furniture, and other heavier goods. Though Jews could own land in America, for the first time in fifteen hundred years, they avoided farming for the most part and chose to follow this route. As a result, Jewish peddlers leveraged their skills into ownership of retail stores and banking businesses. The great financial powerhouse families spawned by the Seligman and Lehman brothers, Marcus Goldman (Goldman Sachs), Solomon Loeb (Kuhn, Loeb), Meyer Guggenheim, and Julius Rosenwald (of Sears Roebuck) all started with peddling. Julius Ochs, the father of Adolph Ochs, future owner of the *New York Times*, had ambitions to go to college after emigrating from Bavaria in the 1840s, but his brother-in-law with whom he lived "refused and sent him off with a pack." Isaac Bernheim, after arriving from Germany, sold goods while traveling on horseback through Pennsylvania and went on to make a fortune after founding the I. W. Harper brand of bourbon whiskey in Kentucky. Other stalwarts of the march toward prosperity were Edward Filene from Poznan (who started as a peddler, tailor, glazier); Lazarus Straus (a peddler and country store owner); Adam Gimbel from Rheinland-Pfaltz (who started in farming); Jacob Kaufmann (a peddler and son of a horse and cattle trader); Henry, Emanuel, and Mayer Lehman, from Würzburg, who started with a dry goods store in Montgomery, Alabama, expanded as cotton merchants and traders, and eventually founded the investment firm Lehman Brothers; and the owners of Goldsmith's department store in Memphis, Rich's in Atlanta, and Sanger Brothers in Dallas. In San Francisco after the Gold Rush, Levi Strauss (born in Bavaria) opened a dry goods business and later collaborated with Jacob Davis, a tailor, to create a new kind of denim work pants using rivets at the seam, known eventually as blue jeans. All these fortunes were started with German-speaking people who arrived in America with little wealth.[6]

It was a hard life. Peddlers led a lonely existence, trudging along fields and dusty or muddy roads in rain, snow, and sweltering heat, often with

packs weighing more than 150 pounds. They slept in open fields or in derelict barns and rooming houses, deferred marriage and friendship, scrounged
for food, and relied on family networks for sales and credit.

"The greater part of the Jewish young men went peddling," a practi-
tioner recalled about his days in New York in the early 1800s. "There were
two or three Jewish merchants who supplied peddlers with 'Yankee notions,' which they called *Kuttle Muttle*."[7] ("Cuddle-muddle" was a popular
American expression referring to a secret language or mumbling jargon.) Of
course, Jews did more than peddle. They ran boardinghouses and were artisans, seamstresses (a popular job for women), bakers, paper hangers, pock-
etbook makers, gold and silver smiths, lace weavers, engravers, shoemakers,
hatters, tailors, and cigar makers. One of their goals was to achieve self-em-
ployed status. Showing some defensiveness, *The Occident*, a popular paper
published and edited by Isaac Leeser, reported in 1857 that while peddling
was the best known occupation of many Jews, everyone should "know well
enough that we have lawyers, medical doctors, bankers, some politicians, a
few teachers, authors and ministers, some shipping merchants and auction-
eers, and a very few farmers, and here and there a butcher, a baker, a distiller,
a brewer, a tavern-keeper, a manufacturer, a miner, a billiard-table maker, an
apothecary, a smith, a produce and cattle-dealer, a painter and glazier. . . ."[8]

The story of the Seligman family was instructive of how Jewish identity came under pressure. The Seligmans came originally from Baiersdorf, a
tiny village in Bavaria, and rose to become known in the nineteenth century
as the "American Rothschilds." The old-world patriarch, David Seligman,
had been the village weaver. Joseph, the eldest son, was persuaded to go to
America by his mother when the weaving business faltered under pressure
from mechanized textile making. David feared that his son, while overseas,
would drift from his religious teachings, including Sabbath observance and
keeping kosher. Rumors had it that many Jews in America were succumb-
ing that way. The challenge confronted Joseph immediately when pork and
beans were the only foods available in steerage to America in 1837.

Joseph Seligman's first job was as a cashier clerk in a small town in eastern Pennsylvania, to which he moved because a cousin lived there. Restless

for other work, Seligman noticed that men and women on nearby farms had to come into town for necessities, so he invested his small savings in jewelry, watches, rings, knives, bolts of cloth, ribbons, lace, thread, hand-kerchiefs, underwear, shawls, tablecloths, sewing equipment, and other wares. Placing these items in a heavy pack, Joseph Seligman headed off on foot through rural Pennsylvania. Soon he asked his two brothers, William and James, to leave Bavaria and join him in America. "They were a strange-looking lot, the three Seligman brothers and peddlers like them—bearded, shaggy-headed, their faces dusty from the road, in long ill-fitting coats and baggy trousers, walking in mud-caked shoes, with a shuffling gait, stooped under their packs—but how they looked didn't matter to them," Stephen Birmingham writes evocatively in *Our Crowd*. They were also plagued on their routes by attacking dogs and children calling them "sheeny" or "Christ-killer." But by 1840 the brothers made enough to open a headquarters and later a shop in Lancaster, Pennsylvania, and they sent for still more family members. [9]

Determined to become an American businessman, Joseph shaved and combed his hair back, just as his father feared. James invested in a horse and wagon and headed south, returning with $1,000 in profits. In 1841, the Seligmans moved to Mobile and then back north again to New York, hav-ing set up a network of stores in the South. The rest of the family, including the weaver David and his wife, Fanny, joined them in 1843. They shifted some of their operations to upstate New York, and in Watertown, the Selig-mans befriended a young first lieutenant named Ulysses S. Grant, stationed nearby. By the time of the Civil War, Seligman had moved into banking and finance, helping to raise funds for the Union cause with bond sales. In the Gilded Age, J. & W. Seligman & Co. was one of the country's leading fi-nanciers, investing in railroads, steel industry, shipbuilding, mining, and the Standard Oil Company.

The dramatic upward climb of the Seligmans and other storied Jewish families has contributed to Jewish American lore. The tales are authentic. But many Jews fared far less well, ending up in poorhouses, orphanages, asylums, and other places where charities looked after them. They had to improvise and innovate in their business challenges while also remaining anchored in Judaism, a difficult task. Many Jews failed in business and remained impoverished, though their stories are less celebrated. "Jewish economic mobility in the nineteenth century has intrigued historians, just as it has been enshrined in American Jewish mythology," writes the historian Hasia Diner. "The self-congratulatory 'rags to riches' saga has been held up as the paradigmatic Jewish experience. The mobility seems to have been real, although less universal and less rapid than usually thought."[10]

The world these Ashkenazi immigrants left behind had been governed in all aspects of life by Jewish law, Jewish courts, and rabbinical decree. Jews in Europe had been guided by an elaborate code of behavior—how to observe the Sabbath and holidays, the clothes one wore, relations between husband and wife, and all manner of other regulations, some derived from the Torah, reputed to contain 613 separate commandments, and others from later tradition and Talmudic interpretation. In the new world of individual choice on religion, peddlers were often the first Jews to arrive in various towns or regions in cities ranging from Rochester, New York, to Sioux City, Iowa, to Atlanta and San Francisco. In such far-flung places, isolated and lonely, distant from the framework of Jewish life, they had to adjust their traditions.

One of the biggest challenges was keeping kosher. Inevitably, the practice declined. Ritual slaughtering calls for swift action with a specially sharpened knife. Trained kosher slaughterers had to be sought out far and wide, but rabbinic authorities who could ensure that their duties followed proper procedure were scarce. As a result, internal squabbling erupted within Jewish communities over whether kosher butchers were following the correct practices. Many communities gave up on the possibility of kosher-style meats, which were often prohibitively expensive.

Another problem was social. Because of dietary restrictions, Jews could not easily sit down with non-Jews at a meal. Avoiding pork was easier than adherence to other dietary restrictions, such as not mixing dairy and meat, and having separate dishes for each, and many nonobservant Jews fell away, while trying to keep more strictly kosher during Passover and other holidays. Ads in papers sought to recruit a Jewish "jack-of-all-trades" for smaller communities—someone who could slaughter meat, teach, chant during services, and also perform circumcisions.[11]

Keeping the Sabbath, which Jews are commanded to observe by not working, was also difficult. Many states had "blue laws" requiring retail stores to close on Sunday, which meant that Jews closing their stores on Saturday lost significant business from Christian customers doing weekend shopping. Many contemporary accounts note instances of Jews giving in and keeping their stores open, and others who went out of their way to observe the day of rest. A missionary to the Delaware Indians recalled, for example, a visit to a Jewish merchant in Lancaster, Pennsylvania, to fill a business order but was told he could not pay him until the next day, a Sunday. Instead, the merchant got a doctor neighbor to pay the missionary, presumably to be repaid himself the next day, which certainly puzzled the visiting missionary who later complained that "he might as well have done the business himself."[12]

Diaries left by peddlers made it clear that for all those who tried to follow Jewish laws, others had little choice but to abandon the rituals of their faith, however tortured they were by the dilemma. "God of Israel," a peddler wrote in his diary in 1843, "Thou knowst my thoughts. Thou alone knowest my grief when, on the sabbath's eve, I must retire to my lodging and on Saturday morning carry my pack on my back, profaning the holy day, God's gift to His people Israel."[13] Another diarist, Abraham Kohn, a native of Bavaria, wrote of the Jews he discovered upon arriving in New York: "O misguided fools, led astray by avarice and cupidity. You have left your friends and acquaintances, your relatives and your parents, your home and your land, your language and your customs, your faith and your religion— only to sell your wares in the wild places of America, in isolated farm houses and tiny hamlets. . . . For the first time in my life I have desecrated the Sabath in such a manner. But circumstances give me no choice. May God forgive me!"[14] (Kohn himself went on to Chicago eventually, opened a store there, and became acquainted with Abraham Lincoln.[15])

As in the colonial period, intermarriage posed a major challenge for

Jews as they spread through the country in the early nineteenth century. To avoid such a prospect, Jews often had to import brides or return to Europe to seek mates. Sometimes they advertised for brides in old-country newspapers and paid for them to make the arduous ocean journey to the United States. Thus, many Jews, primarily men, married outside the faith, amid popular fiction portraying instances of families heartbroken over such occurrences.

For all their gravitation to integrate in secular society, Jews left a record in diaries, letters, and other accounts of their fear of letting down their forebears and forgetting their roots. Typical of these accounts was the letter from a religious teacher to Moses and Yetta Alsbacher as they journeyed from Unsleben (Bavaria) to Cleveland. "Resist and withstand this tempting freedom and do not turn away from the religion of our fathers," the letter beseeched the couple. "The promise to remain good Jews must never and should never be broken during the trip, nor in your home life, nor when you go to sleep, nor when you rise again, nor in the rearing of your children."[16]

To counter such enticements, Jews brought prayer books, Bibles, prayer shawls, phylacteries, shofars, and Torah scrolls from Europe to their new communities. They counted on fellow Jews who knew the way of the law, including kosher butchers, ritual circumcisers, teachers, and cantors— confident, but perhaps not so confident, that their traditions would be maintained. To some foreign visitors, it was impressive that the Jews of America tried so hard to hang on to their traditions. "The religious rites, customs, and festivals of the Jews are all strictly observed," a Canadian visitor wrote in 1812.[17] But Rebecca Samuel, a young woman, wrote to her parents in Hamburg, in Yiddish, that she was pulling up stakes in her home in Petersburg, Virginia, to move to Charleston: "Jewishness is pushed aside here," she lamented. The handful of Jews in the community "are not worthy of being called Jews. . . . The way we live now is no life at all."[18]

A powerful factor contributing to the decline of rabbinical rules in these decades was a kind of Jewish genius for organizing themselves along secular lines outside the authority of the synagogue. In the Old World of the ghettos of Europe, the *kahal*—the name of the organizational structure of government in ancient Israelite society—served as the autonomous government of Jewish communities authorized by the secular governments under which Jews lived. These organizations undertook taxation and law enforcement, but they answered to the clerical authorities that prescribed laws of civil conduct. Such an arrangement was not applicable to the United States, which obviously did not authorize official self-governing institutions among Jews.

To replicate self-governing institutions of their tradition, the Jews turned to their own voluntary civic organizations that in many cases supplanted the authority of the rabbis and other religious figures. It was these organizations that they turned to for economic security and support in times of crisis, friendship, and community. They were grassroots groups that did not seek to impose doctrines. Rather, they embodied a new American attitude of live and let live among Jews.[19]

These organizations involved themselves in education, philanthropy, recreation, community service, and "defense" of Jewish identity against proselytizing or attempts to convert. Some also became activists on behalf of those Jews persecuted overseas. A major cause célèbre was the arrests in Damascus of thirteen prominent Jews accused of murdering a Christian monk to carry out a religious ritual. Another was the seizure by papal authorities of a six-year-old boy, Edgardo Mortara, abducted from a Jewish family in Bologna in 1858 on the grounds that a former servant had baptized him when he fell sick as an infant. Jews from around the world, and across the United States, rallied in protest, marking one of the earliest episodes of their organizing over a political cause. Their activism was to no avail. Edgardo eventually became a priest, taking the name Pius after Pope Pius IX, who defended the kidnapping. News of these outrages was spread through a proliferating group of secular publications, such as the *Asmonean* (1849–58), the *Jewish Messenger*, founded in 1857, and the *Hebrew Leader*, founded in 1859. They helped galvanize the Jewish community as a unified political force among disparate communities.

The preeminent civilian group implicitly challenging rabbinical authority was B'nai B'rith (Children of the Covenant). Founded in 1843 by recently arrived German immigrants at Sinsheimer's saloon on Essex Street in New York, it spread across the country rapidly, in some communities where there was no synagogue. Initially the Germans called themselves Bundes Brüder (Brothers of the Covenant), but they chose a Hebrew name to be more universally appealing to all Jews.

B'nai B'rith's mission was to serve the struggling Jewish community by taking care of the poor, sick, disabled Jews and those widows and orphans from broken families. Maintaining Jewish practices was not high on its agenda. A distinguishing characteristic of B'nai B'rith was its adoption—soon to become common among many Jewish organizations—of various practices of the Masonic movement, universally popular among many religious adherents in the United States, including secret handshakes, regalia, and passwords sometimes adopted from Hebrew ("Shalom Aleichem!") that were secret only to the world outside Judaism. Soon other nationwide fraternal societies sprouted, such as the Order of B'rith Abraham, the Free Sons of Israel, Masons, and Odd Fellows. The men who joined could do good and also do well. While performing community service, they could network on behalf of their businesses.

Some of these organizations inevitably revolved around the Polish, Eastern European, Hungarian, and of course German ethnic identity of the immigrants, known as *landsmannshëftn*. Women's organizations and literary societies grew up around them, and they sometimes hired rabbis and held religious services for High Holidays when there were no synagogues. They did not ignore Sabbath and dietary rules entirely. Many, for example, debated whether they should keep open on Sabbath, for activities not proscribed by the Talmud. In 1874, the New York YMHA (Young Men's Hebrew Association) came up with an ingenious compromise. It decided to keep the building open on the Sabbath for "light" exercise only, a ruling that banned the trapeze and horizontal bars as "too strenuous" and thus a violation of the ban on work.[20]

In the early decades of the nineteenth century, some rabbis complained that the various newly founded lodges and clubs undermined their authority, drew members away, and actually encouraged indifference to religion.

They warned that these secular organizations were weakening Jewish prayer, study, and traditions, not strengthening them.

But it was undoubtedly true that these organizations filled a spiritual need among adherents. Jews founded a New Israelite Sick-Benefit and Burial Society in 1841 in New York, which was an overtly secular effort to provide alternatives to synagogue-based burial. After B'nai B'rith, various Hebrew Benevolent Societies arose, along with Young Men's Hebrew Associations (the first of which was established in Baltimore in 1854). Such groups built boardinghouses and set up cemeteries, orphanages, and hospitals in the spirit of *tsedakah*, the Hebrew word for "charity." These organizations helped Jews navigate the new world, including its criminal justice system, while improving their community in the eyes of Jews and non-Jews alike.

Synagogues were expanding at the same time that secular groups took root. But ironically, the proliferation and fractiousness of synagogues—many of them with differing rites, ideologies, and ethnic backgrounds—contributed to their loss of collective influence. Communities throughout the country struggled to provide for kosher procedures, cemeteries, Hebrew education for children, and adjustments of prayers in Hebrew, sometimes in conflict and rivalry with one another. As congregations proliferated, the number of congregations increased in older communities, such as New York, Philadelphia, Baltimore, Cincinnati, New Orleans, and St. Louis. Many congregations split apart from others, and various attempts to unify synagogues failed.

No single synagogue or organization could claim that it alone represented Jews, and no single organization of synagogues had the ability to raise funds to thrive in the new landscape. In New York, the growing number of synagogues disagreed over such matters as the ritual slaughter of animals and the baking of matzo. In San Francisco, a dispute between immigrants of German and Polish ancestry in a tiny Jewish community led to two separate synagogues being established in the years after the Gold Rush. Temple Emanu-El represented the wealthier German-born Jews, a source of resentment among the Polish-born Jews at Sherith Israel. In Boston, at

Ohabei Shalom, ethnic animosity simmered for years, erupting over the engagement of a new rabbi in 1854 as Germans and Poles split into angry factions. "The dissension grew hotter and hotter until the minority bolted," Rabbi Solomon Schindler of Temple Adath Israel recalled many years later. The defectors angrily ran off with the synagogue's accounts and even its shofar for the new congregation. To fill the middle ground in such disputes, commercial butchers and bakers wrested responsibility for keeping kosher away from synagogue leaderships.

In the field of education, the role of synagogues also waned in the nineteenth century, as cities established public school systems that could draw students of all faiths. In 1854, New York had seven schools attached to congregations. Nonreligious private schools also sprang up. But the shortage of religious school teachers made it difficult for these institutions to continue. Teachers were constantly being hired and fired, and many of them had to carry out other responsibilities, like serving as hazans or even doing housekeeping chores, like taking care of the mikveh, or ritual bath. B'nai Jeshurun set up an "educational institute" in 1852, but it foundered and closed three years later. Scholars looking into the state of education in this period find records replete with complaints about bad teaching and chaotic classrooms. At Rodeph Shalom in Philadelphia, a teacher was reprimanded for beating his students. Maybe his frustration was understandable. The records show that students were setting off firecrackers, urinating in front of the girl students, and attempting "to imitate a circumcision."[21]

In 1853, New York City took over the schools of the Public School Society, shortly after state law in New York forbade religious instruction in 1842, making it possible for Jews to feel more comfortable in secular schools. As a result, the takeover dealt a blow to religious schools and by extension, it dealt another blow to the authority of many New York synagogues.[22]

The Jews of mid-century America were thus becoming more prosperous, more willing to challenge authority, and more willing to adjust their beloved traditions to fit into secular society. Understandably, they wanted their rabbis to accommodate their wishes. But the path toward that goal would prove contentious.

*Five*

# GERMAN RABBIS IN AMERICA

In the early decades of America, many educated Jews fulfilled the role of rabbi as congregations established themselves. They even called themselves rabbis in some cases. But it was not until the 1840s that the United States was able to welcome fully trained rabbis into the Jewish community.

For the most part, the rabbis came from German lands, part of that wave of new German immigrants. But if there was any hope among traditionalists that the new rabbis would impose order, history was to dictate otherwise. By the time rabbis could exert control, Jewish communities had grown accustomed to deciding rules and customs on their own. Some of the German rabbis brought rigid doctrines and rules embodied by the Talmud's 613 commandments that they then sought to dictate to the Jewish communities they served. But many others came bearing the culture of ferment and change that had started and spread in their homelands two decades earlier. Either way, the world of the American synagogue was not what they were accustomed to back home. Isaac Leeser, the preeminent traditionalist figure in Jewish circles of mid-century America, was taken aback, if not appalled, by what he found in America. "We have no ecclesiastical authorities in America, other than the congregations themselves," he wrote. "Each congregation makes its own rules for its government, and elects its own minister, who is appointed without any ordination, induction in office being made through his election."[1]

The pattern of secular, or lay, control of religious practices was similar to that of proliferating sectarian identities in American churches. Christian religions underwent turbulent change as Americans turned to different and conflicting paths toward God. That tumult and "awakening" of Christian fervor was destined to influence the character of American Judaism.[2]

Such influences were inevitable in a society founded on religion from the beginning. The Puritans of the Massachusetts Bay Colony sometimes saw themselves as heirs of Jewish tradition by establishing a "New Jerusalem" in the New World. In some respects, the Puritans convinced themselves that they, not the Jews, were the inheritors of the legacy of the Hebrew Bible, even as they continued to express intolerance of the Jews themselves.[3]

In the eighteenth century colonial era, America experienced a wave of religious revival known as the First Great Awakening, mirroring a similar evangelical wave in England. This period seems to have been a time of "awakenings" in general. Although historians find virtually no connection between this first "awakening" of Christians and anything comparable among Jews, it is striking that Hasidism—a movement of Jews searching for a personal connection with God through pious devotion to their *rebbes*, or grand rabbis—arose in Poland and later throughout Central Europe around the same period.

The First Awakening was characterized by powerful preaching and a yearning for salvation epitomized by the fire-and-brimstone sermonizing of Jonathan Edwards, who extolled the absolute sovereignty of God's judgment over human conduct. There is little evidence of any influence of this first "awakening" of the early 1700s on early American Jewish life, except that these Christians uniformly viewed Jews with toxic sympathy—heirs to a great tradition but errant in their refusal to recognize that their doctrines should yield to those put forward by followers of Jesus Christ.

The Second Great Awakening was almost a century later, in the first decades of the 1800s. It echoed the first, spreading spiritual values throughout the newly independent nation, especially in the frontier states and territories. This epoch delivered two divergent pressures and influences on Jews. On the one hand, Jews felt threatened as emotional Presbyterians, Baptists, Methodists, and other Protestant denominations held rallies that went on for days with preaching and prayers, confession, and repentance, and with worshippers jumping, shouting, and moaning to do battle against Satan. Calls for conversions—targeted at Catholics, African Americans, and Indians as well as Jews—were a regular part of these "come to Jesus" revival sessions. The fervor represented what the historian Gordon S. Wood says may have been "the greatest explosion of Christian religiosity since the seventeenth century or even the Reformation." The deism and secularism of the American founders such as Jefferson and Madison were swept aside in the frenzy, replaced by a dominant belief in an ever-present God with whom people sought a direct relationship.[4] As in South Carolina, Jews integrating into American life found themselves subjected to conversion crusades. Indeed, as Jews assured Christians that theirs was just another religion similar to Christianity, traditionalist Christians wondered why Jews did not take one further small step and accept Jesus Christ as their savior. Many evangelicals started to embrace the idea of restoring Jews to their homeland in Palestine as a prelude to the "ingathering" of Jews and their being converted in the Second Coming of Jesus.

Whatever the intention, the implication of Christians endorsing the ancient Jewish prayers for returning to Palestine reinforced the unwanted perception that American Jews had divided loyalties. Intellectuals admired the Jews' survival throughout history, but there was a body of literature holding that the arrival of Jews in American society meant they would disappear eventually. In the summer of 1852, for example, the poet Henry Wadsworth Longfellow visited Newport, Rhode Island, on a vacation and became entranced by an old Jewish cemetery protected by an iron fence, not far from the pounding surf. The cemetery had been established in 1677, but the Jews of the town had long since died out or left for other communities. Long-fellow wrote a poem, "The Jewish Cemetery at Newport," that evoked the graveyard as a metaphor for the Jews as they faced assimilation and oblivion.

The cause of proselytizing Jews was often taken up by those crusading against various sins, including intemperance—alcoholism was epidemic in some communities—gambling, public obscenity, and profanity. Religious organizations also drove reforms for the treatment of criminals and the mentally ill, and they sought improved higher education standards, the expansion of women's rights (the first women's rights convention at Seneca Falls took place in 1848), and the abolition of slavery.[5] But in cities where Jews lived, various missionary organizations and Bible societies had a familiar goal: bringing nonbelievers into their fold. Some Christians even visited Jewish charity hospitals to seek deathbed conversions. In cities with substantial Jewish populations, conversion efforts spread to public education, even in places where Jewish women were becoming public school teachers. In New York, Jews allied themselves with Catholics in the 1840s to oppose Bible reading and mandatory prayers in schools.

There was a second aspect to the Second Great Awakening that had a subtler influence on Jewish lives. As Protestants splintered into different denominations with their own practices, beliefs, and doctrines, they compelled state governments to loosen their last vestiges of established religions—to "disestablish" religion in their communities. These steps benefited the Jews. In what the historian Sydney Ahlstrom calls "the great tradition of the American churches," denominations in this period established five basic rights to religion: religious freedom, separation of church and state, the right of various denominations to adhere to their own practices, free choice of individuals, and religion infused by patriotic devotion to the United States. In this atmosphere it became easier for Jews to see themselves as one of many threads in the multicolored tapestry of religion in America. It was something they had no ability to do in Europe, where they had lived apart under their own rules for many centuries.[6]

Mainstream Protestantism in this period was also growing more hospitable to commingling with Jews. As America prospered, American Protestants could focus less on the afterlife and more on how to live in the new world they were creating. They embraced the idea that just as reason guided humankind to freedom, culminating in the American experiment, reason could guide humankind to God without requiring belief in miracles recounted in Scripture. Jonathan Edwards's older, bleak vision of mankind as destined to eternal damnation unless saved by divine grace—"Sinners in the Hands of an Angry God," as his most famous sermon put it—yielded to a more optimistic, benevolent depiction of a God of love, and an emphasis on the importance of individual dignity, self-improvement, and man-made progress in the temporal world. As one proponent of this new view, the Reverend William Ellery Channing (1780–1842) rejected Edwards's doctrine of atoning for original sin as equivalent to the idea of the Creator erecting gallows upon which to execute humankind. If life was not merely a preparation for the hereafter, it must follow that life should be cherished for its own beauty and value. After all, the founding father John Adams declared in 1755 that the great principles such as loving your neighbor as yourself were available to all persons of reason, not just to Christians, because they were universal truths understood by everyone.

Elite Protestants especially believed in the power of reason, an inheritance of Enlightenment thinking in Britain and France, and so held that science and rational analysis (in the tradition of Kant) were the paramount vehicles for understanding religion and ethics, even if the masses of less educated people still needed to believe in divine revelation as the foundation of truth for understanding God and morality.[7]

The implication of such views is that while one could well believe that God had created the universe, one could also believe that it was up to humans to carry out God's work and protect his creation. Going further, Unitarians held that Jesus was mortal and the founder of a great religion but not the son of God. Man, according to these teachings, was by nature good, and since God was merciful and loving, not vindictive, each person must search the Scripture for his or her own truth. These doctrines also helped perpetuate tolerance of different faiths, especially Judaism.

Even before the American Revolution, a strong strain of anticlerical thinking ran through Protestant teachings, mirroring the overthrow of the Crown. These anticlerical attitudes also affected Jewish communities. "I believe in the equality of man, and I believe that religious duties consist in doing justice, loving mercy, and endeavoring to make our fellow creatures happy," Thomas Paine declared in *The Age of Reason*, adding that churches were "human inventions set up to terrify and enslave mankind and monopolize power and profit."[8] He further described the Bible as replete with "obscene stories . . . voluptuous debaucheries . . . cruel and torturous executions [and] unrelenting vindictiveness."[9] The hero of Ticonderoga, Ethan Allen, had argued in *The Only Oracle of Man* (1784) that "natural religion" was achievable without the Bible and "priestcraft," so much so that he was attacked as anti-Christian. The "deists" of the Revolution—Paine, Jefferson, and Benjamin Franklin—had all doubted the divinity of Jesus, the concept of the Trinity, and even the status of the Bible as a product of divine revelation. Their central argument was that although God created the universe, it was up to humans to shape its future.

## NOT ONE BUT MANY JUDAISMS

At least eleven rabbis came to the United States in the divided religious environment of the 1840s. Four of them brought both secular and rabbinical degrees, attesting to their training in areas beyond the Talmud. Others came with questionable and likely embellished credentials. But the rabbis who had trained in Europe and earned university degrees generally arrived better educated and more culturally attuned than the Jews they were coming to serve. That situation hardly made their jobs easier. In fact, their educated status probably opened a difficult divide between them and their congregations.

At the same time, the American anticlerical environment of the Second Great Awakening contributed to the willingness of Jews to question their own doctrines as handed down by rabbis. The fights among rabbis, and between rabbis and their congregations, focused on how much Hebrew to include in the service, which prayers to eliminate, and whether to permit men and women to sit together. In some cases, practical considerations were paramount—as when Jewish worshippers looking for houses of worship had to acquire or purchase old church buildings, which had no balconies or separate sections where women could sit. Seated as equals among their family members, women increasingly took charge of religious schools, and the increasing role of women forced adjustments in the traditional rules against women participating in official Jewish religious ceremonies.

In Europe there had been chief rabbis in cities who established clerical authority among synagogues, but no such hierarchical structure was recognized in the United States. No synagogue could lord its practices over others. Writes the historian Jacob Rader Marcus: "There were almost as many Judaisms as there were individuals." It was ironic that so many of the new synagogue congregations adopted the word *shalom* ("peace") as part of their names, since at the time, peace and brotherly love were often more aspirations than realities. Attempts by rabbis to dictate practices as they had in Europe were doomed to failure. Nearly all the first generation of rabbis experienced rejection and dismissal. It was not unusual for rabbis to be hired and fired in rapid succession, migrating from synagogue to synagogue to satisfy their congregations. In Cincinnati, Congregation Bene Yeshurun had five spiritual leaders in five years. Rabbi Bernard Illowy (1814–1871) served six pulpits in sixteen years. Rabbi Isidor Kalisch served in eight pulpits in twenty-five years. Generally speaking, rabbis instituting reforms followed the wishes of their congregations, not the other way around.[10]

The first ordained rabbi on record to settle in America was Abraham Rice (originally Reiss), who arrived in 1840 from Gochsheim, Bavaria. Fervently Orthodox, he had difficulty getting a job in New York and so ended up in Nidchei Yisroel (The Dispersed of Israel) in Baltimore, a congregation established in 1830 that was still holding services above a local grocery. Moving to new quarters in 1845, the congregation changed its name to Baltimore Hebrew Congregation.

At Baltimore Hebrew, Rice stood firm in favor of observing the Sabbath and against intermarriage, deviation from kosher laws, and the shortening of prayers, especially some of the more esoteric ones handed down over the centuries, known as *piyyutim*. (A general term for liturgical poems, *piyyutim* derives from Greek, and the same root as *poietes*, "poet.") He also never mastered English, a refusal that nettled at least some in his congregation. Many Jews in that congregation and elsewhere had advocated such changes to make the service more palatable—and comprehensible—only to be rebuffed by Rice. As a result, he never felt completely at home in his adopted country.

Rice insisted that violators of the Sabbath not be permitted to read from the Torah at Sabbath services, which led to an early dispute with his congregation. He also lashed out at the "heathenish rites" he said were being performed at funerals, evidently referring to secularized rituals taken from Masons and Odd Fellows. In protest, several members of the congregation resigned and formed Har Sinai Verein (Mount Sinai Association) in 1842, holding services that were close to Orthodox in nature, but with modifications. They met in a private home until 1849, when they obtained their own building on High Street in Baltimore and became Har Sinai Congregation, now considered the oldest congregation in the United States that has been affiliated with the Reform movement since its inception.

An irony of the protests against Rice at Baltimore Hebrew was that the rabbi actually wanted to adjust some of the ritual practices. For example, he attempted to accommodate the modernists by eliminating some prayers regarded as overly obscure. But that move drew counter-objections from traditionalists, some of whom were flexible on other matters. The rabbi was frustrated by the congregation's inconsistent approach of enforcing Jewish law in the congregation but permitting latitude among its members in their private behavior. Writing to his friend in Germany, Rice declared, "I dwell in complete darkness, without a teacher or a companion. . . . I am tired of my life. . . . I often think of leaving and going to Paris and put my trust in the good Lord." Eventually his congregation grew dissatisfied, and Rice had to resign in 1849. He tried to establish another more orthodox synagogue but was forced to support himself by opening stores selling dry goods and groceries; he died in 1862.[11]

The second emigrant rabbi to settle in America is generally agreed to have been Rabbi Leo Merzbacher, also a Bavarian native. He is often identified as the first official "reform" rabbi in America. But like Rice, he encountered a turbulent series of setbacks. Merzbacher's own biographical profile referred to his university and rabbinic degrees, but some scholars say the evidence is lacking. After arriving in New York in 1841, Merzbacher took up teaching at Congregation Rodeph Sholom in New York. In 1843, he became preacher at Congregation Ansche Chesed, which had broken from B'nai Jeshurun in 1829. But when Merzbacher delivered a sermon criticizing the practice of women covering their hair, as demanded by Orthodox tradition, his contract was not renewed. Instead he went to Temple Emanu-El (God is with us), a new congregation in New York established by thirty-three German Jews in 1845, after they had earlier started a *Cultus-Verein* (worship association) to attract young people. They held their first services in a second-floor loft on the Lower East Side and later moved to successive new synagogues uptown.

Even at Emanu-El, Merzbacher engaged in disputes with his lay leadership over various practices. At one point the board members told him they were tired of his pursuits and "did not wish to receive further protests, admonitions and rebukes and would feel themselves necessitated to leave them unanswered." The board went further, advertising for an assistant who could speak English. No assistant was found by the time Merzbacher collapsed and died while walking home from the synagogue in 1856. He was succeeded by Rabbi Samuel Adler, a renowned scholar in both Jewish and secular studies and son of a prominent rabbi in Germany, who was persuaded to emigrate from the Rhineland town of Alzey to take up the post.[12]

Another important figure from the era was Rabbi Max Lilienthal (1815–1882), who had served as a director of a network of state-sponsored Jewish schools in the Pale of Settlement in western Russia, where Jews were confined under the decree of Catherine the Great and her successors. Fearing an eventual plan by Russia to turn his schools into instruments of conversion to Christianity, Lilienthal fled to the United States at age thirty. Famous for his courage and pioneering efforts in Russia, Lilienthal was warmly welcomed and recruited to serve simultaneously at three different synagogues, including Ansche Chesed. Many began referring to him as New York City's "chief rabbi."

Lilienthal advocated several changes in Jewish practices while in New York City, including adoption of a ceremony allowing the widow of a deceased man to release his brother from the ancient biblical obligation to marry her. He also tried to set up a *beit din*, or rabbinic court, to rule on religious law for all congregations, but the effort never got off the ground because of resistance among New York's Jews to any obligation to answer to one overarching authority. Eventually, Lilienthal's efforts to serve three different congregations fell into a familiar pattern of mutual recrimination. When a member of Ansche Chesed asked Lilienthal to help form a minyan for blessing a sick child, the rabbi sent word that he was unavailable. For that rebuff, he was brought before the board, whereupon he refused to cooperate and left in a huff. The board suspended him for insulting them. Lilienthal later went into business for himself, establishing a private Jewish day school before heading off to Cincinnati to Congregation Bene Israel. While continuing to serve as a rabbi, he joined Hebrew Union College's faculty in 1875.[13]

Still another outspoken and consequential émigré was David Einhorn (1809–1879), a brilliant, passionate follower of German Jewish enlightenment figures, such as Abraham Geiger, under whom he had studied. In 1855, Einhorn was recruited to serve as the first rabbi of the Har Sinai Congregation in Baltimore. There he produced his own prayer book for reformers that became a model for the *Union Prayer Book* toward the end of the century. Einhorn later took up duties in Philadelphia during the Civil War.

At Har Sinai Verein, Einhorn used the Hamburg Temple prayer book for Rosh Hashanah, and its members went so far as to question whether Jews needed to observe Tisha B'Av, the day of mourning for the destruction of the Temple in ancient times. Einhorn was influenced by the concern among some Jews that Christians would conclude that Jewish desires to return to Jerusalem would open them to charges of disloyalty. Like other reformers, Einhorn belittled the idea of such a return, declaring: "The one temple in

Jerusalem sank into the dust, in order that countless temples might arise to thy honor and glory."[14]

Not only was Baltimore the location of the first congregation to officially identify itself as "reform," but it also established the American paradigm for what later became the three principal branches of Judaism. In the antebellum era, Baltimore had synagogues representing each. On the left was Einhorn and his flock. On the right was the traditionalist, Rabbi Rice. In the middle, but to the right of Har Sinai, was Congregation Oheb Shalom (Lovers of Peace), established in 1853, which in trying to find a middle ground served as a precursor to the denomination later known as Conservative Judaism. Benjamin Szold, its rabbi, composed a prayer book, *Abodath Israel*, which was used by congregations of reform and conservative leanings in later years. The existence of three rabbis in Baltimore, each with a different prayer book, augured the paths that Judaism would develop later in the nineteenth century.[15]

## HASKALAH AND MASKILIM IN GERMANY

What these and other rabbis brought with them was a spirit that had been brewing in Germany among so-called emancipated Jews in a handful of cosmopolitan centers where they were accepted as equals in Christian society. As Jews grew in influence, especially as financiers, secular leaders of Europe turned to them for assistance in raising money for business, government, and military enterprises. It became expedient—and intellectually appealing—for Jews to recognize the legitimacy of the governing authorities in their communities. In Europe, especially Germany, the quid pro quo by which Jews felt welcome if they abandoned their separate identities was an arrangement that would prove tragically doomed to failure. But it set the pattern for a similar if unstated bargain in the United States, where it has been a foundation of Judaism's development.

Jews in Europe began to prosper as merchants and financiers, first in the Netherlands and England, and later in France and Germany, with the rise of the first nation states after the Thirty Years' War in the seventeenth century.

By 1806, less than two years after declaring himself emperor of France, Napoleon Bonaparte summoned more than a hundred notable Jews to an assembly in Paris designed to cement their loyalty to French society. In return for recognition as equals, the delegates to what was called a Sanhedrin (evoking the council of Jewish sages in the Roman Empire period) affirmed that they were subject to French law and no longer "a nation within a nation" in France. In doing so, they effectively abandoned the primary goal of praying for the restoration of the Kingdom of David in the Promised Land.[16] As Napoleon sent troops eastward, conquering German lands as a prelude to invading Russia, this "emancipation" of Jews became an order of the day in German-speaking territories as well.

The Jewish Enlightenment (*Haskalah*) movement and its followers, or *maskilim*, were an outgrowth of the European Enlightenment generally. The core principle was the elevation of rationalism and individual autonomy as superior to social and religious governing constructs. It became important for all Enlightenment figures to declare that religious beliefs could be derived from reason, irrespective of whether one believed that God revealed himself to those who wrote the Bible. For Jews, such beliefs meant that they could place their religion in a more universal context. Accordingly, for enlightened Jewish educators, it was important to establish curricula that emphasized secular knowledge, philosophy, and modern languages—along with the study of Jewish history and ancient Hebrew—as a means to revive Jewish consciousness. Jewish educators also wanted to convince Christians that Judaism was not an obscurantist cult devoted to arcane rituals and rules but a broadly humanist set of ethical beliefs from which Christianity was descended. Some went so far as to align themselves with the deistic possibility of believing in God while rejecting the idea of God intervening in the daily affairs of humankind, and playing down prayers in religious services for such intervention.

It was thus necessary for Enlightenment Jews to deemphasize their distinctive racial identity as direct heirs of biblical patriarchs. They also downplayed themselves as "chosen" by God to observe certain commandments, yet punished by God with forced exile from Jerusalem. Instead of embracing the goal of reestablishing the Kingdom of David in the Holy Land, Jews defined themselves as having a different sort of "mission"—to convey a message of ethical monotheism to the rest of the world. It was not hard, of course, for traditionalist critics of reformers to see such new doctrines as a cynical—and likely to be futile—ploy to abandon their legacy in exchange for equal status in supposedly secular societies.

Even before Napoleon, Jews had risen sufficiently in standing to produce the circumstances for these ideas to flourish. As Jews in the seventeenth century in Europe rose to become doctors and students of philosophy and the physical sciences, they became increasingly attracted to secular pursuits and learning. The leading forerunner of such thinking in the eighteenth century was Moses Mendelssohn (1729–1786), the son of a scribe, who moved to Berlin at a young age and came to be known as "the founder of modern Jewish thought."[17] Mendelssohn, a contemporary and friend of Immanuel Kant, was a rigorous traditionalist who nonetheless advocated an education in secular subjects and vernacular languages for Jews. Mendelssohn was reformulating the fundamental definitions of traditional Judaism along the lines of a religion of reason. In some of his writings, Mendelssohn spoke respectfully of Spinoza's contribution to understanding the nature of religion. But unlike Spinoza, Mendelssohn embraced the concept of laws given to Jews on Mount Sinai and the importance and logic of Jewish practices and identity. He saw Jewish ethical precepts as applicable to all humankind, however. Scholars note that it was not as if Mendelssohn was inventing something entirely new. Since Maimonides, Jewish sages had often declared that Judaism and the belief in God could be understood by reason rather than by acceptance of revelation from biblical times.

Perhaps Mendelssohn's most important historic contribution was his advocacy of the separation of religion from the state. In a secular state, he argued in *Jerusalem*, published in 1783, Judaism could take its place as an equal of Christianity or any other religion, governed by a regime that did not discriminate between one religion over another. Following Mendelssohn's death, as prosperity and the status of Jews rose, increasing numbers of Jews in Germany were admitted to universities and other civic institutions. Influenced by the philosopher Georg Wilhelm Friedrich Hegel, they accepted the intellectual approach of historicism—applying rationalism to the understanding of evolving historical context—to the history of Judaism itself. In 1819, Jews in Germany established the Society for the Culture and Science of Judaism. These Jews adopted the term *Wissenschaft des Judentums* (scientific study of Judaism) as their method and accepted the idea that the first five books of the Bible were a product of many authors over time, not the handiwork of God delivered directly to Moses.

Going further, these scholars sought to create a critical and historical understanding of Jewish history and literature. They saw themselves as expressing their allegiance to tradition with scholarship focused on the entirety of Jewish writings. By implication, the "science of Judaism" was a method to break down the barriers that separated Jews from their fellow citizens and inspired mistrust among non-Jews.

The *maskilim* (adherents of the Jewish Enlightenment) effectively revolutionized the way Jews understood their religious identity. They had set aside the bewildering array of Jewish practices to focus on what they defined as Judaism's essence, i.e., its moral truths. They contended that just as the rabbis of old reinvented Judaism by emphasizing prayer, readings, and laws after it was no longer possible to carry out animal sacrifices at the Temple of Jerusalem, so Jews of the modern era were adjusting Judaism to contemporary exigencies. They did not see themselves as rejectionists but rather as revisionists. They declared, in fact, that they were adhering to the Talmudic tradition of reinterpreting laws to accommodate circumstances unforeseen when the laws were first codified.

Some of the modern Jewish scholars in Germany became increasingly radical. They included Leopold Zunz (1794–1886) and Nahman Krochmal (1785–1840), who theorized that Jews were like many other nations that go through cycles of change and renewal. Another influential figure was Heinrich Graetz (1817–1891), whose multivolume *History of the Jews* was renowned for its analysis of Jewish political experience in the ancient and modern worlds. Following these teachings, certain Jewish practices were bound to fray. In Westphalia, Jews established their own "consistory" to direct their affairs, instituting decorum and sermons in German. Elsewhere, Jews shortened and modified the liturgy to make it more accessible, and Jewish education, which was until this period focused entirely on the Talmud and Jewish law, expanded into secular subjects. In Cassel, religious services featured hymns and German sermons as well as prayers. A confirmation ceremony was instituted in some cases, replacing or complementing the traditional bar mitzvah, the ceremony commemorating a young man's first reading of the Torah.

Increasingly, Germans called their synagogues "temples." The term had been in some use in France and Germany, but modernizers in Germany saw the name as more palatable than the foreign-sounding word *synagogue*, a Greek word meaning "gathering place" or more specifically a gathering place for prayer.[18] In Seesen, a town in Lower Saxony in Germany, Israel Jacobson, a Jewish community leader and philanthropist, established a "temple"— one of the first uses of the word—as part of a school he founded in 1810. Its building had Latin inscriptions along with Hebrew, an organ, a choir, and a pulpit facing the congregation, from which German prayers and a sermon were delivered. The original plan for this temple called for a clocktower and bell, clearly designed to resemble a church, but that plan was scrapped in the face of objections from Jewish and non-Jewish authorities. Instead, the temple was topped by a belvedere, or rooftop gallery, and a short bell tower and bells. The building so clearly evoked a church that many Jews in Seesen and elsewhere objected. So did Christians. Other revised practices were carried out in Congregation Adath Jeshurun in Amsterdam in 1796 and the Beer Temple in Berlin in 1815. But historians generally argue that the first completely reform temple was established in 1818 in Hamburg. It featured prayers in German (as opposed to Hebrew) and omitted any references to the coming of a messiah or a return to Zion. More "temples" proliferated in the 1830s, signaling the intent of some reformers to make them serve as a substitute for the destroyed Temple of Jerusalem.[19]

Another important figure of the period was Abraham Geiger, often called "the spiritual father of the reform movement."[20] Geiger mobilized perhaps the most extensive arguments that the essence of Judaism was its universal tenets of humanism, monotheism, and ethics, whereas the rabbinical rulings of the Talmud were the product of historical conditions confronted by Jews in exile and unsuited to the modern world. "The Talmud must go," he declared. "The Bible, that collection of mostly so beautiful and exalted—perhaps the most exalted—*human* books, as a divine work must also go."[21]

These were all powerful forces. But reform did not survive as a significant movement in Europe. It suffered from many doctrinal and practical differences, including the role of Hebrew. Rabbis and Jewish intellectuals sought to iron them out at conferences in Brunswick in 1844, Frankfurt in 1845, and Breslaw in 1846. But the movement to reform Judaism could not cope with the recrudescence of anti-Semitism and crackdowns on Jewish citizenship and activities throughout Europe in the mid-century. The Jewish embrace of an identity as equal to others became a fiction, swallowed up by waves of anti-Semitism.

It thus fell to rabbis and Jews in the United States to take what they had seen in Europe and turn Judaism into an American religion. The rabbi most responsible for transforming American Judaism in this era arrived inconspicuously in New York as part of the German influx. He did not see himself as a reformer so much as an Americanizer. But he would profoundly change the character of American Judaism before he was done.

*Six*

# THE TURBULENT ISAAC
# MAYER WISE

In the summer of 1846, a twenty-seven-year-old rabbi named Isaac Mayer Wise left his home in Bohemia and traveled to the United States aboard the sailing vessel *Marie*, accompanied by his wife and baby daughter. On board, he and the family endured weeks in lice- and rat-infested steerage and kept kosher by consuming nothing but onions and herring.

One evening late in the trip, the captain of the *Marie* told Wise that if the wind kept up, they would arrive in just a couple of days in New York City. Alone on the ship's deck, Wise surrendered to his emotions. "How foolish and daring it is, thought I, to have left home, friends, position, and future prospects in order to emigrate to a strange land without means or expectations!" Wise later recounted. Back in steerage, the emotional traveler fell asleep and lapsed into a nightmare that he later described with characteristic grandiloquence. He dreamt, he said, that his boat had crashed in a storm at the foot of a steep mountain, where an army of "hollow-eyed, ghostly, grinning dwarfs," "lascivious, ragged goblins," and "tiny poodles" blocked his path. But in his reverie, Wise "dashed them aside" and reached a beautiful meadow at the summit, a harbinger of his new life in the New World.[1]

In the Bible, as Wise well understood, dreams sometimes represent prophesies. The rabbi was no doubt using his memoirs to convince readers that he foresaw his future as the embattled hero of Judaism in America. Hero or not, Wise changed the course of Judaism as it settled and integrated itself into the fabric of religious life in America. At his first congregation, in Albany, New York, he was to participate in a fateful conflict and fistfight on Rosh Hashanah over doctrines and practices, particularly the concept of the Messiah—perhaps the most important physical brawl in the annals of American Judaism.

After moving from Albany to Cincinnati, he established the first Jewish seminary to graduate rabbis in America, an important new American Jewish prayer book, an organization of reform American rabbis, and what was to become the largest organization of Jews in the United States, now known as the Union for Reform Judaism. His lifelong goal—to create a single unified American Judaism—failed spectacularly, amid opposition from both modernizers and traditionalists. He was condemned for apostasy by conservatives, and advocates of reform reviled him for not going far enough. He was hardly the only prominent Jew to try to redefine a new American Judaism, and others made possible what he had begun. But he was the pivotal figure in creating a new normal for American Jewish beliefs.

Wise's early years did not suggest that he would be suited to a life of combat and crusading. Plagued with depression, hypochondria, self-doubt, and death wishes, Wise somehow managed to transmute these handicaps into "a supreme, manic self-confidence that enabled him to face enemies and personal defeats with near equanimity, always certain that eventually he would succeed," as the historian Michael Meyer puts it.[2]

Success for Wise was not necessarily "reform." Rather, his goal was one of uniting all American Jewry under one denomination—to create a distinctly American Judaism commanding the loyalty of all, and not a separate brand of "reform" Judaism that some, but not all, would follow. He lived to see that dream nearly reached and then blown apart by discord over practices, doctrine, and faith. The coup de grâce for that dream at the end of the century was the influx of Jews from Eastern Europe and Russia, whose descendants nonetheless over time were bound to be influenced by his legacy.

"To understand Wise, we must see him above all as an Americanizer," writes Nathan Glazer in his book on American Judaism. "He had a passion for America as the land of freedom. It permitted him to do what he wished without restriction." But Glazer notes that Wise's pragmatism made him seem more like an opportunist than a traditionalist or a radical. At times, he was willing to accept the Talmud as legally binding and even of divine origin, but it was doubtful that he really believed such a thing, and more likely that he was only trying to accommodate disparate points of view in his search for unity.[3]

Instead of unity, Wise's efforts produced disputes. But even these disagreements defined the history that all American Jews have inherited.

## FROM STEINGRUB TO ALBANY

It is not clear that Wise actually came to America with the intention of becoming a rabbi, though his grandson and biographer Max May later recounted that he "came to America with definite plans and purposes," including the goal of liberating Jews from their "bigoted environment" in order to become respected citizens of their country.[4]

At the time of his arrival, New York City was an energetic and prosperous community of 370,000 and a major port because of its connection to the West via the Erie Canal. Wise settled at Temple Beth El (House of God) in Albany, the capital of New York State and a gateway of commerce established by the canal, which had opened a couple of decades earlier and connected the Great Lakes to the Hudson River and to the port of New York.

Born in the village of Steingrub in what later became Czechoslovakia,

Wise was the oldest son of a poor Jewish schoolmaster. Orphaned at an early age, Wise grew up in poverty. He studied at a yeshiva, or seminary, outside Prague and apparently attended university courses there and in Vienna. But the precise character of his rabbinical training remains obscure. Like his father, he served as a schoolmaster in another village, Radnitz, in Bohemia, where he recalled that he was constantly restless and yearning for larger horizons.[5]

The evidence is not abundant, but Wise appears to have been influenced by the practitioners of Haskalah, including such figures as Isaac Noah Mannheimer, who in 1863 was one of a group that defended Heinrich Graetz in a court in Vienna after Graetz had challenged the concept of the Messiah. Wise was also acquainted with Salomon Sulzer, a prominent Viennese cantor and composer, whose singing was admired by Schubert and Liszt. (Sulzer incorporated three-quarter waltz time into some of his chants, including the Shema, the central prayer of Jewish liturgy, in a tune that remains a favorite in Reform congregations today.) The record shows that in 1845 Wise attended the rabbinical conference in Frankfurt and read the antiestablishment writings of German Jewish liberals Gabriel Riesser and Samuel Hirsch and other works of Wissenschaft des Judentums.[6] Not all his biographers agree on the extent of these influences. But one, James G. Heller, argues that in Frankfurt and elsewhere, Wise absorbed such ideas as introducing decorum into the service, elevating the status of women and other practices circulating in Germany. Wise did not speak much of such influences, however, apparently out of determination to define his calls for change as driven by American rather than European influences. Whatever Wise's beliefs before he left the Old World, he was evidently frustrated by the constraints of Europe, including the poverty and ignorance of its Jewish peasants, and his poor prospects for improving on his humble place in its firmament.[7]

Reaching out to like-minded clergy upon his arrival in New York, Wise turned to Max Lilienthal, who had arrived in the city only a few years earlier from Riga. Lilienthal appears to have been the one to encourage Wise to become a rabbi and to substitute for him at consecration ceremonies in

New Haven, Connecticut, and Syracuse, in upstate New York. On the way there, Wise stopped in Albany, where he preached at Temple Beth El and gave a sermon that he later said did not sit well. The congregation, he later wrote, "aggravated and humiliated" him, though for some reason he got an invitation to come back later for the Jewish New Year and was surprised by the more favorable reaction at that time. Meanwhile, a second synagogue in Albany, Temple Beth El Jacob, also invited him, and that sermon was so successful that policemen had to be stationed to keep the crowds under control, at least in Wise's recollection. Temple Beth El was now ready to make him an offer. "My fortune was made as far as Albany was concerned," he wrote in his *Reminiscences.*[8]

Albany was not necessarily a propitious or welcoming place, however. Originally it was part of the Dutch colony controlled by its director general, Peter Stuyvesant, who, as earlier noted, did not welcome Jews. Among his early actions was a rejection of a petition from three Jews seeking permission to trade throughout the colony, including Fort Orange, the tiny settlement on the Hudson River that would later became Albany. Fort Orange was even then an important entrepôt for trade in furs and other goods, which were shipped down the river to the city. The Jews had come from Amsterdam with permission from the Dutch West India Company, but Stuyvesant was uneasy about their presence so soon after the arrival of Jews in New Amsterdam from Brazil the year before. Dutch financiers got Stuyvesant to change his mind, up to a point. Jews were permitted to live and trade in the colony, including in the Hudson River Valley, but they could not hold public service jobs, operate retail shops, or build a synagogue. Instead, they were to worship in their homes as long as these homes were to be "close together in a convenient place."[9]

As traders, the Jews quickly prospered. But their fortunes as a community in Albany faded after the fur trade subsided in the seventeenth century. Individual Jews returned to Albany in the eighteenth century, but no Jewish community emerged until the early nineteenth century as refugees from persecution in Central Europe arrived. By 1838, German Jews established a Jewish society in the city and set up a meeting place in a private home in the city's South End. A few years later, they bought a small church at 76 Herkimer Street, near the banks of the Hudson River, on a plot of land owned by the Dutch Reformed Church. In 1841, Jews dedicated the building as Beth El Synagogue, the first in the city. Five years later, Wise arrived.

Wise, displaying a bit of snobbery, was not exactly enamored of his new community of peddlers and small-time merchants with little English and many Old World customs. In his memoirs, he listed their professions—basket peddler ("altogether dumb and homeless"), trunk carrier, and pack carrier ("who carries 100 to 150 pounds upon his back and indulges the thought that he will become a businessman some day"). There was an aristocracy of richer folk—shop owners, owners of wagons pulled by horses, peddlers who graduated to running their own stores. In that group was Louis Spanier, president of the congregation, the wealthiest Jew in the city, whose business interests included owning and operating a schooner that brought lumber from the Great Lakes.[10]

An initial irritant and harbinger of difficulties in the future between Wise and his congregation occurred when he was offered the job of teacher and preacher, but not rabbi. It was common for smaller congregations in that period not to have a rabbi. The hazan usually served as the main religious celebrant and in some cases the persons filling that role actually opposed the installation of rivals to serve as rabbis in their synagogues. "If you wish to elect me, you must elect me as a rabbi," Wise told the congregation of 130 members, however.[11] The congregation granted his request, and although his own status was "not brilliant financially," Wise later wrote, it set him in reasonable comfort. He was paid $250 a year, plus $9 for each student he taught. Wise went on to establish the Jewish Academy of Albany, where students learned English, arithmetic, history, and geography as well as Hebrew and Jewish studies.

In typical fashion, Wise emanates the soul of reason and the spirit of a revolutionary in recalling his Albany period. "The reforming spirit was innate in me," he wrote. "It was my foremost characteristic."[12] But at other times he described himself as a cautious moderate and not a rebel at all. Yet his difficulties in persuading others to go along with his initial minor adjustments to Jewish practice and observance were so frustrating that at times he considered abandoning the rabbinate for a legal career, returning to Europe, or at least moving to another congregation in America.

There appears to be no evidence of a contract between Wise and the synagogue at the outset. In 1849, however, the congregation insisted on establishing a contract for his continued employment. To Wise's chagrin, the document contained legalistic wording making it clear that Wise could not change any of the temple's rituals without the congregation's consent. The contract also stipulated greater control by the trustees over the school set up by Wise. If Wise didn't obey these strictures, the temple board could meet and declare the contract null and void. In Wise's account, he tore up the contract and prepared to board a steamer for New York City, where he had earlier been interested in forming a union of congregations. A new contract was agreed to by the spring of 1849 but did not ease the anxieties on both sides.

It appears that even Wise's more moderate reforms rankled some in the congregation. One was the introduction of a choir, evidently modeled on those Wise had been familiar with in Germany and Vienna. To find space for the expanded choir, he moved the singers over to the front of the separate women's seating area. This action provoked protests from the women and other members of the congregation. In his memoirs, Wise acknowledged that the choir was "a thorn in their [his critics'] side," and that "there were constant bickerings over it."[13] Another major focus of dispute was over *piyyutim*, the traditional obscure prayers that Wise wanted to eliminate from the service, especially because he disliked those associated with the theme of mourning over the Jews' exile. But some of these prayers were sentimental and traditional favorites of congregation members. Wise said he wanted to honor the authors of these ancient prayers but preferred not to pick and choose among them, so eliminating all of them seemed like a sensible solution.

Other upsetting steps by Wise included the introduction of German and English hymns, a confirmation ceremony that replaced the bar mitzvah, and abolition of the sale to congregants of "honors," such as opening the ark or removing the Torah from it. In another break with precedent, he had the congregation remain seated during the reading of the Torah. Several attempts to repeal these innovations were rebuffed by Wise and his allies.[14]

But no doubt problems arose as well from Wise's overbearing personality and ambitions, too great to be confined in a small congregation on the upper Hudson River. Some members grew suspicious of those ambitions, especially when he expressed interest in joining with Rabbi Lilienthal, who had originally recommended Wise for the Albany post, in creating an American *beit din*, or rabbinical court. In 1846, Lilienthal announced establishment of such a court and selected Wise as one of four members. The little quartet of rabbis immediately declared larger goals. The court would offer its rulings to American Jews in general, they said. But like other attempts to set up religious bodies to rule across the board in the Jewish community, Lilienthal's gambit failed. American Jews were not ready to organize themselves under anyone's authority, let alone his.

It was in Albany that Wise also nurtured what would be a lifelong dream of creating a uniquely American prayer book, which he wanted to call *Minhag America* (*American Custom*). The idea of such a prayer book was not by itself anathema, but inevitably—as with the setting up of a rabbinical court—its execution was going to provoke discord. A Jewish periodical established in 1843, *The Occident*—its founding editor was Isaac Leeser, a lifelong traditionalist and sometime friend and rival of Rabbi Wise—commended the effort but noted the difficulty of a text seeking to unite disparate elements of the Jewish community, coming as they did from different parts of Europe with varied traditions and languages. The problem, said *The Occident* in 1847, was that "the German will not give way to the Polish, nor he to the English, nor the latter to the Portuguese Jew." Like Lilienthal's *beit din*, the prayer book project foundered in these early years of Wise's career. But Wise still harbored a dream of unifying Jews in America around something, whether a prayer book or an organization. In 1848, he called for an "association of Israelitish congregations in North America, to produce one grand and sublime end—to defend and maintain our sacred faith, to the glory of God and for the benefit of Israel and all mankind."[15]

The problem to be overcome, as Wise began to see it, was the splintered nature of Judaism in America, which, in his view, left Jewish beliefs to be defined by ignorant laypeople. "Each congregation pursues its own way, has its own customs and mode of worship, its own way of thinking about religious questions, from which cause it then results that one Jew is a stranger in the Synagogue of the other Jew," he lamented, warning that if Jews did not unite around universal doctrines in the United States, they risked falling by the wayside or even converting to Christianity.[16]

To implement his vision, Wise tried to forge an alliance with Leeser, the publisher of *The Occident*, though it was fated to unravel as Wise moved away from tradition. Leeser had had his own dream of unifying Judaism in America some years earlier, revolving around a more traditional approach. A familiar point of disagreement between them was the role of prayers that called for restoration of the Temple in Jerusalem and the return of animal sacrifices. After Wise gave a lecture declaring that he saw "no reason to pray for the restoration of sacrifices," word of his views reached *The Occident* and Leeser, who disagreed vehemently, as he had earlier over such changes in Charleston.[17] In response, Wise sought to assure Leeser that he was not trying to impose a radical agenda on his countrymen. He wrote in *The Occident* in 1849 that although certain changes were inevitable, he was not a revolutionary. The two rabbis then discussed the idea of holding a meeting of Jewish congregations to discuss various matters, but the plan fizzled out. Its failure occurred just as Wise signed another three-year contract with his balky Albany congregation. He turned his attention to writing and to what he found to be the misinformation and denigration of Judaism by Christian preachers and leaders, with whom he had begun to mingle.

## MORE SQUABBLING IN ALBANY

A family tragedy accelerated Wise's growing breach with tradition. In 1849, shortly after signing up again in Albany, his two-year-old daughter and second child, Laura, died in a cholera epidemic. At his daughter's funeral, members of the congregation beseeched Wise to perform a ritual tearing of his garment, in the tradition known as *k'riah*, as was customary at such occasions. Jewish ritual called for parents, spouse, children, and siblings to make a tear in an article of clothing (usually a shirt or blouse) as an expression of mourning. The supposed biblical precedent is Jacob's rending of his clothes in mourning over Joseph, his son, whom he believed at the time was dead (Genesis 37:34), but the Bible connects mourning and grieving with rending of clothing in other verses as well. At the time of Wise's mourning, it was customary for someone else to use a knife, as opposed to scissors, to start the tear on the mourner's clothes, and then for the mourner to tear it further while reciting a blessing.

For whatever reason, possibly because the rite seemed barbaric in the presence of his tiny daughter's body, Wise recoiled for himself and others. "I repelled them and forbade the women to even suggest this observance to my wife," he later wrote. He also refused to sit on the floor or low bench and remove his shoes, both also customary. These rebuffs were scandalous in the eyes of some of those present, leading to gossip that spread through the streets, shops, and saloons of the Jewish community in Albany. Discouraged and hurt, Wise turned inward and started to give thought to writing books and other pieces that might further the cause of establishing a unified Jewish organization, including essays in a new publication that started in 1849, *The Asmonean*, based in New York. Though Wise had earlier refused to rend his garment, his writing suggested that he was gifted at dramatic gestures aimed at illustrating what he maintained was a tortured conscience. "I am candid enough, sir, to know, and sufficiently meek to confess publicly, that I myself am cause of the disappointment," he wrote in *The Asmonean* in 1849, suggesting that it was his own fault, and perhaps a lack of traditional piety, that led people to suspect him of self-aggrandizement and attention grabbing. The accusations against him were unjust, he said, but he took the blame for insensitivity to the community's concerns. Nevertheless, Wise vowed to continue his quest for Jewish unity in America—focused, he said, on core principles of Jewish faith and law.[18]

Wise's emotional self-justification was itself attention grabbing. In

Philadelphia, Leeser found it overweening. Leeser believed himself to be
the author of the drive for Jewish unity. Shortly after Wise's essay in *The Asmonean, The Occident* ran an ad from Congregation Beth Elohim in Charleston, South Carolina—the congregation that a few years earlier had divided
emotionally and legally over installation of an organ. They were looking for
a rabbi. That Wise took an interest in Beth Elohim indicated that he was
restless.

*Seven*

# A FISTFIGHT IN ALBANY

Following the organ dispute, Congregation Beth Elohim in Charleston struggled to recover a sense of unity and harmony. Despite the favorable court ruling, Rabbi Poznanski continued as a target of disapproval from conservative circles, in Charleston and elsewhere, for what one critic called "German neologistic [i.e., Reformist] doctrines of faith." The city's Jewish traditionalists remained determined to make their breakaway congregation, Charleston's Shearith Israel, a refuge against radical reform. Its members built a new synagogue on Wentworth Street, not far from Beth Elohim. Jacob Rosenfeld, one of their leaders, promised that the new congregation would worship God "as in the days of yore, in the holy tongue, in which He revealed His divine will to His servants the prophets." He called the changes back at Beth Elohim "arrogant, baneful, and preposterous" and praised the loyalty of the traditionalists for "bringing back to the fold those who were indifferent or astray."[1]

Poznanski, obviously still bruised from the organ fight at Beth Elohim, resigned in its wake and presided over a committee to find a successor. At around the same time, the conservatives at Shearith Israel invited Rabbi Morris S. Raphall (1798–1868) from New York to speak in Charleston in 1850, setting off the next battle over reform.

Raphall, a staunch traditionalist, thus became another important emigrant of the 1840s caught up in the arguments over Jewish practices in America. Born in Stockholm, Sweden, the son of a prosperous banker, Raphall was also a renowned speaker—he spoke with a plummy British intonation, having lived in England for some years—who championed an orthodox approach to Jewish practice but with some modernist touches that emphasized preaching, education of the young, and an esthetically pleasing service that still adhered rigorously to tradition. Such was his fame that he commanded the highest salary of any American rabbi of the time: $2,000.[2]

Raphall had studied religion at a Jewish grammar school and seminary in Copenhagen and secular subjects in Germany and England, where he had served as a rabbi in Birmingham before emigrating to the United States. At the time of his invitation to Charleston, he was serving at B'nai Jeshurun in New York, the congregation that had earlier broken away from New York's first congregation, Shearith Israel. Later, on February 1, 1860, Raphall became the first Jew to deliver a prayer at the opening of a session of the United States Congress. Still later, he would play a more notorious role as the most prominent Jewish religious figure in America to defend the institution of slavery. But while in Charleston in this antebellum period, slavery was not an issue. Instead, he lectured on "The Poetry of the Hebrew Bible." In a separate talk, he attacked the reformers at Beth Elohim, mocking them for their belief that as Americans they could forsake the coming of the Messiah. The Messiah, he said, would come one day "without fail."

It appears to have been a coincidence that Wise was visiting Charleston at the same time as Raphall's appearance, apparently to seek the rabbinical post in the wake of Poznanski's resignation. He may also have wanted to get away after grieving over his daughter's death. Overworked, depressed, suffering from a cold, and feeling unappreciated, Wise had been advised by doctors to travel to a warmer climate. The synagogue gave him a leave of absence to do so, perhaps without knowing of the job opportunity. In addition, upon learning (at a stopover in Philadelphia) that Raphall was going to be in town, Wise may also have wanted to use the occasion to meet up with him.

On his way to Charleston, Wise stopped off in Washington, D.C. He was prominent enough in New York's capital to meet on this visit with Senator William Henry Seward, a former governor of New York and a future political mastermind and member of Abraham Lincoln's cabinet. Even more notably, Seward brought him to meet his fellow Whig, President Zachary Taylor, onetime hero of the Mexican War whose presidency was to last less than a year and a half. Wise also attended sessions of the Senate, met Daniel Webster, and wrote later that it was a powerful experience for him, a recent immigrant, to be welcomed by so many distinguished public servants.

To one scholar who has examined the events in Charleston, Rabbi Naphtali Rubinger, Wise was clearly motivated by his desire to change jobs, even though he may have wanted his congregation to think he was traveling to Charleston for his health, or for the exclusive purpose of participating in a debate with Raphall.[3] Many details of the Wise-Raphall encounter have been lost to history, in part because the records of Congregation Beth Elohim were destroyed during the Civil War. But according to Wise's autobiography, the two rabbis decided to meet just as Wise arrived in town. As fate would have it, the subject of Raphall's presentation turned out to be on whether it was appropriate for Jews to still believe in the coming of a "personal" messiah to deliver them back to Palestine. It was this proposition, of course, that Beth Elohim had omitted when it posted only ten of Maimonides's thirteen principles on the wall of its new synagogue. Raphall was to square off with Poznanski in a kind of smackdown in Charleston. Wise would play a crucial, fateful, and decisive role.

But first it is important to understand the nature and history of the dispute over that most important Jewish doctrine.

## "EVEN THOUGH HE TARRIES . . . I AWAIT HIS COMING"

"With some exaggeration, we may say that Judaism's messianic belief makes it unique among world religions," writes the Reform Jewish scholar and theologian Eugene Borowitz. He notes further that while other religions project a vision of eventual redemption, none holds out the vision of a specific redeemer as instrumental to its identity.[4]

The role of Maimonides in enshrining the doctrine of the Messiah and the resurrection of the dead as essential principles of Judaism has long been recognized as historically important, along with Maimonides's other innovative teachings. In his great work *The Guide for the Perplexed*, for example, Maimonides said that the stories of the Bible were to be understood as parables or allegories written to illustrate the existence of God, whose precise identity was beyond human comprehension. But it was Maimonides's exaltation of a messiah in his "Thirteen Principles" of Jewish faith that proved especially pivotal for American Jews in the nineteenth century. To anyone doubting the centrality of the Messiah, Borowitz evokes the heartbreaking spectacle of Jewish martyrs in the Holocaust singing a refrain that alluded to Maimonides on their way to the gas chambers: "I believe with perfect faith in the coming of the Messiah and even though he tarries, I daily await his coming."

Some scholars, on the other hand, have discerned a distinct ambiguity over the prospect of the Messiah going back many centuries. Leon Wieseltier, the author and essayist, notes that throughout history, some rabbis—including Moses ben Nahman, the thirteenth-century sage known as Nachmanides—had mixed feelings about the return of a king who would restore the House of David, as the prophets seem to have predicted. Some rabbis were concerned that if Jews were to fall into the belief that the Messiah had indeed come, some Jews would no longer feel obliged to perform God's commandments; indeed, they might be lured by imposters into such a belief. "For the Jews, the history of messianism is the history of false messianism," Wieseltier writes. "More often than not, the longing for salvation is to be mastered rather than fulfilled."[5]

Yet the historic and scholarly record shows that what one historian calls the "self-contradictions" of messianic belief—praying for a return to the Holy Land just as Jews were becoming more successful and settled in Europe—emerged in the seventeenth century and perhaps even earlier. It was then that principles embraced for two thousand years began showing the effects of the rise of Jewish status—economic if not political—and the parallel rise of rational thought when it came to their religion. These trends began in Holland, then England, and eventually in France and Germany.[6]

The word *messiah* derives from the Hebrew *mashiaḥ* (literally, "the anointed one"), which came into usage as an elegant synonym for *king*. While Jews were living under the thumb of a series of conquerors—Assyrian, Babylonian, Persian, Greek, and Roman—they started yearning toward the end of the biblical period for a reversal of their misfortunes. A belief arose that the time was at hand for God at last to restore his people to their former greatness. That heavenly restoration would revive the long-defunct Davidic monarchy in the person of a divinely sent and anointed king. Such a *mashiaḥ* might singlehandedly lead God's people to the military, political, and religious dominance that they had enjoyed (or believed they had enjoyed) under King David a thousand years earlier. The nations of the world would, in turn, recognize that Israel's God was the one, true deity, and the coming of this *mashiaḥ* would open a period of unparalleled well-being for Israel and the world in general.

As the hope for such a messiah grew in strength, a number of potential candidates presented themselves. Most notably, many of the followers of Jesus of Nazareth believed him to be the long-awaited one, and his crucifixion—a particularly cruel and humiliating form of punishment practiced by Israel's Roman overlords—only strengthened the belief of some Jews that Jesus was indeed the fulfillment of the messianic dream. (The word for *messiah* in Greek is "Christos.") Other Jews continued to look elsewhere. In the early second century CE, the leader of an abortive revolt against Rome, Simon bar Kokhba, was proclaimed by his followers to be the Messiah. But after some initial success, his revolt floundered, and with it the hope for an immediate upturn in the life of Israel. When, by the end of the fourth century CE, Palestine itself came to be a difficult place for Jews to inhabit, its population gradually migrated to more favorable sites: eastward to Babylon and other parts of the ancient Near East, or westward to Europe. Later, a second westward move took place, so that for several centuries a great percentage of world Jewry lived in Iberia and its environs. But after their final expulsion from Spain in 1492, those Jews joined their brethren in North Africa, Italy, Turkey, and other communities on the eastern Mediterranean and beyond. New pretenders to the messianic title arose, but none succeeded long in winning over the hearts of their coreligionists.[7]

Throughout their historic travails and travels, many Jews continued to believe that the Messiah would come if Jews could only adhere to their strictures laid down by the ancient rabbis, and indeed that their devotion to these laws and traditions could *hasten* the coming of the Messiah. No doubt these beliefs helped keep Judaism alive in the face of cultural and political pressures.

A new frenzy for the coming of the Messiah grew out of the mystical movement known as Kabbalah, which spread throughout Europe as early as the medieval period, culminating in the seventeenth century. But this fervor led to some disasters as well. Among these was the apostate Sabbatai Zevi, who emerged in Anatolia in the 1600s to proclaim himself the Messiah, and later Jacob Frank in Poland, claiming to be Sabbatai's successor. Sabbatai's following was vast, spreading throughout the Jewish world. But it came to a bad end, with his imprisonment by the Ottoman Turks and apparent conversion to Islam to avoid death. Yet the mystical attraction of Kabbalah and messianism lived on. It was reborn in the extreme piety embodied by Hasidism in Eastern Europe in the eighteenth century, and kept alive by Hasidic Jews of the modern era.

"Suffice it to say that we Jews believe we will know the Messiah when we see 'him,'" writes Borowitz. For more than two thousand years, as Borowitz says, this fundamental argument about the identity of the Messiah—especially the one between Christians and Jews over whether Jesus was the Messiah—has continued in religious circles. One aspect of this debate concerns the Messiah's lineage. Certain passages in the Bible clearly suggest that the future Messiah was to be a direct descendant of King David. Early Christians struggled to reconcile this claim with the tradition of Jesus's immaculate (i.e., divine) conception. Christian teachings resolved the matter by holding that Jesus was in fact a descendant of David, via the union of Ruth, a Moabite, and Boaz.[8]

The biblical texts referring to the Messiah also speak of a messianic epoch, or political era, as well as an individual: "A sprout will come forth from the trunk of Jesse [King David's father]. . . . With righteousness he will judge the poor / And bring justice to the little people of the land. . . . The wolf will live with the lamb / The leopard lie down with the kid. . . ." Other passages alluding to a messianic era, from both Isaiah and Micah, refer to the day when nations will beat their swords into plowshares and abandon war, and that in this epoch everyone will sit under his own vine and fig tree "and no one will make them afraid." The importance of the prophets' vision of the future is not that an individual will one day come to save humanity, but that one day there will be an era of justice and mercy for which humans must pray.

Thus, for some centuries, some Jews held that the Messiah would be a king of flesh and blood, an altogether mortal if remarkable monarch whose ascension to the throne would herald the beginning of better times. At the same time, other Jews saw in the Messiah a worker of miracles whose appearance would inaugurate a new Golden Age, "the messianic era," leading to the resurrection of the dead in the World to Come.

The varying interpretations about who and what a messiah represented made it possible for Jewish scholars of the Haskalah era to jettison the idea of a "personal" messiah in favor of a coming Messianic Age, as the prayer book for the Hamburg Temple did in 1841. It was further possible for the reformers to discard the accompanying messianic idea of the dead being resurrected as a creation of ancient rabbis not found in the Bible. Indeed, they noted that many passages of the Bible suggest that death is permanent. The Haskalah-era rabbis thus embraced what was becoming an accepted alternative idea—that the soul is immortal in some undefined way and would be "redeemed" in some future era, but not through a specific revival of the dead.

But what to make of the many passages from the Bible suggesting that God had "chosen" the Jews to carry out His commandments? The Haskalah reformers pioneered the concept that the Jews themselves were a messianic *people* designated by God to guide the world to its eventual redemption. This, the reformers said, was Israel's priestly "mission," in keeping with God's words to the Israelites in the Torah: "You shall be to Me a kingdom of priests and a holy nation" (Exodus 19:6). Judaism for these Jews was a religion with a universal priestly message but a particular assignment from God. If Jews were "chosen," it was to carry out this goal.

The Jewish reformers of the nineteenth century were happy to compare what they saw as rabbinic Judaism's sometimes far-fetched interpretations with what they also argued was the Christian misreading of prophetic passages in the Hebrew Bible. For example, Christian scholars translated a crucial passage of Isaiah as: "Behold, a virgin shall conceive, and bear a son, and shall call his name Immanuel." Holding that the Hebrew Bible conveys the word of God, these scholars have pointed to this passage, and many others, as literally prophetic—predicting the coming of Jesus. The normal Jewish translation of the passage, however, is simply that a "young woman" will conceive a restorer to the Davidic line. Reforming Jews of the nineteenth century regarded the supposed foretelling of the coming of Jesus in Isaiah, as asserted by Christian theologians, as precisely the sort of tortured and fallacious interpretation that Talmudic rabbis were sometimes guilty of applying.

How exactly did the overthrowing of belief in a "personal" messiah take root in the nineteenth century? A crucial reason, as the historian Jacob Katz writes, was that the granting of rights as citizens in Germany, France, and elsewhere broke "the spell" of a messiah delivering Jews as a nation back to the Holy Land: "Accepting citizenship in a non-Jewish state was regarded both by the Jews and by their emancipators as incompatible with the messianic belief that was an uncontested article of Jewish faith."[9]

Borowitz cites two additional factors. First, Jews (and Christians) schooled in science and reason could no longer believe in the literal truth of the miracles of the Bible, especially the magical idea of a king returning them to a Jewish state in Jerusalem. Second and still more important, Jews in self-governing states felt that Scripture had given too much importance to God intervening in the world and too little to the power of human beings to seek social justice on earth. If the concept of a messiah grew as well out of Jewish despair over foreign domination, the destruction of the Jerusalem Temple, and Israel's subsequent persecution and exile, then it was time in the modern era to recognize that Jewish redemption must likewise be the work of human hands, and not a deus ex machina sent from heaven. "Instead of God sending an ideal king, they foresaw all humankind working together and by social reconstruction producing a perfected world," Borowitz writes. "In place of people being relatively passive, performing their religious duties but relying on God to redeem history, they would become activists, applying their reason and conscience to effect their salvation."[10]

These are the factors—coupled with similar trends under way among Christians in the Second Great Awakening—that crested in the fateful dispute in South Carolina in 1850 attended by Isaac Mayer Wise.

## "A LOUD AND DECISIVE NO"

At least initially, Wise appears to have thought that any debate involving the traditionalist Rabbi Raphall over the existence of a personal messiah would not be serious. As a skeptic, he was also characteristically disdainful of the debaters themselves. A table, he recalled, was set up for the two to do battle—Raphall "a rotund little man with a black velvet skullcap" and Gustavus Poznanski "in full dress, stiff, cold and self-satisfied." Each had brought a claque of supporters, and Wise sat with the Poznanski group. "The whole affair seemed to me most laughable and ridiculous," he wrote later.

Poznanski began by citing the reinterpretation of the Messiah concept in the writings of a litany of German reform Jews: Isaak Markus Jost of Frankfurt (author of many volumes of Jewish history and interpretation), Abraham Geiger, Leopold Zunz, Samuel Holdheim, and many others. According to Wise, Raphall ignored these latter-day German scholars and even seemed unfamiliar with them, citing instead the work of Maimonides and other thinkers in the ancient and medieval tradition.

"When he began to murder Talmudical passages, I began to grow angry," Wise said of Raphall. "But I held my peace." Not for long, however. Wise clearly felt that Poznanski was the better debater and was winning the argument, much to Raphall's irritation. "Finally, Raphall grew angry, and glowed with holy zeal," Wise recalled. "Instead of arguing, he began to cate-chize. He asked the public, and finally myself personally: 'Do you believe in the personal Messiah?' 'Do you believe in bodily resurrection?' I have never refused to answer a direct question; therefore, I answered Raphall's ques-tion with a loud and decisive No! This ended the drama. Raphall seized his books, rushed angrily out of the hall, followed by his whole party. He had apparently given up the fight."

But the fight did not end. In fact, it only began and grew. In his pub-lished *Reminiscences*, Wise recalled that he told Raphall that "we will see within ten or twenty years what will be left in America of Jewish orthodoxy."

Wise's version was corroborated by other witnesses, including leaders of other congregations who wrote a letter to Louis Spanier, president of Wise's Albany congregation, that his rabbi was running amok. After preach-ing in Charleston for a week after the debate, Wise returned to New York by steamer. Soon the Charleston congregation decided to offer Wise a position as its rabbi. Wise accepted, writing a letter in *The Asmonean* that he was resigning his position in Albany to return to Charleston in the spring. But then he changed his mind and re-upped with the Albany congregation, to the chagrin of the Charleston group, which demanded that he return the money they had spent to bring him there to discuss their job offer. (Wise refused, and the Albany congregation also refused to compensate Charles-ton.)

Wise's new three-year contract required him not to change any rituals without the trustees' approval. "The joy was great; feasts of reconciliation were celebrated," Wise wrote. "I was overwhelmed with costly gifts; the heavens were without cloud."[11]

The reconciliation was not to last, neither in Albany nor in Charleston. After Wise rejected the offer at Beth Elohim, the synagogue selected a rabbi named Julius Eckman to succeed Poznanski, who stayed on as a member of the congregation. But the succession only renewed tensions within as Eckman sought to rescind some of Beth Elohim's reforms while keeping the organ and some of the English in the sermons and prayers. Once again, the issue was Poznanski's placement of the abridged version of Maimonides's creed on the wall, the one omitting references to the Messiah, restoration of Jews to Palestine, and the resurrection of the dead. Reformers called on Eckman to resign over his decision to remove the abridged creed. In an apparent artful compromise, the board yielded to the protests, accepted Eckman's resignation—but then removed the creed, replacing it with the simple Shema.[12]

In Albany, meanwhile, it soon became apparent that Wise's Charleston idyll had poisoned the atmosphere. Concern remained that he was in breach of his promise not to change the synagogue's traditions without the approval of its lay leadership. It was only a matter of time before these ill feelings caught up with him. Wise's reputation was battered, and he wrote to the newspaper *Asmonean* in April citing a supposedly anonymous letter as praising him for advocating "reform" but responding that while he felt bad about jilting Congregation Beth Elohim in Charleston, he was obliged to not abandon his efforts in Albany. He said his main calling was to save Judaism from extinction and that he would be ready to preach anywhere to do so—"to the Pole, or to the Equator, to Ethiopia, or to Patagonia."[13]

What is striking about these comments is Wise's implication that Albany seemed to agree with him. He had earlier repeatedly disavowed attempts to seek radical change. In this interval, he wrote, the Albany congregation "must know" his position on adjusting key traditions and laws to modern times, since he had many times publicly identified himself as an advocate for change. "Did I ever hesitate to pronounce my inmost conviction?" he wrote. "Or did my congregation ever oppose my views? They did not; and they gave me the best proof of their agreement with my views by the re-election of my humble self."[14]

While Wise was using his rehiring in Albany to press full steam ahead with his agenda, despite whatever promises he made to stick to tradition, the Orthodox wing of his congregation viewed the same rehiring as a mandate of a different sort. They regarded it as authorization for them to ensure that he not impose his views on the traditionalists. The divergence of their perspectives was a formula for confusion and eventually for breach.

## "AN UPROAR . . . I HAVE NEVER EXPERIENCED"

The summer of 1850 brought a perhaps inevitable downward spiral of relations between the rabbi and traditionalist members of his congregation. The central issue continued to be Spanier's mounting distress over Wise's denial of the messiah doctrine and refusal to recognize the sensitivity of the matter. Accordingly, Spanier wrote to *The Asmonean*, citing an affidavit he had obtained from three Orthodox leaders in Charleston, asking whether any rabbi who denied the principles of resurrection and the Messiah could be a "fit and proper person" to serve as spiritual leader of a Jewish congregation. (Wise called Spanier's letter "a new bull of excommunication.") The editor of *The Asmonean* responded by describing Spanier as a "firebrand" who had launched "outpourings of indignation" against Wise.[15]

But in his study of the controversy, the historian Naphtali Rubinger notes that while the Orthodox faction in Albany tried to capitalize on the Charleston episode, other factors were creating enmity toward Wise. One was the rabbi's fervent insistence on enforcing Sabbath laws against work, in keeping with a petition signed years before he first arrived. That document demanded that trustees not "desecrate the Sabbath by either buying or selling," and that they faithfully attend Sabbath services. A resolution approving that principle was adopted after Wise joined the temple. Indeed, for all his heterodoxy, Wise was a Sabbath absolutist. He had warned one trustee, Solomon Levy, threatening to denounce him publicly. But when Spanier heard about Wise's threat, he directed Wise not to preach that day, June 1. Ignoring the directive, Wise approached the bima and, according to his memoirs, Spanier came up and tried to stop him. Wise ignored him and continued in a loud voice, provoking several worshippers to leave. "It was probably this incident that provoked the enmity between the president and the rabbi," Rubinger writes. In his memoirs, Wise claims that following the June 1 episode on the bima, Spanier was asked to resign and even brought before the police magistrate on a charge of disturbing divine worship and was given a mild reprimand by the judge. But Rubinger finds "no documentary evidence to substantiate or negate this aspect of Wise's recollections of his encounter and difficulties with Spanier."[16]

A related divisive issue centered on kosher butchering practices. It flared when Wise sought to dismiss the synagogue hazan, or cantor, who was also a leading butcher specializing in the ritual slaughter of animals for kosher purposes. Wise maintained that the butcher, Veist Traub, had been seen visiting saloons, drinking, and playing cards. More complaints arose when Wise urged Jews not to purchase meat slaughtered by Traub.

With these events in the background, distrust between Wise and his Beth-El congregation grew out of control. Traditionalist members of the congregation demanded that Wise release the text of his sermons ahead of their delivery. Wise refused. On June 2, several members wrote Spanier about Wise's "hellish plans for Judaism" and that they intended to "strive not to let our holy religion be desecrated by an apostate." For good measure, they termed Wise a "wicked person" bent on installing "a reform temple service" and attempting "to disobey our religion and to declare our forefathers who have instructed us to be stupid and crazy people." They further accused him of rejecting "the beautiful prayers which our renowned scholars have composed" and dismissing Hebrew as a "dead language."[17] Still another strike against Wise, they said, was his ridicule of the concept of the mikveh, or ritual bath. "Such a man we declare unworthy to occupy the position of Rabbi and preacher," they added, declaring—in a most telling comment that spoke volumes about this pivotal intellectual passage in Jewish history—that Wise was trying to substitute "a God of reason, while the congregation believed in the God of Abraham, Isaac and Jacob."[18]

The issue of Wise's denial of the Messiah and resurrection returned when another group of conservative members of the congregation accused him of blasphemy and declared that he was "not worthy to occupy the position of Rabbi in a Congregation." They called on Spanier to investigate and suspend Wise from his duties while the inquiry was under way. Three days later, on June 26, still another letter—this one from two Jewish butchers—revived the issue of his hiring a new butcher without approval of the congregation. "Is Rabbi Wise empowered to split the congregation over the matter of food provisions?" they asked.[19]

Under pressure from all these fronts, the synagogue board met on July 1 and debated a series of charges against Wise, now including his discarding of the prayer paraphernalia known as *tefillin* (the two small black boxes with black straps, known as phylacteries, that observant Jewish men place on their head and arm while performing prayers) and *tzitzit* (fringes or tassels worn by Jewish men). The conservative dissidents demanded restoration of the *piyyutim*, and they accused him of disloyalty because of his flirtation with Charleston. For good measure, they said they had actually seen him desecrating various bans on work—by writing at a desk over the High Holidays. Improbably, they said he was even seen swinging on a swing during the Sabbath!

With rising indignation, and with characteristic bombast, Wise responded on July 12, citing such biblical passages as "Who made thee a ruler and a judge over us?" which was said by Moses's accusers after he had separated two fighting Hebrew men (Exodus 2:14). "Am I or anybody else obliged to answer writings in which I am called an apostate, a liar, a hypocrite and so, etc. etc.?" Wise asked. Despite what he said were the "grammatical and spelling mistakes" of his accusers, he vowed to defend himself at a fixed time and place. Wise later claimed in his memoirs that at a subsequent meeting of the board of trustees, there was a vote vindicating him three to two. But Rubinger, who went through the records, concluded instead that on July 24, the board voted three to two to suspend Wise's salary until his future was brought before the entire congregation.[20]

In this boiling atmosphere, Spanier wrote to Charleston to get details of what he surely already knew—what exactly the rabbi had said about the Messiah and the resurrection of the dead. Since the events in South Carolina had been fully documented, Spanier's motive seemed to be to build an airtight case, free of secondary matters like the firing of kosher butchers. The documentation was readily available, since Raphall had published his own "excommunication" against Wise and followed up with articles denouncing him.[21] *The Asmonean* also contained the charge that Wise was a "deist," meaning someone who espoused the idea that God abandoned the universe after creation and left its operation to natural laws, which could be discerned by science and discovery. The newspaper's publishing of charges that Wise was a near heretic gave Spanier the doctrinal rationale to proceed with the rabbi's ouster. Wise continued without his salary through the fall until the congregation could meet on September 5, two days before Rosh Hashanah, to decide Wise's fate. August passed without any more meetings, but the storm was gathering.[22]

By the time of the board meeting on September 5, Wise knew that the odds against him were becoming insurmountable. He later recalled that the session's being scheduled for the daytime meant that his supporters, many of them local peddlers and businessmen, could not attend, some of them because they were busy at a state fair. At the end of a lengthy session, Wise's backers moved to adjourn without a vote. Wise recalled in his memoirs that the motion to adjourn, made by the vice president of the congregation, Joseph Sporberg, passed and that Sporberg and many others left. After they had gone, Spanier declared that the meeting was *not* adjourned and engineered another vote, this time ousting Wise from office along with other officers supporting him.

As it later happened, Wise's view that the meeting had officially adjourned was upheld the following year in a court ruling, in which it was ruled that Spanier had insulted Wise in the presence of the congregation. (The court ordered Spanier to pay $1,000 to Wise, but Wise refused the award.) But by then, the court decision was moot. On September 6, Spanier and Traub, the aggrieved kosher butcher, informed Wise that his contract with Beth El was "considered void" and that he was discharged as of September 5, without back pay.

In response, Wise's supporters hatched a subversive plan. Since the temple had continued the practice—over Wise's objections—of selling various honors, such as the honor of opening the ark, carrying the Torah to the reading desk, and offering a prayer, they quietly purchased that procedure for Wise for the morning of Rosh Hashanah. Spanier, sensing trouble, first tried to cancel the sale and then asked the Albany sheriff to send in police to monitor the situation. Wise's description in his memoirs is worth quoting in full:

> I went to the synagogue on New-Year's morning, appeared in my official garb, but found one of Spanier's creatures, who had been the cause of the altercation about the Sabbath, sitting in my chair. I took another seat. Excitement ruled the hour. Everything was quiet as the grave. Finally the choir sings [Solomon] Sulzer's great *En Komokho* ["There is none like you . . ."]. At the conclusion of the song I step before the ark in order to take out the scrolls of the law as usual, and to offer prayer. Spanier steps in my way, and, without saying a word, smites me with his fist so that my cap falls from my head. This was the terrible signal for an uproar the like of which I have never experienced. The people acted like furies. It was as though the synagogue had suddenly burst forth in a flaming conflagration.[23]

In the ensuing melee, worshippers of Polish and Hungarian heritage rushed in to fight on behalf of the rabbi, and the riot was quickly joined by young people in the choir. The Albany sheriff's force moved in, stopped the rioting, arrested several congregants, and cleared the synagogue as men and women spilled out onto Herkimer Street. The sheriff then locked the doors and took the keys.

Wise recalled that he confronted the synagogue president and declared that "there is the law to which I can appeal," whereupon Spanier replied: "I have a hundred thousand dollars more than you. I do not fear the law. I will ruin you." Wise went home, "bowed with pain and inexpressible grief." The sheriff's constables pursued him and arrested him as "the ringleader of a rebellious mob at a public service." One constable seized Wise by his coat and led him to a nearby police station. "Upon our arrival there, the whole rabble was present in order to feast their eyes on the sight of their rabbi appearing before court on New-Year's Day," Wise wrote. "But their hopes were disappointed, for the police judge went into an adjoining room and received me there. My friends had informed him of what had taken place, and he dismissed me on my word of honor. Three months later the constable died of a stroke of paralysis, one day after his discharge. Who can describe that terrible day? Not I. It was agonizing, hellish torture. This victory of orthodoxy proved its grave wherein it was buried. . . . The battle had been fought, and I was prepared to enter upon a new path of life."[24]

The episode made all the papers in the state capital. The *Albany Evening Atlas* reported that the Hebrew Congregation on Fulton Street was "not at all united in love for the Rev. Mr. Wise," with the result that "a strife arose" on the morning of September 7 "between the two sections as to whether the Rev. Mr. Wise should, or should not officiate."[25] The newspaper concluded: "Sheriff Beardsley repaired promptly to the spot, accompanied by a strong force, and soon cleared the synagogue of both parties, locked the doors, and took the keys in his possession. This had the desired effect, and the riot and disturbance then terminated." The paper's account then said that several in the melee applied to the police for warrants charging each other with assault and battery.

Wise was not to be deterred. On the second day of Rosh Hashanah, he conducted the service in his house, with a choir in the front hall and the congregation in his parlors. His supporters did not fail him. They decided immediately to split off from Beth El and form a new congregation. The congregation, Ansche Emeth ("People of Truth"), held services in a nearby house before purchasing a Baptist church on Herkimer Street for its new location—the same church where an anti-Semitic cleric had earlier delivered sermons against the Jews.

Ansche Emeth grew as a new place for the "American Judaism" that Wise envisioned. Wise was to leave Albany in 1854 for Cincinnati. In following years, Congregation Beth El instituted reforms and in 1885 merged with Ansche Emeth to form Temple Beth Emeth. Wise returned to Albany in 1889, at the age of seventy, to preside over the dedication of its new synagogue.

Was the debacle in Albany avoidable? Wise had, after all, lost favor with a considerable number of congregants and acted perhaps arbitrarily to dismiss the ritual slaughterer and hire another in his place without consulting the congregation. He had gotten himself embroiled in a lawsuit with Traub and been charged with libel. He was accused of heresy on several grounds and had created turmoil in the congregation, with Traub threatening to resign as cantor and secretary. Spanier was perhaps understandably concerned that Wise's behavior was overbearing and disruptive, making the president's job of keeping peace within the congregation all but impossible. "The story is not the black and white one depicted by Wise and repeated by his admirers," writes Seftin D. Temkin, noting that Wise seemed to be spoiling for a fight and had a tendency to bluster and to be evasive on embarrassing details.[26]

Only in retrospect has the significance of the riot loomed large in the history of American Judaism. The cause of "reforming," modernizing, or "Americanizing" Judaism was hardly the only thing dividing the rabbi and his congregation. There were many other sources of the breach, which would flare up over many periods of time and over many issues.

Nevertheless, the strife in Albany marks an undeniable turning point in American Jewish history, accelerating American Judaism down its path toward division. Though Wise was still evolving in terms of the specific practices and beliefs of Judaism that would be kept or discarded, he nonetheless clung to his dream of establishing a universally accepted American religion, though such a goal would seem obviously difficult in light of the Albany fracas.

Because of the coverage of the controversy in *The Occident* and *The Asmonean*, Wise's name became known throughout the American Jewish community, putting him in the forefront of the cause of "reform." His notoriety, however, made it all the more difficult for him to be accepted as the unifying figure he wished to become.

The rabbi who posed the strongest challenge was an accomplished but awkward and withdrawn traditionalist in Philadelphia.

*Eight*

# THE "TWO ISAACS"

I do not pretend to be a great Talmudist," Isaac Leeser wrote later in life. "At fourteen years old I left the Hebrew school and learned worldly things."[1]

But Leeser emerged in the nineteenth century as the most important figure in American Judaism to stand athwart the onrush of history and yell Stop! His opposition to reform adjustments did not rule out accommodating to the pressures of American contemporary life. Though not a formally trained rabbi, Leeser is thus considered a founder of what today is called modern Orthodoxy and also a contributor to the establishment of the Conservative movement later in the twentieth century. Leeser emigrated from Westphalia in 1824 at the age of eighteen and first took up work in Richmond and then later became hazan at Mikveh Israel, the Sephardic congregation of Philadelphia. There he pioneered in the delivery of sermons in English and then did English translations of German texts, prayers, and other commentaries, winning considerable fame as a writer. A favorite subject was his campaign against missionaries. To the shock of some German Jews, he supported the establishment of the first Jewish Sunday school—controversial because it was a clear attempt to mimic a Protestant tradition on the Christian Sabbath.

Beyond Sunday schools, Leeser was an advocate of all-day religious schools, necessary in his view to counter Christian attempts at conversion. Wise and others disliked the idea, favoring secular education for Jews, supplemented by religious education in the afternoon or weekends. Leeser went further, developing special materials for children. Among the popular works studied by Jewish children were Leeser's *Catechism, Elementary Introduction to the Scriptures for the Use of Hebrew Children* by Simha Peixotto, and Max Lilienthal's *Sabbath Visitor*. Jewish schools were frequently started by women in such places as Atlanta; Petersburg, Virginia; Fort Wayne, Indiana; Woodland, California; and Calvert, Texas. The best-known pioneer was Rebecca Gratz, who worked with Leeser to establish the first Jewish Sunday school, in Philadelphia, in 1838, seizing control of education that was a province of men in Europe.

A nationwide Jewish protest led by Leeser over the treatment of a group of Jews in Damascus accused of murdering a Catholic priest in 1840, allegedly for using his blood for rituals, also helped to vault him into prominence in the United States. He later published a monthly journal in English, *The Occident and American Jewish Advocate*. But though he tirelessly sought to produce texts and journals for observant Jews, Leeser received little support from his own congregation, in part because of his aloof and didactic manner and in part because of disputes over getting members to pay their dues and Leeser's demand to deliver sermons without prior approval of the board. In the end, he was forced out of his congregation in 1850. But his influence was immense. His prominence illustrates the fact that well before the much later immigration of Yiddish-speaking Jews in the 1880s, many Jews in America sought to establish more conservative congregations in reaction against the advocates of reform.

Leeser was not alone in his advocacy of tradition, however. In 1852, Jews from Lithuania and Poland established Beth Hamidrash, "house of study,"

New York's first East European Orthodox synagogue, though it was beset by conflicts and later split into other competing synagogues.[2] Though it was less prominent than Reform, Leeser, Abraham Rice, Bernard Illowy, and Moshe Aaronsohn developed a kind of subculture of more traditional and even pietistic Judaism, in which they debated the complexities of Jewish law. Some were quite arcane, such as the debate over whether Muscovy duck was kosher and whether one could use the same false teeth for eating dairy and meat dishes or for Passover, which require a separate set of dishes altogether.

Illowy, like Leeser, made adjustments to Orthodox practices, such as conducting the service while facing the Congregation (not the Torah) and embracing the confirmation ceremony. Illowy had received his PhD in Budapest and served congregations in New York, Philadelphia, St. Louis, Syracuse, Baltimore, New Orleans, and Cincinnati. Various disputes followed him in many of these places. Despite his conservative bent, he was adamant about enforcing decorum in the service, insisting that there be "no screeching, or shouting" and that everyone pray in unison and not engage in the "indecorous scramble and rush to get out" of the synagogue even before the closing of the service.[3] Illowy felt aggrieved by the loss of Jewish discipline in the United States, but he could not avoid his own controversies. He had to leave his post at Rodeph Shalom in Philadelphia after a flap over charges (later dismissed) that he had used a razor to shave, failed to wash his hands before praying, failed to cover his head, and even that he had eaten a goose that had not been properly slaughtered. The traditionalist rabbis of this era published books and pamphlets to help guide the perplexed about how to apply Jewish law in the hurly-burly of the modern world. They were not a majority or even sizable part of the American Jewish community, but what they accomplished established a precedent for the waves of Jews who would come later in the century and into the twentieth century.

## ISAAC LEESER'S TRAVAILS

Leeser was an improbable guardian of tradition in many ways. Twelve years older than Wise, he appears to have suffered from depression and led a life

marked by lifelong bachelorhood, family tragedy, isolation, and bitter conflict with lay leaders of his congregation, who failed to appreciate his accomplishments.

Like Wise, Leeser envisioned a "union" of American Hebrew congregations, though based on conservative principles and practices. But Leeser's
painfully reticent, doctrinaire, and sanctimonious personality was no match
for Wise's self-confidence, rhetorical bluster, and gift for self-promotion. If
Wise succumbed to delusions of grandeur, Leeser suffered from an inferiority complex. "He was a difficult person," Leeser's biographer Lance Sussman
writes. "People were not naturally attracted to him. He was often defensive
and argumentative. Similarly, his physical appearance worked against him.
He was very short, nearly blind, and badly scarred by smallpox for most of
his adult life. Finally, his literary style was far from felicitous and his argu-
mentation often flawed by digression or lack of balance. He basically lived
a hard, lonely life. His greatest comfort and his greatest source of tension
came from his work, not from close friends or family."[4]

Born in a tiny village in Westphalia, Leeser was the son of a struggling
merchant. The early deaths of his father and mother left Isaac orphaned at
age fourteen. Raised by a grandparent, he attended school in the town of
Dülmen, in North Rhine–Westphalia, where he befriended Rabbi Abraham
Sutro, a revered figure among Jews in the region who had battled for civil
rights of Jews in the German lands after Napoleon decreed the Jewish people to be emancipated in France. Sutro was also in the forefront of opposing
the nascent movement in Germany for Reform Judaism, a harbinger of what
Leeser was to face later in life in the New World.

Invited by an uncle, a dry-goods merchant, the young rabbinically
trained scholar traveled to America at age seventeen, settling in Richmond,
Virginia. He gained early renown for an essay defending Judaism, written
under a pseudonym in response to a critical article published in London.
The essay attracted the attention of a Sephardic synagogue in Richmond,
Beth Shalom, which recruited him to serve as a cantor and teacher. He later
described his time there as unusually welcoming and compatible with his
traditionalist inclinations.

Gershom Mendes Seixas, spiritual leader of Congregation Shearith Israel in New York, fled when British forces captured the city at the start of the Revolutionary War. He was the first Jew to become part of the early American religious establishment.

President George Washington visited Newport, Rhode Island, in 1790, famously assuring its Jewish community that the government "gives to bigotry no sanction, to persecution no assistance." The Touro Synagogue of Newport, dedicated in 1763, is the oldest surviving synagogue building in the United States.

As the Revolutionary War opened, Hessian soldiers set fire to the sanctuary of Shearith Israel on Mill Street (South William Street today) in Lower Manhattan. Seixas fled with the damaged scrolls, one of which is pictured here, and returned them after the war.

Congregation Mikve Israel in Savannah rebuilt its synagogue after it was destroyed in a fire in 1829, returning two fifteenth-century Torah scrolls that had been brought originally to its sanctuary in the 1730s. This one had been brought from England in 1737. The two scrolls are believed to be the oldest in the United States.

In Charleston, home of the largest American Jewish population in the early 1800s, the fractious congregation at Kahal Kadosh Beth Elohim (interior depicted here) divided over reforms demanded by younger members. After a fire destroyed the synagogue in 1838, a battle erupted over whether to install an organ in the new synagogue.

Installation of an organ in the newly rebuilt Beth Elohim in Charleston, which opened its doors (flanked by Doric columns) in 1841, led to a historic court case. The judge ruled that religious institutions "cannot withstand the agitations of free, active and progressive opinion."

At the age of eighteen, Esther (Hetty)
Barrett married Gustavus Poznanski,
newly arrived from Poland, helping
to secure his social and financial
position in Charleston. Poznanski
stood up to traditionalists and presided
at a fateful debate over whether a
messiah will one day redeem the
Jews and return them to Palestine.

Abraham Rice, the first ordained
rabbi to settle in the United States,
arrived from Bavaria in 1840. "I dwell
in complete darkness," he bitterly
complained to a friend, referring to
Jews abandoning traditional practices.

Combative and self-confident, Rabbi Isaac Mayer Wise sought to forge a distinctly American Judaism, modifying traditional teachings over the Messiah, the Talmud, and the role of Jewish law. His fistfight with his congregation president in Albany led to a brawl that had to be quelled by the police. Wise became the most consequential Jewish leader of the nineteenth century.

Isaac Leeser, the foremost American advocate of traditional Judaism in the nineteenth century, was a friend but also a stubborn rival to Wise. By opposing Wise's "reforms," he became the father of modern Orthodoxy and Conservative Judaism. But he was a prophet without honor at his own congregation in Philadelphia.

Jewish immigrant peddlers crisscrossed the countryside on horse-driven wagons, on horseback, with mules, and on foot, often with packs of 150 pounds on their backs. They struggled to keep Jewish practices, including kosher laws. Many storied Jewish families were founded by peddlers—Seligman, Lehman, Goldman, Loeb, Guggenheim, Filene, Straus, Gimbel, and on and on.

12

Isaac Bernheim, a German
Jewish immigrant, peddled
goods in the Pennsylvania
countryside before
establishing the
I. W. Harper brand
of bourbon whiskey
in Kentucky.

13

Rebecca Gratz was the most
influential Jewish feminist
pioneer of the nineteenth
century, contributing to the
important role of women in Jewish
communities. She established a
women's benevolent association
and the first Jewish Sunday
school, in Philadelphia.

The Congressional Medal of
Honor was awarded to David
Urbansky, a Union soldier who
had emigrated from Prussia,
for his heroism at the battles
of Shiloh and Vicksburg.
He was the first American
Jew to be so honored.

Rabbi Morris Raphall, an ardent
traditionalist during the Civil
War, proclaimed that the Bible
legitimized slavery, though not
necessarily the way it was practiced
in the South. His defense of the
concept of a human messiah to
redeem the Jewish people led
to a rupture with Rabbi Wise.

16

Rabbi David Einhorn attacked slavery as antithetical to Judaism and had to flee death threats in Baltimore during the Civil War. From his pulpit in Philadelphia, he accused Isaac Mayer Wise of timidity as a reformer and paved the way for "classical" Reform Judaism.

17

Secretary of State of the Confederacy Judah P. Benjamin was the target of anti-Semitic attacks in both North and South. He escaped to London as the war ended, avoiding possible prosecution by the victorious Union. He was a slaveholder but is little remembered today in the pantheon of Confederate luminaries in the South.

18

A poem by Penina Moïse, a prominent educator and woman of letters, celebrated the reopening of Beth Elohim in Charleston by calling for "choral harmony." But her plea fell on deaf ears amid discord over the contentious decision to install an organ.

Dedicated in 1866, the Plum Street Synagogue in Cincinnati symbolized a confident new American Judaism in the Gilded Age. Its minarets and arched entrances were meant to evoke the Alhambra and the Golden Age of Judaism in Spain.

A celebration for the first ordained rabbis in America in 1883 in Cincinnati produced a faux pas heard around the Jewish world: the feast included shellfish and frog legs—foods considered *trefa* or nonkosher. Shocked traditionalists stormed out of the banquet hall.

21

Felix Adler broke with his father, a prominent rabbi at Temple Emanu-El, to embrace atheism and renounce Judaism. He founded the New York Society for Ethical Culture, and his ascension as head of the nondenominational Free Religious Association caused Reform Jews to break away from his organization.

22

Ralph Waldo Emerson, the eminent essayist, lecturer, and founder of the Transcendental movement, addressed the opening of the Free Religious Association in 1867, attended by Rabbi Wise. But Wise turned against the association when Felix Adler became president and renounced Judaism.

23

Rabbi Wise, toward the end of his career, took pride in the creation of the major institutions of Reform Judaism. But in reality, he rushed to the front of a parade that was largely led and defined by other more radical reformers.

24

Patriarch of one of the most established Jewish families in America, Joseph Seligman was refused admittance to the Grand Union Hotel in Saratoga Springs, New York, in 1877. The incident revived fears of anti-Semitism throughout the American Jewish community.

Alexander Kohut, an ardent traditionalist and Talmudist, squared off with the reformist Kaufmann Kohler in competing sermons in the 1880s. He declared that anyone who abandoned Judaism's Oral Law "has banished himself from the camp of Israel."

Kaufmann Kohler, a protégé of German Jewish scholars, championed reforms in America in the tradition of his passionate father-in-law, David Einhorn. He brought the Pittsburgh Platform into fruition and succeeded his archrival, Isaac Mayer Wise, as head of Hebrew Union College.

Starting in the 1880s, 2 million Jews from the shtetls of Russia and Eastern Europe immigrated to the United States, depicted here arriving in New York Harbor. They engulfed the existing Jewish population of 250,000 but were welcomed with an array of charity organizations. Some reform leaders were wary of their Old World practices, however. Most of their descendants eventually embraced reforms established in the nineteenth century.

Leeser's reputation as an outspoken foe of attacks on Jews in Damascus and other far-off lands led him to write a book in 1841, entitled *The Claims of the Jews to an Equality of Rights*. His expanded prominence soon got him a position as hazan at Mikveh Israel in Philadelphia, where he was active on a variety of fronts, writing a primer for the Sunday school he established with Rebecca Gratz. He was also a prolific translator of a range of scholarly works from German, Spanish, French, and Hebrew. His English translation of what became known as the "Leeser Bible" was widely used until later versions supplanted it in the early twentieth century. In his book, *The Jews and the Mosaic Law*, Leeser argued in 1834 that the Pentateuch was of divine origin and then went on to write many works of sermons, theological analysis, and a ten-volume *Discourses on the Jewish Religion*. He is generally considered the first Jewish leader to give sermons in the synagogue in English. But perhaps his most lasting achievement in letters was his publication of *The Occident*, a weekly journal of news and opinion that was read among Jews throughout the country.

Philosophically, Leeser regarded Talmudic law and restrictions, including those devised by generations of rabbis from antiquity through the Middle Ages, as divinely inspired, thus imbued with divine authority, and not subject to revision or reinterpretation in a secular context. He also believed American Jews could change their outward dress and approach some traditions with flexibility—so long as they did not violate Jewish law and made sure to embrace inward piety and its rules—what the historian Michael Meyer calls "a linguistic, cultural and patriotic adaptation" of observant Judaism to modern circumstances, in some ways akin to the reform practices while broadly rejecting reform principles.[5]

But Leeser was also ground down by his quarrels with the lay leadership at Mikveh Israel in Philadelphia. The disputes continued, on and off, over Leeser's sermons, which he delivered in English, rather than German or Hebrew. He preached the importance of Jewish rules but did acknowledge that certain Jewish "superstitions" could be discarded. But there were continuous disputes over the board's insistence that he clear his sermons ahead of time. In addition, Leeser was constantly forced to ask for salary increases when his contract was renewed, only to be rebuffed in what would be a string of rejections over many years—a not uncommon situation in synagogues of the time.

An initial dispute arose in 1831, shortly after he came to Philadelphia, over the board's vote to excommunicate one of its members, whose crime was insulting a fellow board member. Objecting that the board had no such power, Leeser refused to read the edict in the synagogue, infuriating the lay leadership. They summoned Leeser to explain his defiance, but he refused to attend and was effectively censured by the board. He responded with more confrontation, lecturing congregation members over their factionalism, failure to contribute funds, showing up late, and general lack of observance of standards.

Just as his hectoring behavior failed to endear him to board members, Leeser's landlord asked him to move out, concerned that Leeser had taken a romantic interest in one of his daughters. Leeser's new living quarters was a sublet in a building owned by a Gentile seamstress, a Mrs. Deliah [sic] Nash Cozens. (Leeser maintained that while living there, he adhered to strict kosher rules by eating no meat, but he failed to dispel suspicions of laxity on dietary rules among some of his critics, including Wise.)

It was in the sublet that he came down with smallpox in 1833. A younger brother, Jacob, came to Philadelphia to look after him, arriving to find his stricken brother in a coma. Jacob then succumbed to the disease himself and died, while Isaac recovered, scarred for the rest of his life by a hideously pockmarked face and guilt over the death of a beloved sibling who had sacrificed his life to nurse him back to health.

Leeser's stormy tenure came to a head with a confrontation in 1849 over yet another renewal of his contract as hazan, in which he asked for terms allowing him to address the congregation on matters of religion without the president's approval. Their rebuff on this and other demands, without a proper hearing, filled Leeser with despair and anger, he later wrote. "Such an unceremonious act of tyranny, that will listen to no reason, but demands absolute submission, roused my indignation," he said. Improvidently, he attacked his own board in *The Occident*, comparing them to "English iron-clad barons." To which the board responded with its own attack on Leeser in a resolution accusing him of "an absence of the good feeling" toward his superiors.

The following year, the board adopted a motion of censure over his behavior but offered him a meager salary for ten years. The board further raised the sensitive issue of his status as a renter in a house owned by a Gentile, suggesting he may not have followed proper dietary precautions. The board's clear intention to force Leeser's ouster filled him with what his biographer described as a "sense of loss and failure." Weakened physically, he tried to keep up a good front, but he later wrote that on his last day that September, as he was poised to leave office, he was "too ill to walk to the synagogue" and remained puzzled that so many had turned against him. In an unfeeling gesture, Leeser's principal tormenter, the congregation president, Abraham Hart, asked him to continue leading the services for the remainder of the high holy days. "I would not do it for a million dollars," Leeser responded. Instead, he spent Yom Kippur fasting alone in his house, mentally shattered, and for many years refused to set foot back in his old synagogue. The motion of censure was eventually repealed in 1856, but by then Leeser had moved on to a new career of writing, lecturing, and teaching—but not performing in services at any congregation. He continued his influential work as editor of *The Occident*, however. In his final years, he led another congregation, Beth El Emeth, in West Philadelphia.[6]

## ISAAC AND ISAAC TRY FOR ENTENTE

The story of the friendship, rivalry, enmity, recriminations, but eventually mutual respect between the two Isaacs, Leeser and Wise, begins in 1846, with Leeser's paper *The Occident* taking note of Wise's arrival in America as one of a handful of rabbis in the country at the time. The paper referred to him as "a young schoolmaster who also preaches, and is said to possess some Hebrew learning."[7] While in Albany, Wise corresponded frequently with Leeser and chafed under the same conditions that Leeser endured—the requirement that his sermons be approved by the president of the congregation.

In Albany, Wise's ambitious drive to organize Jews in America under one umbrella had naturally brought him notice in other parts of the country. The initial step, as earlier mentioned, was to work with New York rabbis to set up a rabbinic court to rule over the city's many synagogues. Leeser, lacking official rabbinic credentials, was not invited to join the project. But Wise and the others needed to disseminate their plans through *The Occident*, and it was in a contribution to that paper that Wise proposed his idea for a prayer book *Minhag America*. Leeser allowed Wise to promote his idea while dissenting from some of Wise's beliefs, including omission of the traditional Jewish prayers for restoration of the destroyed Temple and reestablishing animal sacrifices.

At their first meeting in Albany in 1847, shortly after Wise's arrival there, Wise described Leeser as "a lean pock-marked, clean-shaving little man, clad in black" who was "worthy of respect" because he was "honest and well-meaning in his orthodoxy." Leeser evidently returned that respect.[8] As a result, Leeser overcame his wariness of Wise's doctrines and allowed him to use *The Occident* to promote his idea of a national union of American Jews.

But the Wise-Leeser friendship foundered over the events leading up to and including Wise's firing in Albany, starting with Wise's challenge in Charleston to the concept of a personal messiah. Those comments were what led Spanier, the Albany synagogue president, to get Leeser to publish details of the rabbi's scandalous behavior in *The Occident*. Wise, Leeser wrote, needed to "look into the matter [of the Messiah] more deeply." The "glorious doctrine" of the Messiah and resurrection of the dead derived from sacred sources, he added. "Would there be any disgrace in Dr. Wise acknowledging in calmer moments that he was mistaken?" As a conciliatory gesture, Leeser expressed his personal respect for Wise and offered him the opportunity to respond in *The Occident*, though Wise had already addressed the matter in *The Asmonean,* claiming that some members had waged a vendetta against him because of his enforcement of Sabbath and kosher laws.[9]

A separate source of contention was also revealing. Wise believed in the elimination of scriptural readings calling for murderous vengeance on the Amalekites and other enemies of the Jews depicted in the Bible. While

Leeser went along with Wise's favoring sermons in the services, he could not go as far as Wise on such matters and said so. Yet Wise kept up his challenges to Leeser, saying that Jews, on their own, were already abandoning many of their supposedly outmoded traditions and were in danger of defecting from Judaism altogether. Writing in *The Occident,* Wise argued that the Bible did not forbid the reforms he advocated and again disputed the textual basis in Scripture for the concepts of a messiah and resurrection. Eventually, Leeser could not tolerate what he saw as Wise's heresies, saying it pained him to publish what Wise had to say. Wise promptly withdrew as a contributor, telling Leeser: "I pity you, and I hope the day is not far distant when *The Occident* will advocate the doctrines of reform." Vowing to remain "an honest friend" of Leeser, he nevertheless bade "a hearty farewell" to the readers of *The Occident*. Leeser had the last word in his own paper, saying no Jewish "minister" had the right to deny the truth of Jewish teachings. But in a final letter, Wise retorted that the Talmud and its successor laws were written by humans, and humans are fallible and subject to a reconsideration of their conclusions.

Challenged on the resurrection, Wise added fire to this exchange by indulging in a fanciful case of reductio ad absurdum in still another communication. What if the prediction of a resurrection were true, and all the human beings now dead had suddenly come back to life? Who would feed them? And where would they find places to live? Wise said they could live in a "supernatural" state but asserted that all such speculations were preposterous. He wondered whether, having come back to life, humans would die again eventually. His rejoinder then turned personal, as Wise accused Leeser of turning a philosophical dispute "into personal invectives of the most abusive kind." Leeser fired back, saying he had no wish to declare Wise a heretic, but that it appeared Wise wanted martyrdom.[10]

The irony was that Wise was still determined at this stage to be a compromiser. He also found it useful to dissemble when it came to doctrine, professing unity over radical reform, with his familiar goal of creating an American Judaism around which all Jews could rally. Parting company with some reformers to seek the right balance, he asserted that Judaism had indeed derived in some fashion from divine revelation. He thus consistently maintained that God revealed himself to Moses and that Moses composed the Torah (or most of it). But he was a rationalist and did not believe in magic or miracles such as the parting of the Red Sea, which he said must have occurred because of natural causes. He never accepted the ancient rabbinic traditional view that God imparted hundreds of commandments orally to Moses. But he never doubted the story of Moses receiving the Ten Commandments from God.

This conviction enabled Wise to argue that all interpretations that came after the revelation were subject to revisiting. He contended that the Bible's and the Talmud's condoning of such practices as slavery, bigamy, vengeance and killing of enemies, and a hereditary priesthood, could be discarded as outmoded. But the concept of divine revelation on some level was not disputed. "For all of his reformist stance, there was an undeniable strain of fundamentalism in Wise," writes the historian Michael Meyer. He could not abide the view of critics that the Pentateuch was written by many authors, because interpreting it that way undercut the existence of one eternal God. He believed that something real and important happened at Sinai. Within the boundaries of these doctrines, Wise maintained what Meyer calls "ambiguous formulations" in which he could maneuver with some latitude. "Consistency, moreover, was simply not his highest value," Meyer writes delicately. Instead, Wise harbored a "strain of opportunism" and "penchant for self-aggrandizement." Wise wanted to transform Judaism but understood that he had to show some deference to rabbinic authority if he was to succeed in persuading others to follow him.

To this end, Wise argued that it was not until sometime after the tenth century that rabbinic interpretations from ancient times ceased to be the sole authority of law. It was then, he said, that new schools of interpretation, using philology and philosophy, took their place and began what he maintained would become a new tradition adjusted to modern demands. His contention was that Maimonides and Moses Mendelssohn were the avatars of this new contemporary Judaism that crested in the "scientific" studies of Judaism in Germany but culminated in America. Wise used the

word *reform* on occasion, but he did not see himself as leading some sort of
"Reform" denomination or movement. Instead, he spoke of an Americanized religion. As he put it: "American Judaism, i.e., Judaism reformed and
reconstructed by the beneficent influence of political liberty and progressive enlightenment, is the youngest offspring of the ancient and venerable
faith of Israel. . . . It is the American phase of Judaism."[11]

For all these differences over orthodoxy, Isaac Mayer Wise and Isaac
Leeser did not abandon their hope for common ground. But in 1853 when
Leeser proposed in *The Occident* that a conference be convened of all Jewish
clergy in America, Wise opposed it—even though he had long favored the
idea in principle. There were too few responsible rabbis in America for such
a conference to avoid dictating to others, he asserted. The following year,
Wise published his book, *The History of the Israelitish Nation:From Abraham
to the Present Time.* At the time, few if any such histories of the Jewish people,
daring to provide a narrative that departed from the miracles in Scripture,
existed in English. Drawing on his knowledge of such histories in German,
Wise's work was an attempt to set aside what he viewed as myths and miracles in order to discern an actual history of Jews starting with Abraham.
Its purpose was to record only "facts" and not interventions by God, which
Wise said could not be verified. Various miracles like the parting of the Red
Sea and the descending of darkness as part of the plagues of Egypt could be
explained by science, he asserted. Seeking to get his book published, Wise
won approval from two New York statesmen of the day, Horace Greeley and
William Seward. He also got favorable letters from such other public figures
as Harriet Beecher Stowe. Unable to find a publisher, Wise produced the
book at his own expense with help from friendly benefactors, prompting a
firestorm of conservative criticism, Leeser among them, in some cases calling for his excommunication as a heretic.

But the dream of binding the disparate Jewish communities in the
United States refused to go away. Both Isaacs agreed that it had to be undertaken without the hierarchy associated with Jewish communities in Europe, where "chief rabbis" of individual cities and countries were the norm.
Wise, at least, was influenced no doubt by the phenomenon of rabbinical

conferences in Europe earlier in the 1800s, including the group of Jewish notables who had met with Napoleon and declared themselves to be French citizens. Later parleys to discuss reforms in Judaism took place in Germany, particularly one in Wiesbaden in 1837 (called by Abraham Geiger, an early advocate of a modernized reading of Jewish tradition), Brunswick in 1844, Frankfort-on-the-Main in 1845, and Breslau in 1846.

By 1854, Wise had transplanted himself to a new perch in Cincinnati, following the debacle and change of congregations in Albany. Wise took over as rabbi at B'nai Yeshurun, a leading synagogue in one of the United States' largest and most prosperous Jewish communities. Cincinnati, a booming Ohio River commercial center and entrepôt known as the "Queen City of the West," swelled in population in mid-century, especially with an influx of German immigrants. With his powerful reputation, Wise had been able to dictate many of his own terms to the congregation, avoiding certain customs (such as "antiquated chanting" of the Torah) as beneath his dignity. Over the objections of some in the congregation, he introduced a choir and abolished the wearing of prayer shawls. Again, as in Albany, he discarded several obscure prayers in the liturgy and decreed that the Torah did not need to be read in its entirety throughout the year. Instead, the Torah was to be read in a cycle of three years.

The year he arrived in Cincinnati, Wise began publishing a newspaper, *The Israelite*, in 1854, with the expectation that it would compete with Leeser's *Occident*. Its masthead modestly proclaimed: "Let there be Light." He found time in his work to write a few forgettable and unsuccessful novels and engage in verbal combat with adversaries, Jew and non-Jew, mobilizing what his biographer calls "a rough, uncultivated voice" that "snorts or bellows" when getting its point across. Though *The Israelite* lost money, Wise went on to establish a German companion newspaper, *Die Deborah*, aimed at women, another signal of the rising importance of women in Jewish daily life. He also persisted in his plans to produce a prayer book worthy of his goal of Jewish unity. He was determined to build on an idea introduced in 1847 by his friend, Rabbi Max Lilienthal of Congregation Ansche Chesed in New York, who set up an advisory committee authorizing Wise to submit a prayer book manuscript for eventual use by all congregations in the United States.

In the pages of *The Israelite*, Wise also called for a national parley of rabbis in 1855, scheduled to take place in Cleveland. In an ecumenical gesture, invitations went out to Orthodox as well as Reform congregations. Nine accepted the summons by August, and the conference planners set an agenda of establishing a common liturgy (including his *Minhag America*) and a proposal to expand Jewish education. The planning got off to a rocky start when three of the original Orthodox signatories to the summons of the conference pulled out. But other Orthodox rabbis showed up, along with lay representatives from several cities, setting up potential obstacles to reaching agreement.

As the conference began in October, the attendees elected Wise as president. He immediately sought again to mediate between radical reformers and conservatives, who distrusted each other so much that they refused to sit together and instead scowled at one another throughout the session.[12] To overcome their differences, Wise, Leeser, and Rabbi Leo Merzbacher worked all night to hammer out a compromise. The next day the conference adopted a call for a synod based on two major principles: the divine origin of the Bible and the authority of rabbinic traditions as derived from "the traditional, legal, and logical exposition of the biblical laws which must be expounded and practiced according to the comments of the Talmud."[13] The language fell short of the Orthodox belief in the outright divine nature of the Talmud's authority. But upon hearing this presentation, Leeser got up from his seat in the back of the hall and walked to the front, declaring at the podium that it had eased his fears. His statement may have been a reflection of hope rather than conviction.

The adopted platform at Cleveland clearly went further than Wise might have preferred in making concessions to conservatives. But Wise knew that compromise was necessary to fulfill his dream. In *The Israelite*, Wise recalled that Leeser "beamed with delight" over the declaration, and that the other orthodox delegates were surprised and nonplussed.[14] The conference also set up a committee with Wise as a member to set up a common liturgy and

then to report on its progress at the next conference, to be held in Philadelphia the next year, in 1856.

But in the end, Wise's efforts to compromise backfired. Leeser was
vilified by some of his Orthodox brethren for reaching out to Wise. And
on the other side of the spectrum, vehement objections to Wise's gesture
erupted. The most heated dissent came from Rabbi David Einhorn of Baltimore, who had rejected the Talmud's divinely inspired authority. Einhorn,
in his attack, also accused Wise of reprinting one of his own sermons in a
mangled form in the *Israelite* and omitting passages that conflicted with
the Cleveland meeting's conclusions. The Cleveland platform abandoned
Jews who did not consider the Talmud as binding, Einhorn declared, and
in so doing, it condemned Judaism itself to "perpetual stagnation" and obscurantism.

In raising these objections, Einhorn started on his path to becoming
the most passionate and doctrinaire reformer in the United States. He was
destined over time to wield enormous influence on the transformation of
American Judaism. Like the careers of other rabbis, Einhorn's journey was
a mixture of European and American intellectual and social trends. Born
in Dispeck, Bavaria, in 1809, Einhorn had attended a traditional yeshiva
in Furth, earning a rabbinical diploma at age seventeen. He later studied
at various universities in Erlangen, Würzburg, and Munich, where his religious views turned increasingly radical. After several rabbinical posts, he
succeeded Samuel Holdheim, a champion of Jewish rights and of the view
that Jews were adherents to a religion and not a nation, as chief rabbi of
Mecklenburg-Schwerin.

Einhorn was part of the noisy group of followers of the enlightenment
figure Abraham Geiger. In his book, *The Principles of Mosaism*, published
in 1854, Einhorn elaborated on the well-known German enlightenment
argument, for which Geiger was the leading exponent, that reason, not revelation from thousands of years in the past, must serve as the foundation
of Judaism. Even Moses, in this view, perceived God not externally telling
him to seek freedom for the slaves in Egypt but from within himself. By
extension, the Sinai revelation was not a onetime event but a moment of

comprehension in a continuous process that each new generation can experience. The Talmud may have played a progressive role in the past, he said, but it was not owed deference as divine in and of itself.

"Judaism in its essence is older than the Israelites," Einhorn wrote. "As pure humanity, as the emanation of the inborn divine spirit, it is as old as the human race. . . . It was not a religion, but a religious people, that was newly created at Sinai, a priest people called upon, first of all, to impress the ancient divine teaching more deeply upon itself and then to bring it to universal dominion."

In 1855, when Einhorn immigrated to Baltimore and Har Sinai Congregation, he continued to press his liberal views, although he also defended the peoplehood aspect of Judaism by opposing intermarriage. These views aligned with his opposition to slavery and his view that while the Bible condones slavery if interpreted narrowly and literally, its underlying moral principles dating from antiquity oppose it, if one is to look at such precepts broadly and dispassionately. Equally deserving of his wrath was the treatment of poor people and what he called an excessive pursuit of wealth in America. In part because of his taste for ostentatious displays of material possessions in America, Einhorn could thus not help but remain a Germanophile, seeing scholarship in Germany as exemplary for Jews and the language of German bringing Reform to life. (As late as 1874, most American congregations continued to use German as the main language, including for sermons.) "As proud as I am of my adopted citizenship," Einhorn said, "I will never forget that the old home is the land of thinkers, presently the foremost land of culture, and above all the land of Mendelssohn, the birthplace of Reform Judaism."[15]

Einhorn's attack on Wise after the Cleveland conference was carried out in the name of the president of his synagogue, Har Sinai Verein, and others in the congregation, though they were unnamed. The Cleveland compromise, their criticism said, was not a healing gesture but rather "demoralizing" and backward, singling out its acceptance of the law requiring the widow of a man who dies before they have children to marry the man's brother (a practice called levirate marriage). Einhorn declared that he honored the desire of Jews to accommodate one another's traditions, but in this case, it had gone too far, keeping Jews in chains and raising the prospect of such servitude being enshrined in the universal liturgy that Wise was seeking. More specifically, Einhorn warned against any plan to install any hierarchy of authority among Jews, effectively accusing Wise of trying to establish himself as a Jewish American Pope. "It is not difficult to sum up the difference between Wise and Einhorn," writes Temkin, Wise's biographer. "Wise was fighting for union, Einhorn for reform." And the breach that opened up would last for another twenty-five years. [16]

Defending himself against the criticism, Wise accused Einhorn and his cohorts of atheism and even suggested they should abandon Judaism altogether. Coming to Wise's defense was, of all people, Leeser, who praised the Cleveland platform. "Were these not welcome words?" Leeser asked. "Were they too little compensation for travelling seven hundred miles while laboring under a severe indisposition, in not the most pleasant season of the year? Indeed they were; and we should have travelled farther yet, and labored much to have been sure that this would have been the result of all the contests in which we have been engaged." But Leeser's praise was far from welcome for Wise, who later backtracked and maintained that the Cleveland principles were guidelines, not rules, not intended to dictate to any individuals or congregations. He denied that he had "repented" his ways and was "a traitor to the cause of reform and progress." [17]

Writing in *The Israelite* after Leeser's double-edged praise, Wise saw himself as a victim of a multitude of foes. This was the Wise who later in his memoirs recalled his prophetic dream on board the *Marie* sailing to New York, in which he was attacked by enemies on all sides. Recalling that he had struggled all his life "when he had scarcely bread to eat, or the means to support his family," Wise (speaking of himself in the third person) forswore any ambition for wealth and fame but only for "the sacred cause of Israel." In an astonishing display of self-love, Wise reminded his readers that he, Wise, had become the most famous rabbi in the country, looked upon with "profound respect" by one and all. "What, please tell, what can make a traitor of a man who cares not for money, wealth, reputation or position? What can silence him who fears none, dreads none, and regards but the cause for which he labors?" Wise asked. Reformers who accused him of treachery were themselves frivolous and deceitful. He concluded with a rhetorical flourish, asking whether it was right or wrong in Cleveland to have sought unity among the Jewish people of America. "The opposition waste in vain their words and their paper," he declared. "Truth will triumph."

## EXIT LEESER, WISE ASCENDS, AND THE BATTLE OF PRAYER BOOKS BEGINS

The discord of Cleveland subsided temporarily after the conference. Ordinary Jews may well have been oblivious to the doctrinal and self-serving thunderbolts that religious factions had hurled at each other. Instead, each congregation in the 1850s preferred to set its own course. But Wise seemed to know that the great leap forward toward Jewish unity remained distant. In his German-language publication *Die Deborah*, Wise wrote with resignation that while living in an immense and disputatious America, Jews would also inevitably split into warring camps and accuse each other of betrayal. Jews, Wise observed, were simply too busy and preoccupied with the daily business of making a living to pay attention to their Judaism. He depicted a world in which most American Jews had become so sophisticated that they had no need of Judaism, whereas the traditionalists among them had become enslaved to their ancient ways. Wise portrayed himself, on the other hand, as a "rational Jew" standing between extremes, both hero and victim of his own farsighted and magnanimous quest—again, as foretold in his dream aboard the *Marie* ten years earlier.[18]

Yet Wise refused to set aside his effort to write a shared liturgy, a "book of common prayer" for American Jews, *Minhag America*, even in the absence of a mandate to produce it. Jewish prayers needed to be revised, he believed, "because the belief in the coming of a personal Messiah descended from the house of David had disappeared from among the people." A new universal prayer book, or *siddur*, could perhaps strengthen the cause of unity among

Jews. Accordingly, for all its departure from orthodoxy, *Minhag America* was written to retain the basic structure of Jewish prayers while eliminating the passages that Wise found objectionable in the hopes of appealing to a broad consensus in the middle.

Nevertheless, despite his gratitude after Cleveland, Leeser objected to the book, asserting that the Cleveland Conference had not authorized such an effort. Wise, writing in *The Asmonean* (and trying to be polite), praised Leeser as "a theologian of the first class" but asserted that he had every right to proceed with it. On the other side of the spectrum, Rabbi Einhorn's monthly publication, *Sinai*, excoriated plans for *Minhag America* as excessively compromised. In its place, Einhorn promoted his own prayer book entitled (in German) *Prayerbook for Israelite Reform Congregations*, later called *Olat Tamid* ("perpetual offering," as a tribute to ritual and the role of worshippers to serve God). Drawn from liturgy in Frankfurt and Berlin and from the scientific Jewish studies of Leopold Zunz, a German founder of Wissenschaft des Judentums, Einhorn's book repeatedly emphasized the priestly and messianic role of the people of Israel among all nations. *Olat Tamid* also effectively transformed the concept of resurrection of the dead ("who revives the dead") into immortality of the soul ("who plants within us eternal life"). On one hand, it eliminated the symbols of the palm frond and citron associated with the Sukkot (harvest thanksgiving) festival as having no modern meaning. Yet it also embodied a certain traditional and spiritual approach to the legacy of Judaism appealing to those who did not want to abandon tradition altogether.

Wise's *Minhag America* was finally published in 1857, in a first edition. Like Einhorn's book, it eliminated references to the Messiah and the return of Jews to Zion and restoration of sacrifices at the Temple. Its service was shortened, though not as much as Einhorn's. But Wise, in keeping with his attempt to moderate between factions, included a large number of Hebrew texts and rubrics. The prayer for resurrection of the dead that is part of the Eighteen Blessings, known as the Shemoneh Esreh (or Amidah) that is the central prayer of Judaism, recited three times each day in traditional Judaism, was deemed too central to tradition to discard outright. But Wise kept it only in Hebrew, not in English. Once again, it was clear that Wise was seeking to appeal to the broadest array of congregations, at the expense of consistent or uniform ideology on these controversial matters.[19]

In the competition between these two prayer books, history declared Wise the winner, despite the fact that many members of Reform congregations found it overly traditional. *Minhag America* was adopted in many congregations, thanks in part to Wise's travels and proselytizing, especially in the South and Midwest. (Wise later claimed that as many as one hundred congregations used it at its peak of popularity.)

Wise's views about the nature of his faith were also outlined in a book *The Essence of Judaism*, published in 1861, fleshing out his contention that the understanding of God derives from nature, history, and reason, as well as an acceptance of God's revelation contained in Scripture. Jews also believe in progress, he wrote in the book, and progress must be driven not by miracles or God's intervention but by human beings themselves. He embraced those biblical precepts found in the work of prophets, and related to the carrying out of justice. Rabbis, he said again, had never hesitated to change practices and laws in the religion to conform with their times, as they did after the fall of the Temple in Jerusalem.

Realizing that his reputation for idol breaking had extended to the non-Jewish world, Wise also began to speak out more directly in challenging the miracles in the story of Jesus and the origins of Christianity, as if to say that these stories were no more and no less credible than the ones in the Hebrew Bible. It is easier, he implied, for Jews to question such supernatural deeds of Jesus, such as his walking on water, turning wine into water, and raising Lazarus from the dead, if one was equally skeptical about miracles in the Old Testament. Like Jewish scholars throughout the centuries, Wise felt compelled to dispute the widely embraced and promoted libel among Christians that the Jews killed Jesus. (The historian Stephen Prothero has found that American Jews were reluctant to fully recognize even the existence of Jesus as a historical figure until the twentieth century.[20]) Wise's purpose was twofold: to rebut missionaries seeking to convert Jews and overturn claims dating from the colonial era that America was a Christian nation. Like other Jewish leaders, in 1858–59, he took up the cause of Edgardo Mortara, the Jewish child in Rome who was forcibly abducted and baptized. But in these disputes, Wise "preferred to fight alone than to fight as a member of a team of which he was not the captain," writes Temkin, his biographer. He thus declined to join the Board of Delegates of American Israelites, an Orthodox-led movement in New York to press for greater rights for Jews after the Mortara case. In his antipathy toward traditionalists, he refused to support the establishment of Maimonides College as the first Jewish seminary in America, which chose Leeser as president but which foundered quickly thereafter.

The death of Leeser in 1868 removed from the scene the man with whom he had first tried to collaborate to unite American Jewry. Death seemed to offer the possibility of a new phase in which the differences between the two Isaacs could be relegated to the past. A few months before his passing, Leeser even expressed admiration for Wise for his leadership of his congregation, noting that only the "antagonistic" and "radical" influence of Einhorn prevented American Jews from rallying around him. Wise appears to have been moved by the passing of his longtime friend and occasional antagonist, hailing him as "the banner bearer of American Jewish conservatism," and adding that for all their disagreements, "We know of no man in America who will replace Isaac Leeser in the orthodox camp. . . . He had a cause to plead, and he did it without fears or favors. He did not yield an inch to anybody. He unfurled his true colors on every occasion, and proved himself by far more consistent and by far more honest than many in that camp who are prudent enough to be everything to everybody."[21]

With Leeser gone, no single figure in the Orthodox community had the stature to stand up to Wise. As a result, the Cincinnati rabbi was fated to engage in combat with those on his left instead of his right.

## DENOUEMENT IN CHARLESTON

Back in South Carolina, while Leeser and Wise jockeyed for influence in the 1850s, Congregations Beth Elohim and Shearith Israel struggled to overcome their differences with mixed success. Poznanski, after his resignation, evidently lived in Charleston until the Civil War and then went north, spending time in New York, but it is not clear where or when. A son, Gustavus Jr., died defending Charleston during the war. Two other sons became musicians in Europe and later inherited the rabbi's estate. To this day, Beth Elohim cites his name at its annual memorial service on Yom Kippur.

Poznanski's departure from Beth Elohim cleared the way for it to declare its allegiance to reform. The organ was there to stay. Beth Elohim proclaimed that its sermons and some prayers would be in English, and that hymns and psalms would employ both Hebrew and English. The Torah would be read in a three-year cycle, the Haftarah (passages from the Prophets) and some parts of the service were eliminated, and second days of holidays were discarded. In 1855, Beth Elohim held a "confirmation" for students—five females and one male—following the first such adaptation of a church Sunday school practice in New York City in 1846.

But it was also a period of financial difficulties for both Beth Elohim and Shearith Israel. In 1858, the new rabbi at Beth Elohim, Maurice Mayer, threatened to resign because he was not being paid on time. The congregation continued disputes with him. They complained, for example, that he had not covered his head while appearing in public. His response was to accuse the board of hypocrisy, arguing that if they were that conservative, the synagogue should remove the organ and reinstitute the second day of festivals. Mayer sought permission to leave in 1858, citing ill health, and finally resigned in 1859 after moving to New York. Yet another new hazan, Abraham Harris, began his duties in February 1860, only to resign the following year as Confederates bombarded and seized Fort Sumter.

As Beth Elohim and Shearith Israel continued their feuds, a new group of Jews recently emigrated from Poland created another new synagogue congregation in 1855, Berith Shalome (today Brith Shalom-Beth Israel), so that by the time of the Civil War there were three synagogues in Charleston. For the most part, they were loyal to South Carolina and the Confederacy.

Once Charleston was occupied by the Union, Shearith congregants asked Union army authorities for permission to take over their former synagogue, on the ground that the occupants had "no rights in the premises." The Union forces agreed, notwithstanding its citation of "a decision of a civil court previous to the Union forces occupying the city," a reference to Judge Butler's decision approving the organ.[22]

The two synagogues decided to reunite in 1866, a development made easier as Shearith Israel grew more receptive to the reformist sentiments of Beth Elohim. The two feuding congregations also sought a unified front against the new Polish upstarts. Of course, disputes over ritual and music continued to flare, as it has at many synagogues in America.

The organ, meanwhile, continued its perilous and discordant journey into history. When Charleston was bombarded during the Civil War, the organ was taken one hundred miles away for safekeeping to the interior of the state in Columbia, along with the chandelier and Torah scrolls. But these treasures ended up burned by Union forces racing through Columbia under General William Tecumseh Sherman in 1864.

The merger of Shearith Israel and Beth Elohim after the Civil War was accompanied by a new constitution shortening the Orthodox service and discarding the practice of members making offerings in return for the honor of reading from the Torah. No instrumental music was part of the service, but there was to be a choir with women.

Charles H. Moïse, the new president of Beth Elohim, called himself "an enlightened Orthodox Jew." He declared that he did not wish to adopt new practices just because they were new—and that he would not reject old practices just because they were old. Jews throughout the country took an interest in the doings of the two synagogues. Before his death, Rabbi Leeser even expressed regret over the discontinuation of selling the honor of reading from the Torah. The practice was reinstated. The synagogue, despite its new unification, fell on hard times, forcing the resignation of its president. But when the five-year contract of union was renewed, an organ was restored to a place of honor in 1872.

Penina Moïse, Charles's aunt and a celebrated poet regarded as the first woman of Jewish letters in America, whose hymn was sung when Beth Elohim opened with its new organ in 1841, fared less well in these years.

Having published a collection of sixty poems in 1833, many of which first appeared in South Carolina newspapers, she was famous for her rhapsodic paeans to nature, heroism, Jewish faith, and loyalty to the people of South Carolina and their traditions.

In her heyday, Moïse wrote poems that lamented the death of the ardent slavery advocate and white supremacist John C. Calhoun and that praised the Confederate forces of the Palmetto State. She wrote poems about the fire that destroyed Beth Elohim and its rebuilding: "Behold, O Mighty Architect, / What love for Thee has wrought; / This Fane arising from the wrecked, / Beauty from ashes brought." When the schism opened up and traditionalists seceded, she wrote a poem, "Lines on the Issue of the Late Hebrew Controversy," that expressed "the sound of a brother's farewell." She rejoiced when the struggle was resolved.

During the Civil War, Penina Moïse fled from Charleston and then returned after the war, by then blind from old age, impoverished, and forced to teach school to make ends meet. But her legacy remained in Charleston for evoking the American sounds of Protestant church music, a fusing of traditions that would mark the journey of Jews toward the mainstream of American religion. She saw the Jews as forever yearning for their God-given destiny—for example, in her poem evoking Israel at the Red Sea, before crossing to a life in the Promised Land:

Hallelujah! Symbol bright
Of divine, impartial light
Is the sun that taketh heed
Of the flower and the weed.
Hallelujah! Even so
Mercy beams on all below;
Nor to Saints its smiles confines
But on guilt forgiving shines.

Hallelujah! May our race,
Heirs of promise and of grace,

Enter Heav'n beyond Life's goal,
Blessed Canaan of the soul![23]

Moïse's poetry echoed with themes of freedom and redemption for Jews, but it was also a voice of the Old South. That voice gave poetic eloquence to the stormy efforts in Charleston to reconcile tradition and change in an ancient religion. American Judaism on the eve of the Civil War was to become as divided as the rest of the Union. Jews, citing Scripture as their basis, could not help but be divided, not only over their own practices but over the greatest moral issue of the era and one that would sunder a nation and its Jewish community.

*Nine*

# JEWS IN THE CIVIL WAR

South Carolina, home of one of the largest concentrations of American Jews, had many reasons to distrust the North, well beyond the issue of slavery. It was in South Carolina that the doctrine of nullification—in which the state argued it was entitled to abrogate federal laws imposing tariffs on imports—provoked a constitutional crisis in the 1830s. Tariffs were anathema to the state's trade-based economy from which many Jews prospered.

The state's rebellious tendencies boiled over with the election of Abraham Lincoln in 1860. Immediately following the vote, a South Carolina state assembly, fearing that slavery would soon be abolished, voted to secede. Federal property was taken over by Confederate forces throughout the South. Union troops defending Charleston retreated to Fort Sumter, on a small island offshore. Once in office in 1861, Lincoln sent a fleet of unarmed ships to relieve the island garrison, provoking the rebels to open fire and seize the outpost, forcing Union troops to surrender. The Civil War had begun.

Socially and politically, the Civil War marked a turning point for American Jews, in ways beneficial and baleful. The conflict hastened Jewish integration into the military and, in the process, into the fabric of American society. Yet war also brought forth a new and virulent wave of American anti-Semitism in both the North and the South, underscoring the detestable but indestructible stereotype of Jews as obsessed with money and material possessions, and willing to pursue them at the expense of the war effort. Above all, Jewish loyalty to their regions—both North and South—was a sign that Jews were proclaiming their identity as full Americans, shedding their affinities with the countries they left behind.

"For Jews in America, the Civil War was a watershed that involved Jewish soldiers from all over the nation," writes the historian and biographer Eli N. Evans. "Jews served in both armies and helped in the war effort in many other ways. Serving their countries under fire and fighting side by side with their Gentile comrades in arms accelerated the process of acculturation, not only through their self-perceptions, but also because of the reactions of the community around them."

Of the 150,000 Jews living in at least 160 identifiable Jewish communities in the United States (25,000 of them in the South), Evans estimates that the number of Jews serving in the South was 2,000 to 3,000 and 6,000 in the North—more than 5 percent of the total population, a remarkably high number. In addition, this number included generals, surgeons, and medal winners. David Urbansky, a Union soldier who had emigrated from Prussia, was the first American Jew to be awarded a Congressional Medal of Honor. It was for his heroism at the Battles of Shiloh and Vicksburg. On the home front, Jews supported myriad relief activities, and Jewish women made clothes, prepared bandages, and treated the wounded.[1]

Diaries and journals attest to the experience of Jews feeling at home in military service but also struggling with the pain of a war that split Jewish families and relations, just as it did for the rest of Americans. "I have now become a respected man in a respected position," Louis Gratz, a peddler, wrote upon becoming a first lieutenant in the cavalry of the Union. "I move in the best and richest circles and am treated with utmost consideration by

Jews and Christians." But the children of Abraham Jonas were divided—four for the South and one for the North. Septima Levy Collis's brother died fighting for the South while her husband was wounded fighting for the North. Southern Jews were chagrined that Northern Jews were among the invaders—in one case guarding the house of a Southern Jew. A memoirist recounted how Northern soldiers attended services in Natchez, Mississippi, giving offense to the Jews of that congregation.[2]

Jewish themes also abounded in the statements of Jews praying for victory for the sides on which they fought. A Jewish Confederate captain compared the North to Egypt and the South to the Israelites seeking freedom from Egyptian slavery. Rabbi Maxmilian J. Michelbacher of Richmond charged that the enemy of the North had "dissolved fraternal love" and threatened "to desecrate our soil, to murder our people, and to deprive us of the glorious inheritance which was left to us by the immortal fathers of this once great Republic. . . . O Lord, God of Israel, be with me in the hot season of the contending strife; protect and bless me with health and courage to bear cheerfully the hardship of war. . . ." Rabbis in the South had a special difficulty when the Union Army captured their cities. In New Orleans, Rabbi James K. Gutheim, who had earlier served in New York and Cincinnati, refused to take an oath of allegiance to occupying forces. Ordered to leave, he installed himself in Montgomery, Alabama, where he remained loyal to "our beloved country, the Confederate States of America," which he hailed for defending "our liberties and rights and independence, under just and equitable laws."[3]

In the North, religious figures, such as Rabbi David Einhorn of Baltimore, prayed for victory and condemned slavery by invoking the story of Exodus. It was not always easy for Jews to serve and remain faithful to their traditions, but the evidence suggests that Jews in the military sought to keep their identities and beliefs in the field, including attempts on both sides to keep kosher and observe the Sabbath and at least the major Jewish holidays. General Robert E. Lee, a devout Christian, pledged in 1864 to try "to facilitate the observances of the duties of their religion by the Israelites in the army." The historian Jonathan Sarna poignantly cites two accounts of Passover in 1862, one on the Union side and the other Confederate, as they sought to obtain matzo and kosher meat for the Seder. On the other hand, some Jews serving in the army hid their identities, to the disappointment of rabbis who sought to reach out to them.

As if by Providence, news of the Union victory and Lee's surrender coincided with the arrival of Passover in 1865. Jews in the North readily compared the victory to their own freedom from slavery celebrated by that holiday. But then five days later Lincoln was dead—the eve of the fifth day of Passover—and also Good Friday. Sermons in synagogues compared Lincoln not only to Moses but also to Abraham and King David. Some three thousand Jews marched in Lincoln's funeral pageant in New York and mourned his loss as one of their own.

In defeat, the Confederacy's Jews mourned the looting and burning of some of their synagogues. Southern rabbis compared the rout of their forces to the fall of the Temple and the Jews' expulsion in ancient Jerusalem. "As Israelites, we are passing through another captivity which relives and reenacts all the troubles so pathetically poured forth by the inspired Jeremiah," Henry Hyams of Louisiana wrote of the Northern occupation, in 1868. A group called the Hebrew Ladies' Memorial Association, founded in 1866 after the war, distributed a circular echoing the emerging sense of grievance and loss that was to characterize the South for decades after the war. The association said that because of their history of suffering, Jews had a special reason for remembering those who had "so nobly perished" for the "glorious cause" of the Confederacy. The Jewish sculptor Moses Ezekiel, a Confederate veteran, created sculptures and busts of Robert E. Lee, Stonewall Jackson, and the Confederate Memorial at Arlington Cemetery.[4]

## ANTI-SEMITISM IN NORTH AND SOUTH

Despite their service and loyalty to both North and South, and perhaps because they were heavily integrated into the war efforts on both sides, anti-Semitism reared its ugly visage and caused great pain for Jews both ordinary and prominent.

On the Union side, anti-Jewish prejudice flared over the role of Jews in businesses that profited from the war, often featured in news stories and cartoons depicting Jews as avaricious, disloyal, and greedy. These focused especially on poorly made uniforms made from shredded or discarded fiber known as "shoddy." *Shoddy* became an anti-Semitic slur, so widespread was the assumption that it was Jews who produced such goods. "In the media, the theme of 'shoddy,' the purported manipulation of financial institutions, the alleged subversive complicity with the Confederacy, the supposed exploitation of military personnel by Jewish camp followers, and the claims of foreign intervention against the interest of the North continued unabated to plague the image of Jews," the historians Gary L. Bunker and John J. Appel write.[5]

Some anti-Semitism in the North was also driven by the conspicuous role of Jews in the South. A particular target of such hatred in the North was the Confederate secretary of state, Judah P. Benjamin (1811–1884), a former senator from Louisiana and a close confidant of the Confederate president Jefferson Davis. A number of damaging episodes in the military were also painful. In 1861, the Union Army decreed that chaplains had to be of "some Christian denomination." (The Confederate law was more inclusive, specifying only that a chaplain had to be a "minister of religion.") Jewish chaplains in the North were even barred from ministering to soldiers in the field. But the ruling was overturned in 1862, with Lincoln's support, in a historically significant milestone for all religions other than Christianity.

Far more damaging than the ban on Jewish chaplains was the notorious General Order 11 of General Ulysses S. Grant. Issued December 17, 1862, it expelled Jews from all areas under Grant's command, threatening Jews with imprisonment if they did not obey quickly. If there was a rationale to the order, it derived from Grant's advancing into Mississippi to join with General William Tecumseh Sherman and take Vicksburg. Once Grant permitted citizens in these areas to resume their business livelihoods, various traders swept in. Seizing abandoned cotton and other goods, they sold them and offered gold and weapons to Confederate sympathizers whom Grant feared would resume hostilities.

Investigations into these activities implicated soldiers, traders, and civilians of all persuasions. No doubt some were Jews. But Grant blamed the Jews, in part because of antipathy toward his father, whom he believed was engaging in such trading in conjunction with Jewish partners. Grant further suspected his father of trading on the son's status as general in seeking a license to trade cotton. The order was what the historian Stephen V. Ash calls "a logical culmination of the history of anti-Semitism in Grant's army and his own intensifying bigotry, a culmination shaped by the penchant of the soldier for quick and decisive remedies based on military considerations alone."[6]

General Order 11 was largely not carried out, but it was enforced in certain areas. Many Jews in northern Mississippi and Kentucky were ousted from their homes—fleeing north, in some cases on foot. But one of them, Cesar Kaskel of Paducah, Kentucky, managed to make his way to Washington and, accompanied by Congressman John Addison Gurley from Cincinnati, got an appointment with President Lincoln. Legend has it that the following exchange took place: "And so the children of Israel were driven from the happy land of Canaan?" the president said to Kaskel. "Yes, and that is why we have come unto Father Abraham's bosom, asking protection," came the reply. "And this protection they shall have at once," Lincoln is supposed to have said.[7]

Whether or not the exchange occurred precisely this way, Lincoln did ask General Henry Halleck, general-in-chief of the US Armies, to direct Grant to rescind the order. Lincoln later stated that "to condemn a class is, to say the least, to wrong the good with the bad. I do not like to hear a class or nationality condemned on account of a few sinners." The episode was significant not simply because it demonstrated that prejudice was still a burden for Jews. It also showed Jews that they could fight back. Grant never apologized for the order but clearly regretted it when he ran for president in 1868 and later wrote in his memoirs that the order was issued "without reflection." As president, Grant appointed Jews to public office and sought to reassure them of his intentions.[8]

In the South, meanwhile, Jews faced their own share of anti-Semitic prejudice. Nearly every major Southern city had Jewish populations—from

New Orleans and Charleston to Savannah, Atlanta, Memphis, Nashville, and Houston. As everywhere, Southern Jews ranged in professions. They were peddlers, teachers, musicians, lawyers, doctors, druggists, and of course storekeepers and merchants. Scholars presume that anyone prosperous enough to own slaves did. But Southern Jews' chief reason for supporting the secession had less to do with defending slavery than with expressing loyalty to their communities.

Many accounts suggest that although most Jews did not own slaves, they may have been especially comfortable in the South because they were part of a slave-owning class that could look down on the underclass of slaves as inferior, a rarity in any society in which Jews had lived in the world. "Whether so many Jews would have achieved so high a level of social, political, economic, and intellectual status and recognition, without the presence of the lowly and degraded slave, is indeed dubious," writes the historian Bertram Korn.[9]

Jews in the South had many reasons to enlist in the Confederate army, including social pressure and the lure of adventure. "Letters, memoirs, and obituaries all reflect Jewish soldiers' chief reasons for fighting: to do their duty, to protect their homeland, to protect southern rights and liberty and, once the war began, to support their comrades in arms," writes Robert N. Rosen, a historian of Jews in the Confederacy. But he also notes that Jews knew that they had to align themselves with monarchs and conservative regimes for self-protection.[10] Indeed, as the cause of secession faltered, anti-Semitism flared among those looking to cast blame for the South's difficulties. "The Jews are at work," a Confederate diarist wrote in 1861. "Having no nationality, all wars are harvests for them." Localities in some parts of the Confederacy sought to drive out Jews as dangerous and disloyal.[11]

While Judah P. Benjamin was seen in the North as a sinister Israelite Svengali and manipulator, he received much blame in the South for its disastrous diplomacy, including the failure to win support from France and Britain, and the imploding finances of the Confederacy. An irony lay in the fact that Benjamin was among a number of Jews in the South

who had intermarried and shed or at least downplayed their Jewish identity, including Lieutenant Governor Henry M. Hyams of Louisiana, and
Louisiana House Speaker Edwin Warren Moïse. Benjamin possessed impressive political and personal skills and was the first Jew to serve in the
United States Senate, from Louisiana. (David Levy Yulee of Florida had
earlier become the first person of Jewish heritage to serve as a senator,
from Florida, but he had formally converted to Christianity.) Benjamin
served as the Confederacy's attorney general before his appointment
as the South's top diplomat. Round-faced with curly hair and a close-
cropped beard, Benjamin was hailed as the smartest and wiliest member
of the Dixie cabinet by various commentators—the "brains" of the Confederacy, some said.

Benjamin may have left his Jewish identity behind, but it did not leave
him. When as senator he walked out of a debate about slavery and secession,
Henry Wilson, the abolitionist senator from Massachusetts, derided him as
a descendant of "that race that stoned Prophets and crucified the Redeemer
of the World."[12] On the other hand, after meeting with him in New Orleans,
Salomon de Rothschild of the Paris branch of the great banking family said
he found it "astonishing" that high positions in the Confederacy should be
"occupied by our coreligionists, or rather by those who were born into the
faith and who, having married Christian women, and without converting,
have forgotten the practices of their fathers." In a letter home, Rothschild
added that Benjamin had "a Jewish heart" and said he took an interest in him
"because I represent the greatest Jewish house in the world."[13]

In fact, Benjamin's biographer, Eli Evans, argues that he was "much
more steeped in Jewish culture and tradition" than most records indicate.
Though he did not speak or write about his religious beliefs, Evans argues that Benjamin was not a nonbeliever. He was, for example, son of a
founder of the Reform Society of Israelites in Charleston, South Carolina.
On the other hand, the evidence suggests that he led an unhappy personal
life, in part because of anti-Semitism. He had been expelled from Yale for
"ungentlemanly conduct," which has never been detailed. There has been
speculation that the charges could have involved anything from gambling

to petty theft, carousing, and homosexuality, stimulated perhaps by a whiff of religious prejudice. In New Orleans, he married Natalie St. Martin, of Catholic and Creole descent, whom he tried to please by purchasing a plantation near the city called Bellechasse, where he kept a retinue of 140 slaves. "Since Bellechasse was not a plantation handed down to him by an earlier generation, he came to slave owning late in life from an urban background," writes Evans. Benjamin never believed slavery was part of some divine order justified by the Bible and he "hated the cruelty of the overseers" of others in the Confederacy, Evans argues.[14]

A dozen years after marrying in 1833, Benjamin was abandoned by his wife and Ninette, their only child, who moved to France. During their separation, the couple saw each other only about once a year. The marriage was obviously a stormy one. Diaries from the era describe her as openly unfaithful with a string of men in Paris. But Benjamin never abandoned her. Instead, he threw himself into his work and became a confidant of Jefferson Davis, whom he helped persuade in the war's waning days to offer freedom to slaves in exchange for military service on behalf of the Confederacy—one of the oddest turns in a war based on the South's claims that the slaves were happy in their status.

As the Union overran Richmond and headed for a crushing victory, Benjamin burned his papers and escaped to England, where he rose to prominence as an international lawyer; he never returned to the United States. In the postwar era, his reputation was plagued by continuing suspicions of involvement in the conspiracy behind Lincoln's assassination, predicated evidently on the role he played in establishing a Confederate "spy ring" in Canada that was to function after the war, possibly as an insurgent group. Evans concludes that the evidence absolves both Benjamin and Davis in the assassination plot, though Davis served two years in prison on treason charges. (Three men and one woman were executed in 1865 for their roles in the assassination.) But anti-Semitism may have accounted for his decision to flee. Evans speculates that Benjamin knew that if he were captured, religious hatred would have prevented him from getting a fair trial. (Benjamin is buried at Père Lachaise cemetery in Paris.)[15]

## JEWS AND SLAVERY

As the case of Benjamin illustrates, it is impossible to talk about the Jews of the South in the Civil War without discussing their role in owning slaves and their disagreements over the institution itself. In some accounts, Jews have been singled out for an allegedly outsized role in slavery and the slave trade. In light of their history as traders of other goods from Europe to the Western hemisphere, there is little doubt that Jews had something of a role. The slave trade, which flourished between 1450 and 1800, has been examined carefully by scholars, who have documented the important role of Muslims, Catholics, Protestants, and pagans in Africa, as well as Jews. The conclusion from these examinations is that Jews did not play an exaggerated or disproportionate role.

One historian who has looked at the records, Seymour Drescher, contends that it was unlikely that more than a fraction of 1 percent of the 12 million people enslaved and transported from Africa were purchased or sold by Jewish merchants. "At no point along the continuum of the slave trade were Jews numerous enough, rich enough, and powerful enough to affect significantly the structure and flow of the slave trade or to diminish the suffering of its African victims," he concludes, although some of the slave trade was conducted by so-called New Christians, who were often Jewish converts whose abandonment of Judaism was forced on them by the inquisition in Spain and Portugal.[16]

Only a small proportion of Southern Jews were planters or plantation owners, and thus most were not slaveholders on a grand scale. Benjamin was a conspicuous exception with his plantation. He lived there in a mansion of spiral staircases and silver doorknobs, and had his slaves tend the rose gardens on the grounds—all in an effor to placate his wife. Scholarly examinations of wills show that a number of Jewish slaveholders were sensitive to the slaves' condition and treated them humanely. Some prominent Southern Jews emancipated their own slaves and openly supported the abolitionist cause. On the other hand, like many slaveholders, some Jews used their slaves as concubines. There is little doubt that

Southern Jews were supportive of slavery overall. One defender, Jacob N. Cardozo, editor and political economist, wrote: "Slavery brought not only great wealth to the South but to the slaves a greater share of its enjoyment than in many regions where the relation between employer and employee was based on wages." He also argued along with some Jewish scholars that the black race was obviously inferior to whites, as decreed by God.[17]

More striking perhaps is the fact that many Jews in the North, even those who supported the Union in the Civil War, were reluctant to condemn the institution of slavery or support the abolitionist cause. Their uncertainty stemmed from a lingering feeling of precariousness about their role in society. This Jewish reluctance irritated and disappointed some abolitionists who had hoped they could be allies. "The Jews of the United States have never taken any steps whatever with regard to the Slavery question," a report to the American and Foreign Anti-Slavery Society said in 1853, noting that Jews seemed reluctant to mobilize their community to address such explosive political issues.[18]

Abolitionist hopes for Jews to call upon their celebrated history of freedom from slavery in Egypt to be more sympathetic to the abolitionist cause thus were unfulfilled. What seems clear is that, lacking a clear direction or interpretation of the Bible, Jews tended to adhere to the beliefs of their neighbors, whether North or South—another example of their desire to Americanize their identity. In addition, many Jews maintained that it was inappropriate, if not dangerous, to speak in one voice on issues ostensibly outside their expertise and their own laws. This reluctance came at a time of genuine debate among Jews over whether slavery was acceptable or a moral sin, since the Bible seemed to countenance slavery even while imposing strict rules on how slaves should be treated and under what circumstances it was forbidden to return runaway slaves to their masters.

Another factor in Jewish uneasiness was that many fundamentalist Christian groups supporting abolition were not themselves tolerant of Jews. Some abolitionist leaders—including white preachers and pamphleteers like William Lloyd Garrison but also the great African American reformer and statesman Frederick Douglass—had gone so far as to denounce Jews as evildoers and killers of Christ. Garrison had attacked Mordecai Noah for Noah's anti-abolitionist writings, labeling him "a Jewish unbeliever, the enemy of Christ and Liberty." In another publication he called him "the miscreant Jew" and a "lineal descendant of the monsters who nailed Jesus to the cross between two thieves."[19]

The Jewish leaders most likely to side with abolitionists in the North came from the "reformer" camp, led by Rabbis Max Lilienthal of Cincinnati, Liebman Adler and Bernhard Felsenthal of Chicago, and S. M. Isaacs of New York. But it was not always easy for them. Isaacs's appeal for Jews to stand with the Union prompted a torrent of protests calling him Brutus and canceling subscriptions to *The Jewish Messenger*, where he was editor.

Perhaps the most active among these Northerners was the Reverend Sabato Morais of Mikveh Israel in Philadelphia, who referred to the Confederates as "misguided . . . disaffected children."[20] But his case also illustrates the problems of speaking out against slavery among Jews. Born and educated in Italy, where his father had been imprisoned for agitating with other revolutionaries to establish a republic, Morais passionately championed democracy in his sermons. Though not an outright abolitionist, he opposed the South's secession as a threat to democracy and stability. "We must have peace, but not at the cost of our national existence," he wrote. Morais was even more notable for his affection for Lincoln. He delivered a moving sermon when Lincoln's son, Willie, died in 1862, and some of his preaching stirred unease among those in his congregation sympathetic to the Democrats and the South. In 1864, when he seemed to advocate Lincoln's reelection, the board demanded that he get its approval for future sermons, provoking a counterreaction among his defenders. Disputes within the congregation continued to rage, culminating in another vote in 1865, granting him blanket permission on sermons.[21]

These change-oriented Americanizing rabbis acknowledged that African Americans were, on the whole, and with obvious exceptions, less

well educated than whites were. But they argued that the unequal status of blacks was not racial but the result of generations of mistreatment, subjugation, and deprivation of rights to education and of liberty. In doing so, they were mindful that lethal racial stereotypes had been used against Jews themselves, who were looked down on not simply because of their customs and traditions but because of their caricatured racial identities as big nosed, hunched over, and swarthy. The racial stereotypes of African Americans, to many Jews, ominously resembled anti-Semitic bigotry. Rabbi Felsenthal compared the plight of blacks specifically to the restrictions on Jews that kept them in backward conditions in the West for centuries. "The Jewish antislavery crusade was extraordinarily sensitive to charges of innate inferiority and civic inequality," writes the historian Jayme A. Sokolow. "They believed that slavery was not only wrong but dangerous. Its defenders could use their arguments against other groups, and thus all minorities had a stake in showing that the Blacks' shortcomings had environmental, not racial causes."[22]

It was easier for reform-oriented rabbis to condemn slavery despite its existence in the Bible. They had already been arguing that events depicted in Scripture should not be taken literally and instead understood in the context of their times. But slavery posed a tough dilemma for Isaac Mayer Wise, who criticized literal readings of the Bible but opted to stay out of the issue of whether the Bible justified slavery. Wise never made the argument advanced by many Jews that equated abolitionism with the story of Jews freed from slavery in Exodus, for example. His political leanings in Cincinnati were to the Democrats, the dominant party in the South. He supported Illinois senator Stephen A. Douglas against Lincoln for president in 1860 and even considered running for the state legislature in 1863 as a Democrat, only to be blocked by his synagogue board members.

In the years and months before the Civil War, as Democrats and antislavery Republicans argued over the issue, Wise's view was: a plague on both your houses. He worried more specifically that a war over secession would jeopardize the hard-won security of the Jewish people. "The fanatics in both sections of the country succeeded in destroying the most admirable

fabric of government," he wrote in *The Israelite* at the end of 1860. But he was repeatedly more willing to label the party of Lincoln as the fanatics who drove the nation to war, blasting antislavery politicians as disrupters bent on destroying the Union. During the war, he sided with the so-called Peace Democrats, or Copperheads, who urged a negotiated end to the conflict as argued by General George B. McClellan, fired by Lincoln only to run against him as the Democratic nominee in 1864.

Wise was never a personal fan of Lincoln, who stopped in Cincinnati on his way to his inauguration. The rabbi said the president-elect came across as "a country lawyer" likely to be overwhelmed by the job. "We have no doubt he is an honest man, and, as much as we can learn, also quite an intelligent man," Wise wrote. "But he will look queer in the White House, with his primitive manner."[23] But Wise's deeper concern was that the war would shatter the support systems for his own people and impede the cause of a unified Judaism sheltered by a secular American government. He thus held that peace was more important than using force to keep the South from seceding. Throughout the war, Wise sought to keep in touch with Jewish congregations in the North and the South and was determined to inform his own community in Cincinnati of how both sides were faring.

Isaac Leeser, Wise's traditionalist rival, had similar views, trying to straddle the middle in a conflict that spiraled down beyond compromise. Leeser was fearful that Jews taking anything like a collective stand on the issue would send a wrong message and jeopardize Jewish status. But his attempts at conciliation and discretion only drew fire from the combatants. "If anyone tried with desperate sincerity to occupy the unhappy, sad position of neutrality during the entire war period, it was the bachelor rabbi of Philadelphia," writes the historian Bertram Korn. Slavery proved another issue in which Leeser lacked the diplomatic skills to avoid antagonizing people. He tried to offer prayers for both sides in the war, while maintaining starchily that Jews must participate in politics individually but not collectively. But when he commended Confederate Jews for their loyalty to their cause, he was rebuked by a prominent Jewish lawyer in Philadelphia, Moses A. Dropsie. "You better take care what you say," Dropsie warned. "You are already on

the suspected list, and you may be compelled to quit the city before long!"
Leeser was so shaken by the warning that he wrote a letter to the mayor of
Philadelphia suggesting that he might leave the country altogether if the atmosphere was that hostile, and he sought reassurance that he would not be
expelled. The mayor replied that he should have no such fears.[24]

## SERMONS IN CONFLICT: RABBI RAPHALL "MUST KNOW"

The interregnum following Lincoln's election in November 1860 height-
ened fears of war throughout the soon-to-be disunited States. President
James Buchanan, hapless in the face of catastrophe, including the seizure of
Fort Sumter, proclaimed a National Fast Day on January 4, 1861, to pray for
the survival of the Union. There followed an extraordinary set of sermons
by rabbis that argued the cause of slavery on both sides. The debate stands
out as testimony not only to the division among Jews but to the divergent
ways that Jews in the mid-nineteenth century were hewing to their Talmudic traditions of literal interpretation of Scripture.

On one side, the pro-slavery argument was forcefully delivered by
Rabbi Morris Raphall, the renowned German-educated orator, linguist,
translator, and lecturer who had debated Poznanski about the Messiah in
Charleston. His New York congregation, B'nai Jeshurun, was a citadel of tradition, and Raphall's speech recapitulated his literalist take on the Talmud
and Scripture, impervious to modern conditions, rationality, and even, it
could be argued, common sense. It echoed the arguments he had outlined
when debating with Poznanski and in front of Wise a decade earlier.

Raphall's sermon, delivered to honor the day of fasting and sponsored
by the American Society for Promoting National Unity, was highly influential because of the rabbi's stature and because its arguments were widely
seen as effectively giving God's blessing to the very concept of slavery. The
remarks were a great comfort to slavery supporters and stirred more attention than any other sermon ever delivered by an American rabbi up
until that time. Many non-Jewish slavery advocates hailed Raphall for

supposedly settling the matter, an implicit (if ironic) endorsement of the authority of Jewish scholars over biblical interpretation, as if to say, "He's Jewish—he must know." The sermon was widely disseminated in the press. The *Richmond Daily Dispatch* praised it as "the most powerful argument delivered" by a clergyman. The Virginia governor, Wyndham Robertson, cited it as vindicating the South's battle for legitimacy, and it persuaded some clergy in the South to defend Jews as loyal citizens of the Confederacy.

On the other side of the debate were Rabbi Michael Heilprin, a Polish-American scholar, and Rabbi Einhorn, the militantly reformist leader based in Baltimore. Their arguments revealed how reformers and liberals were trying to apply broader interpretations to Jewish texts.

Raphall was hardly an outlier in his own community. His pro-slavery (or anti-abolitionist) stance probably reflected those of many Jews in New York City, a pro-Confederacy outpost at least at the outset of the war. New York was a Democratic-controlled commercial center with an economic base dependent on financing the cotton trade in the South. The mayor, Fernando Wood, a Tammany Hall sachem, spoke of the city seceding from the Union to side with the Confederacy. The New York City draft riots of 1863, in which white working-class protesters ransacked neighborhoods and murdered scores of blacks, were an outgrowth of the city's antipathy toward the Union cause. The city at the time was also the home of some forty thousand Jews on the eve of the conflict, or 5 percent of the city's population. Like commercial operations in the city as a whole, Jewish businesses were often tied to the South. The banking sector facilitated transactions between the regions, and the garment industry, where many Jews worked, produced 40 percent of the nation's clothing, dependent on cotton from the South and on Southerners (including slaves) as consumers of their goods. A prominent Jewish politician, Emmanuel Hart, who served in Congress in the early 1850s, was a leader of Wood's Tammany Hall and allied with its opposition to the abolitionist movement. But not everyone was pro-slavery. A cluster of anti-slavery Jews worshipped at Temple Emanu-El, already known as a reform-oriented congregation. Among its leaders were the Seligman family, which played a role in financing the war on the Union side, including the sale of bonds in their native Germany. After the war broke out, many Jewish leaders in the city like the Seligmans rallied patriotically to the Union's side.[25]

Raphall's sermon bears additional significance because of its explicit attack on rationalism as antithetical to religious faith, turning the teachings of Maimonides (among others) upside down. Beginning his sermon with a recollection of various biblical injunctions to humanity to cover itself in sackcloth to repent for its sins, Raphall noted the Southern slogan, "Cotton is King." But he had a telling riposte. The North, he charged, was asserting in effect: "Thought is King," as if rational thought would lead to a condemnation of slavery. "No, my friends, 'Cotton' is not King, and 'Human thought' is not King. . . . Hashem alone is King!" he declared, using a Hebrew word for God. He added that God countenances humans enslaving their fellow humans; it was a "pernicious fallacy" to argue otherwise.

Raphall's explication of the Bible included a discussion of the conditions of slaves in biblical times. Slavery in antiquity, he noted, is usually associated with wars, in which the victor had the right to enslave the conquered. One could also sell oneself into slavery to pay off a debt, and the Bible distinguishes between a Hebrew and a Canaanite slave. In Scripture, those in captivity in such circumstances were sometimes referred to as *eved* (sometimes spelled *ebed*), which is translated as both "slave" and "servant." "Facts are facts," he said, adding that there was not a single biblical text "which directly or indirectly denounces slaveholding as a sin."

To buttress his claims, Raphall began with the story of Noah's cursing his grandson Canaan, as recounted in Genesis 9:20–25. According to the biblical account, Noah planted a vineyard, got drunk from the wine it produced, and passed out naked in his tent. Noah's son Ham then saw his father's condition and related the fact, apparently disparagingly, to his brothers outside. Realizing what Ham had done, Noah mysteriously cursed Ham's son Canaan (rather than Ham himself), condemning Canaan to be "the slave of slaves" to his brothers. The passage is generally viewed by scholars as an ex post facto justification of the Israelites dwelling in the land bearing the name of Canaan. But traditional biblical interpretation at the time of Raphall held that, since Noah had granted much or all of the African continent to Ham (Genesis 10:620), the Canaanites of contemporary time were none other than "the African race," as Raphall put it in his sermon. In other words, Ham's descendants were the American slaves of modern times, Raphall reasoned—though a literal reading of Scripture makes no such claim.

If one could pick an example of Raphall's manipulation of scriptural interpretation, it would be his acknowledgment that Noah condemned an entire race to slavery without even knowing about slavery, since no slavery existed at the time of Noah. Taking the Bible's truth to be inviolable, Raphall theorized that Noah must have recalled slavery from an unnamed era before the Flood. The proof of the Bible's truth, he asserted, is the fact that the Jews did indeed conquer the Land of Canaan, just as the Bible predicted.

It is difficult not to see Raphall's reading of the Bible as fundamentally racist. "To this day it remains a fact which cannot be gainsaid that in his own native home, and generally throughout the world, the unfortunate negro is indeed the meanest of slaves," Raphall said, just as Noah had predicted. "Much has been said respecting the inferiority of his intellectual powers, and that no man of his race has ever inscribed his name on the Pantheon of human excellence, either mental or moral," Raphall asserted. "But this is a subject I will not discuss. I do not attempt to build up a theory, nor yet to defend the moral government of Providence. I state facts." As for the fact that the Hebrews were for at least four hundred years slaves in Egypt, he cited various biblical passages to suggest that the particular enslavement *of Jews* was *not* willed by God.

One of the contemporary figures condemned by Raphall in his sermon was the Reverend Henry Ward Beecher, of Brooklyn, a distinguished abolitionist and brother of Harriet Beecher Stowe, author of *Uncle Tom's Cabin*. Beecher, Raphall declared, was especially ignorant of both the Old and the New Testaments, which authorized slavery by "all Christian nations during many centuries." He further noted that the Ten Commandments as reviewed in Deuteronomy 5:14 commanded a day of rest for "thy male slave and thy female slave," and because the Ten Commandments had also prohibited coveting a neighbor's slaves (Exodus 20:14, Deuteronomy 5:18), slavery must be legitimate in the eyes of God. As if speaking to Beecher, Raphall demanded: "How dare you, in the face of the sanction and protection afforded to slave property in the Ten Commandments—how dare you denounce slaveholding as a sin?" By what right, he went on, did Beecher have to insult the many God-fearing, law-abiding people of the South and denigrate their moral worth and patriotism, equating them with murderers, adulterers, thieves, and other sinners?

And yet the rabbi, perhaps feeling ill at ease over the subject, offered a note of caution. Scripture, he concluded, makes clear that slaves must not be coveted, mistreated, or subjected to cruelty and lust of the slave owner— protections not prevailing in the United States. In effect, he seemed to be saying that though slavery exists in the Bible, the South's system did not necessarily deserve biblical approbation. "This, indeed, is the great distinction which the Bible view of slavery derives from its divine source," Raphall said. "The slave is a *person* in whom the dignity of human nature is to be respected; *he has rights*. Whereas, the heathen view of slavery which prevailed at Rome, and which, I am sorry to say, is adopted in the South, reduces the slave to a *thing*, and a thing can have no rights."[26] His sermon is thus seen by some as a plea for mutual tolerance between North and South, though it is most remembered for its defense of the peculiar institution.

## SLAVERY AS A "MORAL EVIL"

There were two major rebuttals to Raphall's defense of slavery. One by Michael Heilprin—a scholar descended from generations of rabbis, and an editor at the *New American Cyclopaedia*, who had supported the 1848 revolution in his native Hungary—probably gained the wider audience. Published in the *New York Daily Tribune* less than a week after Raphall's Sermon, it presented a sweeping rejection of his analysis.[27]

"I had read similar nonsense hundreds of times before," declared Heilprin. But now he was dismayed to find that Christian churches were validating Raphall's conclusions. "Day after day brings hosannahs to the Hebrew defamer of the law of his nation; and his words are trumpeted through the land as if he were the messenger of a new salvation," Heilprin lamented, tarring Jews as worshippers of a "God of Slavery." The idea that the curse of Ham justifies slavery is no more logical, he said, than saying that the story of Cain and Abel justifies murder. He asserted that the proper translation of the word *eved* was as "servant" rather than "slave," and that such people were in any case accorded a variety of protections and privileges under Jewish law. Under some circumstances, depending on whether a slave was a Hebrew or a Canaanite, a runaway had to be returned to his or her master, he noted, alluding implicitly to the divisive issue of the rights of runaways in the Dred Scott decision of the Supreme Court.

The depiction of Ham as the progenitor of "the negro," Heilprin declared, was "full of falsehood, nonsense, and blasphemy!" Condemned throughout history as "cursed" killers of Christ, Jews especially should see the dangers of such calumnies, he said. If slavery should be considered legitimate, why not also condone biblically sanctioned practices, such as prostitution, polygamy, and incest? Or even the rule of kings, since the prophets appeal to Israelites not to install a king—described as a sin against God. Must Jews see all kings in that light, or only the kings described in Scripture?

Of interest in Heilprin's critique is its implication for the role of the Talmud itself. Echoing the comments of "reformers" seeking to overthrow the authority of rabbinical rules, he noted that the Talmud itself commands scholars not to take every passage of the Bible literally—for example, the prescription of an eye for an eye in punishment. Rather than endorsing slavery, people must instead embrace the "divine spirit of truth, justice, and mercy" pervading the Bible, rejecting those parts of it that are "contradictory, unjust, and even barbarous."

If Heilprin's stirring appeal can be read as filled with compassion and scholarship, Rabbi David Einhorn's rebuttal comes across as argumentative, sarcastic, and contemptuous. Underlying his sermon is the familiar argument that interpretation of the Bible must rest not on universal or immutable meaning of words, but on the cultural context of the historical period in which the words were written. We do not sit in judgment on Abraham and his slaves, not to mention polygamy, he said, "because we look upon him from the standpoint of his time."

But that does not mean that slavery is anything less than a "moral evil," he noted. Unjustly subjugated across the globe, Jews must not shrink from labeling it as such. At stake, he said, is the very concept that humanity is capable of achieving progress, eradicating disease, and correcting injustices, including no longer burning witches and heretics at the stake or sacrificing children—practices sanctioned in ancient times. Freeing the Jews from slavery in Egypt would have made no sense if God intended slavery as it existed to be continued in perpetuity. Freedom, he said, must triumph over ancient prejudices and the "hallowed atrocities" of the past.

Raphall's attempt at humility—he had said he was not making a personal judgment about slavery, only discerning God's intent—was derided by Einhorn as an attempt to replace his head covering with a glittering "crown of martyrdom." By implication, Einhorn was declaring a nearly existential redefinition of the foundations of Judaism. Yes, Judaism is a religion based more than any other on the reading of text. But what is that text? Is it the word of God? Is it history? Is it something that must guide human relations for a Jew even if one has to torture the reading of it to find justification? If Noah's curse applies to Canaanites, what could one make of the fact that Canaanites—as modern ethnologists had begun to note—were also Semites, like Hebrews? The "negro" slaves "must decline the honor of having been destined by Noah," said Einhorn. And if the Ten Commandments outlaw coveting a neighbor's property, including servants or slaves, did it then mean that the neighbor's wife was also his property, just as his house, field, ox, or ass were his property? And if the Bible was so sacrosanct, did that mean that a man could acquire a second wife of his own free will, as the Bible allowed? If so, Scripture would seem to have justified the acquisition of twenty wives!

Raphall's supposed high-minded criticism of the Confederacy for its cruel treatment of slaves was also dismissed in withering terms by Einhorn as a "gross contradiction" of everything he said to justify the practice. A Bible declaring that God created man in His image, and that all humans are descended from Adam and Eve, can never approve of slavery, Einhorn said at last. A book that commands man not to deprive the mother bird of the birds in her nest cannot be the same book that forces a human mother to be deprived of her child.

"The [Ten Commandments], the first of which is: 'I am the Lord, thy God, who brought thee out of the land of Egypt—out of the house of bondage' can by no means want to place slavery of any human-being under divine sanction," Einhorn declared. Raphall, he added, had further "entangled himself in his own net" by trying to lay out rules for extradition of runaway slaves, inadvertently *strengthening* the case for a ban on slavery.

In conclusion, Einhorn acknowledged that some in his own Baltimore congregation might disagree with him about these issues. Such concern about speaking out as war clouds gathered was justifiable. "The Jew has special cause to be conservative, and he is doubly and triply so in a country which grants him all the spiritual and material privileges he can wish for," Einhorn said, with evident feeling. "He wants peace at every price and trembles for the preservation of the Union like a true son for the life of a dangerously sick mother.... From the depth of my soul, I share your patriotic sentiments, and cherish no more fervent wish than that God may soon grant us the deeply yearned-for peace."

Yet the sanctity of Jewish law and teachings must not be disgraced in the interest of politics, Einhorn said. The principles of Judaism had served as a weapon for its people for thousands of years: "This weapon we cannot forfeit without pressing a mighty sword into the hands of our foes. This pride and renown, the only one which we possess, we will not and dare not allow ourselves to be robbed of. This would be unscrupulous, prove the greatest triumph of our adversaries and our own *destruction,* and would be paying too dearly for the fleeting, wavering favor of the moment."

Had Christians in Europe justified their oppression of Jews based on Scripture, Jews would have protested to the heavens, rightly declaring such actions blasphemy, Einhorn declared. They can do no less now. "And are we in America to ignore this mischief done by a *Jewish* preacher?" he asked. "Only such Jews, who prize the dollar more highly than their God and their religion, can demand or even approve of this!"[28]

Einhorn acknowledged that he was "no politician," which was certainly an understatement. As the war erupted, his antislavery sermons, delivered in German, proved to be his undoing in his adopted city of Baltimore. The city was a crucial staging area for Union troops, an essential line of defense for the nation's capital, against what Lincoln feared would be attacks from the north and east as well as the west in Virginia. Baltimore was also a heavily Democratic city with strong sympathies to the South, stirring incessant fears on the Union side about keeping its loyalty to the North in tow.

Like New York City, Baltimore had also become a major center for American Jews, with perhaps 5,000 to 7,000 families on the eve of the Civil War. Many if not most of them were Democrats who believed that the Constitution protected slavery. The first ordained rabbi in the United States, Abraham Rice, who was serving at Baltimore's Congregation Nidche Israel, was a defender of slavery, as was Rabbi Bernard Illowy of Baltimore Hebrew Congregation. Illowy said one could not blame the South "for seceding from a society whose government cannot or will not protect the property, rights and privileges" of slaveholders. Like other traditionalists, Illowy cited the Bible's several references to slaveholding by the patriarch Abraham.

Caught in the center as sympathetic to both sides were Rabbis Henry Hochheimer of Baltimore Hebrew Congregation and Benjamin Szold of Temple Oheb Shalom. Both pleaded for reconciliation of North and South lest war destroy what they regarded as a new and secure refuge for Jews. Szold, a change-oriented rabbi who used a prayer book omitting references to the Messiah, spoke of America as a place where God "hast given us another home in place of that which we lost in the land of our fathers." Szold explicitly shied away from the issue of whether the Bible countenanced slavery, acknowledging truth on both sides—and that "free reasoning" could find the ultimate truth.

Einhorn's refusal to mince words made him an outlier in his adopted city, and in its Jewish community. He was controversial not just for his fiery beliefs and withering attacks on Raphall and others, but also because of his argument that Jews should not hide their religious beliefs from public view, even if they ran counter to the beliefs of the majority outside the Jewish community. He thus challenged the long-held concern among Jewish leaders that their Judaism was their business and that they had better not speak out collectively as Jews and jeopardize their sense of belonging in the United States. His beliefs were a foreshadowing of the emerging doctrine that Jews were exponents of universal ethical precepts, and that it was their "mission," their duty, to disseminate them to the world. "Jews for thousands of years consciously or unconsciously were fighting for freedom of conscience," said Einhorn, adding that they must "fight for the whole world" and not their narrow interests.[29]

Given the volatile situation in Baltimore—where mobs favoring secession attacked places believed to be sympathetic to the North, including abolitionist publications affiliated with Einhorn—concerns mounted for the rabbi's safety. Fearing for his life, Einhorn asked his congregation for permission to leave the city and fled to Philadelphia. Because of threats of reprisals even after he left, Har Sinai asked him not to speak out even in his new redoubt, in another of the many instances of synagogue boards questioning the freedom of speech of their rabbis. In this case, inevitably, Einhorn refused and remained bitter about his experience with his board members and other slavery sympathizers in Baltimore. He never returned to his home city.

## LINCOLN AND THE JEWS: A LAST TESTAMENT

On March 4, 1865, as the Union armies overran the South and moved closer to securing victory in a catastrophic war, Lincoln took the oath of office for a second term on the Capitol's eastern steps. It was a blustery rain-drenched day that turned the entire area into a sea of mud. But the sun burst through the clouds as the beleaguered president stepped to the podium, lighting up the inaugural stand as if God had cast celestial light on the day's momentous proceedings.

God's will and judgment figured throughout Lincoln's address, as it had throughout his presidency. He asserted that if all the wealth accumulated and blood spilled from 250 years of slavery were to be repaid by an equivalent loss of treasure and blood in the Civil War, such a fate must be accepted as God's will. Lincoln's biographer, David Herbert Donald, has termed this cold reference to divine retribution, even at the horrific level caused by the war, "one of the most terrible statements ever made by an American public official."[30]

Yet Lincoln clearly knew the dangers of invoking God to justify one's actions, especially when he observed, speaking of North and South: "Both read the same Bible and pray to the same God, and each invokes His aid against the other." It was a statement true of Jews as well as Christians.

A month and a half later, on the morning of April 15, 1865, Rabbi Elkan Cohn was about to ascend his pulpit for Shabbat services at Congregation Emanu-El, the reform-oriented synagogue in San Francisco, when someone handed him a note. Cohn, an émigré from Poland with a graying beard and wire-rim glasses, silently read the news: Abraham Lincoln had been shot and killed the night before, on Good Friday, in Washington. Overcome with shock, the rabbi wept and sank to the floor. After getting to the bima, Rabbi Cohn made the announcement: "Lincoln, the twice-anointed high priest in the sanctuary of our Republic, has fallen a bloody victim to treason and assassination, and is no more," he intoned. The congregants then burst into tears themselves. "Arise, my brethren, and bow in humble devotion before God!" Rabbi Cohn declared. "Arise, and honor the memory of the blessed, whose life was a blessing to us."

In Philadelphia, Rabbi Leeser shed his mixed feelings about the war as he also lost his composure on the same morning and apologized to his congregation for doing so. In another part of Philadelphia, Rabbi Morais told Congregation Mikveh Israel: "I loved every action, every word of that godly man." Sadly, he added, Lincoln's critics could not see underneath his rough-hewn exterior to the "inestimable and precious" qualities that Lincoln brought to his office. Rabbi Einhorn, speaking his German vernacular, told the Philadelphia congregation to which he had moved that Lincoln, like Moses, had "led his people through a long, bleak desert to the border of Canaan, and was not allowed to enter it." If Lincoln had a flaw, Einhorn said, it was his "excessive leniency towards the rebels" in the South. And in Kentucky, Lewis Naphthali Dembitz, a prominent attorney, said the Jews of Louisville referred humorously to Lincoln as "Rabbi Abraham." Rabbi Isaac Mayer Wise called Lincoln a messiah for his country and a man of great principle—and even asserted the dubious proposition that Lincoln was of Jewish heritage. In an essay in *Die Deborah* on April 28, 1865, Wise elaborated on his improbable claim that "Lincoln maintained before four witnesses, I being one of them, that he believed he was descended from Jewish parents, and he insisted that his face had Jewish features, which was indeed so."[31]

Lincoln has the unique distinction of being revered as both an American Moses and an American Jesus. For Jews, like Moses, Lincoln freed the slaves only to be barred from the Promised Land. For both Jews and Christians, he was a man of godlike humility who died for American sins. It was almost as if his prophetic second inaugural address only a few weeks earlier had come true—that the "terrible" assertion that the war's bloodshed had served as divine restitution for the sins of slavery had been fulfilled. Now Lincoln had been nailed to the cross and murdered so that America might experience the "new birth of freedom" he had called for in the Gettysburg Address. It was hard for Americans, especially Jews, not to see him and his murder in a deeply religious and redemptive context.

Just as historical interpretations of the Civil War have evolved over time, so too have the interpretations of the role of Jews in the war and its causes. In the first century or so after the war, Jews continued to seek to weave their experience into the mainstream narrative of American history, retelling and almost fetishizing stories about Abraham Lincoln's encounters with Jews.

Perhaps the best-known Jew to interact with Lincoln was Isachar

Zacharie, a foot doctor who treated the president's bunions and is often cited as a key to what was the president's sympathy for Jews in general. The conversations between Lincoln and his doctor were said to have ranged through many subjects and included a share of gossip, since Zacharie also treated various members of Lincoln's cabinet, the Senate, and the Union's commanding general and thorn in Lincoln's side, George P. McClellan. Lincoln even dispatched Zacharie to New Orleans after it fell to Union forces. There Zacharie treated a number of prominent people for their foot problems and sent back impressions to the White House.

Zacharie's most famous mission entailed a trip to the Confederate capital of Richmond in 1863 to discuss a possible accommodation between North and South. When aspects of his discussions came to light— supposedly involving a scheme for the Confederacy to attack Napoleon III's French troops in Mexico, oust Emperor Maximilian, and install Jefferson Davis as president of Mexico—they were widely ridiculed. Although Zacharie presciently proposed establishment of a Jewish homeland in Palestine, which Lincoln apparently found worthy of consideration, he was clearly part clever ingratiator, part self-promoter, part genuine patriot, and perhaps even part spy. He was certainly one of the strangest characters in the annals of Jewish American history, not to mention Lincoln's personal associations.[32]

Many other Jews appear to have interacted with Lincoln, among them Edward Rosewater, who is said to have transmitted the Emancipation Proclamation by telegraph; Samuel Huttenbauer, who sold Lincoln suspenders and collar buttons from his peddler's pushcart; and Samuel G. Alschuler, a photographer who captured Lincoln in an early portrait, having lent his own coat to the future president for the sitting. Another figure, Abraham Jonas, was a political activist who befriended Lincoln in his Whig Party days in the Illinois legislature and supported his nomination at the Republican convention in 1860.

After Lincoln's death, the Gettysburg Address was translated and recited in Yiddish. The identification of Lincoln as "Rabbi Abraham" and "Father Abraham" later figured in a landmark publication in 1927 of *Abraham*

*Lincoln: The Tribute of the Synagogue,* which consisted of sermons and eulogies by rabbis and prominent Jews following his assassination.

Jewish histories in the century after the Civil War paralleled the histories of the war written for all Americans. The political bargain that installed President Rutherford Hayes in the White House in 1877 officially ended Reconstruction and ushered in the depredations of Jim Crow laws reinstituting racial subjugation and the deliberate amnesia and romanticizing of the South and its "Lost Cause." Initially sanitized accounts of the role Jews played in the war emphasized that the conflict was caused by many factors—sectional, economic, cultural—beyond the dispute over slavery. Jewish histories in turn bought into the interpretation of the conflict as a painful domestic disruption interrupting the progress that accompanied the making of modern America, a time of shared sacrifice and common cause, with Jews playing the role of loyal citizens of whichever part of the country they inhabited.

"The key elements of the dominant depiction of the war—loyal Jewish service to the North and South, the reciprocated Jewish love of Lincoln, and the braininess of [Judah P.] Benjamin—echoed the reconciliatory spirit of the broader historiography in the early decades of the twentieth century," writes Adam Mendelsohn, adding that this was a "convenient" way of looking at history, allowing historians to overlook Jewish slaveholding, support for slavery, and other unpleasant facts. This approach "allowed a superficial discussion of Southern Jewish slaveholding that avoided troubling questions about morality and responsibility and enabled the resurrection of Judah P. Benjamin as a communal hero."[33]

In *The American Jew as Patriot, Soldier and Citizen* (published in 1895), Simon Wolf, who was the B'nai B'rith representative in Washington, D.C., sought to demonstrate the loyalty of Jews to their new country. His book, an encyclopedic account of Jewish participation in both sides, showed that Jews signed up to fight in larger proportions than adherents of other religions. It was largely written as a rejoinder to Mark Twain, who had earlier denigrated Jews as soldiers.

In 1896, Max Kohler, a New York lawyer who wrote frequently for the American Jewish Historical Society, argued that slaveholding in general by Jews, and the slaveholding of Benjamin, demonstrated that Jews were "receptive and assimilative" to their environment. Acknowledging that Benjamin was not an observant or practicing Jew, Kohler hailed him as the "most distinguished statesman, orator and lawyer, that American Jewry has produced."[34] On the other hand, not one statue of Benjamin appears to have been erected throughout the South in the post-Reconstruction period, despite his supposed reputation as "the brains" of the Confederacy. Jews in the region were not exactly rushing to honor him.

Scholars argue that a historiographic sea change after World War II brought a new willingness by researchers to look hard at the darker sides of the American Jewish experience. By the 1950s, the weight of growing impatience over the legacy of Jim Crow and the stirrings of the struggle over civil rights burst forth. It was time for Jews themselves to confront the issue of Jewish support of slavery, and to explore the reality behind the myth that Jews were loyal to the South because they were trying to integrate themselves into American society.

The main Jewish advocate of this revisionism was Bertram Korn, an ordained rabbi who had served as a chaplain in the Marines during World War II. His 1951 book, *Jews in the Civil War*, raised multiple questions about the Jewish role, including their participation in slavery. Korn joined with a handful of other historians to challenge the consensus and he took it even further, looking fearlessly at Jewish slaveholding and at Benjamin himself.

Still, the reverence for Lincoln has permeated Jewish American tradition down through the ages. After Lincoln's assassination, a Jewish shopkeeper in Buffalo, New York, Julius E. Francis, collected Civil War and Lincoln memorabilia, displaying them in his store and campaigning for Lincoln's birthday, February 12, to be a national holiday—the cause of his life, he said. Francis died in 1881, after founding the Buffalo Lincoln's Birthday Association, which continued work that is widely credited with the success of making Lincoln's birthday the holiday it has become. In 1909, to commemorate the one hundredth birthday of Lincoln, Victor David Brenner, a Jewish sculptor originally from Lithuania, designed the profile of Lincoln in bronze that remains on the penny. In 1942, the composer Aaron Copland wrote his stirring "Lincoln Portrait," a musical accompaniment to Lincoln's words. Most recently, Steven Spielberg's 2012 movie *Lincoln*, with its screenplay by Tony Kushner, was another case of two Jews enshrining Lincoln as a saint.

The attachment of Jews to Lincoln is historically appropriate. There is after all little doubt that the Civil War transformed the status of Jews in the United States, fusing their religious identity with the fate of their adopted country. Brought to a new level of status and prosperity, American Jews were ready to transform their own relationship with Judaism. But that challenge was to be fraught with peril, discord, and struggle.

Ten

# PROSPER AND DIVIDE

As the Gilded Age beckoned after the Civil War, Jews shared in the turbulent but steady economic growth of postbellum America, attaining greater material, social, and cultural status than Jews had ever enjoyed in modern history. The Civil War shattered the South, reducing it to smoldering ruins, but most of the country thrived despite intermittent economic crises through the rest of the century. Leaders of the increasingly prosperous Jewish community optimistically proclaimed that a new era had arrived in which they could take their place alongside non-Jews, enjoying American secular values as virtual coreligionists. The term *Judeo-Christian*, which had begun as a derisive way of describing Jewish converts, was becoming a phrase characterizing the common spiritual and ethical legacy of two Abrahamic religions.

Signaling their self-confidence and prosperity, Jewish communities built monumental synagogues of Moorish or Byzantine design and marble and gilt décor throughout the country, copying the fashion in some parts of Germany. Especially in the big cities, synagogues moved into statelier houses of worship that reflected Jewish self-confidence and prosperity. "The acquisition of a synagogue edifice with the accompanying display of civic recognition and patriotic affirmation became a symbol of belonging in the new society," writes the scholar Leon Jick. By the 1860s, he writes "there was hardly a congregation in America which did not build a large and sumptuous new edifice."[1]

Isaac Mayer Wise's congregation, Bene Yeshurun, which he joined after leaving Albany in 1854, started construction of its synagogue in downtown Cincinnati on Plum Street while the Civil War was still raging. With three arched entrances crowned by minarets and dedicated in 1866, it became the second largest Jewish temple in America, located proudly near city hall and the leading Unitarian and Catholic churches. A prominent Cincinnati architect, James Keys Wilson, designed the building to evoke the Alhambra, the fortress and castle at Granada in Spain, and by implication the Golden Age of Judaism in Spain before the Inquisition. Following the German trend, the edifice was called the Plum Street Temple. Its vaulting interior was lit by gaslight chandeliers and candelabras, and a rose stained-glass window seemed to conjure the atmosphere of a Gothic cathedral, improbably flanked along the walls by Hebrew texts, primarily from Psalms. Other Jewish congregations in New York, San Francisco, and Philadelphia followed suit with similar ornate and grandiose constructions. Like the new building in Cincinnati, those synagogues included such Christian-inspired innovations as a choir loft, an organ, and mixed seating in pews.

Wise had joined Bene Yeshurun in Cincinnati only after telling its leadership to ignore what he said were false stories about his alleged "disbelieving in the immortality of the soul, future reward and punishment and the final redemption of Israel." These allegations, he said, were "positively not true." Under his leadership, in addition to erecting its new building, Bene Yeshurun set about enforcing decorum, eliminating obscure prayers, and banning the sale of "honors" or *mitzvot*, such as the honor of making a blessing over the Torah before the Torah reading. A choir was organized, an organ was introduced, and Wise disseminated his first draft of *Minhag America*, omitting prayers for the return of Palestine and the restoration of the Davidic dynasty.[2]

It was from this Jewish cathedral that Wise would later establish the foundations of modern Reform Judaism: the Union of American Hebrew Congregations (1873), the Hebrew Union College (1875), and the Central Conference of American Rabbis (1889). The tripartite architecture of these institutions came over time to be adopted by all American Judaism branches: seminary, rabbinical conference, and congregational organization.

Similar reform practices in this post–Civil War period spread throughout many congregations and many parts of the country, including the western frontiers, where Jews began to see themselves as trailblazers far from home. They were not so much bent on Reform but on creating synagogues compatible with their new community consensus, which was not easy when there was diversity of views, whether traditional vs. nontraditional, or Polish vs. German, or Bavarian vs. Bohemian.

The first Reform congregation in Chicago, established as the Juedische Reformverein (Jewish Reform Society) in 1858, followed the pattern. In 1861 it took the name Chicago Sinai Congregation and recruited Bernhard Felsenthal, a former teacher in Bavaria who had been teaching school and writing for Jewish periodicals, as its rabbi. Felsenthal didn't think of himself as a rabbi, but the Sinai congregation hardly seemed to care.

Sinai was one of the early American exponents of the redefinition of the Jewish people as the equivalent of the Messiah. As its preamble put it: "We are deeply convinced that Israel has been called by God to be the Messiah of the nations and to spread truth and virtue on earth. In order to fulfill this high mission, Israel has to undergo a process of purification in its own midst. . . . The special mission of American Israel, therefore, is to place Judaism before the world, purified in doctrine and conduct, and so to become a shining example for Israelites the world over."

In accordance with its reform spirit, Sinai reduced the observance of holidays from two days to one, read the Torah in Hebrew in a cycle of three years, and read the Haftarah in English. The congregation called for a solemn service accompanied by choral and organ music, no discrimination against women, no "bombastic words" or "bad taste" and "unnecessary repetition," and finally a ban on "wailing over oppression and persecution." The congregation also called for the omission of "prayers for the restoration of the sacrificial cult, for Israel's return to Palestine, the expression of the hope for a personal Messiah and for a resurrection of the body."[3]

The historian Marc Lee Raphael has discerned at least twenty such reforms that were the most popular. Many were clearly adopted from church practices or with an effort to streamline the service so that it did not try the patience of worshippers. After the Civil War, the organ became increasingly popular; dozens of congregations installed one. The organ at Temple Emanu-El in New York, which moved in 1868 to its newly built and immense Moorish structure with two minaretlike spires on Fifth Avenue and Forty-Third Street, was said to be the biggest in the country except for the one in the Music Hall in Boston.

In addition to the organ, and the increasingly widespread use of the word *temple*, many synagogues continued to embrace such rules of decorum as making sure that prayers be chanted in unison, and that sitting and standing be done together. The motives for such changes was complex, but historians agree that one purpose was overriding. "They generally liked the idea that their houses of worship resemble those of their Christian neighbors," writes Hasia Diner. "They wanted to give the synagogue all the dignity of an American religious institution."[4]

Some synagogues went further, demanding "orderly dress" and others imposing fines on those who talked loudly out of turn, cracked jokes, wandered in and out, or even engaged in "loud kissing" of their *tzitzit*, or fringes on their prayer shawls. There were even disagreements about who was supposed to impose the sense of dignity and correctness that the new Jews aspired to. "Apparently one source of disorder was the cacophony of loud calls for order," comments the historian Leon Jick.[5]

In addition to halting the bidding wars for blessings over the Torah, the congregations moved in this period to eliminate special blessings recited by the *kohanim*, i.e., descendants of the Jewish priestly caste, typically those named Cohen. They also trimmed the number of verses read in each service and moved to the three-year cycle of reading the Torah. Another widespread practice, eliminating the second day of Jewish holidays, was a recognition of modern communications in the world Jews were living in. The practice of celebrating such holidays for two days began in ancient times, dictated by Judaism's lunisolar calendar. The rationale was that people living some distance from Jerusalem could never be sure when the new month had been officially proclaimed. Because of this uncertainty, it became customary to sanctify the new month as well as the start of any festival occurring in that month two days outside the land of Israel. In later times, although the Hebrew calendar came to be systematized and the uncertainty disappeared, the two-day observance of holy days and festivals was continued nonetheless. To reformers, the second day was no longer justified. Another popular reform came with the introduction of choirs that included men and women singing together. Some also included non-Jews. More than a few congregations substituted a cornet or trumpet for a shofar (ram's horn) in celebrating the Jewish new year. Insisting on prayer shawls and yarmulkes was also left by the wayside, even on Yom Kippur, the Day of Atonement, when wearing a shawl is intended to remind male worshippers of a shroud, evoking their mortality.

Another increasingly popular step was moving the hazan to the front of the sanctuary facing the congregation rather than in the midst of the congregation facing the ark. (The ark was traditionally placed to the east, so that worshippers would be facing Jerusalem, but this practice also was adjusted for practical or architectural reasons.) This step continued the earlier trend of making the service into more of a theatrical experience and reinforcing the feeling that worshippers were in an audience rather than in a participatory exercise. Some congregations went further, eliminating outright the singing or chanting of prayers by the congregation in favor of leaving the music entirely to the choir and an organist. Though some critics worried that Jewish services were emulating church services, many congregations carried the steps out precisely for that reason.

The broad impetus for these changes was both high-minded and cynical. On the one hand, they were aimed at attracting younger, Americanized Jews, but they also sought to make Jewish ritual more acceptable and comfortable to non-Jewish friends and Gentile visitors. Yet in subtle ways the changes had a profound impact on the nature of Jewish worship. In exchange for the participatory and familiar cacophony of tradition, they bought into a more docile and even submissive experience. The old rowdy atmosphere gave way to services that came to resemble a distant spectacle, in which worshippers were instructed on what to read, when to sing—and of course when to stand and when to sit. Welcome as the changes were to many Jews, going to the synagogue lost a great deal of its endearing boisterousness.

Along with mixed seating, many synagogues joined the trend of eliminating the requirement that male worshippers cover their heads, usually with *yarmulkes* (*kippas*). (Congregation Keneseth Israel in Philadelphia prohibited head coverings outright.) Bar mitzvahs (the ceremony of reading from the Torah for boys turning the age of thirteen) were often replaced by a confirmation ceremony, usually associated with older teenagers, as conducted by churches. Aside from eliminating many of the ancient prayers composed by anonymous sages many centuries earlier, congregations took another significant step: discarding prayers and passages deemed offensive to cosmopolitan sensibilities, such as the chapter in the Book of Esther (invoked during the Purim holiday) reporting that the Jews in Persian times had avenged the threats against them by killing 75,000 of their enemies. Torah readings on the Sabbath were in many cases spoken rather than chanted. The Haftarah was read in English or omitted altogether, and more English was introduced for prayers in general. To counter the declining attendance at Shabbat services on Saturday morning, often because of work demands on congregation members, many synagogues promoted Friday evening services at a fixed hour, though not as a substitute for morning services the next day. Friday services welcoming the Sabbath (Kabbalat

Shabbat) had long been customary, but were first introduced by Temple Emanu-El in New York in 1861 as a possible alternative to Jews unable to attend services the next day. The practice spread after by Isaac Mayer Wise adopted it in Cincinnati in 1866, when he set the services at a fixed time rather than sunset. Today these services are a common occurrence in more traditional congregations as well.

The sermon was also becoming an increasingly standard feature of the service, not only in reform-oriented but also more traditional congregations, which had no problem with the practice that had been reintroduced in America by Leeser decades earlier. Sermons had long existed throughout Jewish history, but in the newly revised worship services, rabbis found that sermons were an especially effective way to communicate and establish bonds with their congregants. The earliest sermons in many congregations were in German, the native language of the new wave of immigrants. English gradually replaced German starting in the late 1840s. In 1850, Wise printed a sermon "on the theology of Moses" that was highly publicized, helping to popularize the use of English in sermons. Jews realized that sermons had served as a popular drawing card and social occasions for churches, and a practice that if emulated could draw in more worshippers. Speechifying had become increasingly popular on the American scene generally, with politicians, professional lecturers, and preachers entertaining sizable crowds with their rhetorical skills. Sermons for many thus became the centerpiece of the service, an educational experience that attracted Jews and persuaded them to bring their Gentile friends so that they could experience the meaning of Judaism. Once synagogues saw that sermons would attract members, they began to seek out rabbis for their ability to speak eloquently from the pulpit. Orating became an essential qualification for aspiring rabbis, and for recruiting them.[6]

Along with these changes came the important cultural shift then under way throughout the United States, in non-Jewish as well as Jewish circles— the elevation of the status of women. Segregation of the sexes in synagogues had been a feature that non-Jews found curious for some time. In 1744, a visitor to Shearith Israel in New York City deplored the balcony seating area for women as a "hen coop." The spectacle had not changed more than a century later when James Gordon Bennett, editor of the *New York Herald*, visited Shearith Israel on Yom Kippur in 1836 and spoke of the "degradation" of women as "the great error of the Jews." Bennett deplored what he said were women "separated and huddled into a gallery like beautiful crockery ware, while the men perform the ceremonies below." He added that the Hebrew prayer "I thank thee, Lord, that I am not a woman" ought to be superseded by the Christian prayer "I praise thee, Lord, that I and my wife are immortal."

Segregating men and women in synagogues, which remains the rule in Orthodox services today, has long been an emotional issue, pitting the goal of strengthening family unity against the relegation of women to a partitioned-off place to prevent contact, including eye contact, between the sexes. The lower status of women in Judaism is reinforced by their being barred from official roles in the religious service. (In the modern world, the ancient principle of segregating men and women can be seen on airline flights in which ultra-Orthodox Jews demand to be separated from women.)[7]

The actual binding nature of this rule is not clear. Traditional Judaism held that the mixing of men and women was a violation of Jewish law, and an unacceptable concession to assimilation and loss of Jewish identity, as well as a step intended to make Judaism more like Christianity. In fact, Christian churches often had the same practice in medieval and later times—usually men and women sat on opposite sides of the central aisle. But many churches abolished segregation of the sexes in the eighteenth and nineteenth centuries. As they did so, pressure accelerated on Jewish congregations, whose members were becoming increasingly acquainted with practices outside their Jewish milieu. Though Temple Emanu-El in New York started mixed seating. Rabbi Wise maintained in his memoirs that he popularized the practice in Albany, at the Ansche Emeth synagogue, where he served after being ousted at Beth El. In part, the move was a necessity because the second congregation moved into a church where there was no balcony or upstairs where women could sit separately.

Traditionalists felt so strongly—there was also a genuine belief that mixed seating would promote sexual promiscuity—that they sometimes tried to block the changes in court, as they had done in opposing the installation of an organ in South Carolina. That is what happened in New York, where B'nai Jeshurun—the second oldest congregation in the city—had long hewed to the conservative side.

The congregation, located at Thirty-Fourth Street (the current site of Macy's), was going through travails as it navigated the pressures of tradition and change. B'nai Jeshurun's founding Ashkenazi members had adopted less formal practices of Jewish services when it left the Sephardic-oriented Shearith Israel in 1825. But it remained relatively traditional, having played a role in 1859 in establishing the Board of Directors of American Israelites, a conservative group uneasy with changes instituted by reformers. B'nai Jeshurun had earlier introduced reforms in the category of "decorum," including the chanting of prayers in unison. It moved the hazan's desk to the front of the synagogue, introduced special robes for the rabbi and cantor, and initiated a confirmation ceremony while abolishing obscurantist prayers. The issue of family seating had been much discussed in the 1860s under the reign of Rabbi Raphall, the staunch traditionalist who had denounced Wise over the issue of the Messiah and defended slavery during the Civil War. But Raphall, who opposed such a step, died in 1868. His death paved the way for internal soul searching over adapting to modern times. Finally, after many years of disputing the issue, each time amid resignation threats, a majority elected to conform with "modern taste and culture" in 1874. They voted 55 to 30 not only to introduce an organ into the service but also to adopt the practice of men and women sitting together, hoping to satisfy its younger members.

Dissenters, feeling betrayed, turned for help to Israel Salomon, son of Jonas Salomon, a longtime member of the congregation. Young Salomon had once been antiestablishment himself, having led the battle for more voting rights for the congregation. He had withdrawn in protest from B'nai Jeshurun and formed a new breakaway congregation, only to return and serve as B'nai Jeshurun's president (parnas). To block the change to mixed seating, Salomon did what traditionalist Jews in South Carolina had done before: he went to court.

At issue in the case of *Israel Solomon* [sic] *v. The Congregation B'nai Jeshurun* was the prerogative of the synagogue to make rules against the wishes of a pew "owner." But in his complaint, Salomon said men and women sitting together was "immodest" and "unchaste," and that adopting mixed seating had unlawfully deprived him of the seats he had purchased. He filed affidavits from several Orthodox community leaders and rabbis at other synagogues attesting to the practice as "promiscuous" in a divine setting and in violation of German-Polish traditions.

The congregation countered that its changes were well within its prerogative and that mixed seating was a practice recognized "throughout the civilized world"—and that bringing households together in prayer would strengthen ties of each family to God and Judaism. Among those brought in by change advocates to file affidavits were Einhorn and Wise, all of whom assured the judge that family seating "is not antagonistic to the teachings of the Holy Scripture and the Talmud." The judge in the matter sided with the congregation, saying—as the judge in the organ case in South Carolina had—that the decision was for the synagogue itself to make.

Once again, the ruling dealt a blow to the Orthodox claim that they could use the government's judicial branch to enforce tradition, as had been the practice in the days of ghettos in Europe. Unhappy with the decision, more than thirty congregation members resigned in protest. They were quickly replaced by new members. Under a new rabbi, Henry Jacobs, hired in 1877, B'nai Jeshurun later adhered to a middle ground and remained a conservative-leaning congregation in a sea of reformers in New York. The advocates of family togetherness and women's equality had won. For the traditionalists, the victory represented not only the rejection of tradition and law, but also "Christianization" of the service and the encouragement of sexual license.[8]

Meanwhile, changes at Temple Emanu-El in New York were proceeding, in many ways more quickly than those introduced by Wise in Albany.

The synagogue maintained separate seating for men and women in the 1840s but installed family pews, a mixed choir, and other innovations in the 1850s. It also abolished the prayer shawl and the second day of most festivals. Later came the installation of an organ, abolition of the sale of honors at the Torah, and use of a hymn book with German hymns. By 1868, a bit late by the standards of some other temples, Emanu-El introduced some English into the service when it moved to its new structure on Forty-Third Street off Fifth Avenue. The temple also established religious schools and drew worshippers from the most prosperous part of society in New York City before the Civil War. Rabbi Merzbacher had compiled a new English prayer book in 1855, *Seder Tefilah: The Order of Prayer for Divine Service.* Known as the "Merzbacher prayer book," its pages were arranged to be read from right to left. Though it referred to the resurrection of the dead and the restoration of the Temple, it omitted references to angels, animal sacrifices, and passages from Scripture that referred to revenge and death visited upon the enemies of Israel.

Another striking change in Temple Emanu-El's liturgy was the elimination of *kol nidre* ("all vows"), the Aramaic proclamation annulling vows made before God, which is sung by Jews at the opening of the Day of Atonement service on the eve of Yom Kippur. The prayer, perhaps first introduced to nullify forced conversions or other acts of adherence to another faith, developed an emotional following despite the fact that many authorities had questioned its legal validity. Though understood by those who recite it as an effort to clear one's conscience and reconcile with God, the prayer had been expunged from many prayer books in Europe out of concern that it might reinforce a Christian prejudice that Jews could not be trusted to keep their promises.

The prayer book also changed the liturgy from saying that God "resurrects the dead" to one that says God "renews everything." Merzbacher was a major believer in what he called Enlightenment terminology embracing reason, progress, and truth and said that many parts of the traditional worship service were "thoughtless" and unintelligible, filled with "dogmatic particularism," and "inappropriate to our present social and political condition." His prayer book was used only in some congregations. Merzbacher's successor at Emanu-El, James K. Gutheim, declared that he wanted a Judaism "stripped of ritualistic observances" so that "rational progress" would "chase away the dense clouds of superstition that darken the religious horizon." He rejected the traditionalist belief that Moses's encounter with God at Sinai produced the Oral Law with its hundreds of rituals and observances. Instead, he said the "mission from Sinai" was the "spirit of God" calling humanity to a high level of ethical behavior.[9] Merzbacher's prayer book, later amended by his successor, Samuel Adler, never caught on among other Reform-minded Jews, and many Orthodox Jews banished it as heretical.

For all these changes, it took some time for women to gain status in American synagogues. The irony was that although congregation membership in the United States was frequently restricted to men, it was increasingly the women who made the Torah covers, brought their children to services, taught Sunday school, contributed to fundraising, and served as the mainstays of synagogue attendance. Through female auxiliaries and ladies' benevolent associations, women took some synagogue activities away from men. In the process, they grew comfortable with their authority and began pressing for equal status, rights, and decision making. Women's fiction also began appearing in periodicals like the *Occident* and *Jewish Messenger*.

The best-known pioneer for women in mid-century, Rebecca Gratz of Philadelphia, the daughter of a wealthy merchant, was active in civic organizations that were opening up to women. From her involvement in Philadelphia's Protestant-dominated charities, Gratz went on to establish the Female Hebrew Benevolent Society in 1819—the first Jewish women's benevolent organization and the first Jewish charity in Philadelphia outside of the synagogue. It was a precursor to the creation of Jewish charitable organizations functioning apart from synagogue control and to women playing a prominent role in it. She later helped to initiate the Jewish Sunday school movement.

Women also aspired to positions of leadership in synagogues and in

these outside organizations, and rebelled against the traditional requirement that they go through a ritual bath in a *mikveh* seven days after men-
struating. Some but not all synagogues built mikvehs, and some were built
independently for the whole Jewish community. Debates flared over the
appropriateness of women bathing in such circumstances, a fact causing
some chagrin in a country where such matters were not considered acceptable as a publicly discussed subject.

Yet even these reformers adhered to traditions to retain their Jewish
identity. They festooned their buildings with the Star of David (which appears to date from the seventeenth century as a popular symbol to compete
with the Christian cross) and depictions of the tablets of the Ten Commandments. The tablet was an image originally created to depict a medieval notebook—two slabs of wood with rounded tops, hinged together to
protect the wax surfaces on which words could be inscribed. Sometimes,
as in the Plum Street Synagogue, these images appeared alongside or near
stained-glass windows evoking the décor of churches. The Star of David
eventually became ubiquitous on books, tombstones, and other objects
of religious significance. There were of course the prayers at the center
of these objects: principally the Shema, "Hear O Israel," from Deuteronomy, recited as a daily reminder of Jewish belief in one God and inscribed in mezuzahs on the doorposts of synagogues and Jewish homes.
In another tradition, some Reform congregations continued to employ a
non-Jew to light candles or ovens on the Sabbath, functioning as a figure
sometimes called the "Shabbos goy." Prominent New York Reform Jews
such as Jacob Schiff refrained from working on the Sabbath. Diaries of
other Jews in this period recalled keeping the Sabbath as well. The Jewish press reported that major businesses around the country shuttered
on Saturdays, although some businesses opened on Saturday afternoons.
Even those who worked kept to other customs on the Sabbath, such as
the ritual blessing of children, blessings over wine and bread, and saying
Grace or reciting appropriate Psalms. In a striking continuation of this
pattern, Jews did tend to close their stores for the High Holidays. Some
Jewish congregations that had introduced mixed seating during the year

reverted to separating the sexes during Rosh Hashanah and Yom Kippur. Many synagogues baked matzo and shipped it to other parts of the country during Passover.

Yet fealty to Judaism was far short of universal. A census in 1850 had calculated that only 35 percent of America's Jews could be accommodated by the number of synagogues then in existence. As many as half of America's Jews are believed to have been unaffiliated in the middle of the nineteenth century, and Jewish leaders were beginning to deplore their disaffection or indifference. A separate study in 1870 found that a third of Jews in the United States were still hewing to religious traditions, another third were in varying degrees of Reform congregating, and another third neglected Judaism except for the High Holidays.

What seemed to be happening was that as long as their leaders and rabbis kept up the traditions, Jews felt they did not have to do so themselves. Toward the end of the century, at least some of the nonbelievers further broke away and became active in their hostility to religion. Some took up socialism and free thinking, including holding dinner parties on Yom Kippur in deliberate violation of the rules of fasting. These challenges grew bolder with the arrival of Jews from Eastern Europe and Russia after the 1880s.

Still there is little doubt that the post–Civil War period gave Jews a sense of triumph in their adopted land. The Christian church at the time was itself divided into an array of branches, so Jews could more easily see themselves as part of a rich variety of different religious branches while sharing common roots in the Hebrew Bible. Judaism in America thus evolved into a kind of cafeteria approach in which Jews could select different choices emphasizing everything from deep faith in God to those doubting that God intervened in the daily existence of the world.[10]

The "Judaism as marketplace" fit in with a new spirit of freedom. Jews felt they did not need to explain to others why they chose some practices over others. Instead they sought to adopt those parts of Judaism that fit in with their lifestyles and self-definitions as Americans, even as they were determined to keep their Jewish identities. The records kept by synagogues and communities show that Jews across the country wanted to support their places of worship, be buried in Jewish cemeteries, and have their boys circumcised—even if it meant summoning mohels to travel hundreds of miles to carry out the practice. There were some cases of the Jewish press containing advertisements for mohels—sometimes expressing the hope that a mohel could come to a community and also function as a kosher butcher![11] (Psalm 149:6 was often cited as biblical proof that these two professions went together.)

Because of all these developments, Wise could probably be forgiven for declaring that rigidly traditional Judaism was in retreat if not outright defeat. Yes, nearly every urban Jewish community in the mid-nineteenth century had at least one traditional congregation. Their existence was important historically, because these communities were positioned to welcome the Eastern European Jews who migrated in such large numbers toward the end of the century. But the handful of Orthodox congregations in post–Civil War America appear to have had little impact on the Jewish community and even on Jewish consciousness. A commentator observed in the 1870s that "the meager residues of Orthodoxy which one still finds in this land are insignificant."[12]

Wise took pride in this phenomenon, declaring in 1866 that perhaps only 50 congregations out of 300 in the United States adhered to "what used to be called orthodoxy." He said he was proud of the innovations that included men and women singing together in choirs and sitting together in the synagogue; organs; sermons and hymns in English; and abandonment of prayers for the Messiah, resurrection of the dead, and returning to Palestine to carry out animal sacrifices at the Temple in Jerusalem.[13] "Everywhere the temples of Israel, the monuments of progressive Judaism, as though touched by a magic wand, rise in proud magnificence, and proclaim with a thundering voice, we are right, and you are wrong," he declared, insisting that the few traditionalist synagogues left in America were "harmless remnants of bygone days." He asserted that Orthodoxy was withering away, and that the goal was within reach of uniting Judaism in America under one roof. Within fifty years, he predicted, Judaism would be seen as a universal heritage of the American people based on Jewish teachings enshrining the principles of God, justice, virtuous behavior, and perfecting humanity. These goals, he confidently declared, would be seen as the shared legacy of Jews and Christians alike.[14]

But first Wise would have to forge unity among Jews themselves, a task that proved more difficult than he acknowledged.

*Eleven*

# REFORMISTS AND RADICALS

The success achieved by rabbis and Jewish leaders in establishing an American Judaism persuaded Wise to try to institutionalize his goal of Jewish unity, including the general adoption of his prayer book *Minhag America*. The *Israelite*, his weekly newspaper that was a rival to the *Occident* in Philadelphia and the *Asmonean* in New York, gave him a platform for his agenda. He grandly compared himself to nothing less than Isaiah as the avatar of modern Judaism, citing the passage as applying to himself: "And I heard the voice of the Lord saying: whom shall I send and who shall go for us? And I said: behold here I am, send me."[1]

Another opportunity for working toward these goals emerged as Wise and other Jewish leaders laid plans for the next big conclave of Jewish rabbinical leaders. It was to be in Philadelphia in 1869 and was convened by Samuel Adler of Temple Emanu-El in New York, the German-born scholar who had succeeded Merzbacher a few years earlier. Only a dozen like-minded reformers seemed to be invited, and they conferred at the private home of Samuel Hirsch, a former chief rabbi of the Grand Duchy of Luxembourg who had moved to Congregation Keneseth Israel in Philadelphia a few years earlier. Both Adler and Hirsch had previously attended reform-minded European rabbinical conferences, where they probably got the idea of organizing similar meetings in America. The Philadelphia group met in November for four days, with Wise show-ing up on the second day. On the whole, the conference went smoothly, though there were disagreements under the surface over the direction of reform. Wise did clash with his nemesis, David Einhorn, on a few key matters.

But this Philadelphia conference achieved consensus on the important matter of opposing prayers calling for the restoration of the Jewish state in the Holy Land. The conferees also discarded the principle that the destruc-tion of the ancient Temple in Jerusalem was the product of God's wrath over the sins of the Jewish people. This idea of God's retribution, implicit in the Hebrew Bible prophets inveighing against the sins of the Jews and no doubt written by authors seeking to explain the destruction, had been a theme of Jewish teachings throughout history.

In the place of the traditional view of God punishing the Jews for their sinful and wayward conduct, the conference endorsed the teaching that the Temple's destruction and the Jews' dispersal was part of a divine plan "for the realization of their high-priestly mission, to lead the nations to the true knowledge and worship of G-d." At one level, this revisionist theme of punishment leading to a blessed outcome reflected a longstanding belief in the redemptive power of religious devotion overcoming sin and destruc-tion, a powerful theme in Scripture since ancient times. This theme also has echoes in the Catholic teachings of St. Augustine, St. Thomas Aquinas, and most majestically in John Milton's *Paradise Lost*, in which the expulsion of Adam and Eve from Eden—the "original sin"—is interpreted theologi-cally as a "happy fall" ( *felix culpa*) because it leads to eventual redemption for humankind following the teachings of Jesus Christ (*Paradise Regained*). But for the Jews of Philadelphia to explicitly revise the concept of being punished for ancient sins, and to embrace a new "high-priestly mission" in the world vouchsafed by God, marked a significant redefinition of their role, now woven into a larger sense of national purpose that had been a part of American history and culture as well. Jews were thus aligning themselves increasingly with the ethos of America—the "city upon on a hill"—and consciously assigning themselves the role of delivering the ethical message at the heart of the Hebrew Bible and the center of the American spirit.

The rabbis in Philadelphia, echoing the trend sought to make explicit their commitment to jettison prayers for the Messiah, the resurrection of the dead, and the restoration of ancient rites of the Temple. The Philadelphia attendees declared further that prayer in Jewish services should be in an intelligible language to reduce the alienation among younger Jews.

The Philadelphia conference proved a landmark in the Jewish effort to distance itself from identity as a "nation" or "people," as well as from Jewish traditional practices. In doing so, it effectively fulfilled the legacy of the principles enunciated in 1824 in Charleston, South Carolina, that "this country is our Palestine, this city our Jerusalem, this House of God our Temple."[2]

Some other steps by the delegates in Philadelphia illustrated evolving attitudes toward the condition of women and families. In weddings, the Philadelphia rabbis slightly elevated women's status by calling for the bride to give a ring to her husband and utter the same vow in Hebrew as he did. The rabbis declared their opposition to polygamy, which was then practiced by Mormons in America and some Jews (as well as Muslims) in parts of the Middle East. Also disavowed were extramarital relations and marriage restrictions between Jews from priestly lineage and other Jews. They accepted civil divorce and discarded the use of the *get*, the divorce document by a husband to his wife in order to effectuate their divorce. Substituting civil divorce for the religious ritual did concern some of the rabbis, who felt that divorce was altogether too easy in some states. They insisted on retaining the right of rabbis to refuse officiating in a second marriage if they felt the civil divorce was too flimsy to observe.

Wise and Einhorn clashed over what proved to be the most contentious disagreement at the 1869 Philadelphia conference—circumcision,
a sensitive matter theologically, racially, and of course physically. Both
rabbis agreed that the son of a Jewish mother was a Jew, whether circumcised or not, a principle that remains universally accepted in Judaism.
But Wise went further, believing that Judaism was more of a universal
religion and asserting that a Jewish convert need not be circumcised.
That was too far for Einhorn, who generally opposed efforts to convert
non-Jews. Einhorn argued (no doubt correctly) that the circumcision requirement—if the person was already circumcised, it was carried out by
a ritual cutting and drawing of blood—would deter conversions, which
was his objective. His argument carried the day, and requiring circumcision for conversions was retained. Einhorn's uncompromising view about
circumcision demonstrated that even for a reform-minded Jew, the religion of sense of Judaism as a distinct people with a tribal legacy should
not be entirely obliterated.[3]

Philadelphia marked another milestone in the tactical calculations of
Isaac Mayer Wise. His participation signaled a willingness to join the van-
guard of reform, even radical reform, if the ultimate objective of unity was
attained. But as soon as the Philadelphia parley concluded, it came under
attack by tradition-minded rabbis. Nervous that Philadelphia had gone too
far, Wise later backtracked, complaining that the manifesto from that conclave was excessively negative and "Einhornian"—a case of "innovations for
the sake of innovation, and reform for the sake of reform." The Philadelphia
manifesto, he said, was not binding, an assertion that only served to arouse
the suspicions of liberal reformers.[4]

## MINHAG AMERICA STRUGGLES
## FOR ACCEPTANCE

In the wake of the Philadelphia conclave, Wise and his allies pursued three
major new objectives. First was to establish a union of Jewish congregations for reform-minded believers and as many traditionalists as they could

encourage to join. Second was to establish a seminary to train rabbis along the same ecumenical lines. Third was to establish Wise's beloved *Minhag America* as a prayer book for all American Jews.

First proposed as a goal by Wise in 1847 shortly after he came to America, *Minhag America* had its first incarnation in Cincinnati in 1857. Although it was accepted among many congregations, Wise was continually open to making changes to widen its usage. But as previously noted, it started with such reforms as removing references to a "personal" messiah, rebuilding the Temple, and the restoration of the priesthood and the Davidic dynasty. Instead of the resurrection of the dead, the prayer book referred nonspecifically to the immortality of the human soul.

For all its reforms, Wise's prayer book hewed to tradition in its structure. It was thus more conservative than a rival prayer book introduced and used by David Einhorn called *Olat Tamid* (*Eternal Offering*), first published in 1856. Never one for understatement, Einhorn condemned Wise's moves to establish *Minhag America* as a universal prayer book, excoriating it as "an abortion" and Wise as "the Barnum of the Jewish pulpit" who "arrogates to himself the role of dictator." Yet Wise pressed ahead with negotiations to make more revisions of *Minhag America*, adopting such additional reforms as an abandonment of the second day of festivals and permitting worshippers to attend without head coverings. His prayer book group decided to complete its revision the next summer in 1871 in Cincinnati. The group also supported Wise's dream for establishment of a seminary in Cincinnati and still another synod of like-minded congregations.

Wise's dreams seemed to be on the verge of fulfillment—until he once again stumbled into controversy. This time it was over his proposals to reconstruct the Yom Kippur (Day of Atonement) service. To the surprise of even some allies, he declared that the most sacred holiday of the Jewish calendar, a time of Jews atoning their sins and asking God's forgiveness, was based on a fallacy. Seeking forgiveness for one's sins on a specific day of the year made no sense, he declared, because of the underlying assumption that God is a "personal" entity who forgives individuals once they atone. Asking forgiveness, and even beseeching God for comfort and blessings, certainly implies that God actually does forgive or provide such sustenance—which Wise denied. In reasoning this way, Wise was getting perilously close to questioning a core principle of prayer itself. Even for Jews moving away from belief in a God who could answer prayers and intercede in the affairs of humankind, it was a jolt to hear Wise belittle such prayers as effectively delusional.

Wise's comments were heatedly rejected by numerous colleagues, many of whom declared in the Jewish press that Wise and his supporters were echoing the heresies of Spinoza. Wise responded with a further explanation. God, he declared, is infinite and absolute in embodying love, justice, holiness, and universal values—"unlimited, eternal and infinite" in nature—but not "personal," in the literal sense of a bearded elder intervening with his fingertips in the manner of Michelangelo's depiction of God as Zeus. Though these comments might have seemed unobjectionable to any reform-minded Jew who had thought through the implications of a nonpersonal God, the opportunity for Wise's rivals in the nontraditional camp was irresistible. The animus toward Wise on the left drove many reformers into the camp of traditionalists attacking Wise. It was a historic stumble for him. He may have viewed his remarks as honest, reflecting his willingness to challenge orthodox thinking. But Wise's enemies seized on his comments to use against him.[5]

Leading the charge was an indignant Einhorn. Having been attacked himself as a heretic, Einhorn now could turn the tables and accuse Wise of heresy. In addition, a phalanx of fourteen rabbis of various persuasions denounced Wise as "utterly incompetent to represent Judaism." It was not the defense of a noncorporeal God that bothered them. Rather it was the implication that prayer was meaningless. They accused him of "flagrant blasphemies," "impious desecration" of truth, an embrace of "heathen" beliefs, and of renouncing Judaism itself. Judaism, these rabbis asserted, teaches divine grace and mercy through Scripture and holds out forgiveness for the repenting sinner. More rabbis joined the free-for-all as the weeks went on.

As usual, Wise ignored the substantive charge and attacked the motives, fitness, and competence of his critics. "They started from falsehoods, progressed in wickedness, and landed in a hell of absurdity," he wrote. "We pity the innocent poor individuals who have been beguiled by Satan to set their names to that protest." He even went so far as to accuse them of waging an Inquisition.[6]

Wise had his defenders, but the planned Cincinnati meeting of 1871 foundered on the issue of—of all things—God. Supporting Wise was Rabbi Jacob Mayer of Cleveland, a well-known radical who had himself been accused of apostasy. "I believe not in a personal God, neither do I address my prayer to a personal God," Mayer said. But so many other leaders denounced Wise that his scheme for a congregational union and seminary was set back, at least for the time being.[7]

## FATEFUL PARLEY IN CINCINNATI

Immobilized by controversy over his ill-advised comments on prayer, Wise was compelled to yield in the 1870s to the lay president of the Bene Yeshurun congregation to propose another conference to set up a union of Jewish congregations, a seminary, and a body of laws that all could accept. This parley was to involve leaders from the Midwestern and Southern regions. Chagrined and feeling sidelined, Wise still expected to manipulate events to his advantage. His reasoning was that his ideas might gain better currency and be less toxic if promoted by lay leaders rather than by himself.

The call went out, accordingly, from Moritz Loth, president of Bene Yeshurun and a successful businessman, author, and traditionalist, to set up a conclave that would bring these issues to a head. The conference then called for a Union of American Hebrew Congregations, provided that no doctrines or rules be imposed on any of its members. The proposed seminary, or theological institute, would also be careful not to promote one doctrine over another.

The seminary proposal was part of an American trend that coincided with efforts by many Protestant denominations to set up their own religious academies. The Berkeley Divinity School at Yale and the Warburg Theological Seminary (Lutheran) in Dubuque had been established in 1854, and the Wesley Theological Seminary (Methodist) was planned for 1882 in Washington, D.C. Loth called for the Jewish seminary to publish teaching materials and, for the most part, to adhere to traditional laws on the Sabbath, circumcision, and diet. These conservative principles had the effect of bringing at least some Orthodox congregations in the city into the process. Previously, all American rabbis had been trained in Europe.

The proceedings also led to the Union of American Hebrew Congregations (UAHC), born in Cincinnati in July 1873, which brought together thirty-four congregations and two thousand members from thirteen states and proudly boasted that it was the first such body in Jewish history. (The Union later changed its name to the Union for Reform Judaism in 2003 and represents, through congregations, about a third of American Jews who consider themselves to be members of a synagogue.) But in its inception, the Union was more of a regional than a national organization. Most members were from smaller towns throughout the West and South. Loth was elected president of the new union, and the board was dominated by Cincinnati representatives. Though not its progenitor, Wise recognized that Loth had fulfilled one of his dreams, likening it to the coming of the Messiah or at least the restoration of the rule of King David.

The Union quickly grew to seventy-two congregations by 1874, though congregations in New York and other parts of the East looked askance and remained holdouts until a few years later. A major step forward occurred when the Board of Delegates of American Israelites, the East Coast Orthodox grouping founded before the Civil War, and previously derided by Wise, merged with the Union in 1878. (The Board had opened its own seminary, Maimonides College, in 1867 in Philadelphia with Leeser as provost, but the college foundered after Leeser's death and none of its students ever received rabbinical ordination from that seminary.) By the end of the decade of the 1870s, the Union commanded allegiance from 118 congregations, including some more traditional in nature and had become one of the largest Jewish organizations in the United States.

The Union of American Hebrew Congregations begat its sister institution, Hebrew Union College, which had only one paid instructor and Wise as part-time head of the faculty. In 1873, Wise had persuaded Henry Adler, a wealthy businessman in Lawrenceberg, Indiana, to put up $10,000 as a challenge grant to establish the seminary. Adler agreed, provided that the seminary opened in two years; otherwise he would take back the funds. As a result, a grand total of nine teenage students showed up when classes started in the fall of 1875. Most of them attended regular studies in their secular schools, but at the College they were confronted with a rigorous classical Jewish education and taught to read the Talmud and other commentaries. Again, at least at the outset, Wise did not want to stir controversy with a wholesale abandonment of ancient teachings. The seminary's formula for success was its determination to bring in both conservatives and radicals to teach and participate in panels. Wise and his cautious tactics drew praise even from long-standing skeptics such as Rabbi Bernhard Felsenthal, a Chicago-based Reform advocate who declared that with the new institutions established in Cincinnati, Wise had become head "of all Israel in the United States. . . . It is he who gives shape and color and character to our Jewish affairs. He is the central sun, around which the planets and *trabants* [satellites] are moving, some near to him, some more distant. That is all right, and we submit to the hard facts. He has succeeded, and 'nothing is so successful as the success.'"[8] Proud of his triumph in including the Board of Delegates and other traditionalists, Wise later declared: "I managed very well with Orthodoxy, with which later I ate very heartily, drank and launched toasts."[9]

Yet signs of restiveness persisted among traditionalists in this same period. In the nation's capital, the citadel of reform was Washington Hebrew Congregation, established in 1852 by twenty-one German-speaking worshippers as the city's first Jewish congregation. They first met at a private home on Pennsylvania Avenue. Fearing that Jews might be denied the right to build a synagogue, they petitioned President Franklin Pierce for permission to build one and he signed an order establishing it in 1856. In 1863, a converted church at Eighth and I Streets became its first permanent location. The congregation quickly adopted mixed seating and other reforms, but when an organ was added in 1869, thirty-eight members resigned in displeasure and established Adas Israel (Congregation of Israel). Adas located itself in a series of rented buildings, including a loft over a carriage factory near the Capitol. By 1873, though struggling over funds, the members managed to build a brick synagogue with a small cupola at Sixth and G Streets, NW, and President Ulysses S. Grant—his record of anti-Semitism during the Civil War apparently forgiven—attended the dedication in 1876. (The location is today the Lillian and Albert Small Jewish Museum.)[10]

Another schism opened in 1871 in Baltimore, where conservatives established Congregation Chizuk Amuno (Strengthening the Faith) and broke away from Baltimore Hebrew Congregation, which had started out as strictly Orthodox in 1845 under Rabbi Rice but more recently had adopted a variety of reforms over the objection of conservatives. In Rochester, New York, Congregation Beth Israel was founded in 1874 by traditionalists seeking to differentiate themselves from Reform-oriented Berith Kodesh.

By the mid-1870s, Wise could surely take some satisfaction over the trend toward both unity and reform in the mid-1870s. But he was also feeling restless. His wife, Theresa, was suffering with a debilitating illness beyond his ability to handle. (She died in 1874 after a long and painful decline.) He changed the name of his newspaper from *The Israelite* to *The American Israelite*, signaling a belief that he was fulfilling his dream of an American Judaism. In late 1873, despite his triumphs, he flirted with quitting Bene Yeshurun, but eventually decided to stay and build on his accomplishments.

Instead, the 1870s brought a conflict between Wise and Jewish establishment reformers on one side and a surprising new force on the other—one that rejected tradition so thoroughly that it broke from Judaism altogether. To Wise, Einhorn, and other mainstream Jewish figures, this threat was potentially more lethal to American Judaism than the rearguard actions of the traditionalists.

## CHALLENGE FROM THE ATHEISTS:
## THE FREE RELIGIOUS ASSOCIATION

The origins of the new conflict between the Jewish establishment and those who rejected God altogether had been long in coming. One might even trace its roots to Spinoza. But one modern point of origin occurred in the spring of 1867, when Ralph Waldo Emerson—the essayist, lecturer, poet, and founder of the Transcendental movement—was invited to address the opening session of a new organization called the Free Religious Association. In the audience in Boston were adherents of a wide range of religious views, from Quakers and Unitarians to agnostics, feminists (including the abolitionist and women's rights advocate Lucretia Mott), and spiritualists. Also in attendance and embracing Emerson were Rabbis Isaac Mayer Wise and Max Lilienthal.

Emerson, the son of a Unitarian minister, had seemed destined from his early age to follow in his father's footsteps. After his graduation from Harvard, he spent time in South Carolina and Florida and became an ardent foe of slavery. He then attended Harvard Divinity School and became a pastor in Boston. The death of Emerson's beloved wife, Ellen, in 1830 was one of many blows to his faith, however. Complaining about the church's outdated practices and doctrines, he resigned the ministry in 1832 and founded the Transcendental Club with like-minded intellectual skeptics of religion in 1836. In a speech at Harvard Divinity School in 1838, Emerson challenged the existence of miracles in the Bible and proclaimed that Jesus was not divine.

Now at the Free Religious Association in 1867, Emerson went even further. He declared that churches and religious creeds had become obsolete. The audience, he said, should look elsewhere for spiritual sustenance. "The church is not large enough for the man," he declared. "It cannot inspire the enthusiasm which is the parent of everything good in history, which makes the romance of history. For that enthusiasm, you must have something greater than yourselves, and not less."[11]

Revered as the apostle of individualism and New England rectitude—and a friend of Melville, Thoreau, Hawthorne, and Emily Dickinson—Emerson was a magnetic but seemingly unlikely figure for Jews seeking common cause. In fact, Wise was paying careful attention to the Free Religious Association and had maintained strong ties with some Protestant religious reformers as he rose to prominence. His acquaintances included Octavius Brooks

Frothingham, a prominent Unitarian and the first president of the Free Religious Association. Wise, no doubt flattered to be asked to find common
ground with the Protestant aristocracy, became a board member of the association and a vice president. Wise had also been in regular contact with the
reform-minded abolitionist minister, the Reverend Theodore Parker of the
Unitarian Church in Boston, whose advocacy of "a church without tyranny,
a society without ignorance, want, or crime, a state without oppression" influenced Wise's writings about modernity and the origins of Christianity.[12]

But another Jewish intellectual eager to become involved in the association was destined to play a divisive role in American Judaism. That figure
was Felix Adler, son of the chief rabbi at Temple Emanu-El in New York.
Expected by his family to succeed his father in that position, Felix Adler had
other plans and broke with Judaism altogether. He later established the New
York Society for Ethical Culture in 1876, to the consternation of his family
and also of Rabbi Wise.

The story of the fraught relationship between Wise and Adler begins,
however, with the legacy of the Second Great Awakening of the early nineteenth century in America. Advances in science and philosophy had accelerated the trend of religious believers rethinking some of their most basic
assumptions. Along with their more skeptical view of religious dogma, Emerson and like-minded reformists opposed what they saw as the crass materialism of contemporary life. They believed in the power of the individual
to discern right and wrong and defy authority, including the church. This
liberationist view led to Thoreau's retreat to Walden Pond and his paean to
civil disobedience in 1849. But Emerson and other transcendentalists did
not seek withdrawal from society—they wanted to ameliorate it. The documentary evidence that their fervor influenced Wise and other Jews is scant,
but there is little question that Wise was familiar with their beliefs, and that
his own agenda was aligned with theirs.

Jews and Christians of a liberal bent had also been powerfully affected
by startling scientific developments in the first half of the nineteenth century. The study of geology led the way in shaking up inherited religious beliefs. In 1788, the Scottish scientist James Hutton had published his *Theory*

*of the Earth*, and Sir Charles Lyell's *Principles of Geology* (1830–32) studied prehistoric patterns of Earth formation and fossils. These works provided powerful evidence that the earth was hundreds of millions of years old, overthrowing the Bible's account of Creation.

Various Americans of faith had earlier wrestled with these findings. Benjamin Silliman, professor of chemistry and natural history at Yale (whose son Benjamin Jr. later discovered how to refine and distill petroleum into fuel), was one of those religiously inclined scientists who pioneered in the reinterpretation of Scripture in light of irrefutable scientific facts. Silliman, a protégé of the Yale president Timothy Dwight (who was himself a grandson of Jonathan Edwards), argued in 1836 that in light of these geological truths, the Bible should not be taken literally. He proposed instead that the concept of a "day" in the Creation story should be understood as an "aeon" in the eyes of God. His pupil, the geologist Edward Hitchcock, later president of Amherst, wrote *The Religion of Geology* in 1851, echoing this view, explaining that the earth's long history was evidence of God's glory. It was what some historians call the "Silliman-Hitchcock compromise" to the conflict between science and religion.[13]

Echoing the plea for science to inform religious faith, Henry Jones, a founder of B'nai B'rith, called on Jews to recognize "the mighty levers which move mankind in the onward march of events of development and progress." Julius Bien, a German emigrant who established a lithographic business that published many scientific works in the mid-nineteenth century, declared: "*Science* is the *Messiah* of the human race, leads to human happiness and leads toward the realization of the brotherhood of man."[14]

Against this backdrop came Felix Adler, who argued that if the goal of religion was universal brotherhood, why was it necessary to embrace any particular religion at all?

Felix Adler was in many ways destined to become the beau ideal of Reform Jews. He certainly had the lineage. His father, Rabbi Samuel Adler, was a prominent champion of reform and an ally of Abraham Geiger in Germany. When Samuel Adler moved with his family to America in 1857 to take up duties as rabbi at Temple Emanu-El, the most elite reform synagogue in America, Felix was only five years old.[15]

Succeeding Merzbacher at the synagogue, the elder Rabbi Adler revised his predecessor's prayer book, shortened the Sabbath service, removed a partition separating men and women, and made it mandatory for men to keep their heads uncovered during the service. In 1869, Adler had helped convene the conference of reformist rabbis in Philadelphia, where they adopted basic reforms intended to discard Jewish identity as a separate nation. Still, the atmosphere in which Felix grew up was decidedly traditional, at least in terms of his education. As a teenager, Felix had already imbibed the writings of Jewish sages as well as an array of German enlightenment thinkers. The elder rabbi fully expected his son to succeed him at Temple Emanu-El.

For all that, Felix's home life was lonely and unhappy; he very likely found it difficult to move out of his father's shadow. At the age of fifteen, he attended Columbia College, probably as the only Jew in his class, and had trouble making friends because of his young age, shy manner, and ostentatious display of learning. At the same time, Felix was drawn to sympathy for the slums, poverty, and disease of the surrounding city, where full-scale rioting to protest the draft had erupted during the Civil War. "I think I was always sensitive to suffering," Felix later wrote.[16] (Whereas Felix was sympathetic to the African American victims of the Civil War draft riots, his father was careful not to oppose slavery, in keeping with the conservative leanings and Southern sympathies of many Temple Emanu-El congregants.)

Samuel Adler remained deeply devoted to his belief in God, even though he contended that contemporary rabbis with whom he studied in Germany had as much right as the ancient sages of the Talmud to reinterpret Jewish law. Felix embraced the idea of God through most of his teenage years. He also accepted what historians, including his biographer, have called the "mission theory" of Judaism—the concept that the Jewish people, far from being punished for their sins as exiles, possessed a mission handed down by God to use their dispersal to espouse the universal truth of God's existence and to pray for the eventual establishment of a just world. Felix revealed his embrace of a distinctive Jewish identity when he wrote a scathing essay at the age of eighteen denouncing the practice of some Jews to put up Christmas trees in their homes.

Still, he was plagued in this period by doubts over many matters. He questioned why Jews had to fast on Yom Kippur and expressed revulsion over the stories of Abraham's willingness to sacrifice his son Isaac, or God "hardening the heart" of the pharaoh in order to perpetuate his lethal miracles. His doubts mounted as a result of his growing indignation over conditions of the poor in New York and his own interest in science. Reading Alexander von Humboldt's *Cosmos*, with its accounts of the origins of the universe and various aspects of geology and astronomy, Felix increasingly questioned the authenticity of Scripture while proclaiming his awe at the inability of humans to fully understand the universe.

Troubled by doubts, Felix headed off to Europe in 1870 after graduating from Columbia. He intended to pursue rabbinic studies in Berlin and Heidelberg, but he grew increasingly lonely and put off by the doctrinaire teachings of Protestant and Jewish theologians, especially by the continued insistence of Jewish teachers that Jews had a special mission given to them by God. He was also revolted by what he felt was the sexual depravity and excesses he found in Germany and developed what his biographer calls an "excessive zeal for sexual purity" that later became a dominant theme of his philosophical pronouncements.

Influenced by his studies of science, history, and philosophy, especially Darwin and his followers, and also by the school of German biblical criticism, young Adler finally made a clean break. "I look back with dread to that time when everything seemed sinking around me," he later wrote, "when the cherished faith which seemed at one time dearer than life itself was going to pieces under me, and it seemed to me that I could save nothing out of the wreck of all that seemed holiest to me." As much as he wanted, Adler could not accept Geiger's theory that the Jews had evolved into a special people with a mission for humankind.

Samuel Adler was overjoyed when Felix got his doctorate in Heidelberg but soon learned that his son was determined to effectively reject Judaism in favor of universal principles, based on Kant, that morality could be discerned through reason apart from belief in the divine. These beliefs joined with his passion for social justice, even socialism, as a cure for human debasement in a modern capitalist society.

Alarmed by Felix's messages home about his new leanings, Adler family members beseeched him to give them up. "Take my advice," his mother wrote. "Leave Berlin, its philosophy, and prepare yourself for life with good practical knowledge and common sense. That will be of more use to you in our calling than all the philosophy in the world." The advice went unheeded.

Upon his return to New York in 1873, Felix went on to deliver a sermon at Temple Emanu-El that was to be his big tryout for serving as rabbi there. Instead, the sermon ensured that it would be his last at the synagogue. Speaking on "The Judaism of the Future," Adler outlined a series of principles of importance to religion but never once mentioned believing in God. "We discard the narrow spirits of exclusion, and loudly proclaim that Judaism was not given to the Jews alone," he declared. Many in the congregation welcomed his comments, but the leadership found them unacceptable and even insulting, especially to the prosperous listeners alarmed by his talk of social revolution. Adler immediately withdrew as a candidate to serve as rabbi and developed a new interest in the proceedings of the Free Religious Association and its president, O. B. Frothingham. At that time, the association was primarily preoccupied with issues of religious freedom, and only later—when Adler became the association president in 1878—did it adopt a social and economic agenda.

As for Felix's father, Samuel, he was "almost heartbroken," writes Adler's biographer, Benny Kraut. "The long-standing rabbinic tradition in the Adler family was broken," he writes. "Three years of preparatory education seemed to have been wasted." But the elder rabbi continued to support his son's journey and never fully severed his relationship with him. Felix responded with reverence and loyalty to his father throughout his life.[17]

To promote his ideas outside Temple Emanu-El, Felix embarked on a series of Sunday lectures laying out a social reform agenda based on moral principles that were religious in their fervor if not in name. These upset his Jewish colleagues all the more. Many saw his talks as an attempt to supplant both Jewish and church services on a day set aside for worship. But some in the Jewish community found his talks informative and provocative, according to accounts in the Jewish press. For a few years, Adler also took up teaching duties at Cornell, where his controversial views did not sit well among anti-Semites in upstate New York. His contract in Ithaca was not renewed. Back in New York, he turned to his associates and friends at the Free Religion Association and became acquainted with Emerson and others in the Transcendental circle. Increasingly, commentators in the Jewish press grew uncomfortable with his preaching and began suggesting that he was a traitor, heretic, and apostate.

In 1876, Adler built on the success of his lectures to establish the New York Society for Ethical Culture, aimed at advancing the cause of social justice through moral actions detached from religious belief. The society was incorporated the following year and in later years established a nursing service, a kindergarten, and a school that eventually became the Fieldston School.

It was obviously painful for Felix to assert that Reform Jews were no longer really Jews anyway, even though they did not recognize it. Reform Jews felt threatened by his teachings, but most sought to ignore him. Once he founded the Ethical Culture organization, many Jews were happy that he was no longer trying to redefine Judaism itself. Among those who sought to ignore him was Isaac Mayer Wise, who nonetheless derided the movement with a mocking disdain: "There is no God and Felix Adler is his prophet," Wise declared sarcastically.[18] Wise, however, resigned from the Free Religious Association after Adler became its president.

Hoping to rid his brand of Judaism from the taint of atheism, Wise prepared to expand his scope of influence by doing battle with both traditionalists and reformers. He ended up having to rush to the front of the parade in order to lead it.

*Twelve*

# THE TREFA BANQUET

Ten years after the founding of Hebrew Union College, which had established itself in a three-story building in downtown Cincinnati, a historic moment arrived for the seminary to hold what was proclaimed to be the first ordination of rabbis on American soil. Furious planning went into what Wise and others hoped and expected would be a landmark event to take place in Cincinnati on July 11, 1883. More than a hundred leaders from seventy-six congregations around the country descended on the city to see four young men installed as rabbis. Also attending were Jews in town to celebrate the tenth anniversary of the Union of American Hebrew Congregations, and members of the Rabbinical Literary Association, a forerunner of the Central Conference of American Rabbis (CCAR).

The ceremony began at 2:30 p.m. at the Plum Street Synagogue and featured a choir of five women and three men singing Jewish hymns, as well as speeches by two of the graduating students. Guests, also including

Christian clergy and professors at the University of Cincinnati, rode cable cars to the top of Mt. Adams, where they gathered at Highland House, a banquet and entertainment hall, and were greeted by a full orchestra and elegant menus laying out nine courses and various alcoholic drinks. The official banquet host was Julius Freiberg, who had made his fortune producing bourbon whiskey and was active in a multitude of civic organizations in the Queen City.

The banquet reflected a growing comfort level among American Jews to celebrate milestones at festive occasions, but it was hardly unique in that respect. Many other groups held banquets featuring music, decorations, toasts, and elaborate displays of food.[1]

But the disastrous decision of the caterer to provide crabs, shrimp, clams, and frogs legs—prohibited by kosher dietary laws—to Jews of all persuasions, including Orthodox rabbis in attendance, provoked a backlash. At least two of the observant clerics stormed out of the event, according to an eyewitness. Articles in Jewish journals around the country gleefully condemned Wise's beloved seminary for colossal insensitivity.

How could such a thing have happened?

Historians note that the caterer did not serve pork at the banquet, which might have been an even graver provocation, even though pork was a popular food in a city with a large non-Jewish German population. The absence of pork demonstrates that at least someone was sensitive to Jewish dietary practices. (Pork has always had a special status as a nonkosher food, perhaps because pork played an especially pernicious role during the Spanish Inquisition, when Jews were forced to eat it as a test of their conversions.) But in fact, though the reform movement itself had generally not broken with kosher laws in its early years, dietary restrictions were fraying by the 1880s.

As to the explanation for the faux pas, the question was whether it was carelessness rather than a deliberate provocation. Much of the evidence suggests that it was at least not an accident. A caterer, Gus Lindeman, was accustomed to reform practices that had begun to loosen the dietary laws, and the record shows that banquets held by B'nai B'rith and other secular Jewish organizations were accustomed to eating certain forbidden delicacies. But whatever the motives, Wise was in no mood to apologize. Instead, he derided the critics as adherents to "stomach Judaism" or "kitchen Judaism," adding that kosher practices of Judaism were clearly out of date. In his callous dismissal of the dissenters, Wise seemed unworried that his attitude might weaken his cause of a universal "union" of American Judaism.

The practical result of the controversy was to accelerate, at least on a symbolic level, the division of Jews into two warring camps that could not, so to speak, even break bread together. Several congregations resigned from the Union of American Hebrew Congregations. Some years later, they and their supporters called for the establishment of a new seminary along traditional lines, though the banquet was only one of many reasons behind their determination to break away. Why the mistake, if it was a mistake, actually took place is a matter of dispute. It may not matter much in the larger context of historical schism among Jews. But the mystery of the event sheds light on the chaotic but also intricate state of play within American Judaism at the time.

Not everyone agrees that the uproar was that major. The historian and Isaac Leeser biographer Lance Sussman asserts that an account by one eyewitness, David Philipson, a member of the first ordination class, contained many inaccuracies. Philipson had written that "terrific excitement ensued when two rabbis rose from their seats and rushed from the room." In fact, writes Sussman, the dinner may not have been that dramatically disrupted. A separate history of the Trefa Banquet by John J. Appel, a scholar at Michigan State University, concluded that the serving of shellfish reflected the "ambivalent, sometimes contradictory attitude" of Rabbi Wise and "was deliberately arranged by some Cincinnati businessmen."[2]

The central figure in the drama, of course, was Lindeman, the caterer and food manager of a local Jewish club. Years after the banquet, Lindeman's granddaughter wrote that "my grandfather, though Jewish, had no knowledge of whom the guests were to be and had merely followed instructions to provide 'an elegant and sumptuous meal.'" Wise's own accounts varied. At first, he claimed that he assumed the caterer, being Jewish, would know not to violate Jewish norms and that "we do not know why he diversified his menu with multipeds and bivalves." Later, Wise changed his account, saying that the banquet committee had explicitly allowed "a few dishes" forbidden for Jews.

The food elements of the banquet have been examined carefully by scholars. According to surviving texts of the menu, the first course was indeed littleneck clams, followed by a consommé, beef tenderloin with mushrooms, soft-shell crabs, a shrimp salad, and potatoes in a lobster bisque sauce. The entrée was sweetbreads, and the fifth course featured frogs legs, breaded chicken, and asparagus, and then pigeon and squab embedded in pastry. There were also desserts and rivers of French wines and other drinks. As Sussman points out, it was not just the shellfish that violated dietary laws. The meat (including the sweetbreads) was also non-kosher, and the dinner promiscuously mixed dairy and meat. It seems possible that by omitting pork, the hosts thought they had at least not gone overboard.

As for how big a fiasco the banquet really was, a Jewish reporter writing in the New York Herald noted the presence of forbidden dishes but said everyone sat down at the table in acceptance of them. Another writer, Henrietta Szold, who had accompanied her father, Rabbi Benjamin Szold, to Cincinnati, wrote differently in a Jewish journal. Szold was only twenty-three at the time, but she later rose to become a prominent educator, essayist, social activist, and founder of Hadassah (the women's Zionist organization) revered for her philanthropic work in Israel. "I would be outraging my own feelings were I to omit recording the indignation which was felt by a surprisingly small minority at the manner in which the banquet was served," Szold wrote. "There was no regard paid to our dietary laws, and consequently two rabbis left the table without having touched the dishes, and I am happy to state that I know of at least three more who ate nothing and were indignant but signified their disapproval in a less demonstrative manner."

As word of the banquet spread in Jewish circles, Wise turned from being defensive to firing back with charges that his critics were hypocrites

who themselves were less than observant on dietary matters. But the board
of Rodeph Shalom Congregation in Philadelphia concured Wise in April
1884. After an investigation, the Union of American Hebrew Congregations
exonerated Wise of charges of improprieties, prompting some traditionalist
Jewish writers in the east to declare that the inquiry had been a whitewash.
The banquet did appear to strike a blow at Hebrew Union College, where
attendance dropped off for a time after the fiasco.

Sussman's scholarship on the Trefa Banquet included a thorough examination of the history of dietary laws in a broad range of religious traditions,
not simply among Jews, who, archeological records show, had avoided pork
at least since ancient times. Among American Jews in the nineteenth century, it was hardly uncommon to not eat pork (many Jews understood that
pork was especially susceptible to contamination and disease) yet eat other
forbidden foods, in much the same way that they had become accustomed
to eating meat that had not been slaughtered in strictly kosher fashion. Jewish skepticism about keeping kosher was underscored by the many disputes
among kosher butchers over whose practices were the most stringent.

Oysters, on the other hand, were harvested up and down the East and
Gulf Coasts and were no doubt enjoyed by Jews throughout the United
States. "By analogy, it might be said that oysters were for nineteenth-century
American Jews what Chinese food became for their twentieth-century de-
scendants," Sussman writes, a reference to the well-known Jewish habit of
going to Chinese resturants on Christmas.

A footnote to history: three years after the Trefa Banquet, a kosher meat
business was established in Cincinnati, and became one of the leading sup-
pliers in the United States.


## THE SCHISM DEEPENS

The seeds of a counterrevolution among American Jews dismayed over the
excesses of the reform movement were planted well before the Trefa Banquet.
But the fiasco in Cincinnati helped bring the emerging schism to a head.

The focus was a storied debate in the 1880s between two prominent rabbis and research scholars, Alexander Kohut on the traditional side and Kaufmann Kohler of the reformers. Their long-running dispute, embodied by a series of competing sermons published in the *American Hebrew* journal in 1885, exposed what was becoming obvious: American Judaism was evolving into two warring denominations—traditional and change-oriented, with the potential for traditionalists later splitting themselves into Orthodox and Conservative.[3]

The conservative backlash against reform had been a long time in coming, going back to the orthodox exemplar Isaac Leeser, who died shortly after the Civil War. A little more than a decade after his death, a group of traditionalist Jewish leaders met in Philadelphia in 1879 to discuss their alarm over the fraying discipline and self-serving revisions of doctrine by Jews in their community. They called their group Keyam Dishmaya, the "divine covenant," and pledged to bring Jews back "to the ancient faith" and to "re-create the ancient Hebrew Sabbath" at a time when Jewish observance of the day of rest was falling by the wayside under the enormous pressures of business and a desire to fit in with the rest of the world.[4]

A revealing example of their approach lay in their determination to revitalize Hanukkah as a holiday. Hanukkah, the Jewish "festival of lights," had since Talmudic times been relegated to a minor status. Reformers were comfortable ignoring the holiday as well because of its obsolete (in their view) association with the importance of restoring the ancient Temple in Jerusalem by the Maccabees. The Maccabees were fiercely traditionalist religious zealots opposed to the Hellenic and pagan influence on Judaism during Judea's occupation by the Ptolemaic and Seleucid dynasties, which ruled Judea from Egypt and Syria respectively following the death of Alexander the Great in 323 BCE.

Maccabean warriors took control of Jerusalem and established a new Jewish dynasty, the Hasmoneans, who ruled from 164 to 63 BCE. Their triumph is today depicted in Jewish storytelling as a victory of freedom of religion and liberation from Greek persecution and tyranny. The eight-day festival of lights—celebrated by the lighting of candles on a Hanukkah menorah—is associated with the rededication of the Temple in Jerusalem and the miracle of its lamp oil lasting eight days.

As a revolt against anything Hellenistic, however, the Maccabean conquest was mostly a failure. The Hasmoneans soon proved to be every bit as Hellenizing as the rulers they displaced. The period during and after the rule of Alexander the Great and his successors was one in which the Jews were divided. Many lovingly embraced Greek secular culture in literature, the arts, and sport; they ate pork and even worse, some went along with idol worship as they tried to assimilate Greek ideas and practices. Such accommodations might have been benign, like having a Christmas tree or celebrating Halloween in today's world. But their conduct set an example of Jews, not for the first or last time, seeking to integrate themselves in the majority culture, to end their isolation, and to avoid persecution based on the Jews' supposed long-standing desire to identify themselves as "the other." Some Jews went so far as to abandon circumcision out of a desire not to be embarrassed in the Greek-style gymnasium, where young men competed naked in sporting events along with non-Jews and homosexuality was not unusual. And also not for the first or last time, traditionalists vehemently objected to all such practices, warning that they would bring down the wrath of God and perhaps spell the end of Judaism's covenant with the Almighty.

In popular culture, the Maccabean revolt is now depicted in Hanukkah as against the Greeks. But a close examination of the record by scholars has demonstrated that it was sparked by internal discord over the supposed apostasies of these "Hellenized" Jews. (Indeed, Orthodox Jews in Israel today still use the term "Hellenic" to deplore secularized Jews.) As the scholar of Hellenistic Judaism Elias Bickerman states: "The Maccabean movement was primarily a civil war, a religious battle between the orthodox and the reformers."[5]

Thus, the traditionalists meeting in Philadelphia saw the reestablishment of Hanukkah as an echo of what the Maccabees were trying to do: saving Judaism and even monotheism. They wanted the holiday to celebrate not only the restoration of the Temple in Jerusalem and religious freedom, but also to remind Jews to pray for the restoration of the Temple as part of their adherence to Talmudic commandments, the very practice that reformers were discarding. Reviving Hanukkah, in other words, was a way for conservatives to revive the hope of the people of Israel to return to their ancient birthright in the Promised Land. The implicit goal of tradition-bound Jews was thus to restate Jewish "nationhood" and its roots in Jerusalem, just as Reform Jews had moved away from their identity as a nation, people, or tribe yearning for the restoration of power in the Holy Land.

Of course, Hanukkah was also a way of counteracting the increasing appeal of the Christmas holiday among Jews. The 1879 Hanukkah festival held by traditionalist Jews was declared a success in fulfilling their objective. "Every worker in the cause of a revived Judaism must have felt the inspiration exuded from the enthusiastic interest evinced by such a mass of Israel's people," an organizer wrote afterward.[6]

The traditional Jews also started a newspaper in New York called the *American Hebrew* edited by young activists, two of them rabbis, who tried to retain the principles of Orthodoxy while adjusting it to a modern context, including the respect for a more elevated role for women. The magazine, according to one adherent, would be edited by "a group of young American Jews who, while not inordinately addicted to Orthodoxy as a rigid standardization of thought and conduct, was yet opposed to the wholesale and reckless discarding of everything that was Jewish simply because it was inconvenient, oriental, or was not in conformity with Episcopalian custom."[7] It was in the *American Hebrew* that the dispute between Kohut and Kohler played out in 1885, in a series of published sermons.

Another pillar of the new traditionalist organization was Cyrus L. Sulzberger, a prosperous cotton goods merchant and patriarch of the Sulzberger family, which had emigrated from Bavaria earlier in the century. As president and director of several Jewish philanthropic organizations, he sided with conservative Judaism in one important respect, as an advocate of reestablishing Jewish identity as a people seeking to return eventually to the land of Israel. (Sulzberger's son, Arthur Hays Sulzberger, much later became a foe of Zionism after World War II. Back in 1917, Arthur Hays Sulzberger had married Iphigene Ochs, daughter of Adolph Ochs, who had bought the

*New York Times* in 1896 and was himself married to Effie Wise, the daughter of Isaac Mayer Wise. After succeeding Ochs as publisher of the *New York Times*, Sulzberger became the progenitor of the Sulzbergers, the family that continues to control the newspaper.)

The traditionalists in Philadelphia were among the forerunners of what would later become known as Zionism, the movement that supported establishing a Jewish homeland in Palestine. The movement was getting increasing support in the 1880s from the influx of Jews from Eastern Europe and Russia. New Jewish news organizations and journals began to take note of the early trend, calling it a "revival" or "renaissance" of tradition.

The reestablishment of the Jewish Publication Society in 1888 also led to a proliferation of Jewish-oriented histories, novels, scholarly works, and organizations determined to educate Jews about their own faith and traditions. These organizations included Gratz College in Philadelphia, which trained women to teach Jewish studies in school; the Jewish Chautauqua Society; and the National Council of Jewish Women. The increasing participation of women infused American Judaism in the late nineteenth century with a new energy and determination to preserve a distinctly American identity, combining tradition with indigenous culture and even literature. (Among the leading female literary figures was Emma Lazarus, whose 1883 sonnet "The New Colossus"—"Give me your tired, your poor, / Your huddled masses yearning to breathe free. . . . "—was written to raise funds for the pedestal of the Statue of Liberty and is now inscribed on a plaque at its base.)

The 1885 Kohut-Kohler dispute pivoted around two of the biggest issues vexing Jews in the latter part of the nineteenth century: the God-driven primacy and authority of Jewish law and the emerging field of biblical criticism holding that Scripture was not handed down by God through revelation, but written by human beings and thus susceptible to reinterpretation or revision.

Alexander Kohut (1842–1894) was a distinguished rabbinical scholar, author of a Talmudic dictionary, and advocate of tradition with some adjustments allowing for contemporary demands. Descended from a long line of rabbis in Hungary and Palestine, he was unable to attend Hebrew school at a young age because his family was poor. While selling tarts to make ends meet for his family, according to the *Jewish Encyclopedia,* an odd and extraordinary episode occurred: He was briefly abducted by gypsies— "because of his extraordinary beauty." No further elaboration is offered.[8]

Returned to his family, young Alexander started studying Talmud and came up with the idea of producing a lexicon of Talmudic words and terms. He went on to get a PhD from the University of Leipzig in Germany and was ordained as a rabbi at the Jewish Theological Seminary in Breslau, an institution devoted to following a middle ground between radicalism and orthodoxy. Famous as an orator in Hungary, he drew crowds from distant parts of the country and was invited to speak to the Hungarian parliament as a representative of the Jews. Kohut largely devoted his scholarly labors to his early project of producing a Talmudic lexicon. The result was a Hebrew *Dictionary of the Talmud,* much of it copied by hand, which took twenty-five years to complete and is widely considered a major achievement in Hebrew and Jewish scholarly literature.

Having studied, preached, and led congregations in Budapest and other parts of his native land, Kohut took over as rabbi at Congregation Ahawath Chesed (Love of Mercy) in New York in 1885, succeeding its founding rabbi, Adolph Huebsch, a Bohemian émigré who had helped establish Hebrew Union College in Cincinnati. Kohut determined to move the congregation back to an approach that was more conservative than the one taught by Huebsch. (The congregation, housed in a grandly Moorish building crowned by two minarets, on Lexington Avenue, years later merged with Shaar Hashomayim Congregation and became Central Synagogue.) At his new place of worship, Kohut's lectures—which he called "Ethics of the Fathers" in reference to the compilation of ethical teachings of the ancient rabbis—were famous for challenging the revolution wrought by reformers: "A Reform which seeks to progress without the Mosaic-rabbinical tradition is a deformity—a skeleton without flesh and sinew, without spirit and heart. It is a suicide; and suicide is not reform."[9]

Though he was an exemplar of conservatism and tradition, Kohut said he favored "conservative progress" against "nerveless indifference" and "glowing fanaticism."[10] Ahawath Chesed had mixed male-and-female seating and other trappings of Reform, but Kohut was determined to take his flock back to tradition, or what he called a "healthy golden mean" between Orthodox and Reform. On the one hand, he spoke of the Jews' "priestly vocation" and argued that American Judaism was the equivalent of a new Zion, as Reformers had begun to articulate. On the other hand, he stood by the tradition of rabbinic Judaism codifying the Oral Law as believed to be given to Moses, and argued that it embodied divine authority.[11]

Bringing a historical perspective to the argument, Kohut liked to cite heresies of the past as a dangerous precedent for the Reformers of the present. There was, for example, the ancient sect known as Sadducees, a Jewish faction that flourished at the time of the Roman occupation of Judea and the period of Jesus. The Sadducees opposed the authority of the emerging corpus of Oral Laws endorsed by their rival sect, the Pharisees. (The Pharisees ultimately gained dominance and served as the founders of rabbinic Judaism—that is, the form of Judaism that, in one way or another, is represented in all the various traditional branches of Judaism practiced today.)

But rabbinic Judaism did not continue unchallenged. As Kohut noted, a later movement, the Karaites, also arose to dispute rabbinic Judaism with what historians say was the most serious revolt against its authority in medieval times. The antirabbinic Karaite insurgency emerged in Baghdad in the eighth century CE, led by a charismatic if mysterious figure and seer named Anan ben David, and it also sought to liberate Jews from many ancient practices. Reacting to the challenge of Islam, which denied both the written Torah and the later oral traditions of rabbinic Judaism, the Karaites tried to save the former at the expense of the latter. The sect thus held that the source of divine guidance for Judaism was to be found in the words of the Torah itself, but not in the altogether human Oral Law. The Torah alone contained God's divine commandments, they said, and these should be interpreted in strict, literal ways without relying on the elaborate, often highly imaginative, inferences of their rabbinical opponents. Karaitism was a major movement that existed in Spain, Russia, Turkey, Egypt, and other places, and its full extent and collected writings are only being properly assessed by scholars today.[12]

The rivalries between Sadducees and Pharisees, and between the Karaites and the Rabbinites, as their opponents were called, in many ways prefigured the battle between traditionalist and reformist elements in Judaism in the modern era. No doubt, as with any religious practices in any tradition, Jewish law was not always followed by individuals and communities down to the letter in practice, and in any case, practices and customs varied widely across the Jewish world.

Kohut's condemnation of the reform movement of his day as an unwelcome throwback to the ancient heresies of Karaism and the Sadducees was intended as the ultimate insult. In effect, he was questioning the entire body of literary examination of the Bible holding that human writers, and not God, were the authors of the Torah. Kohut's view was that the concept of revelation and the divine authority of biblical and Talmudic texts were essential to Judaism.

At Congregation Ahawath Chesed, Kohut gave lectures that were as popular as his sermons back in Hungary, with crowds lining up to hear him. He saw as particularly dangerous biblical criticism undertaken by Lutherans and others in Germany. A bête noire was the German biblical scholar and Protestant theologian Julius Wellhausen, who pioneered in the historical interpretation of the Bible as written by many authors and not bearing the imprint directly of God. Kohut argued that such criticism, undertaken by Protestants in Germany, had poisoned Judaism when it took root in the so-called Jewish enlightenment and "scientific" study of Jewish texts carried out by Geiger and others in Germany. These studies, he charged, not only undermined the authority of the Bible's moral teachings but also diminished the standing and special status of Jews. "The views of non-Jewish Biblical critics must be banished from the camp of Israel, when they endanger its holy treasures," Kohut wrote. "The results of Wellhausen's researches belong as little to the Jewish pulpit as the religious beliefs of Unitarianism."

As for the authority of the Mishna, the Talmud, and later formulations

of Jewish observance, Kohut maintained that the teachings of rabbinical interpreters, as passed on from generation to generation in these works, was
nothing less than the essence of Judaism. "Whoever denies this; denies this
on principle, disclaims his connection with the bond of the community of
the house of Israel," he declared. He noted that this was the belief even of
those Jews who did not carry out the practices themselves. While acknowledging that not all of the traditional practices were still in force, and that the
status of Jews had changed in America, he declared that a Jew who abandoned the law "has banished himself from the camp of Israel; writes his own
epitaph: 'I am no Jew; no adherent to the faith of my fathers.'" In another
passage, he wrote: "No, we cannot maintain Judaism without the tradition
as it has been orally bequeathed to us from the time of Moses."[13]

## KOHLER PICKS UP KOHUT'S GAUNTLET

The task of defending reform against attacks by Kohut and others was
eagerly seized by Rabbi Kaufmann Kohler (1843–1926), another German
émigré and protégé of Abraham Geiger and exponent of Geiger's studies of
biblical criticism. Like Kohut, Kohler was descended from a family of rabbis in his birthplace of Fürth, Bavaria. He got his rabbinical training under
Samson Raphael Hirsch, a strict traditionalist who nonetheless affirmed
the importance of secular culture and modernization, as well as Geiger. In
1869, Kohler moved to America, first to Detroit and then to Chicago, and
in 1879 he succeeded his father-in-law, David Einhorn, as rabbi of Temple
Beth-El, in New York City. (Beth-El merged with Temple Emanu-El many
years later, in 1927.) In 1903, three years after the death of Isaac M. Wise,
Kohler became president of Hebrew Union College, in Cincinnati.[14]

    Kohler and his brother-in-law, Emil G. Hirsch (1851–1923)—they
each married a daughter of Einhorn—are considered the giants of what has
become known as the era of "classical" Reform Judaism, ardent champions
of radical reform, and foes of the old guard. "The gauntlet thrown in our
faces must be taken up at once," Kohler declared. In a series of lectures entitled "Backwards or Forwards," he asked: "Which are we to espouse, the

Underlying Kohler's freethinking dissertation was the German Reform view that no biblical text was to be taken at face value, an idea inherited from Wellhausen and other earlier Christian scholars. His thesis maintained that the blessing was thus not literally something spoken by Jacob but "put into the mouth of Jacob" by later writers, well after the time of the original biblical patriarchs of Abraham, Isaac, Jacob and Jacob's twelve sons. Yet Kohler sought to be respectful of traditional readings at the same time. He argued that it was important for Jews to know and understand the text and its various interpretations from the rabbinical period to medieval times, and that they owed at least some respect to the scholarly forebears who preserved and refined Judaism in trying times of exile and persecution. But the criticism of his dissertation among conservative rabbinical authorities in Germany evidently contributed to his decision to emigrate to America.[16]

Kohler's brother-in-law Emil G. Hirsch, the son of a German Reformer, Samuel Hirsch, was also an early pioneer in bringing together German secular philosophy and Judaism. Emil Hirsch attended the University of Pennsylvania, but his influence was concentrated in Chicago, where he was a professor of rabbinic literature and philosophy at the University of Chicago, and served as rabbi at Chicago's Sinai Temple. He also founded a journal, the *Reform Advocate.*

"Modern scholarship has spoken, and its voice cannot be hushed," Hirsch declared. "It has shown that Moses is not the author of the Pentateuch [the first five books of the Bible]; that Sinai is not the cradle of what is highest and best in Biblical Judaism . . . that the whole apparatus of priestly institutionalism is of non-Hebraic origin." In other words, all the dietary and other laws, including the rules of sacrifices and festivals, are not central to Judaism as the rabbis of millennia maintained.

The challenge remained over how to define ancient scriptures as worthy of reverence and holy, while still seeing them as a product of variable mortal and well-intentioned writers in a certain time and place. Both Kohler and Hirsch argued that the sacred meaning of scripture lay in moral precepts that can be venerated as if touched by the divine. As Kohler put it: "The Bible is holy *not because it is inspired, but because and insofar as it does* one that turns the dials of the time backward, or the one that proudly points to the forward move of history?"¹⁵

The debate between Rabbis Kohut and Kohler played out in sermons later published in the summer of 1885 by *The American Hebrew*, the weekly periodical founded in 1879 by traditionalist Jews. Like the Germans who influenced him, Kohler centered his arguments on scholarship of text and whether it should be seen as a product of direct divine revelation or as a more nuanced document with many authors. If it was the latter, the question was whether the text was inspired by divine authority in some mysterious way, bearing God's fingerprints without having been directly dictated word by word.

Kohler had questioned the divine authenticity of text in his doctoral dissertation, published when he was twenty-four. The subject of that study was revealing. It focused on the story of Jacob's blessing of his twelve sons in Genesis chapter 49, singling out Joseph for exemplary praise and others for more restrained praise mixed with harsh criticism and even condemnation. Literary analysis pointed to a fact that would seem obvious: the poem of Jacob blessing his sons was written many generations after the event could have taken place. The passages were obviously meant to justify the fates of the various twelve tribes of Israel, and in particular to explain the divine choice of Judah's tribe as the tribe of all future kings. (King David was indeed a Judean, and it thus seemed likely that this passage went back to his own period of rule: Genesis 49 was essentially designed to "grandfather" the choice of David's tribe back to the time of Jacob—indeed, it was conceivably David himself, or his son Solomon, who commissioned the writing of Genesis 49.) Scholars call such stories "etiological narratives," which are intended to explain a later reality as the result of far earlier events. (The most well-known and perhaps extreme instance of such interpretation revolves around the contention of some scholars that the biblical story of Moses leading the enslaved Jews out of Egypt to the Promised Land of Israel was an etiological narrative to reinforce Jewish possession of the land as promised by God to Abraham and his descendants. Scholars have had difficulty finding historical evidence in Egyptian or other writings of any kind of slave rebellion from that era.)

*still, inspire.* It is not because God has spoken the word, but because in the truth, the comfort, the hope, the final victory of justice which it holds out, you hear God speak to you in soul stirring strains." One might argue, he was suggesting, that the Bible looms all the more powerfully precisely because it was the work of many righteous hands whose inspirational moral authority transcended the arbitrary laws of their texts. Kohler was contending in effect that the sacred status of the Bible derived not from the origins of the text but from within the soul of Jewish believers inspired to write it down. [17]

## THE INESCAPABLE INFLUENCE OF DARWIN

Classical reform in Judaism flowered at the apex of influences that started a half century earlier with the Second Great Awakening, discussed earlier. These influences had been significant all along, but toward the end of the nineteenth century they were buttressed by additional scientific discoveries and the increasingly widespread acceptance of Darwinian theories. These theories served to reinforce the legitimacy of the rigorous application of the textual analysis espoused by Kohler, Hirsch, and others.

Still another influence in this latter period of reform was the broader study of comparative religions, and of the religious practices that were embraced by other occupants of the Middle East. For example, the latest scholarship contended that Jewish practices, which believers felt had been dictated by God, were actually similar to the practices of other early Mesopotamian religions and cults, which worshipped other gods, especially Baal, the god of fertility. Jews were instructed, after all, to worship the God YHWH, who decreed that they must have no other gods before them—an instruction in the Ten Commandments that makes clear that historically speaking, other gods were competing for Jews' fealty. Hirsch and other revisionists saw the dietary laws as borne of totemic cults in antiquity, just as circumcision was a widely observed rite for initiation into one's clan and animal sacrifices were carried out by other cults at the time.

Hirsch also viewed the tefillin, the mezuzah, and the wearing of prayer shawls as fetishistic "talismans" from another primitive time. The irony of these scholarly inferences was that these practices were viewed as discredited in modern times precisely because they were discovered to have existed in ancient times in other non-Jewish contexts and peoples. Judaism, it was increasingly understood, was one of many competing forms of religion from antiquity, affected by a variety of external influences, from Greeks to other Semitic tribes.

Casting a vast and variable shadow over the debate among religious believers in the late nineteenth century was the figure of Charles Darwin (1809–1882), father of the theory of evolution and "natural selection" of species. Earlier in the century, scientific breakthroughs in cosmology, geology, and paleontology (by Charles Lyell documenting evidence of prehistoric epochs, among others) forced a rethinking of religious assumptions held by Christian and Jews alike. But Darwin's conclusions shattered these assumptions altogether. His book *On the Origin of Species* was published in 1859. By the 1870s his theories had generally come to be accepted as fact in educated circles. In 1871, Darwin's further studies in *The Descent of Man* applied his theories to human evolution, including the role of psychology, ethics, and differences between human races and sexes.

Darwin's findings left scant room for serious consideration of the Bible's stories, and the notion that the earth was created in six days 6,000 years previously. Christians seeking to reconcile their religious belief with the concept of evolution sought the authority of John Fiske, who set about a pathbreaking approach by arguing that perhaps biological evolution could be understood as part of God's plan. Other theories were more exotic, if not outright half-baked. A renowned paleontologist and scholar of glaciers, Louis Agassiz, suggested the existence of "special creationism," holding that God created the world as the Bible recorded but that God also created fossils, ancient rocks, genetic material, and other detritus, perhaps to throw off scientists.

Sydney Ahlstrom, the historian of American religion, has argued that Darwinism had a far greater impact on religion than simply undercutting the literal truth of the Bible. Evolution more fundamentally challenged the

religious view of the universe as a tribute to God's harmonious and benevolent purpose, in that "the sun and clouds, trees and grass, seeds, cows, dogs,
and insects—even manure—were all harmoniously interacting for man's
well-being." Instead of such a glorious vision, Ahlstrom contends, Darwin
depicted life on earth as "a relentless struggle for existence, a war of all against
all, with blood dripping from every bough, and man involved in the struggle
not only against the locusts, but against other men, even other races of man,
with victory for the fittest. . . . Never since the scientific revolution completed
by Newton had the humanistic and religious traditions of the West been confronted by a greater need for adjustment and reformulation."[18]

In sociology Darwin's findings opened new vistas to explain how progress and conflict occurred among human beings, and to explicate the advent
of "economic man." His writings paved the way for the "social Darwinists"
William Graham Sumner and Herbert Spencer, who applied the concept
of "survival of the fittest" to economic progress as well as to science. On
the other hand, seeing the Bible—including the life of Jesus—as a story
to be understood for its spiritual lessons rather than the literal truth of the
account seemed to reinforce the role of human agency in "repairing the
world." For Christians and Jews, the late nineteenth century was ripe for
the belief that addressing issues of economic inequality, poverty, social and
racial injustice, worker rights, and an end to war were the best way to implement God's teachings.

For many Jews, Darwinism was initially resisted as materialist and hostile to religion. Both Isaac Mayer Wise and David Einhorn charged that
Darwin had robbed humans of their dignity, but the next generation of "classical" reformers such as Kohler and Hirsch evolved. Kohler did so in a novel
way. He compared biological evolution to the "spiritual progress" embodied by Jewish teachings. Darwinism helped explain the survival of Judaism
over the millennia, as "the necessary outcome of the age of evolution." The
"survival of the fittest"—a phrase coined by Spencer, not Darwin—could
explain that Jews survived as the *morally* most fit of human species. Instead
of their status as "chosen people," Jews could see themselves as a product of
divine "natural selection."

If Jews had evolved in this fashion, Kohler further believed they must evolve further. Just as prayer had replaced animal sacrifices after the fall of the Temple, so too must Jews replace their outmoded doctrines and practices—such as the ban on wearing garments of mixed wool and linens—to embrace the modern world. The influence of Darwin was again apparent. It was the genius of Jews to evolve, so evolve they must yet again! "Can we, or must we believe exactly what our fathers believed concerning revelation and the Law, resurrection, and the Messianic future?" Kohler asked. "Rabbinic-Mosaical Judaism is dead." Reform Judaism was not a break from tradition; it was in the Jewish tradition to revise and amend as history commanded. "I do not believe in the divine origin of the Mosaic law and tradition as our orthodox brethren do," he said. "But I do believe in the divine mission of the Jewish people as the martyr priests of pure monotheism with its true ethics."

Kohut feared that Kohler was turning Judaism into a kind of Christian religion, but Kohler argued that he was saving Judaism from itself. Kohut said to Kohler once: "You are only an ethical Jew!" It was not a compliment, but Kohler took it as such.[19]

In the same period that Kohler was sending incendiary rockets over to Kohut's traditionalist camp, he was preoccupied with defending his own brand of Judaism against the radical departure of Felix Adler. He thus emerged as the rabbi most publicly identified as an antagonist of the Ethical Culture Society.

In 1878, Kohler vetoed an invitation to Adler from the Sinai Literary Association to speak at the Chicago Sinai Congregation, where Kohler was serving as rabbi: "Of what benefit to a society of Jewish young people the lecture of a man who has deserted the Jewish flag, and openly professes his disbelief in God and immortality, I really fail to see, unless the eradication of the Jewish faith is the object contemplated." He further belittled Adler as a figure of no intellectual standing except for being the son of a famous father who happened to have studied under Geiger in Germany.

Adler ended up speaking to an overflow audience of five hundred at the Standard Club, where he expressed pain over the accusations but also

assailed the "immoral conception of the Deity" rewarding virtue and punishing sin. Kohler's response in the *Chicago Daily Tribune* was to accuse
Adler of sacrilege and plagiarizing the work of a German historian and philosopher. "I am very sorry to state that in this very lecture the professor in
calling the God worshipped by Jews and Christians a 'fetish,' corroborated
anew my charge of blasphemy brought against him."

Defenders of Adler denied the plagiarism charge, and commentators in
the Jewish press—where the dispute was lavishly covered—attacked and
defended both disputants. Unlike his fellow rabbis in New York, Kohler
could afford to take his gloves off in the fight; he believed that Jewish intellectuals had a duty to speak out in public and had no concern about of-
fending Adler's supporters. Standing aloof from the controversy was Felix's
father Samuel, who wrote a letter to a friend after the Chicago furor that,
even if he could silence his son, he would refuse to do so. "I am convinced
that the aim and purpose of my son's work is a deeply sacred and religious
one," he said. "If his convictions in some respects are not the same as mine,
they are entitled to as much consideration as my own."[20]

Thirteen

# NEW DIVISIONS

Kohler's debate with Kohut in 1885, coupled with his principled opposition to the Free Religious Association, gave him confidence to seize the reins of Jewish reform. Thus fortified, he called for yet another conference of Jews—this time at Concordia Hall in Allegheny City, just outside Pittsburgh, on November 16–18, 1885. The result was a watershed of what has come to be called "classical" reform Judaism just as it was about to fracture internally and then be overtaken by events overseas.

An impetus for the Pittsburgh parley was the continued anxiousness among Jews to define yet again who they were and how they were determined to assimilate within American society. For as comfortable as the Gilded Age was for Jews, there were reminders of the dangers of complacency.

In a well-publicized episode in 1877, for example, Joseph Seligman, patriarch of one of the most established Jewish families in America and friend

of the Vanderbilts and other pillars in New York society, was refused admittance at the Grand Union Hotel in the spa community of Saratoga Springs
in upstate New York. The incident was widely publicized inside and outside
the Jewish community. The Grand Union Hotel owner offered no apolo-
gies for his policy of barring Jews from his establishment. Another blow to
Jewish self-satisfaction came with an announcement that "Jews as a class"
were unwelcome at Coney Island in 1879. The announcement was delivered by Austin Corbin, a prominent railroad mogul and robber baron who
had founded the Long Island Rail Road and who owned various resorts in
southern Brooklyn. "The highest social element . . . won't associate with
Jews, and that's all there is about it," Corbin declared. American Jews were
increasingly mindful of news demonstrating that anti-Semitism in Europe
had hardly died out— far from it. Jews remained confined to their communities and to the Pale of Settlement in vast parts of Eastern Europe, and
although many American Jews did not identify with the persecution of Jews
they felt were living in backward conditions in the Old Country, they were
acutely aware that their conditions were deplorable.

In pushing ahead for another conference on Reform, Kohler cast a
wary eye on his famous rival, Isaac Mayer Wise, whom he cordially despised and distrusted. Like his father-in-law Einhorn, Kohler once accused
Wise of trying to establish himself as the head of a new "Jewish Sanhedrin," a reference to the great Jewish High Court that existed in late biblical
times. But he knew it was necessary to consult Wise and win him over to
get the conference going. He managed to get Wise's support for this latest effort to produce a "common platform" for Reform Judaism that "in
view of the wide divergence of opinions and the conflict ideas prevailing in
Judaism today" would "declare before the world *what Judaism is and what
Reform Judaism means and aims at.*"[1] Gone was the idea of unifying everyone under the banner of an American Judaism, replaced by the concept of
a Judaism of Reform.

Wise, meanwhile, understood that by joining Kohler and others on the
left, he might lose backing from the conservative members of his Union and

his seminary, which still stood at least in principle for a single American Judaism. But he set aside these concerns, perhaps thinking that over time he would be able to influence the Jewish community as more and more numbers of graduates from Hebrew Union College took their place as leaders around the country. For his willingness to compromise, Wise was elected president of the Pittsburgh conference. By all accounts, however, the conclave was Kohler's show.

Pittsburgh was a logical choice for the reformers' parley. As a banking and steel industry city, it was a center of Jewish prosperity and upward mobility in the 1880s, and home to three thousand Jews and eight congregations. The largest and most prosperous was Rodef Shalom, which embraced reforms advocated by Wise in the 1860s, prompting a revolt from Orthodox members who bolted and established the rival Tree of Life Synagogue in 1864.

A shadowy influence on Kohler's conduct at the conference in Pittsburgh was the memory of his charismatic but stern and doctrinaire father-in-law, David Einhorn, who had died six years earlier. Rabbi Wise's extraordinary prominence as an organizer could not be denied. But Einhorn, though departed, was the guiding spirit in Pittsburgh. "Einhorn was the father of American Reform, its theology and practice, its ideology and thrust," writes W. Gunther Plaut, a leading historian of the movement, noting that it was Einhorn and Samuel Adler of Emanu-El, Felix's father, who had formed a direct line of continuity from the Reform discussions in Germany to the delegates in Pittsburgh.[2]

Many years after Pittsburgh, Kohler paid tribute to his father-in-law as a member of "the Jewish legion of immortals" and a man of "tragic earnestness" who crossed swords with Wise on fundamental matters but nonetheless joined him in the pantheon of the religion's modernizers. Kohler compared Einhorn to the patriarch Abraham as a breaker of idols, and a lonely and persecuted wanderer who sought fearlessly to serve God. Recalling Einhorn's ouster from congregations in Europe and his escape from Baltimore to Philadelphia when his life was in danger because of his opposition to slavery, Kohler said his father-in-law's "continuous martyrdom" in the cause of his religious beliefs made him an exemplar of the German maxim "First Unity and then Liberty," except that for the combustible tempered Einhorn, it was "First Truth and then Peace."[3]

Yet Wise's presence could also not be denied in Pittsburgh. His outsized personality and record of establishing Jewish institutions guaranteed that he would be more famous than his rivals, whereas Einhorn had never commanded more followers than Wise and was perpetually handicapped by his insistence on speaking in dense German sentences. Wise was gregarious, self-important, voluble, and self-indulgent. Einhorn had been scholarly and serious, if occasionally vituperative. Wise could not help but be beloved and disdained, yet people were attracted to him in spite of his outsized personality. Yet Einhorn's fierce and uncompromising approach rather than Wise's flexible pragmatism would win the day at Pittsburgh and indeed in the cause of Reform Judaism as it reached its apex of influence at the end of the nineteenth century.[4]

Einhorn's spirit runs everywhere through his son-in-law's opening speech at the conference, where he laid out ten principles for the Jews in attendance. "We cannot afford to stand condemned as *law-breakers*, to be branded as frivolous and as *rebels and traitors* because we transgress these laws and principle," Kohler declared. Rather, he said, the conferees were soldiers in the war against Jewish assimilation and indifference. He urged them "to unite on a platform. . . . broad, comprehensive, enlightened, and liberal enough to impress and with all hearts, and also firm and positive enough to dispel suspicion and reproach of agnostic tendencies, or of discontinuing the historical thread of the past."[5]

Kohler's address made clear the challenge of saving a younger generation growing "more estranged from our sacred heritage" every day and the urgent need to adopt a new code rather than simply reject the old rules. His first principle called for unity around a platform that would exclude only the most "radical" views and embrace modern research in science, comparative religion, ethnology, biblical criticism, and other developments that force modern men and women to reassess their religious beliefs. Yet it was not enough for Jews to strip away every tradition and simply embrace the

Ten Commandments as the sole governing doctrine of Judaism. Rather, Jews had to find their way through a reinterpretation of all the related customs and laws of their heritage.

At the core of Jewish belief, he argued in his second principle, was broadening access to Judaism, perhaps through Sunday services, and to "awaken and foster the spirit of mutual help and elevation" on social and economic justice. In a striking conciliatory gesture despite his clear difference with Felix Adler and his Ethical Culture Society, Kohler praised those he had denounced as heretics for at least pursuing beneficial social goals. "Why should not each Jewish congregation have the material and moral welfare of the poor within its reach entrusted to its care also, so that religion becomes with each member an active training for the practice of love?" Kohler asked. Echoing Adler, he criticized the "aristocratic" structures of congregations handing out privileges to its wealthiest members and called on congregations to elevate the status of women to full and equal membership.

A third precept in Kohler's address called for a proliferation of Jewish publications and other means to disseminate the Jewish message. A fourth called for expanded religious education, including Hebrew. Related to these education issues, Kohler's fifth "commandment" was to upgrade, shorten, refine, and impose a basic uniformity on religious services themselves. Sixth, moving to a more controversial subject, Kohler called for elimination of the reading of passages that might be offensive to contemporary audiences, including the curses in Leviticus calling for terror, disease, death, barrenness, and defeat at the hands of Israel's enemies should Israel forsake God's laws.

To justify this remarkably censorious approach, Kohler noted that censorship of Scripture was hardly new—the rabbis of old had long discriminated "between offensive and other passages of the Bible," he said, presumably also referring to passages that seemed to condone rape and killing of enemies. In a seventh tenet, Kohler said that other "impure and offensive chapters" could be eliminated at least for children. These included Lot's offering his two virgin daughters to be raped by intruders rather than letting them have sex with two male guests (who in reality were angels) who had come to his house. He cited other cruelties visited on Israel's foes "which ought not to be mentioned before the youth or before a mixed assembly." (The point of the story about Lot is interpreted by many scholars to be that Lot was prepared to go to any length in order not to violate the laws of hospitality. But the passage suggests a more offensive interpretation for many others: that the heterosexual rape of one's virgin daughters is preferable to the homosexual rape of one's male guests.)

On the other hand, in his eighth principle, Kohler renewed a commitment to teaching the Bible and all of Jewish literature. In the ninth principle, Kohler called for Jews to relate more positively to Gentiles, especially Christians, who he said had shown greater tolerance toward Jews. It was also time, he insisted, for Jews to recognize Christians as fellow worshippers of the same God and not as pagans—and that Christians should be welcomed as converts, without subjecting men to the "barbarous cruelty" of circumcision, which he called "a national remnant of savage African life" that had no bearing to Jewish identity. Nor should a child of intermarriage be considered any less a Jew. "I can no longer accept the fanciful and twisted syllogisms of Talmudic law as binding for us," he declare. "I prefer good, sound, common-sense logic to Pilpulistic [i.e., obscurantist] lore and I think, if anywhere, here we ought to have the courage to emancipate ourselves from the thralldom of Rabbinical legality." Finally, in the tenth section, Kohler addressed the need to revive Judaism in the home by celebrating the Sabbath, Passover Seder, Hanukkah, and other rituals and holidays while modernizing them.

Upon concluding his presentation, the assembly approved a motion that his principles be adopted as the basis for its forthcoming deliberations. They whittled his ten points down to eight before adopting the platform. First, the platform explicitly disavowed the quasi atheism of Adler's Ethical Culture Society by recognizing that Judaism, while having "an attempt to grasp the Infinite" in common with all religion, "presents the highest conception of the God-idea." Here the platform dared to tread on new linguistic ground by explaining that the "idea" of God—reflected in Scripture in the context of ancient times—nonetheless remains "the central religious truth for the human race." Second, the platform declared the Bible to be "the record of the consecration of the Jewish people to its mission as the priest of the one God" and "the most potent instrument of religious and moral instruction." Science, history, and literary research "are not antagonistic to the doctrines of Judaism," it said, and the stories of the Bible, including its recounting of miracles, are "primitive" constructs and need not be taken literally.

A third provision declared that the full panoply of Talmudic teachings under the heading of interpreting "Mosaic legislation" should be seen as "training the Jewish people" for their mission but that contemporary Jews need be bound only by "its moral laws." Jews should embrace only those ceremonies that "elevate and sanctify our lives" while rejecting those "not adapted to the views and habits of modern civilization." More specifically, in the fourth precept, the platform asserted that rabbinical laws regulating diet, priestly purity, and dress were "entirely foreign to our present mental and spiritual state." Observing such rules "is apt rather to obstruct than to further modern spiritual elevation."

On the issue of praying for a messiah and a return to Palestine, the platform marked the culmination of many decades of thinking by reimagining and replacing these concepts with a yearning for a "great Messianic hope" for a just and peaceful world. Judaism, the platform made clear, is a religion—not a national identity: "We consider ourselves no longer a nation, but a religious community, and therefore expect neither a return to Palestine, nor a sacrificial worship under the sons of Aaron, nor the restoration of any of the laws concerning the Jewish state." Judaism, moreover, in the sixth plank of the platform, is deemed "a progressive religion, ever striving to be in accord with the postulates of reason." But in a concession to those uneasy about entirely rejecting the national identity of Judaism, the platform proclaimed "the utmost necessity of preserving the historical identity with our great past." In an ecumenical gesture that was also a plea for acceptance, it declared Christianity and Islam to be "daughter religions of Judaism," and that their mission of spreading "monotheistic and moral truth" was appreciated by Jews.

As for bodily resurrection of the dead, and the concepts of Gehenna and Eden (Hell and Paradise) as places of punishment or reward after death, the platform was clear. These ideas were to be rejected in favor of the doctrine "that the soul is immortal, grounding the belief on the divine nature of human spirit, which forever finds bliss in righteousness and misery in wickedness." Finally, in the eighth plank of the platform was a social justice section bearing the influence of Kohler's brother-in-law, Rabbi Emil Hirsch, that was destined to become a central tenet of Reform Judaism. Reminiscent also of the teachings of Felix Adler, this plank declared that "the spirit of the Mosaic legislation" sought "to regulate the relations between rich and poor," and thus it was the duty of Jews "to participate in the great task of modern times, to solve, on the basis of justice and righteousness, the problems presented by the contrasts and evils of the present organization of society."[6]

At a little more than six hundred words in length, the Pittsburgh Platform reflected the most ambitious attempt in modern Jewish history to embrace the goal of social progress among all citizens, while seeking to reconcile Judaism with science, history, modern interpretations of text, and practical realities of the contemporary world. Breaking dramatically with a vast legacy of law, tradition, and history, the platform capped decades of incremental and fitful moves by American Jewish leaders. It essentially signaled the transformation of the campaign to create an "American" Judaism, as advocated by Wise, into a campaign to create a more particular form of what was officially becoming known as Reform Judaism. It is for these reasons that Pittsburgh is known as the foundation of the "classical" phase of Reform Judaism—with its renunciation of traditional doctrines, practices, and "peoplehood"—that flourished into the first decades of the twentieth century. The platform also edged Judaism into increasing alignment with the influential social gospel of Protestantism, Catholicism and—most important—the leanings of many secularized Jews in America toward the belief that religious faith must be fulfilled by pursuing religiously inspired social justice.

In 1985, on the one hundredth anniversary of the platform, a leading synagogue in Pittsburgh assembled a group of Jewish historians and scholars to take stock of the platform's context, antecedents, and significance in a volume of essays. "It is clear . . . that the Pittsburgh Conference owed everything to its German predecessor of a generation before," noted the historian Gunther Plaut. But many other historians have maintained that the platform was quintessentially American, not German, and that it was excessively "triumphalist" in consigning traditions to obsolescence. Certainly, it was filled with optimism about the Jewish role in achieving redemption for humanity, and it abandoned once and for all the rote rituals of ancient Judaism, which it felt had prevented Jews from fulfilling their historic role as a chosen or elect people to achieve justice and virtue for individuals and for society as a whole. But the question was left hanging, whether the platform was an arrogant overreaching for Jews, by asserting that the Hebrew Bible, and especially the prophets, had a distinctive if not unique role in spreading ethics and virtuous behavior to the rest of the world. In retrospect, the platform was bound to be followed by revisionism as Jews came to grips with the difficulty of reconciling their unique role based on Scripture with the fact that Judaism was perhaps like other religions in the world and should not stand accused of a sense of superiority.[7]

Among the most controversial aspects of the Pittsburgh legacy was the way it defined the meaning of the "covenant" between Jews and God, the significance of the fact that Jews would continue living in exile and the redefinition of the Jewish distinction as a "chosen" people. In holding that Judaism reflects the "highest conception of the God idea" and that Judaism has "preserved and defended" this idea throughout history, the platform asserted that Jews undertook this obligation not simply because of history or because of their own virtue as a people, but because their covenant with God transformed them into a priestly people. "We are the heirs to a message, and we are vested with a mission to proclaim that message," Rabbi Samuel E. Karff of Congregation Beth Israel in Houston, and a former president of the Central Conference of American Rabbis, wrote in the platform's anniversary volume. Talmudic sages, Karff argued, assumed that for Jews to observe all 613 commandments at the root of the Talmud (by an ancient reckoning, the total number of positive and negative commandments in the written Torah) was their way of bearing witness to God. The Pittsburgh

Platform, in contrast, saw the mission as one of a higher and more general moral purpose in the broader world of disparate religious beliefs and social welfare challenges. The platform effectively defined Jews as the custodians, not the sole proprietors, of universally applicable ethical rules.

Recognizing that centuries of suffering had brought Jews to America to survive and thrive as full citizens, the authors of the platform demonstrated the readiness of American Jews to redefine the nature of their expulsion from the holy land in antiquity—to effectively rewrite their history. The platform rejected more explicitly than ever the idea that Jews were expelled from the land of Israel because of their sins. Citing certain Talmudic rulings that the Diaspora obliged Jews to bring truth to the world, Reform Jews developed the idea that Jews must achieve God's purpose by "living and working in and with the world," as Kohler enunciated it.

Intertwined with that belief was the important and revolutionary idea that Israel was not a nation but a religious community that did not expect to return to Palestine or to sacrificing animals at the Temple, especially after the dawn of the twentieth century and certainly after World War II. "History has discredited Pittsburgh's attitude toward Zionism," wrote Karff, "but its attitude toward Diaspora remains abidingly valid." Zionism and the establishment of Israel as a Jewish state, need not negate the mission of Jews in the Diaspora, in other words, Karff argued. Jews may carry out their priestly mission wherever they live, including in Zion. Equally important, the platform was revolutionary in embracing Christianity and Islam as heirs to the same origins in Abraham's faith.[8]

The Pittsburgh Platform enjoyed wide dissemination throughout America and Europe and was endorsed by various groups of rabbis who were not present at its creation. Wise reprinted the platform text in his *American Israelite* periodical, welcoming the prospect of healing his breach with radical followers of Einhorn. A new periodical called the *Jewish Reformer* was started by Rabbi Hirsch of Chicago, Einhorn's other son-in-law, who was instrumental in developing its social justice provision, and Adolph Moses, of Louisville, with three portraits on its masthead: Moses Mendelssohn, the great Enlightenment thinker who paved the way for reformist ideas in the eighteenth century; Abraham Geiger, a founder of German Reform; and David Einhorn.

The Pittsburgh Platform also speeded the movement to institute educational, cultural, and family programs at synagogues, elevate the role of women, and refocus attention on some ceremonies that had fallen away, notably Hanukkah and Sukkot, the harvest holiday following the opening of the autumnal new year. American Jews grew somewhat more comfortable calling themselves "Jews" or at least Jewish Americans, rather than using the adjective Hebrew or Israelite. The practice of calling rabbis minister or "the Reverend" took much longer to fade away.

But Pittsburgh also marked the final abandonment of Wise's earlier idea of one Judaism for all. Felix Adler of Ethical Culture condemned what he called its "race pride," still arguing that Judaism could not reform and still call itself Judaism. Conservatives thoroughly rejected its tenets, and some members of Wise's Union of American Hebrew Congregations withdrew from his organization, just as Wise had earlier feared.

Why did Wise embrace the platform after opposing many of its more radical doctrines for years? There is no evidence that Wise was abandoning his belief in the divine status of scripture, which the platform seemed to reject. Normally voluble about everything that crossed his mind, Wise also never produced a thorough rationale for the teachings of the Pittsburgh document. One answer to the question is that he was confident that he would be able to influence the future of Judaism through the members and alumni of the institutions he was creating. In addition, his earlier skepticism of radical adjustment to Judaism was fading. Having forbidden "biblical criticism" at Hebrew Union College, specifically rejecting the "documentary hypothesis" that the Torah was the product of at least four separate writers, as Wellhausen and others concluded, Wise came to embrace the underlying assumption of such analysis. On the other hand, Wise never abandoned his belief in the divine status of the Bible or even the historicity of the revelation on Mount Sinai.

The main answer to Wise's embrace of these radical doctrines was that he continued to be animated by the same spirit favoring unity that compelled him at previous rabbinical conferences. He also did not want to be left behind. Under fire from more traditionalist reformers who felt that Pittsburgh had gone too far, Wise asserted to colleagues that "nothing practical had been done at Pittsburgh" and that another rabbinical conference would soon adopt a more practical platform—a prediction never fulfilled. Despite himself, Wise thus came to be identified with the very reforms that he felt may have gone too far. In the wake of Pittsburgh, many congregations, especially in the east, demanded that he resign as president of Hebrew Union College. He was able to ignore those demands, popular as ever in Cincinnati. He had beaten back some of the more radical moves being discussed by reformers. In the end, Wise termed the "Declaration of Principles" hammered out in Pittsburgh as a "Declaration of Independence" for American Jews, adding in the *American Israelite*: "It declares that we, the much abused reformers, radicals, decried, defamed and debased by the men of the minority who usurped for themselves the titles of conservative and orthodox, or rather the Jews *par excellence*—We *are* the orthodox Jews in America, and they *were* the orthodoxy of former days and other countries. . . . You are an anachronism, strangers in this country, and to your own brethren. . . . We must proceed without you to perform our duties to our God, and our country, and our religion, for We are the orthodox Jews in America."[9]

But the reality was that Wise's dream of a unified liberal Judaism in America was definitively shattered at Pittsburgh. Instead of the high-water mark of Jews speaking in one voice, the charter hammered out at Pittsburgh proved the impossibility of such a goal. Instead of a Declaration of Independence, the Pittsburgh Platform was a declaration of war.

## CHALLENGES TO "CLASSICAL" REFORM

The decade of the adoption of the Pittsburgh Platform had begun with a seismic event in Jewish American history—as historically significant, by some lights, as the forced dispersal of Jews following destruction of the Temple in Jerusalem in 70 CE or the Spanish Inquisition in 1492. But the event was not in America. It occurred as Czar Alexander II of Russia was riding through the central streets of St. Petersburg, near the Winter Palace.[10]

Czar Alexander had undertaken many reforms, including liberation of the nation's serfs, after succeeding his father, Nicholas I, and ascending to the Russian imperial throne in 1855. But he had been unable to suppress the angry revolutionary spirit spreading through his country. Radicals exacted their revenge by planting a bomb on the czar's route on March 13, 1881, mortally wounding its imperial passenger. Alexander's death a few hours later ignited a conflagration of pogroms against Jews throughout Russia, a culmination of rising anti-Semitic attacks building in much of Europe over previous decades.

Russia was hardly a stranger to anti-Semitic violence. But this time a Jewish woman, Gesya Gelfman, was accused in the assassination plot. Along with others, she was later tried and convicted, and she died in prison before she could be executed. There followed a sweeping crackdown on Jews and a wave of oppressive laws barring or limiting them from certain jobs and educational opportunities. These "May Laws"—so-called because they were imposed May 15, 1882—were also accompanied by the forced resettlement of Jews out of cities and back into the rural parts of the so-called Pale of Settlement, a vast western region of Imperial Russia, established in 1791 for the permanent residency of Jews.[11]

From these frightful events ensued one of the largest and most dramatic migrations in Jewish history, as two million Jews from Russia, Romania, and Austria-Hungary fled to American shores from 1881 to 1914. This great migration transformed the face of American Jewry, along with its doctrines, practices, customs, and culture. Many of the Jewish immigrants wore the caftans and fur hats characteristic of the Polish gentry in the eighteenth century, when Hasidic Judaism first began in Europe, in part as a protest against adherents of German-style Orthodoxy who sometimes dressed like their fellow Germans.

The Jewish migration overwhelmed the existing population of 250,000 American Jews, most of whom were of Central European heritage, with an entirely different culture rooted in the Yiddishkeit practices of the Old World.

Not that the Eastern European Jews were homogeneous, either. Mixed in with the many devout believers in traditional Judaism was an agglomeration of renegades, agnostics, socialists, communists, anarchists, Zionists, and others not necessarily devoted to deeply Orthodox practices. Many Reform Jews saw the new immigrants as uncouth and an embarrassing throwback to a world they left behind. Some were shocked by the revival of practices they had sought to discard, and there were efforts to "Americanize" the newly arrived coreligionists. But to their credit, American Jews resisted any temptation to limit immigration. To assist the new immigrants, they set up a remarkable array of social welfare organizations. Jews who had kept to traditional practices during the Reform period, however, were among those who sought most to reach out to the new immigrants.

Reform Jews like Rabbi Wise did not at first see any kind of threat to his efforts to modernize and Americanize Judaism. "There is no danger that the Russian Jews settling down in this country will abide very long in their inherited orthodoxy, which quite a number of them had deserted before they came to this country," he wrote in 1884. But within a few years he deplored the "half-civilized orthodoxy" of the newcomers. "We are Americans, and they are not," he declared, dismissing them as less than liberal, especially in their opposition to emancipation for women. "We appeal to reason and they appeal to their grandparent's habits. We are Israelites of the nineteenth century and a free country, and they gnaw the dead bones of past centuries."[12]

The counterrevolution against the reforms pressed by Wise, Kohler, and others was already beginning. A few months after adoption of the Pittsburgh Platform, a small gathering of Orthodox rabbis met on January 31, 1886, at New York's Spanish Portuguese Synagogue, Shearith Israel. The oldest synagogue congregation in America continued to relish its status as an aristocratic redoubt of traditional Judaism, proudly located in a majestic Palladian-style house of worship with a high octagonal dome and Ionic and Corinthian columns at Nineteenth Street just west of Fifth Avenue.

In attendance were Rabbis Sabato Morais, who had succeeded Isaac Leeser at Mikveh Israel Synagogue of Philadelphia after emigrating from Italy in 1851; Abraham Pereira Mendes of Newport; Henry Schneeberger of Baltimore; Bernard Drachman of New York; and the host, Shearith Israel's

spiritual leader, Rabbi Henry Pereira Mendes. The Pittsburgh Platform, adopted the previous year, alarmed these rabbis over the prospect that Hebrew Union College, with its liberal bent, would overwhelm and suffocate
Orthodox Judaism if allowed to continue unchallenged. This small group
was later joined by Rabbis Kohut, Aaron Wise, Henry S. Jacobs, Marcus
Jastrow, and Aaron Bettelheim—many of them not necessarily adhering to
strict Orthodox teachings but nonetheless still alarmed by the apostasy if
not outright heresies at Pittsburgh.

The gathering effectively marked the birth of Conservative Judaism in
nineteenth-century America, though the term was not in general use at that
time. Their cooperation led to the establishment of the Jewish Theological
Seminary that same year. The seminary held its first classes the next year in
the vestry at the Spanish Portuguese building. Morais, the first president,
prayed that the new seminary would preserve "Historical and Traditional
Judaism . . . by educating, training and inspiring teachers-rabbis who would
stand for the 'Torah and Testimony.'" Graduates would use "their knowledge of Jewish learning, literature, history, ideals and Jewish Science" to
achieve "human uplift" and "world civilization."[13]

Significantly, and as if to express continuity with the narrative of American Judaism, the Seminary and Morais paid tribute at its founding to Isaac
Leeser as one of its progenitors. Rabbi Morais, as an equally important conciliatory gesture, declared that it was both dangerous and impossible for
Judaism to reject Reform Judaism's significance, which "well meaning and
unwise orthodoxy" advised them to do. "Isolation is an impossibility," he
said. "It would be inadvisable if it were possible."[14]

The forerunner of the Jewish Theological Seminary in New York had
been the Jewish Theological Seminary in Breslaw, led by Rabbi Zacharias
Frankel, who is also considered a founder of modern Conservative Judaism.
It was Frankel who sought to reconcile and harmonize modern concepts
of humanity and scholarship with traditional Judaism, but without under-
mining the institutions and practices of the latter. Frankel's signature philosophy—what he called a "positive-historical" approach—was that textual
interpretation and reason must form the basis of changes in Jewish practices

and norms, not the demands of ordinary Jews themselves. To that end, he argued, Judaism must be studied historically because it had always been influenced by its exposure to social, political, and economic conditions, and that these changes should be seen as positive. He had called for some changes in services and prayers based on a reinterpretation of texts, over the objection of both German Enlightenment reformers and also traditionalists. He did not hesitate to criticize Geiger and others for what he charged was shoddy scholarship. But he also defended some changes in practice, such as the use of choirs in the service. His teachings influenced Morais and other founders of the conservative movement in America.

Much more traditionally oriented Jews were also trying to find their way on a more conservative path from the Reformers' or even the founders of Jewish Theological Seminary's. A year after JTS was established on the Lower East Side, a separate group of representatives of what was called the Association of American Orthodox Hebrew Congregations met at Beth Hamedrash Hagadol (Great Study House), in a former Baptist church on East Broadway. There these ultra-traditionalist Jews, many of them part of the new wave of immigrants from Eastern Europe and Russia, sought consensus on a leader who could arrest the "open and flagrant desecration of the Sabbath, the neglect of dietary laws, and the formation of various shades of Orthodoxy and Reform." Their hope was to find an Orthodox sage of such stature that he could organize and defend Orthodoxy as it was besieged by heresy and disbelief in America. Turning to the Old Country, and the seat of some of Europe's leading Jewish intellectuals, they recruited Rabbi Jacob Joseph (1840–1902) of Vilna as their rescuer.

The disparate organizers and rabbis called themselves "Orthodox" Jews, using a term increasingly in vogue and borrowed from usage in Germany and the Austro-Hungarian Empire. But they were deeply divided among themselves over tradition and doctrine. Rabbi Joseph, fluent in Hebrew and Yiddish, looked like a likely savior, having been educated at yeshivas and having achieved a record of scholarship while still in his forties. He arrived in 1888 to become chief rabbi of the Association of American Orthodox Hebrew Congregations, with the ultimate objective of uniting the Orthodox community under his leadership as chief rabbi. It was an effort that eventually failed. The Orthodox community, like the reformers, was split between Sephardim, who were accustomed to interacting with non-Jewish communities around them and also with Jewish Reformers, and Ashkenizim, often from European ghettos, where their experience was untouched by the religious dissent fermenting in Germany and the United States. Formal arguments over doctrine and customs masked the simple fact of fierce ethnic resentments based on loyalties to disparate parts of Jewry in Europe. Rabbi Joseph, a Lithuanian, spoke Yiddish but not German or English, and his overconfident claim to be serving as "chief rabbi" in the city was, inevitably, poorly received among many other Jewish communities.

Despite his reputation as a learned man back in Lithuania, Rabbi Joseph faced ridicule over his speeches in Yiddish, even by many observant Jews, who saw them as an absurd throwback. He stirred special controversy over his feckless efforts to impose order on the notoriously corrupt and unruly kosher meat business in New York, in which a variety of butchers claiming to be kosher had long enlisted their own rabbis to bless their practices, often with kickbacks involved. Joseph and the association tried to institute a uniform tax to obtain its seal of approval, but the move ignited protests among butchers and consumers alike, who viewed it as a shakedown. Eventually, the association fell apart, and Rabbi Joseph died in poverty on the Lower East Side. At his funeral in 1902, thousands followed his cortege through the city streets, but a riot erupted between the mourners and a group of Irish factory workers (the grievance beyond the disruption in their neighborhood is obscure) while the police stood by, watching many Jews get beaten.

The issue of how much disparate Jewish groups could work together for the common good remained salient. The founders of Jewish Theological Seminary, while disagreeing vehemently with Reform Jews on important matters, had no problem working with them to defend the right of Jews to be free from efforts by missionaries to indoctrinate and convert their coreligionists. Rabbi Joseph, by contrast, had no interest in working with the dissidents. "From his European background, he knew of but one expression of Judaism, and it was to help save the faith from America that he had come to this country," writes Jeffrey S. Gurock, a historian at Yeshiva University. The Lithuanian rabbi's goal was to rescue Judaism from the disarray in the fields of observing the Sabbath, keeping kosher, and educating young people in the proper way.[15]

While Rabbi Joseph's efforts to revive orthodoxy on Old World lines failed, the Orthodox modernizers pushed ahead, led by Rabbi Bernard Drachman, who became president of the Union of Orthodox Jewish Congregations of America, known as the Orthodox Union (or "the OU"), which was established in 1898 and devoted to modernizing education by including instruction in English. In effect, Rabbi Drachman and other pioneers were seeking to Americanize *orthodox* Judaism, in the tradition of Isaac Leeser. Drachman, son of immigrants from Galicia and Bavaria, studied at the Jewish Theological Seminary of Breslau and the University of Heidelberg. He was a founder of the Park East Synagogue, sheltered in a grandly Moorish building on New York's Upper East Side. He and other "modern" Orthodox figures argued that the traditionalists like Rabbi Joseph were less than helpful in their efforts to persuade American Jews to turn their backs on modernization. Their purpose, they declared, was to mediate between the modern world and Jewish tradition.

The efforts of Drachman and others included the establishment of an Orthodox Jewish Sabbath Alliance, which sought to get Jewish shopkeepers to close on Saturday. They also petitioned state legislators to repeal blue laws that required closing shops on Sunday, which prevented Jews from opening on a day they did not observe as Sabbath. The disagreement was played out in a matter of emphasis. Rabbi Joseph had beseeched Jews to observe the Sabbath. Rabbi Drachman, by contrast, sought to change laws to help Jews adjust. He and others also sought to lift Jewish education out of the sterile pedagogy that they inherited from Europe. Gurock explains that their differences in the late nineteenth century set in motion the division in Jewish Orthodoxy between "resisters" and "accommodators." The resisters disdained Reform and other breakaway Jews. The accommodators were comfortable with alliances for certain causes.

It was more than ironic, and indeed it was predictable, that the Orthodox factions would split apart much as the Reformers had many decades earlier over the issue of various folk practices from the Old Country and what some called noisy and undignified behavior at services. Acknowledging that such practices were comforting to new immigrant Jews, the Orthodox Union argued that American Judaism had to move beyond its immigrant past and find a new identity rooted in contemporary society. The Jewish Endeavor Society, an initiative that sought to retain the involvement of youth in Orthodox Jewish practice, was founded in 1901 by some students of Drachman. This society called for "dignified services" designed to "recall indifferent Jewry back to their ancestral faith." These services retained traditional prayers and separation of the sexes but also instituted English language prayers and sermons. The "downtown," more traditional establishment was suspicious of them for consorting with Reform rabbis and "deviationists."

## THE NEW CENTURY: EMERGENCE OF THREE MAIN BRANCHES OF JUDAISM

Amid the proliferation of these different groups, it was still possible to say at the dawn of the twentieth century that American Judaism was split into two basic camps, Orthodox and Reform, with the reformers still predominant, at least organizationally. The term *Conservative* was in use but still relatively undefined, even though many applied it to those Jews involved in the establishment of the Jewish Theological Seminary. The name Conservative derived in part from rabbis in Germany who, like their counterparts in America, wanted to adjust Jewish law and orthodox practices to contemporary demands, but who also thought reformers had gone too far. Their aim was to *conserve* what they thought was most valuable in traditional Judaism while accepting certain accommodations to modernity legitimized by their reading of the ancient texts.

At the turn of the century, the Jewish Theological Seminary was struggling under the weight of low enrollment and financial problems following the death in 1897 of its founding president, Rabbi Morais. Believing it was their duty to sustain an Orthodox seminary in spite of their own reformist inclinations, a number of members of Temple Emanu-El, such as Jacob Schiff, Louis Marshall, and Julius Rosenwald, stepped in to support the seminary. In 1902 they recruited a new president, Solomon Schechter, a scholar at Cambridge University renowned for his pioneering study of a collection of rare ancient and medieval Jewish texts discovered in Egypt (the so-called Cairo Geniza). Schechter was no stranger to the reformers' vision of Judaism. He had studied with scholars affiliated with the Wissenschaft des Judentums movement in Berlin. But he believed that this school had "never, to my knowledge, offered to the world a theological platform of its own"—and that no such platform could be legitimately adopted for all Jews without some formal consent.[16] Schechter and his disciples at Jewish Theological Seminary established the United Synagogue of America, later renamed the United Synagogue of Conservative Judaism. And as they sought to define a middle ground for Judaism, various congregations throughout the United States gravitated toward an institutionalization of Conservative Judaism in order to attract the flood of immigrants from Eastern Europe and Russia who might feel uncomfortable with the Reform movement's radicalism.

To some scholars, Conservative Judaism represented a wholly new religion comparable to Mormonism and Christian Science. Other scholars defined Conservative Judaism as a middle-of-the-road branch of Judaism as it was practiced by Americans seeking to make some but not all adjustments to modernity. The followers of Schechter sometimes called themselves Orthodox, but they also used terms like Conservative, traditional, liberal, progressive, or Modern Orthodox. But because they so confidently embraced a variety of adjustments to modernization, they were generally to remain in the middle ground or mainstream "American Judaism" that had evolved in the late nineteenth century.

The cause of Reform Judaism at the turn of the century was also pushed in two different directions. Some congregations abandoned the reading of the Torah altogether, believing that merely displaying it in the arc was sufficient. Advocates of such changes saw them as revealing Judaism in its essential purity. Conversions occurred without ritual baths or circumcision, only instruction and commitment. The matrilineal definition of Judaism, holding that only children of a Jewish mother were considered Jewish, was increasingly overlooked as many Jews wanted children of all mixed marriages to be automatically regarded as Jewish. The Central Conference of American Rabbis, the organization of Reform rabbis, moved increasingly toward breaking with other interpretations, such as allowing cremation rather than burial.

But because it also provoked a backlash, the Pittsburgh Platform was beginning to look outdated among many reformers after the turn of the century. Like all pendulums, the Jewish pendulum of reform started swinging back somewhat to tradition, even among reformers, as Jews looked back to their rituals to find meaning and reexamined the history of their traditions. Accordingly, they started to refine and revive rituals in the marriage ceremony and in the mourning rites. They set about reviving certain holidays like Sukkot, the harvest festival, and they accepted Hanukkah, overlooking its significance as calling for the restoration of the Temple in Jerusalem, because the holiday was especially beloved among children. "There can be no healthy Reform that has not its origin in Orthodoxy," declared Jacob Schiff, the prominent German Jew in New York, suggesting that without tradition, Reform would cause Judaism to disappear. Kohler had also declared in 1898: "Today not Reform, but Judaism, must be the sole object of our solicitude." Not surprisingly, the changes toward both more and less reform provoked disputes between rabbis and congregation presidents, sometimes with rabbis advocating change in opposition to lay leaders, and often the reverse.

For prayer books, Reform Jews primarily gravitated to Wise's *Minhag America* and Einhorn's *Olat Tamid*, but other prayer books proliferated as Reform Jews experimented with different approaches. What emerged from these disagreements among Reformers was the *Union Prayer Book* (*Seder Tefilot Yisrael*), which appeared in 1892, compiled by Rabbi Isaac Moses of Chicago and revised in the next few years by Rabbi Kohler. Heavily indebted to Einhorn, the *Union Prayer Book* opened from left to right, and was written mostly in English. "We rejoice that after the long, dreary night a new morn is dawning," the book declared. "The truths revealed to Israel are becoming the possession of an even greater number of men." The *Union Prayer Book* remained in use by congregations of varied leanings until the 1960s, when the Reform movement sought to accommodate widening support for Israel and a desire to return to at least some traditions in the service and in practices.

Kohler's takeover of Hebrew Union College in 1903, after Wise's passing and a year after Schechter's appointment at Jewish Theological Seminary, solidified its identity as a Reform organization. Biblical criticism became a main part of the academic curriculum and the College also rejected what it called "Jewish nationalism," the ultimate expression of Jewish peoplehood and attachment to the Holy Land. Looking outward, arms of Reform Judaism—the Union's Board of Delegates on Civil Rights—sought to combat anti-Semitism, laws prohibiting work on Sunday, Bible reading in public schools, and restrictions on immigration. Kohler and Schechter maintained good relations with each other as Reform and Conservative Judaism increasingly took over the mainstream of American Judaism.

But one of the most powerful trends within Reform Judaism continued to evolve as it became increasingly identified with the cause of social justice. Rabbinical sermons in all the mainstream parts of American Judaism increasingly focused on social and economic issues. Though long in coming, this trend forcefully cast aside earlier concerns in the nineteenth century about being identified with socialism, or indeed with any cause outside Jewish concerns. Jewish interest in such matters also grew out of the era of protests, strikes, and demands among farmers, workers, and others left out of the general prosperity of the Gilded Age.

These developments fed into the growth of the populist and progressive political movements in the late nineteenth and early twentieth centuries, as well as Christian exponents of the social gospel, many of them citing the biblical prophets along with Jesus as advocates for moral treatment of the poor and the oppressed. In 1891, Pope Leo XIII had issued his encyclical "Rerum Novarum" ("Revolutionary Change") on the "rights and duties of capital and labor," addressing the condition of workers. Jewish leaders could not help but notice, and they too cited the prophets Amos, Isaiah, and Micah. ("What does the Lord require of you, but to do justice, to love kindness, and walk humbly with your God?")[17]

The Jewish version of the "social gospel" of Christians flowered in the 1920s when the Central Conference of American Rabbis, the organization of Reform religious leaders, campaigned against child labor and in favor of worker rights generally. Their interests expanded to white slavery, venereal disease, working conditions and rights, juvenile delinquency, profit sharing, health care, and housing. In 1923, the Central Conference worked with the Federal Council of Churches of Christ and the National Catholic Welfare Council in attacking the seven-day, twelve-hour-a-day work week in the steel industry.[18]

After World War I, a serious divide among Jews opened up, focusing on Zionism—the goal of establishing a secular Jewish homeland or state in Palestine. The First Zionist Congress had taken place in Basel in 1897, provoking disapproval from the Reform establishment. But the Balfour Declaration by Britain in 1917, supporting a "homeland" for Jews in Palestine in response to the efforts of Theodor Herzl and the Zionist movement, appealed to many American Jews, reformers included, who began to see the ancient Jewish homeland as a place of refuge for the dispossessed in Europe and the Middle East, if not for themselves. (Prominent among these Jews was Louis D. Brandeis, elevated to the United States Supreme Court in 1916, a thoroughly secularized Jew who passionately joined the Zionist cause.)

But generally speaking, Reform Jews continued to see themselves as Americans first, and America as their Zion, and the Zionist movement as not for them. American Jews continued to fear being seen as harboring dual loyalties, a perception they worried might fuel anti-Semitism. Not all Reform Jews were anti-Zionist, but over time in the twentieth century, there arose a "Zionization" of the Reform movement.

In 1919, Kohler finally agreed, declaring: "Let Palestine, our ancient home, under the protection of the great nations, or under the specific British suzerainty, again become a center of Jewish culture and a safe refuge for the homeless." The shift toward supporting a homeland for the Jews gathered strength throughout the middle of the twentieth century. After World

War II and the Holocaust, the transformation of American Jewry into sup-porting creation of a state of Israel was complete.[19] Complete, that is, until controversies arose about Israel's policies in the West Bank territories in recent years.

Reform Jews had not been the only ones to resist creation of a secular state for Jews, at least at first. Many deeply Orthodox Jews also saw Zionism in its early phase as a threat, because they considered the Jews' return to the Promised Land something that could be delivered only by God. Moreover, the Zionist movement in Europe was overtly secular, sometimes flagrantly mocking traditional Jewish practices. Over time, many in the Orthodox establishment have accepted the Jewish state as useful but continue to reject its secular authority over Jewish matters.

The Americanization of Judaism continued to develop in the pre–World War II decades with the founding of the Reconstructionist movement by Mordecai Kaplan, a former Orthodox rabbi born in Lithuania. Kaplan founded the Orthodox Jewish Center in 1918 but left Orthodoxy because of his evolving definition of Judaism as a "religious civilization" not depen-dent on belief in a personal and anthropomorphic conception of God, divine revelation, or traditional laws. He was initially most comfortable as a Con-servative Jew, but eventually founded his own Reconstructionist branch of Judaism. Despite Kaplan's declaration that Jews were welcome to embrace traditional Jewish practices, his publication of a Reconstructionist prayer book led to his excommunication by the Union of Orthodox Rabbis in 1945.

In the 1920s, Rabbi Stephen S. Wise of New York established the Jew-ish Institute of Religion, a liberal seminary that sought to compete with Hebrew Union College by being openly Zionist and by embracing some traditions that the College had rejected. The American Jewish Congress was also founded to represent pro-Zionist American Jews. Stephen Wise's institute later merged with Hebrew Union College in 1949.

By 1924, the passage of the National Origins Act severely curtailed the immigration of Jews to the United States by imposing strict quotas on immi-grants from Eastern and Southern Europe. By 1930, the gates to the United States from Eastern Europe were closing, ending the massive migration of preceding decades, putting the number of Jews in the United States at a little more than four million. The advent of Hitler in the 1930s was another cataclysmic event for the identity of American Jews, as Rabbi Stephen Wise led the warnings to the dangers of European Jews posed by Nazism. But reform Jews of this period remained primarily focused on their own domestic concerns, in part because news from Hitler's Germany was fragmentary.

Meeting in Columbus, Ohio, in 1937, the Central Conference of American Rabbis felt the influence of the yearning for a return to tradition. Once again declaring that the Jewish message was "universal, aiming at the union and perfection of mankind under the sovereignty of God" and that it was entirely consistent with science and modernity, the Columbus conference declared its embrace of "the doctrine of the One, living God, who rules the world through law and love," not the "God idea" of Pittsburgh. In another throwback to tradition, the Columbus Platform honored the Torah "both written and oral," though there was no specific reference to the Talmud, the central text of the "Oral Torah." "Each age has the obligation to adapt the teachings of the Torah to its basic needs in consonance with the genius of Judaism," it said, in the only reference to the possible obsolescence of Talmudic teachings cited in the Pittsburgh document.

The Columbus charter also avoided rejection of Jewish "peoplehood" as previous declarations had done. Rather, it spoke of the people of Israel as bound by a common heritage, and of Palestine as holding "the promise of renewed life for many of our brethren." Moving with full force toward the embrace of social justice, the Columbus Platform called for "the elimination of man-made misery and suffering, of poverty and degradation, of tyranny and slavery, of social inequality and prejudice, of ill-will and strife."[20]

Following all the horrors of the Holocaust that came to light after World War II, Jewish synagogue membership grew in the 1950s, along with support for the state of Israel as a signal responsibility for American Jews.

The 1960s buffeted Jewish identity in the United States. American Jews had gradually moved from American cities to its prosperous suburbs, where dozens of new synagogue congregations flourished. Comity with non-Jews was made easier after a milestone was achieved by the Vatican Council,

which declared in 1965 that Jews were collectively absolved for the murder of Jesus. Another turning point for American Jews occurred in 1967, when Israel was besieged by its Arab neighbors and struck back with a stunning military victory, capturing the West Bank, the Sinai, Gaza, and Eastern Jerusalem. American Jews responded across the board with a deeper devotion to Israel's security and perhaps an appreciation of its identity.

The 1960s were also a time of racial turmoil in the United States. Reform and Conservative Jews generally supported the civil rights movement even as some were alarmed by a flare-up of anti-Semitic rhetoric among some African-American militants. By the late 1970s, a series of social upheavals in America challenged all branches of Judaism. The Reform and Conservative movements suddenly had to adjust some of their traditional practices in the face of demands for equal treatment by women and, much later, by gay Americans. They also had to deal with the increasing phenomenon of intermarriage, and whether to recognize the children of these marriages as Jewish if their mother was not. (Recognition of patrilineal Jewish identity, which began in the nineteenth century, accelerated in the late twentieth century in non-Orthodox circles.)

Another quandary for American Jews in more contemporary times has been the growing embrace of Jews—and of the state of Israel—by the evangelical Christian community. This embrace has occurred just as American Jews were growing uncomfortable with that community's opposition to rights for women and gays—and, as recent surveys show, as younger American Jews grow increasingly critical of the treatment of Palestinian Arabs in Israel and the West Bank. Yet, in the face of these threats, American Jews continue to remain in solidarity with the liberal political order and on the liberal side of the Democratic Party in elections all the way through the Obama and Trump eras. Still, the expansion of Jewish settlements in the West Bank, territory held by Israel since the 1967 war, has threatened to drive a historic wedge between Israel and the American Jewish community generally, testing Jewish loyalty to Israel among Reform and (to a lesser degree) Conservative Jews.

In 1976, shortly after the centennial anniversaries of the founding of

Hebrew Union College and the Union of American Hebrew Congregations, the Central Conference of American Rabbis called for yet another Reform rabbinic conference, this time in San Francisco. The conference adopted what it called a "centenary perspective" that accelerated the process of Jews returning to an acceptance of their identity as a people as well as a religion, moving away from the declarations of rabbis in the nineteenth century. "Born as Hebrews in the ancient Near East, we are bound together like all ethnic groups by language, land, history, culture, and institutions," the platform declared. "But the people of Israel is unique because of its involvement with God and its resulting perception of the human condition." Once again, the Reform movement expressed support for "universal justice and peace," noting that a third of all the world's Jews now live "in our people's ancient homeland" and that Jews everywhere "are bound to that land and to the newly reborn State of Israel by innumerable religious and ethnic ties."[21]

Then, in 1999, the most recent iteration of Reform Jewish attitudes again reaffirmed tradition, pluralism, social justice, and tolerance of conflicting views in Judaism. Taking note of the platforms of 1885, 1937, and 1976, the 1999 document said the "great contribution of Reform Judaism is that it has enabled the Jewish people to introduce innovation while preserving tradition, to embrace diversity while asserting commonality, to affirm beliefs without rejecting those who doubt, and to bring faith to sacred texts without sacrificing critical scholarship."

Rather than reject the "sources of our tradition," the Reform movement embraced them as a path to understanding the "holiness" of the Jewish people. It affirmed that humans are created in God's image—as it says in the Bible—again a distant cry from the rejection of an anthropomorphic and "personal" God of the nineteenth century. The 1999 platform held that Jews "encounter God's presence in moments of awe and wonder, in acts of justice and compassion, in loving relationships and in the experiences of everyday life." The Torah, it said, has become a "manifestation of God's love" for humanity and central to Judaism and the focus of study. There must be "renewed attention" to the traditional commandments of Judaism, but there was no specific reference to the body of Oral Law or Halakha that

had been effectively abandoned. The Messiah was again treated metaphorically, and the increasingly popular use of the ancient concept of *tikkun olam*, "repairing the world," was cited to "help bring nearer the messianic age." Seeking to reconcile support for Israel with uneasiness over treatment of Palestinians, the platform rejoiced in the state of Israel, but noted that it did so in support of Israel fulfilling the rights "for all its inhabitants" and striving "for a lasting peace between Israel and its neighbors."[22]

By the end of the twentieth century, American Judaism was characterized by diversity of views on politics and social issues, including a return to tradition in worship and sense of identity as a people with a rich culture. But for the most part, American Judaism at the dawn of the twenty-first century was dominated by the adjustments to custom, Jewish law, ritual, and theology that had been carried out by American forebears of the nineteenth century.

Where the American Judaism community takes these changes in the future is uncertain and in flux, with diversity giving way to polarization as Jews struggle to remain unified—the long-pursued but still elusive goal of most of their history in the United States.

*Epilogue*

# AN AMERICAN RELIGION

J ewish immigrants in the nineteenth century clung to a multitude of ap-
prehensions as well as hopes. America beckoned as a place of economic
promise and unprecedented religious liberty. But Jews understood that
their new land might suffocate the traditions of their faith and obliterate
their roots.

"Friends!" a religious teacher in Bavaria wrote in 1839 to Moses and
Yetta Alsbacher before they departed for Cleveland, "You are traveling to
a land of freedom where the opportunity will be presented to live without
compulsory religious education. Resist and withstand this tempting freedom and do not turn away from the religion of our fathers."[1] But turning
away would be difficult to avoid. To traditionalists such as Rabbi Bernard
Illowy, who emigrated to America from Bohemia in 1848, Judaism faced
a moment of maximum peril. Writing to acquaintances in London and

Frankfurt, he described the United States as "an unclean land, a land that devoureth its inhabitants, whose people . . . are to be considered dead."[2]

The Jews were not alone in predicting that Judaism faced oblivion in the United States. When the poet Henry Wadsworth Longfellow was inspired to write a poem about an old Jewish cemetery in Newport, Rhode Island, he turned it into a symbol of the Jews' vanished past and doubtful future. The poem echoed his nostalgia over the disappearance of the heroic Native Americans in "The Song of Hiawatha" (1855), but in Newport the derelict gravestones reminded Longfellow of the tablets carried by Moses and the crumbling traditions that Jews carried with them:

> But ah! what once has been shall be no more!
> The groaning earth in travail and in pain,
> Brings forth its races, but does not restore.
> And the dead nations never rise again.[3]

For all these predictions of demise, starting with their arrival as a group in New York in the mid-seventeenth century and continuing through the next three centuries, Jews did more than outwit the pessimists and survive. They thrived, in part by adjusting their religion to their new environment's demands. Their motives included a need to accommodate the practical necessity of living and traveling in an alien environment. But the Jews also wanted to make Jewish customs more "American" in their own eyes and the eyes of their fellow citizens. Finally, they embraced an intellectual transformation guiding them to rethink and revise ancient laws, practices, and doctrines to keep Judaism alive for new generations awakening and adhering to modern science and intellectual trends. They effectively redefined what it is to be a Jew, and what the purpose of a Jew in America should be.

Judaism's flourishing in America was not foreordained or inevitable. Neither was it free from conflict and animosity. On the contrary, the disputes among Jews in America were emotional and personal. They were also very American. As Martin Marty has suggested, Jews became pilgrims in their new land, but all religions have made the same pilgrimage and had faced challenges and adjustments. The Jews shaped their experience in America, and they were shaped by the America they found. The push and pull for Jews followed a historic tension. On one side was the American myth that its inhabitants became "new" men and women, evolving into what the critic R. W. B. Lewis called the "American Adam," untethered to the past and setting out anew, and surrendering to the American "melting pot" in which everyone would become like everyone else. On the other side was the determination of Jews and others not to melt away but to adjust in ways that preserved and even strengthened their identity, heritage, traditions—and even their diversity—to be "a part" of America as well as a people "apart."

Today Jews in America face new perils and new predictions of their demise. These take the form of warnings about intermarriage, secularization, low fertility rates, conversion, the failure of Jewish education, and the fear of forgetting if not abandoning their history. Jews are further divided over "peoplehood" versus "religion" in their identity—that is, whether Judaism is a civilization and culture based on blood, rituals, and shared ancestors, or defined strictly by religious principles of belief in God. There are also conflicting demands to make Judaism conform to new definitions of social and economic justice, tolerance, feminism, gay rights, government support for religious education institutions, and religious liberty defined by the law. American Jews on opposite ends of the religious spectrum continue to see many other American Jews on the other end as practicing an alien form of their own religion, so different as to be another religion altogether.

Finally, American Jews are divided over Israel, and the extent of their obligations or loyalty to the world's only Jewish state. They argue over Israel's security concerns, its treatment of non-Jewish citizens, its conduct toward Palestinians in disputed territories, its relationship with its neighbors, and importantly, over its enforcement of Orthodox norms governing marriage, divorce, conversion, prayer, Sabbath observance, and other practices.

The message of the Jewish journey recounted in this book is that the conflicts of today are anything but new. They are rooted in the disputes of the past, and the counsels of despair and doom can take solace that Jews have faced and overcome such trials in that history. It is important for Jews today to remember that the turbulent history of their religion has always been one of division competing with unity. In ancient times, exile forced Jews to turn to prayer, books, and laws rather than animal sacrifices and other rituals at the ancient Temple of Judaism. They then divided over the interpretation of their laws time and time again. The conflicts between Sadducees and Pharisees, between the Maccabees and the Hellenizers, between the Karaites and their traditionalist antagonists, between followers and repudiators of false messiahs, between the pietistic adherents of mysticism and the rationalists, between customs in the Sephardic and Ashkenazic worlds, and between the modern Haskalah school of interpreters of ancient laws and the literalist believers in God speaking through those laws—all are part of a long narrative of division. The message of this volume is that these conflicts formed the foundation of American Judaism as well. As the religious historian Judah Goldin has noted, "it is impossible to say that the Jewish people were perpetually dominated by this or that single idea from the beginnings to now."[4]

But for all these conflicts, what American Jews established in their first centuries in a new land has evolved into what has become the mainstream today, even among many traditionalist-oriented American Jews. Although this book dwells on the period from the mid-seventeenth century to roughly the advent of the twentieth century, the Judaism of today—even after the influx of millions of Jews fleeing persecution and poverty in Eastern Europe in the early twentieth century, and the more modern influx of Jews from Iran, South Africa, the former Soviet Union, and even Israel—rests on the foundation established by the pioneers of this earlier period. And in whatever ways Judaism finds to resolve its contradictory tendencies, the influence of courageous thinkers of the nineteenth century—Isaac Leeser, Isaac Mayer Wise, Gustavus Poznanski, Isaac Harby, David Einhorn, Felix Adler, Alexander Kohut, Kaufmann Kohler, Sabato Morais, and many others—played a central role in shaping the great Jewish community that arose in its new American home.

In exile from their Promised Land for much of the last 2,500 years, Jews have lived through what the anthropologist Melvin Konner delineates as

five great "golden ages." The first brought an outpouring of Talmudic scholarship in the "Babylonian Captivity" following the first destruction of the
Jerusalem Temple in the sixth century BCE. The second was marked by
a similar profusion of scholarship and literature in medieval Spain, ending
catastrophically with the Inquisition. The third took place as Jews prospered
during the Ottoman Empire spanning the Mediterranean. In the fourth,
Jews prospered as global merchants and revived their religious teachings in
the Netherlands. And the fifth, Konner maintains, with all due respect to
the establishment of a thriving modern Israel, has occurred with Jews transplanted in the New World and transforming and indeed revitalizing their
faith for the modern era.[5]

What is that state of the Jewish religion in America today?

In 2013, the Pew Research Center released a lengthy survey concluding
that American Jews overwhelmingly feel that they are proud to be Jewish
and have a strong sense of belonging to the Jewish people. Such surveys
are inherently difficult to conduct, and experts disagree over their accuracy.
But the Pew surveys taken since 2013 have shown the same trend. Despite
concerns of Jews dying out, the number of Jews in the United States is likely
growing, from 3.9 million in 2007 to 4.7 million in 2014—and well over
5 million if one counts Americans who consider themselves Jewish by heritage but not belief—though these numbers are in the middle of a possible
range, and some experts maintain the growth of the Jewish population is
greater than indicated by these numbers. As a percentage of the American
population, the Jewish population has remained fairly stable in recent years,
around 2 percent, about the same that it has been since 1972.

On the other hand, Judaism is following an American trend, in that
the Jewish community is becoming more polarized in its attitudes toward
faith and its demands in the modern world. The "center" of Jews finding a
balance between extremes is holding, but barely. In 2013, according to the
Pew researchers, the Jewish population broke down as followed: 35 percent Reform, 18 percent Conservative, 10 percent Orthodox, 30 percent
no denomination identified. The Orthodox branch is clearly growing, but
among those raised Orthodox, only half remain Orthodox in adulthood,

whereas very few Jews who are raised Reform or Conservative turn to Orthodoxy.

Thus, somewhat more than half of American Jews fit into the mainstream Reform and Conservative branches, and that does not count Jews of
little affiliation who are probably closer to those branches than to others. Not
only do Orthodox Jews face problems of defection, they are also riven by divisions themselves. "Modern Orthodox" are at one end and are adjusting to
contemporary demands in dress, daily rituals, and attitudes toward women.
Ultra-Orthodox are on the other end, including the Haredim, who reject
modern secular culture, dress, and customs and tend to live among themselves in certain neighborhoods and communities. (Accounting for only 10
percent of the Jewish population, Orthodoxy still has more than 40 percent
of America's 3,700 synagogues) The portion of these ultra-Orthodox Jews
is rising, largely because of their high birth rates and marriages occurring at
younger ages. On the other end of the spectrum, the number of Jews who
identify *only* through secular culture, and not any denomination, is also expanding proportionately. What the Pew Research Center calls "Jews of No
Religion" is higher—close to a third—of Jews born after 1980, the so-called
millennials. Thus, one could say that Reform and Conservative Judaism
predominate, drawing on the foundations portrayed in this book, but are
contracting. There is political polarization as well. Most Jews (70 percent)
are Democrats, but most Orthodox Jews (56 percent) are Republican.[6]

In the Pew poll, some 62 percent of American Jews described their
identity as a matter of ancestry and culture, and only 15 percent said it was
purely a matter of religion. Many Jews even say it is not necessary to believe
in God to be Jewish. Yet tradition does not die. It is alive and well in some
ways. Seven in ten Jews said they participated in a Passover meal in the past
year, and more than half said they had fasted for all or part of Yom Kippur
in 2012. Support for Israel remains fairly and perhaps surprisingly strong,
with seven out of ten Jews saying they felt "very attached" or "somewhat
attached" to Israel, even while many hold reservations about its policies toward the Palestinians. Large majorities say they remembered the Holocaust.

A central thesis of this book is that after Jews came to the United States, they evolved in the nineteenth century from believing in a messiah who would return Jews to the Holy Land toward a belief in seeking redemption for humanity through good works—specifically by working for social justice and harmony among all peoples. It is thus important that this tradition—this mission—remains central to American Jews, who believe that "leading an ethical life" is essential to American Judaism. More than half of those surveyed said that "working for justice and equality" is crucial to their Jewish identity. (Four in ten said having a good sense of humor was also essential.) The numbers approach 60 percent for Reform, Conservative, and Modern Orthodox Jews. Accordingly, it is not overreaching to say that this aspect of American Judaism—which can be seen in the way Jews vote and the way they march for everything from treatment of other minorities and rights for women and gays to performing service projects for the homeless and refugees—derives from a foundation established in the nineteenth century by American Jews working with similar "social gospel" adherents in non-Jewish traditions.

Intermarriage—a perennial concern among rabbis and Jewish leaders—appears to have been a double-edged sword, if one considers the loss of Jewish identity from mixed marriages to be a danger to Jewish identity. Although many Jews lose their identity when they marry non-Jews, many others do not, and intermarriage has in the process expanded the number of Americans who are related to Jews. Synagogues, especially Reform congregations, increasingly rely on non-Jews to carry out their activities. Some analysts think intermarriage may have a net positive impact on the Jewish population, pointing to evidence that there has been an increase in the number of mixed marriages raising their children as Jews, and also an increase in the share of children of these marriages identifying themselves in adulthood as Jews. Predictably, intermarriage is more of a trend among Reform Jews than all others.

All these conclusions reflect the strength of the heritage American Jews received from their turbulent past. Jews may read and even pray about a Messianic age of redemption. They may say "Next year in Jerusalem!" at Passover. But for the most part, despite a genuine attachment to the state

---

of Israel, they have left behind the goal of restoring the Kingdom of David in the Holy Land and the return of practices associated with the ancient Temple. The transformation of Judaism into a faith that seeks redemption through adhering to core traditions while practicing good works to hasten a "messianic" age of redemption has become the bulwark of their survival in America. The parallel transformation of American Judaism from a rote devotion to ancient rules of conduct in daily life, to a more spiritual devotion to its ethical underpinnings, while respecting the scholarship of the past, has also strengthened the American Jews' faith in their heritage and their willingness to maintain it.

And it is the determination to survive, more than anything else, that has become the key to understanding the American Jewish experience, as Nathan Glazer in his seminal book *American Judaism*, many times updated, has noted. Glazer reminds us of the powerful message delivered since the Holocaust by such scholars as Emil Fackenheim, a German concentration camp survivor and escapee, who has spoken of the moral and religious imperative of Jews to commit themselves to survival. Jews, Fackenheim has said, "are commanded to survive as Jews, lest the Jewish people perish."[7]

Still other scholars have taken to exploring the meaning of Judaism in the modern world and calling for new commitments to social justice and unity among Jews in the face of threats to their survival. Such threats were underscored by the Yom Kippur War that threatened to wipe out Israel in 1973 and that rise today from Iran and its surrogates in the region.

Despite the attachment to Israel, as American Judaism continues to develop, a striking aspect is the way that, purely as a religion, it has grown away from Judaism as practiced in Israel. Although many if not most Israelis have been less than rigorous in practicing religious traditions affecting all aspects of their daily life, the Orthodox rabbinate remains recognized in the Jewish state as the sole authority over many aspects of civic life. The areas where the Orthodox establishment holds sway, in part because of the political arrangements through the Israeli government, relate to such issues as marriage, conversion, enforcement of the Sabbath (through the shutdown of public transportation in Jerusalem), exemptions from military service, and other strictures on civil activities. Many of these restrictions revolve around basic definitions of "who is a Jew." The barring of women from joining while praying at certain parts of the Western Wall has been particularly incendiary, at the insistence of the Israeli religious establishment, and has divided many American Jews from their Israeli coreligionists. One irony is that ultra-Orthodox Jews more than a century ago were among those skeptical of the establishment of a Jewish state, believing that only God could deliver such an entity at the hands of the Messiah. Today ultra-Orthodox Jews in Israel tend to see themselves as the activist agents of God's will in working through the political system to strengthen the state of Israel, and insist on the authority of the Israeli secular state to enforce Orthodox laws.

In this sense, one could almost say that Orthodox Jews embrace the idea associated with Reformers that it is not enough to pray for results and hope they flow from keeping the mitzvot, but to be actively involved in a political process of bringing them about. A major difference between Judaism in the two countries is that, while American Jews abandoned the European practice of the state enforcing Jewish law, Israeli Jews keep electing governments that favor the state as just such an enforcement agent.

In the final analysis, Jewish belief in the Jewish people's own unique identity, whether as a nation or as a community of faith, has been so strong that it remains a foundation of Jewish life in the United States. Yet that identity has always been and likely always will be one of contention and dispute. The history recounted in this book must be seen as a story that continues. Perhaps the biggest lesson is that Jews should be unafraid to stand up for how they want to pursue their varied religious paths toward meaning and toward faith and worship. Doing so is not only an American tradition. It is a tradition of American Judaism.

The lament of Henry Wadsworth Longfellow over the supposed oblivion of Judaism has long since been met by the stubbornness of Jews not to give up their identity but to fashion it to find their own path. Judaism has been "dying," subject to internal conflicts, and persecuted for as long as there have been Jews. There is no reason to think that will change. But if the past is any guide, as long as there are forces to eradicate distinctive Jewish identities, Jews will find ways to reinforce their identities. They will cherish their heritage and simply refuse to disappear. Traditionalists may bridle at this heterodoxy, but they can take solace at the number of Jews who want to live in the modern world, retain their Judaism, and find new meanings within it. In this sense, the story of this book is the story of Jews revitalizing their religious traditions from one generation to the next and providing lessons for how contemporary American Jews may do the same.

For American Jews, the path forward is strengthened by the path they have followed: change qualified by tradition and faith in God and in divinely ordained ethical conduct, coupled with a determination to seek and define their own way to express that faith. As they head into an uncertain future, Jews will likely continue to see themselves as Jews, defying the warnings of traditionalists and well-meaning predictions of sympathizers like Longfellow. The Orthodoxy is certain to continue to challenge that claim, but Jews have always insisted on finding their own way in the world. They can do so confidently by looking back to the courageous examples of the past as well as forward to the leadership that will surely come in the future.

# Acknowledgments

This book is the result of many years of reading, thinking, and learning from teachers and friends, far and wide, to whom I owe a debt of gratitude. In the early 1970s, for example, I stayed for several days with a childhood friend, Geoffrey Greenfield, who had abruptly transplanted himself after Harvard to an Orthodox seminary in Jerusalem. There I was exposed to a feverish and daunting culture of Talmudic learning the likes of which I had never experienced. It was the beginning of a journey to understand the history and meaning of Judaism, and then to try to write about what I learned.

On that same trip, I traveled across Israel—from the West Bank to Galilee, the Golan Heights, and across to Tel Aviv—in a rented car with another observant friend, James Kugel, who had been a fellow literature major at Yale. Forty-five years later, Jim Kugel, now a renowned biblical scholar, patiently read the manuscript of this book and corrected more errors and omissions than I care to think about. Rabbi Gary Phillip Zola, executive director of the Jacob Rader Marcus Center of the American Jewish Archives in Cincinnati, was another careful reader. He has been a north star for this book project. Erica Brown, the brilliant and prolific author, teacher, counselor,

267

and director of the Mayberg Center for Jewish Education and Leadership at the George Washington University, has been still another tough-minded reader. None is of course responsible for the errors and misinterpretations that may remain.

Several other learned friends contributed to my education. Leon Wieseltier has taught me about these subjects over many decades of friendship. Rabbi Daniel Zemel of Temple Micah in Washington, DC, has been a mentor and friend who has illuminated the great narrative of Judaism for me. Rabbi James Ponet invited me to discuss the early research for this book at a seminar at the Slifka Center at Yale, where he was the Jewish chaplain at the time. The historian John Morton Blum, whose course on American history I took in the 1960s, attended that session and encouraged me to proceed, just as he had with my earlier book on the history of American taxes. It was at Yale, after all, that I learned how to read literature and history—from great teachers like Blum, Bart Giamatti, George Fayen, Michael Cooke, Michael Holahan, and Leo Braudy.

The small miracle of an intermittent study group led by Erica Brown in Washington has enriched my understanding of Judaism. I am indebted to her and others in the group: David Brooks, Franklin Foer, David Gregory, Jeffrey Goldberg, Martin Indyk, and Daniel Silva. I have also learned from Rabbi David Wolpe, Rabbi Steven Leder, and the late Rabbi Harvey Fields of Los Angeles, my hometown. I thank others in the Temple Micah community, especially Rabbi Josh Beraha, Meryl Weiner, Teddy Klaus, Michael Feuer, Martha and David Adler, and Betsy Broder and David Wentworth.

Sidney Blumenthal, ardent student of Lincoln and nineteenth-century American history, has been endlessly encouraging and helpful. I owe a special thanks to Sally Quinn, who has shared her own journey of faith with me, urged me to pursue this subject, and introduced me to people who helped, including John Gray, director of the Smithsonian's National Museum of American History, and the Reverend Gary Hall, former dean of the Washington National Cathedral. Peter Manseau, curator of American religion at the museum, has been most supportive and has advised me on tracking down pictures for this book. Thanks also to Elisa Ho and Joe Weber of the

American Jewish Archives and Dale Rosengarten and her team at the special collections at the College of Charleston for additional help.

Daniel Yergin, my friend and source of encouragement since high school, has heard me out on this subject and others. He sharpened the argument in this book in countless ways. Other friends lending support include Angela Stent, Ken Auletta, Evan and Oscie Thomas, Walter and Cathy Isaacson, Ellen Chesler and Matthew Mallow, Amy and Chick Entelis, Steve Rattner and Maureen White, Steve Pearlstein and Wendy Gray, Geraldine Baum and Mike Oreskes, Gahl Burt, Liaquat Ahamed, Bill Macomber, John Macomber, the late Polly Kraft Cutler, Eitan Urkowitz, Madona Devasahayam, Linda Greenhouse, Eden Rafshoon, David Makovsky, Patsy Glazer, Betsy Gotbaum, Jeffrey Garten, David Freeman, Elizabeth Moynihan, Justice Stephen Breyer, Strobe Talbott and Barbara Lazear Ascher, Caroline and Haywood Miller, Peter Osnos, Priscilla Painton, Chris and Kathy Matthews, Jill Abramson, Michael Kinsley, Hendrik Hertzberg, and Jonathan Lear. Special thanks to Alan Cooperman of the Pew Research Center for helping me understand contemporary patterns in American Judaism. I am immensely grateful to Adam Posen, president of the Peterson Institute for International Economics, for placing his confidence in me and letting me be a part of the institute's quest for a just and sustainable world economy.

Alice Mayhew of Simon & Schuster has been a longtime champion of this book, having waited for it over many years. True to her legendary reputation, she understood what I was trying to do better than I did, seeing this book as a study of American cultural and political history, not just Jewish history. Amanda Urban, dearest of friends, sharpest of critics, and my agent forever, has been exhorting me to finish this project for many years. When she finally said she loved the first draft, I was over the moon. I thank others at Simon & Schuster for helping me bring this book into the world: Stuart Roberts, Philip Metcalf, Ruth Lee-Mui, Lisa Erwin, Amanda Lang, and Kelley Buck.

Finally, I thank my family, especially my children Madeleine and Teddy, who have always cheered me on with humor and love. My late mother and father, Etta and Joe Weisman, taught me that ethical conduct is at the center of Judaism. My brother and sister, Michael Weisman and Lynn Weisman, and my sister-in-law, Betsy Weisman, have traveled their own paths in the Jewish community of Los Angeles and helped me understand my roots there. My California nieces and nephew—Greg Weisman, Lisa Cope, and Annie Weisman—are the most loving friends an uncle could ask for.

To Elisabeth Bumiller, my wife, I owe the most. Despite her success at one of the most important, demanding, and stressful jobs in journalism, she has given me the space to write a book far afield from both our day jobs. She took time to read the manuscript and made multiple editing suggestions that improved it. As an Episcopalian who grew up in Cincinnati a stone's throw from Hebrew Union College, she delighted in this project and has enthusiastically supported my Jewish journey, while undertaking her own Jewish education as we raised our children in that tradition. This book— and my life as a whole—would not have been remotely possible without her support, strength, and love.

# Recommended Reading

Ahlstrom, Sydney E. *A Religious History of the American People,* second edition. New Haven and London: Yale University Press, 1972, 2004.

Birminghan, Stephen. *Our Crowd: The Great Jewish Families of New York.* Syracuse: Syracuse University Press, 1996. Originally published by Harper & Row, 1967.

Diner, Hasia R. *A Time for Gathering: The Second Migration, 1820–1880.* Baltimore and London: Johns Hopkins University Press, 1992.

Eisen, Arnold M. *The Chosen People in America: A Study in Jewish Religious Ideology.* Bloomington and Indianapolis: Indiana University Press, 1983.

Evans, Eli N. *Judah P. Benjamin: The Jewish Confederate.* New York: Free Press, 1988.

Glazer, Nathan. *American Judaism,* Second Edition with a New Introduction. Chicago: University of Chicago Press, 1957, 1972, 1989.

Howe, Irving, *World of Our Fathers: The Journey of the East European Jews to America and the Life They Found and Made.* New York: Simon & Schuster, 1976.

Jick, Leon A. *The Americanization of the Synagogue, 1820–1870.* Hanover and London: Brandeis University Press, 1976, 1992.

Johnson, Paul. *A History of the Jews.* New York: Harper & Row, 1987.

Karp, Abraham J. *Haven and Home: A History of the Jews in America.* New York: Schocken Books, 1985.

Kugel, James L. *How to Read the Bible: A Guide to Scripture, Then and Now.* New York: Free Press/Simon & Schuster, 2007.

Marcus, Jacob Rader. *Memoirs of American Jews, 1775–1865, Vol. 1.* Philadelphia: The Jewish Publication Society of America, 1955.

Meyer, Michael A. *Response to Modernity: A History of the Reform Movement in Judaism.* New York and Oxford: Oxford University Press, 1988.

Miles, Jack, gen. ed., and David Biale. *The Norton Anthology of World Religions: Volume Two.* New York and London: W. W. Norton & Co., 2015.

Raphael, Marc Lee. *The Synagogue in America: A Short History.* New York: New York University Press, 2011.

Sachar, Howard M. *A History of the Jews in the Modern World.* New York: Alfred A. Knopf, 2005.

Sarna, Jonathan D. *American Judaism: A History.* New Haven and London: Yale University Press, 2004.

Satlow, Michael L. *Creating Judaism: History, Tradition, Practice.* New York: Columbia University Press, 2006.

Schama, Simon. *The Story of the Jews: Volumes I and II.* New York: HarperCollins, 2013 and 2017.

Silverstein, Alan. *Alternatives to Assimilation: The Response of Reform Judaism to American Culture 1840–1930.* Hanover and London: Brandeis University Press, 1994.

Sussman, Lance J. *Isaac Leeser and The Making of American Judaism.* Detroit: Wayne State University Press, 1995.

Temkin, Sefton D. *Isaac Mayer Wise: Shaping American Judaism.* Oxford and New York: Oxford University Press, 1992.

Wertheimer, Jack, ed. *The American Synagogue: A Sanctuary Transformed.* Hanover and London: Brandeis University Press, 1987, 1995.

Zola, Gary Phillip, and Marc Dollinger, eds. *American Jewish History: A Primary Source Reader.* Waltham: Brandeis University Press, 2016.

# Bibliography

BIOGRAPHICAL

Donald, David Herbert, *Lincoln*. New York: Simon & Schuster, 1995.

Evans, Eli N. *Judah P. Benjamin: The Jewish Confederate*. New York: Free Press, 1988.

Ginsberg, Benjamin. *Moses of South Carolina: A Jewish Scalawag During Radical Reconstruction*. Baltimore: Johns Hopkins University Press, 2010.

Greenberg, Gershon. *Modern Jewish Thinkers: From Mendelssohn to Rosenzweig*. Brighton, MA: Academic Studies Press, 2011.

Gumbiner, Joseph H. *Isaac Mayer Wise: Pioneer of American Judaism*. New York: Union of American Hebrew Congregations, 1959.

Heller, James G. *Isaac M. Wise: His Life, Work and Thought*. New York: Union of American Hebrew Congregations, 1965.

Key, Andrew F. *The Theology of Isaac Mayer Wise*. Cincinnati: The American Jewish Archives, 1962.

Klinger, Jerry. "Major Noah. an American Patriot, American Zionist." *The Jewish Magazine*, March 2010.

Kraut, Benny. *From Reform Judaism to Ethical Culture: The Religious Evolution of Felix Adler*. Cincinnati: Hebrew Union College Press, 1979.

Levenson, Alan T. *Modern Jewish Thinkers: An Introduction*. Northvale, NJ, and Jerusalem: Jason Aronson, 2000.

May, Max B. *Isaac Mayer Wise: The Founder of American Judaism.* New York and London: G. P. Putnam's Sons, 1916.

Noah, Mordecai Manuel, "Discourse on the Evidences of the American Indians Being the Descendants of the Lost Tribes of Israel." New York: Mercantile Library Association, 1837. Hathi Trust Digital Library.

Philipson, David and Louis Grossmann, eds. *Selected Writings of Isaac M. Wise with a Biography by the Editors.* Cincinnati: The Robert Clarke Co., 1900. Reprinted Kessinger Publishing, Whitefish, MT.

Ruben, Bruce L. *Max Lilienthal: The Making of an American Rabbinate.* Detroit: Wayne State University Press, 2011.

Sharfman, I. Harold. *The First Rabbi: Origins of Conflict Between Orthodox & Reform: Jewish Polemic Warfare in Pre–Civil War America.* Malibu, California: Joseph Simon Pangloss Press, 1988.

Sussman, Lance J. *Isaac Leeser and The Making of American Judaism.* Detroit: Wayne State University Press, 1995.

Temkin, Sefton D. *Isaac Mayer Wise: Shaping American Judaism.* Oxford and New York: Oxford University Press, 1992.

Wise, Isaac M. *Reminiscences.* Translated from German by David Philipson. Cincinnati: Leo Wise and Co., 1901. Also Centenary Edition published by Central Synagogue of New York, 1956.

———. *Reminiscences.* Memphis: General Books, 2012.

## GENERAL HISTORIES

Ahlstrom, Sydney E. *A Religious History of the American People,* second edition. New Haven and London: Yale University Press, 1972, 2004.

Barnavi, Eli, ed. *A Historical Atlas of the Jewish People: From the Time of the Patriarchs to the Present.* New York: Schocken Books, 1992.

Ben-Sasson, H. H., ed. *A History of the Jewish People.* Cambridge, MA: Harvard University Press, 1976, 1997.

Birminghan, Stephen. *Our Crowd: The Great Jewish Families of New York.* Syracuse, NY: Syracuse University Press, 1996. Originally published by Harper & Row, 1967.

Blum, John M., Bruce Catton, Edmund S. Morgan, Arthur M. Schlesinger Jr., Kenneth M. Stampp, C. Vann Woodward. *The National Experience: A History of the United States, Second Edition.* New York: Harcourt, Brace & World, Inc., 1968.

Bright, John. *A History of Israel.* Second edition. Philadelphia: Westminster Press, 1959, 1972.

Burrows, Edwin G., and Mike Wallace. *Gotham: A History of New York City to 1898.* Oxford and New York: Oxford University Press, 1999.

Butler, Jon. *Awash in a Sea of Faith: Christianizing the American People.* Cambridge and London: Harvard University Press, 1990.

Caplan, Samuel, and Harold U. Ribalow, eds. *The Great Jewish Books and Their Influence on History.* New York: Horizon Press, 1952.

Cohen, Michael R. *The Birth of Conservative Judaism: Solomon Schechter's Disciplines and the Creation of an American Religious Movement.* New York: Columbia University Press, 2012.

Davies, Paul. *God and the New Physics.* New York: Touchstone, 1983.

Diner, Hasia R. *The Jews of the United States 1654 to 2000.* Berkeley, Los Angeles, London: University of California Press, 2004.

———. *A Time for Gathering: The Second Migration, 1820–1880.* Baltimore and London: Johns Hopkins University Press, 1992.

Diner, Hasia R., and Beryl Lieff Benderly. *Her Works Praise Her: A History of Jewish Women in America from Colonial Times to the Present.* New York: Basic Books, 2002.

Eizenstat, Stuart E. *The Future of the Jews: How Global Forces Are Impacting the Jewish People, Israel, and Its Relationship with the United States.* London: Rowman & Littlefield Publishers Inc., 2012.

Elon, Amos. *The Pity of It All: A Portrait of the German-Jewish Epoch, 1743–1933.* New York: Henry Holt and Company, 2002.

Endelman, Todd M. *The Jews of Britain, 1656 to 2000.* Berkeley, Los Angeles, London: University of California Press., 2002.

Evans, Eli N. *The Provincials: A Personal History of Jews in the South.* Chapel Hill and London: University of North Carolina Press, 1973, 1977, 2005.

Fitzgerald, Frances. *The Evangelicals: The Struggle to Shape America.* New York: Simon & Schuster, 2017.

Golden, Harry. *Our Southern Landsman.* New York: G. P. Putnam's Sons, 1974.

Goldfarb, Michael. *Emancipation: How Liberating Europe's Jews from the Ghetto Led to Revolution and Renaissance.* New York: Simon & Schuster, 2009.

Gurda, John. *One People, Many Paths: A History of Jewish Milwaukee.* Milwaukee: Jewish Museum Milwaukee, 2009.

Heckelman, Joseph. *The First Jews in the New World: The Dramatic Odyssey of the Early Jews into the Western Hemisphere.* New York: Jay Street Publishers, 2004.

Hertzberg, Arthur. *The Jews in America: Four Centuries of an Uneasy Encounter.* New York: Simon & Schuster, 1989.

Howe, Irving, *World of Our Fathers: The Journey of the East European Jews to America and the Life They Found and Made*, New York: Simon & Schuster, 1976.

Jacob, Walter, ed. *The Pittsburgh Platform in Retrospect: The Changing World of Reform Judaism*. Pittsburgh: Rodef Shalom Congregation, 1985.

Jackson, Kenneth T., ed. *The Encyclopedia of New York City*. New Haven and London: Yale University Press, 1995.

Jick, Leon A. *The Americanization of the Synagogue, 1820–1870*. Hanover and London: Brandeis University Press, 1976, 1992.

Johnson, Paul. *A History of the Jews*. New York: Harper & Row, 1987.

Karp, Abraham J. *Haven and Home: A History of the Jews in America*. New York: Schocken Books, 1985.

Katz, Jacob. *Jewish Emancipation and Self-Emancipation*. Philadelphia: Jewish Publication Society, 1986.

———. *Out of the Ghetto: The Social Background of Jewish Emancipation, 1770–1870*. New York: Schocken Books, 1978.

Kennedy, David M., Lizabeth Cohen, and Thomas A. Bailey. *The American Pageant: A History of the American People, Fourteenth Edition*. Boston: Wadsworth Cengage Learning, 2010.

Kennedy, William. *O Albany: Improbable City of Political Wizards, Fearless Ethnics, Spectacular Aristocrats, Splendid Nobodies, and Underrated Scoundrels*. New York: Penguin Books, 1983.

LaGrone, Matthew, ed. *Judaism and Religious Freedom: A Sourcebook of Scriptural, Theological, and Legal Texts*. Washington, DC: Religious Freedom Project. Berkley Center for Religion, Peace & World Affairs, 2015.

Learsi, Rufus. *The Jews in America: A History*. New York: KTAV Publishing House, 1972.

Leiman, Sondra with Jonathan D. Sarna, consulting editor. *America: The Jewish Experience*. New York: URJ Press, 1993.

Levine, Aaron, ed. *The Oxford Handbook of Judaism and Economics*. Oxford and New York: Oxford University Press, 2010.

Lipset, Seymour Martin and Earl Raab. *Jews and the New American Scene*. Cambridge and London: Harvard University Press, 1995.

Manseau, Peter. *Objects of Devotion: Religion in Early America*. Washington, DC: Smithsonian Books, 2017.

Marcus, Jacob Rader. *The Dynamics of American Jewish History: Jacob Rader Marcus's Essays on American Jewry*. Edited by Gary Phillip Zola. Lebanon, NH: Brandeis University Press, 2004.

————. *Early American Jewry: The Jews of New York, New England and Canada, 1694–1794*, vol. 1. Philadelphia: Jewish Publication Society of America, 1951.

————. *Memoirs of American Jews, 1775–1865*, vol. 1. Philadelphia: Jewish Publication Society of America, 1955.

————. *United States Jewry, 1776–1985*, vol. 2. Detroit: Wayne State University Press, 1991.

Marty, Martin E. *Pilgrims in Their Own Land: 500 Years of Religion in America.* New York: Viking Penguin, first published by Little, Brown and Co., 1985.

Meyer, Michael A. *The Origins of the Modern Jew: Jewish Identity and European Culture in Germany, 1749–1824.* Detroit: Wayne State University Press, 1967.

————. *Response to Modernity: A History of the Reform Movement in Judaism.* New York and Oxford: Oxford University Press, 1988.

Meyer, Michael A., and W. Gunther Plaut, eds. *The Reform Judaism Reader: North American Documents.* New York: UAHC Press, 2001.

Muller, Jerry Z. *Capitalism and the Jews.* Princeton and Oxford: Princeton University Press, 2010.

Nadell, Pamela S., Jonathan D. Sarna, and Lance J. Sussman, eds. *New Essays in American Jewish History.* Cincinnati: American Jewish Archives of Hebrew Union College–Jewish Institute of Religion, 2010.

Noll, Mark A. *America's God: From Jonathan Edwards to Abraham Lincoln.* Oxford: Oxford University Press, 2002.

Plaut, Gunther W. *The Growth of Reform Judaism: American and European Sources Until 1948.* New York: World Union for Progressive Judaism, 1965.

Plaut, Gunther W., ed. *The Rise of Reform Judaism: A Sourcebook of Its European Origins.* New York: World Union for Progressive Judaism, 1963.

Prothero, Stephen. *American Jesus: How the Son of God Became an American Icon.* New York: Farrar, Straus and Giroux, 2003.

————. *Religious Literacy: What Every American Needs to Know—and Doesn't.* New York: Harper San Francisco/HarperCollins, 2007.

Rabinowitz, Richard. *The Spiritual Self in Everyday Life: The Transformation of Personal Religious Experience in Nineteenth-Century New England.* Boston: Northeastern University Press, 1989.

Raphael, Marc Lee, ed. *The Columbia History of Jews & Judaism in America.* New York: Columbia University Press, 2008.

Raphael, Marc Lee. *The Synagogue in America: A Short History.* New York: New York University Press, 2011.

Rosengarten, Theodore, and Dale Rosengarten, eds. *A Portion of the People: Three Hundred Years of Southern Jewish Life.* Columbia: University of South Carolina Press, 2002.

Rubinger, Rabbi Naphtali J. "Albany Jewry of the Nineteenth Century—Historic Roots and Communal Evolution." New York: Doctoral Dissertation for Bernard Revel Graduate School, Yeshiva University. Ann Arbor: University Microfilms, 1971.

Sachar, Abram Leon. *A History of the Jews.* Fifth Edition. New York: Alfred A. Knopf, 1968.

Sachar, Howard M. *A History of the Jews in the Modern World.* New York: Alfred A. Knopf, 2005.

Sæbø, Magne, ed. *Hebrew Bible Old Testament: The History of Its Interpretation. III/1: The Nineteenth Century.* Göttingen: Vandenhoeck & Ruprecht, 2013.

Sarna, Jonathan D. *American Judaism: A History.* New Haven and London: Yale University Press, 2004.

Sarna, Jonathan D., ed. *The American Jewish Experience.* New York: Holmes & Meier, 1986.

Sarna, Jonathan. *JPS: The Americanization of Jewish Culture 1888–1988.* Philadelphia: Jewish Publication Society, 1989.

Sarna, Jonathan, and David G. Dalin. *Religion and State in the American Jewish Experience.* Notre Dame, IN: University of Notre Dame Press, 1997.

Schalit, Abraham, ed. *The Hellenistic Age: Political History of Jewish Palestine from 332 BCE to 67 BCE, Vol. 6 of The World History of the Jewish People.* New Brunswick, NJ: Rutgers University Press, 1972.

Schama, Simon. *The Story of the Jews: Finding the Words 1000 BC–1492 AD.* New York: Harper Collins, 2013.

Seltzer, Robert M. *Jewish People, Jewish Thought: The Jewish Experience in History.* Upper Saddle River, NJ: Prentice Hall, 1980.

Silberman, Charles. *American Jews and Their Lives Today.* New York: Summit Books, 1985.

Silverstein, Alan. *Alternatives to Assimilation: The Response of Reform Judaism to American Culture 1840–1930.* Hanover and London: Brandeis University Press, 1994.

Sorkin, David. *The Transformation of German Jewry: 1780–1840.* Detroit: Wayne State University Press, 1999.

Wertheimer, Jack, ed. *The American Synagogue: A Sanctuary Transformed.* Hanover and London: Brandeis University Press, 1987, 1995.

Zola, Gary Phillip, and Marc Dollinger, eds. *American Jewish History: A Primary Source Reader*. Waltham, MA: Brandeis University Press, 2016.

## JUDAISM AND SCRIPTURE

Batnitzky, Leora. *How Judaism Became a Religion: An Introduction to Modern Jewish Thought*. Princeton and Oxford: Princeton University Press, 2011.

Borowitz, Eugene B. *Choices in Modern Jewish Thought: A Partisan Guide*. New York: Behrman House, 1983.

Cantor, Geoffrey, ed. *Jewish Tradition and the Challenge of Darwinism*. Chicago and London: University of Chicago Press, 2006.

Cohen, Naomi W. *What the Rabbis Said: The Public Discourse of Nineteenth-Century American Rabbis*. New York and London: New York University Press, 2008.

Davis, Kenneth C. *Don't Know Much About the Bible*. New York: William Morrow and Co., 1998.

Dosick, Wayne. *Living Judaism: The Complete Guide to Jewish Belief, Tradition, and Practice*. New York: HarperCollins, 1995.

Eisen, Arnold M. *The Chosen People in America: A Study in Jewish Religious Ideology*. Bloomington and Indianapolis: Indiana University Press, 1983.

———. *Galut: Modern Jewish Reflection on Homelessness and Homecoming*. Bloomington and Indianapolis: Indiana University Press.1986.

Eisen, Arnold M. *Rethinking Modern Judaism: Ritual, Commandment, Community*. Chicago and London: University of Chicago Press, 1998.

———. *Jewish Meaning in a World of Choice*. Philadelphia and Lincoln, NE: Jewish Publication Society and University of Nebraska Press, 2014.

———. *After Emancipation: Jewish Religious Responses to Modernity*. Cincinnati: Hebrew Union College Press, 2004.

Feiner, Schmuel. *The Origins of Jewish Secularization in Eighteenth-Century Europe*. Translated by Chaya Naor. Philadelphia and Oxford: University of Pennsylvania Press, 2011.

Freedman, Harry. *The Talmud: A Biography*. London: Bloomsbury Publishing, 2014.

Gaer, Joseph, and Rabbi Alfred Wolf. *Our Jewish Heritage*. New York: Henry Holt and Co., 1957.

Glazer, Nathan. *American Judaism,* second edition with a new introduction. Chicago: University of Chicago Press, 1957, 1972, 1989.

Goldin, Judah, ed. *The Jewish Expression*. New Haven and London: Yale University Press, 1976.

Goldman, Shalom. *God's Sacred Tongue: Hebrew & the American Imagination*. Chapel Hill and London: University of North Carolina Press, 2004.

Katz, Michael, and Gershon Schwartz. *Swimming in the Sea of Talmud: Lessons for Everyday Living*. Philadelphia and Jerusalem: Jewish Publication Society, 1998.

Kirsch, Adam. *The People and the Books: 18 Classics of Jewish Literature*. New York and London: W. W. Norton & Co., 2016.

Kohut, Alexander. *The Ethics of the Fathers*. New York: private printing, 1920. Reprinted by Forgotten Books, 2015.

Kohler, Kaufmann. *A Living Faith: Selected Sermons and Addresses from the Literary Remains of Dr. Kaufmann Kohler*. Edited by Samuel S. Cohon. Cincinnati: Hebrew Union College Press, 1948.

Kugel, James L. *On Being a Jew*. New York: Harper San Francisco (Harper Collins), 1990.

———. *The Bible as It Was*. Cambridge, MA: Harvard University Press, 1999.

———. *The Great Shift: Encountering God in Biblical Times*. Boston and New York: Houghton Mifflin Harcourt, 2017.

———. *How to Read the Bible: A Guide to Scripture, Then and Now*. New York: Free Press/Simon & Schuster, 2007.

Laytner, Anson. *Arguing with God: A Jewish Tradition*. Northvale, NJ: Jason Aronson, Inc., 1990.

Meyer, Michael A., and David N. Myers, eds. *Between Jewish Tradition and Modernity: Rethinking an Old Opposition*. Detroit: Wayne State University Press, 2014.

Miles, Jack. *God: A Biography*. New York: Vintage Books/Random House, 1995.

Miles, Jack, gen. ed., and David Biale. *The Norton Anthology of World Religions*, vol. 2. New York, London: W. W. Norton & Co., 2015.

Neusner, Jacob. *From Politics to Piety: The Emergence of Pharisaic Judaism*. Englewood Cliffs, NJ: Prentice-Hall, 1973.

Norris, Pippa, and Ronald Inglehart. *Sacred and Secular: Religion and Politics Worldwide*. Cambridge: Cambridge University Press, 2004.

Oz, Amos, and Fania Oz-Salzberger. *Jews and Words*. New Haven and London: Yale University Press, 2012.

Petuchowski, Jakob J. *Prayerbook Reform in Europe: The Liturgy of European Liberal and Reform Judaism*. New York: World Union for Progressive Judaism, 1968.

Parry, Aaron. *The Complete Idiot's Guide to the Talmud*. New York: Penguin Group, 2004.

Pianko, Noam. *Jewish Peoplehood: An American Innovation.* New Brunswick, NJ: Rutgers University Press, 2015.

Sacks, Jonathan. *The Dignity of Difference: How to Avoid the Clash of Civilization.* London and New York: Continuum, 2002.

———. *The Great Partnership: God, Science and the Search for Meaning.* New York: Schocken Books, 2011.

Satlow, Michael L. *Creating Judaism: History, Tradition, Practice.* New York: Columbia University Press, 2006.

Satlow, Michael L. *How the Bible Became Holy.* New Haven and London: Yale University Press, 2014.

Stanislawski, Michael. *A Murder in Lemberg: Politics, Religion, and Violence in Modern Jewish History.* Princeton and Oxford: Princeton University Press, 2007.

Walzer, Michael. *In God's Shadow: Politics in the Hebrew Bible.* New Haven and London: Yale University Press, 2012.

Wieseltier, Leon. *Kaddish.* New York: Vintage Books, Random House, 1998.

Wright, Robert. *The Evolution of God.* New York, Boston, London: Little, Brown and Company, 2009.

## THE CIVIL WAR

Ash, Stephen V. "Civil War Exodus," in Jonathan D. Sarna and Adam Mendelsohn, eds., *Jews and the Civil War.* New York and London: New York University Press, 2010.

Bunker, Gary L., and John J. Appel. " 'Shoddy' Antisemitism and the Civil War," in Jonathan D. Sarna and Adam Mendelsohn, eds., *Jews and the Civil War.* New York and London: New York University Press, 2010.

Drescher, Seymour. "Jews and New Christians in the Atlantic Slave Trade," in Jonathan D. Sarna and Adam Mendelsohn, *Jews and the Civil War.* New York: New York University Press, 2010.

Einhorn, David. "David Einhorn's Response to 'A Biblical View of Slavery,'" translated from the German, in *Sinai*, vol. 6, 2–22, Baltimore, 1861, by Mrs. Kaufmann Kohler; published by Jewish-American Historical Society: http://www.jewish-history.com/civilwar/einhorn.html.

Evans, Eli N. "Overview: The War Between Jewish Brothers in America," in Jonathan Sarna and Adam Mendelsohn, eds., *Jews and the Civil War: A Reader.* New York and London: New York University Press, 2010.

Fein, Isaac M. "Baltimore Rabbis During the Civil War," in Jonathan D. Sarna and

Adam Mendelsohn, eds., *Jews and the Civil War*. New York and London: New York University Press, 2010.

Ferris, Marcie Cohen and Mark I. Greenberg, eds. *Jewish Roots in Southern Soil: A New History*. Waltham, MA: Brandeis University Press, 2006.

Heilprin, Michael. "Michael Heilprin's Anti-Slavery Editorial," New York, January 11, 1861, published by Jewish-American Historical Society: http://www.jewish-history.com/civilwar/heilprin.htm.l

Hertz, Emanuel, ed. *Abraham Lincoln: The Tribute of the Synagogue*. New York: Bloch Publishing Co., 1927.

Holzer, Harold. *Lincoln and the Jews: The Last Best Hope of Earth*. Los Angeles: Skirball Cultural Center, 2002.

Korn, Bertram W. *American Jewry and the Civil War*. Cleveland and New York: Meridian Books, World Publishing Co., and Philadelphia: Jewish Publication Society of America, 1961.

———. "Revolution and Reform: The Antebellum Jewish Abolitionists," in Jonathan D. Sarna and Adam Mendelsohn, eds., *Jews and the Civil War*. New York and London: New York University Press, 2010.

Mendelsohn, Adam. "Introduction: Before Korn: A Century of Jewish Historical Writing About the Civil War," in Jonathan D. Sarna and Adam Mendelsohn, eds., *Jews and the Civil War*. New York and London: New York University Press, 2010.

Raphall, M. J. "The Bible View of Slavery," January 15, 1861, published by Jewish-American Historical Society: http://www.jewish-history.com/civilwar/raphall.html.

Rock, Howard B. "Upheaval, Innovation, and Transformation: New York City Jews and the Civil War." *American Jewish Archives Journal*, LXIV (2012), no. 1 & 2.

———. "Jewish Confederates," in Jonathan D. Sarna and Adam Mendelsohn, eds., *Jews and the Civil War*. New York: New York University Press, 2010.

Ruchames, Louis, "The Abolitionists and the Jews: Some Further Thoughts," in Jonathan D. Sarna and Adam Mendelsohn, eds., *Jews and the Civil War*. New York and London: New York University Press, 2010.

Sarna, Jonathan D., and Benjamin Shapell, eds. *Lincoln and the Jews: A History*. New York: St. Martin's Press/Thomas Dunne Books, 2015.

———. *When General Grant Expelled the Jews*. New York: Schocken Books, 2012.

Sarna, Jonathan D., and Adam Neldesohn, eds., *Jews and the Civil War: A Reader*. New York and London: New York University Press, 2010.

Sokolow, Jayme A. "Revolution and Reform: The Antebellum Jewish Abolitionists,"

Jonathan D. Sarna and Adam Mendelsohn, eds., *Jews and the Civil War* (New York and London: New York University Press, 2010).

Zola, Gary Phillip, ed. *We Called Him Rabbi Abraham: Lincoln and American Jewry—A Documentary History.* Carbondale: Southern Illinois University Press, 2014.

## MESSIANISM

Katz, Jacob, "Israel and the Messiah," in *Essential Papers on Messianic Movements and Personalities in Jewish History,* ed. Marc Saperstein. New York: New York University Press, 1992.

Klausner, Joseph. *The Messianic Idea in Israel: From Its Beginning to the Completion of the Mishnah.* New York: Macmillan Company, 1955.

Levenson, Jon D. *Resurrection and the Restoration of Israel: The Ultimate Victory of the God of Life.* New Haven and London: Yale University Press, 2006.

Saperstein, Marc, ed. *Essential Papers on Messianic Movements and Personalities in Jewish History.* New York and London: New York University Press, 1992.

Scholem, Gershom. *The Messianic Idea in Judaism and Other Essays on Jewish Spirituality.* New York: Schocken Books, 1971, 1972.

Silver, Abba Hillel. *A History of Messianic Speculation in Israel: From the First Through the Seventeenth Centuries.* With a new introduction: 1959. Boston: Beacon Hill Press, 1927.

Wieseltier, Leon. "A Passion for Waiting: Liberal Notes on Messianism and the Jews." In a privately published book in honor of Daniel Bell.

## CHARLESTON

Breitbart, Solomon, compiled by Harlan Greene. *Explorations in Charleston's Jewish History.* Charleston and London: History Press, 2005.

Elzas, Barnett A. *The Jews of South Carolina: From the Earliest Times to the Present Day.* Philadelphia: J. B. Lippincott Co., 1905. Digitized by Internet Archive 2007.

Hagy, James William. *This Happy Land: The Jews of Colonial and Antebellum Charleston.* Tuscaloosa and London: University of Alabama Press, 1993.

Harby, Lee C. "Penina Moïse: Woman and Writer," in *The American Jewish Year Book,* vol. 7, September 30, 1905, to September 19, 1906, 17–31.

Holz, Anthony D. and other authors. *Pocket Guide to Kahal Kadosh Beth Elohim and Charleston Jewish History.* Charleston: Kahal Kadosh Beth Elohim, 2005.

Liberles, Robert, "Conflict Over Reforms in Charleston," in Jack Wertheimer, ed.,

*The American Synagogue: A Sanctuary Transformed* (Waltham, MA: Brandeis University Press, 1987).

Moïse, L. C. *Biography of Isaac Harby, with an Account of the Reformed Society of Israelites of Charleston, S.C. 1824–1833.* Macon, GA: Central Conference of American Rabbis, 1930.

Reznikoff, Charles, with Uriah Z. Engelman. *The Jews of Charleston: A History of an American Jewish Community.* Philadelphia: Jewish Publication Society of America, 1950.

Silberman, Lou H. "American Impact: Judaism in the United States in the Early Nineteenth Century," in *B .G. Rudolph Lectures in Judaic Studies.* Syracuse, NY: Syracuse University Press, 1964.

Tarshish, Allan. "The Charleston Organ Case," in *American Jewish Historical Quarterly.* Johns Hopkins University Press, vol. 54 (June 1965), no. 4, 411–449.

Zola, Gary Phillip. *Isaac Harby of Charleston, 1788–1828: Jewish Reformer and Intellectual.* Tuscaloosa and London: University of Alabama Press, 1994.

———. *Encyclopedia of Southern Jewish Communities—Charleston, South Carolina.* Goldring/Woldenberg Institute of Southern Jewish Life, 2017 (accessed online September 3, 2017).

———. *A Guided Tour of Jewish Community Life: 300 Years of South Carolina History.* Publication of the Jewish Historical Society of South Carolina. Undated.

## ARTICLES AND LECTURES

Appel, John J. "The Trefa Banquet," *Commentary*, February 1, 1966, https://www.com mentarymagazine.com/articles/the-trefa-banquet/ (accessed August 9, 2017).

Ashton, Susanna, "Slaves of Charleston: Beyond the Beauty and Wealth of Jewish South Carolina Lies a Troubled and Troubling History," *Forward*, September 19, 2014.

Baer, Yitzhak F. "From the Ancient Faith to a New Historical Consciousness," excerpt from Galut, Robert Warshow, trans. New York: Schocken Books, 1947. Republished in Goldin, Judah, ed., *The Jewish Expression.* New Haven and London: Yale University Press, 1976.

Bickerman, Elias. "The Maccabean Uprising: An Interpretation," trans. from the German by Krishna Winston. Berlin: Schocken Books, 1937. Republished in Judah Goldin, ed. *The Jewish Expression.* New Haven and London: Yale University Press, 1976, 66–86.

Borowitz, Eugene B. "What Do We Expect in the Messianic Age?" *Liberal Judaism.* New York: Union of American Hebrew Congregations, 1984.

Brook, Daniel. "The Forgotten Confederate Jew: How History Lost Judah P. Benjamin, the Most Prominent American Jew of the Nineteenth Century." *Tablet*, July 17, 2012.

Goodman, Abraham Vossen. "A Jewish Peddler's Diary." *American Jewish Archives*, June 1951.

Gurock, Jeffrey S. "Resisters and Accommodators: Varieties of Orthodox Rabbis in America, 1886–1983." *American Jewish Archives*, November 1983, 100–187.

Harby, Lee C. "Penina Moïse: Woman and Writer," American Jewish Committee Archives, http://www.ajcarchives.org/AJC_DATA/Files/1905_1906_3_Biographies.pdf (accessed July 21, 2016).

Hirsch, Emil G. "Reform Judaism: A Discourse at the Celebration of Dr. Samuel Hirsch's 70th Anniversary, delivered by his son, the Rabbi of Chicago Sinai Congregation." Philadelphia: Edward Hirsch & Co. 1885.

Hoffman, Lawrence A. "Limits, Truth and Meaning: A Foundation for Dialogue." Hebrew Union College–Jewish Institute of Religion, NY, 1988.

Karff, Samuel E. "The Theology of the Pittsburgh Platform," in *The Pittsburgh Platform in Retrospect*, Walter Jacob, ed. Pittsburgh: Rodef Shalom Congregation Press, 1985.

LaGrone, Matthew. "Disagreement and Denominationalism: The Kohut-Kohler Debate of 1885." *Conservative Judaism*, vol. 64 (Summer 2013), no. 4.

Leeser, Isaac, "Letter to the Rev. G. Poznanski." *The Occident and American Jewish Advocate*, vol. 1 (August 1843), no. 5.

Mooney, James E. "Seixas, Gershom Mendes," in Kenneth T. Jackson, ed., *The Encyclopedia of New York City*. New Haven and London: Yale University Press, 1995.

Plaut, W. Gunther, "The Pittsburgh Platform in the Light of European Antecedents," in *The Pittsburgh Platform in Retrospect*, Walter Jacob, ed. Pittsburgh: Rodef Shalom Congregation Press, 1985.

Rock, Howard B. "Upheaval, Innovation, and Transformation: New York City Jews and the Civil War." *American Jewish Archives Journal*, vol. LXIV (2012), nos. 1 and 2.

Ruben, Bruce L. "Max Lilienthal and Isaac M. Wise: Architects of American Reform Judaism." *American Jewish Archives Journal*, vol. LV (2003), no. 2, 1–29.

Rubinger, Naphtali J. "Dismissal in Albany," *American Jewish Archives Journal*, vol. XXIV (April 1972), no. 1.

Sarna, Jonathan D. "The Debate Over Mixed Seating in the American Synagogue,"

in Jack Wertheimer, ed., *The American Synagogue: A Sanctuary Transformed.*
Hanover and London: Brandeis University Press, 1987.

Shalev, Eran. "Revive, Renew, and Reestablish: Mordecai Noah's Ararat and the
Limits of Biblical Imagination in the Early American Republic." *American Jewish Archives,* vol. LXII (2010), no. 1, 1–20.

Singer, Isidore, George Alexander, and Cyrus Adler. "Alexander Kohut," *Jewish Encyclopedia* (1906), http://www.jewishencyclopedia.com/articles/9436-kohut-alexander.

Sperling, S. David, "Major Developments in Jewish Biblical Scholarship," in Magne
Sæbø, ed., *Hebrew Bible/Old Testament: The History of Its Interpretation, vol. III, From Modernism to Post-Modernism (The Nineteenth and Twentieth Centuries).*
Göttingen: Vandenhoeck & Ruprecht, 2015.

Strum, Harvey. "Albany," in *Encyclopedia Judaica 2008.* Republished by Jewish Virtual Library; American-Israeli Cooperative Enterprise.

Sussman, Lance J. "The Myth of the Trefa Banquet: American Culinary Culture
and the Radicalization of Food Policy in American Reform Judaism." *American Jewish Archives Journal,* vol. 57 (2005), nos. 1–2, http://americanjewish
archives.org/publications/journal/PDF/2005_57_01_02_sussman.pdf (accessed August 9, 2017).

# Notes

## INTRODUCTION: JEWS IN AMERICA: A PART BUT APART

1. Alexis de Tocqueville, *Democracy in America*, translated with a preface and introductory notice by Henry Reeve, C. B., edited by Bruce Frohnen (Washington, DC: Regnery Publishing, 2002), 241.

2. Sydney E. Ahlstrom, *A Religious History of the American People*, 2d ed. (New Haven: Yale University Press, 2004), 569.

3. Abraham J. Karp, *Haven and Home: A History of the Jews in America* (New York: Schocken Books, 1985), 7–8.

4. Michael A. Meyer, *Response to Modernity: A History of the Reform Movement in Judaism* (New York and Oxford: Oxford University University Press, 1988), 42.

5. Arnold M. Eisen, 1983, *The Chosen People in America: A Study in Jewish Religious Ideology*, (Bloomington and Indianapolis: Indiana University Press, 1983), 3. Quoted in David Philipson, "The Jewish Pioneers of the Ohio Valley," *Publications of the American Jewish Historical Society 8* (1900), 45.

6. Eisen, *The Chosen People in America*, 14.

## ONE: COMING TO AMERICA

1. Sydney Ahlstrom, *A Religious History*, 569.

2. Simon Scharna, *The Story of the Jews: Finding the Words 1000 BC–1491 AD* (New York: HarperCollins, 2013), 306–406.

3. Arthur Hertzberg, *The Jews in America: Four Centuries of an Uneasy Encounter* (New York: Simon & Schuster, 1989), 19. See also Edwin G. Burrows and Mike Wallace: *Gotham: A History of New York City to 1898* (New York and Oxford: Oxford University Press, 1999), 43 ff.

4. Martin E. Marty, *Pilgrims in Their Own Land: 500 Years of Religion in America* (New York: Penguin Books, 1985), viii–ix.

5. Paul Johnson, *A History of the Jews* (New York: Harper & Row, 1987), 278.

6. Jonathan Sarna, *American Judaism: A History* (New Haven and London: Yale University Press, 2004), 2.

7. Jonathan D. Sarna, *American Judaism*, xv.

8. Jacob Rader Marcus, *Early American Jewry: The Jews of New York, New England and Canada 1694–1794*, vol. 1 (Philadelphia: Jewish Publication Society of America, 1951), 39.

9. Paul Johnson, *History of the Jews*, 283–287.

10. Paul Johnson, *History of the Jews*, 281.

11. Nathan Glazer, *American Judaism*, 2d ed., with a new introduction (Chicago: University of Chicago Press, 1957, 1972, 1989), 16.

12. Abraham J. Karp, *Haven and Home: A History of the Jews in America* (New York: Schocken Books, 1985), 18.

13. Jonathan D. Sarna, *American Judaism*, 26.

14. Abraham J. Karp, *Haven and Home*, 39.

15. Hasia R. Diner, *The Jews of the United States 1654 to 2000* (Berkeley, Los Angeles, London: University of California Press, 2004), 16.

16. Jonathan D. Sarna, *American Judaism*, 27–28.

17. Jonathan D. Sarna, *American Judaism*, 44–45.

18. Leon A. Jick, *The Americanization of the Synagogue, 1820–1870* (Hanover and London: Brandeis University Press, 1976, 1992), 6.

19. Jacob Rader Marcus, *Memoirs of American Jews 1775–1865, vol. 1* (Philadelphia: Jewish Publication Society of America, 1955), 67–68 and 107.

20. Abraham J. Karp, *Haven and Home*, 15.

21. Leon A. Jick, *Americanization of the Synagogue*, 7.

22. Jonathan D. Sarna, *American Judaism*, 16.

23. Jacob Rader Marcus, *Early American Jewry*, 73–74 and 94–99. Also Jonathan D. Sarna, *American Judaism*, 36.

24. Sydney E. Ahlstrom, *A Religious History of the American People*, 573.

25. James E. Mooney, "Seixas, Gershom Mendes," in Kenneth T. Jackson, ed., *The Encyclopedia of New York City* (New Haven and London: Yale University

Press, 1995), 1058. Also Jonathan D. Sarna, *American Judaism, 40–41,* and Leon A. Jick, *Americanization of the Synagogue,* 10.

26. Jonathan D. Sarna, *American Judaism,* 38.

27. Jonathan D. Sarna, *American Judaism,* 14.

28. Jonathan D. Sarna, *American Judaism,* 43.

29. Hasia R. Diner, *A Time for Gathering: The Second Migration 1820–1880* (Baltimore and London: Johns Hopkins University Press, 1992), 149.

30. Jonathan D. Sarna, *American Judaism,* 79.

31. Marc Lee Raphael, *The Synagogue in America: A Short History* (New York: New York University Press, 2011), 17. See also Sandee Brawarsky, 2005, "A History of Congregation B'nai Jeshurun, 1825–2005," B'nai Jeshurun website, http://www.bj.org/Articles/a-history-of-bj-1825-2005/.

32. Leon A. Jick, *Americanization of the Synagogue,* 53–54.

33. James William Hagy, *This Happy Land: The Jews of Colonial and Antebellum Charleston* (Tuscaloosa and London: The University of Alabama Press, 1993), 80.

34. Abraham J. Karp, *Haven and Home,* 45–48.

## TWO: LET HARMONY ASCEND

1. Gary Phillip Zola, *Isaac Harby of Charleston, 1788–1828* (Tuscaloosa: University of Alabama Press Judaic Studies Series, 1994), 2.

2. Charles Reznikoff, with Uriah Z. Engelman, *The Jews of Charleston: A History of an American Jewish Community* (Philadelphia: Jewish Publication Society of America, 1950), 67.

3. Preservation Society of Charleston, "1838 (April 27–28) Fire" (Charleston: Alfred O. Halsey Map Preservation Research Project, 1949), http://www.halseymap.com/flash/window.asp?HMID=48.

4. James William Hagy, *This Happy Land,* 112.

5. James William Hagy, *This Happy Land,* 239.

6. James William Hagy, *This Happy Land,* 245.

7. Charles Reznikoff with Uriah Z. Engelman, *The Jews of Charleston,* 4–6.

8. Susanna Ashton, "Slaves of Charleston," *Forward,* September 19, 2014.

9. Allan Tarshish, "The Charleston Organ Case," in *American Jewish Historical Quarterly,* vol. 54 (June 1965), no. 4, 411–449, 412.

10. Barnett A. Elzas, *The Jews of South Carolina: From the Earliest Times to the Present Day* (Philadelphia: J.B. Lippincott Company, 1902), https://archive.org/details/jewsofcharleston00elzaiala.

11. James William Hagy, *This Happy Land*, 37–39.
12. Solomon Breitbart, compiled by Harlan Greene, *Explorations in Charleston's Jewish History*. (Charleston and London: History Press, 2005), 35–37.
13. Charles Reznikoff with Uriah Z. Engelman, *The Jews of Charleston*, 17–18.
14. James William Hagy, *This Happy Land*, 58–60.
15. Barnett A. Elzas, *The Jews of South Carolina: From the Earliest Times to the Present Day* (Philadelphia: J. B. Lippincott Company, 1902), 150–154, https://archive.org/details/jewsofcharleston00elzaiala.
16. James William Hagy, *This Happy Land*, 61–68.
17. Solomon Breitbart, *Explorations in Charleston's Jewish History*, 113–115.
18. Allan Tarshish, "The Charleston Organ Case," *American Jewish Historical Quarterly*, vol. 54 (June 1965), no. 4, 411–449.
19. James William Hagy, *This Happy Land*, 79–80.
20. L. C. Moïse, *Biography of Isaac Harby, with an Account of the Reformed Society of Israelites of Charleston, S.C., 1824–1833* (Columbia: University of South Carolina Press; Central Conference of American Rabbis, 1931), 32–33.
21. "Memorial to the President and Members of the Adjunta of Kahal Kodesh Beth Elohim of Charleston, South Carolina, demanding religious reform, December 23, 1824," in Gary Philip Zola and Marc Dollinger, eds., *American Jewish History: A Primary Source Reader* (Waltham, MA: Brandeis University Press, 2014), 79–80.
22. Gary Phillip Zola, *Isaac Harby of Charleston, 1788–1828* (Tuscaloosa: University of Alabama Press Judaic Studies Series, 1994) 122, xi, xii.
23. Lou H. Silberman, "American Impact: Judaism in the United States in the Early Nineteenth Century," Syracuse, NY: Syracuse University Press, B. G. Rudolph Lectures in Judaic Studies (April 19, 1964), no. 2.
24. Michael A. Meyer, *Response to Modernity*, 229.
25. See James L. Kugel, *The God of Old: Inside the Lost World of the Bible* (New York: Free Press/Simon & Schuster, 2003), and *The Great Shift: Encountering God in Biblical Times* (Boston and New York: Houghton Mifflin, 2017).
26. Allan Tarshish, "The Charleston Organ Case," *American Jewish Historical Quarterly*, 417–18.
27. Gary Phillip Zola, *Isaac Harby of Charleston*, 141–143.
28. Gary Phillip Zola: *Isaac Harby of Charleston*, 135 ff.
29  Gary Phillip Zola, *Isaac Harby of Charleston*, xii.
30. Gary Phillip Zola, *Isaac Harby of Charleston*, 9.
31. Gary Phillip Zola, *Isaac Harby of Charleston*, 32, 41, 53, 61–3, 94, 96, 112.

## THREE: REBELLION IN CHARLESTON

1.  Gary Phillip Zola, *Isaac Harby of Charleston*, 117.

2.  James L. Kugel, *The Great Shift: Encountering God in Biblical Times* (Boston and New York: Houghton Mifflin Harcourt, 2017), 317–328.

3.  Gary Phillip Zola, *Isaac Harby of Charleston*, 124–125.

4.  Lou H. Silberman, "American Impact," *B. G. Rudolph Lectures.*

5.  Gary Phillip Zola, *Isaac Harby of Charleston*, 125–128.

6.  Allan Tarshish, "The Charleston Organ Case," *American Jewish Historical Quarterly*, 413.

7.  Gary Phillip Zola, *Isaac Harby of Charleston*, 130–133.

8.  Harlan Greene and Dale Rosengarten, in Solomon Brietbart, ed., *Explorations in Charleston's Jewish History* (Charleston, SC: History Press, 2005), 13.

9.  Solomon Breitbart, ed., *Explorations in Charleston's Jewish History*, 56–58.

10. David Ellenson, "A Disputed Precedent: the Prague Organ," in David Ellenson, *After Emancipation: Jewish Religious Responses to Modernity* (Cincinnati: Hebrew Union College Press, 2004), 121–138. The issue of the organ in Hamburg and Prague is also discussed by Allan Tarshish in "The Charleston Organ Case," *American Jewish Historical Quarterly,* vol. 54 (June 1965), no. 4, 411–449, drawing on the scholarship of W. Gunther Plaut, *The Rise of Reform Judaism: A Sourcebook of Its Europe Origins* (New York: World Union of Progressive Judaism, 1963), 34–44 and 165–169. See also James William Hagy, *This Happy Land*, 242 ff.

11. Allan Tarshish, "The Charleston Organ Case," *American Jewish Historical Quarterly*, 411–449.

12. See "Savannah: Historical Overview" in *Encyclopedia of Southern Jewish Communities— Savannah, Georgia; Goldring Woldenberg Institute of Southern Jewish Life*; http://www.isjl.org/georgia-savannah-encyclopedia.html (accessed July 23, 2016).

13. Charles Reznikoff, Uriah Engelman, *The Jews of Charleston*, 140.

14. James William Hagy, *This Happy Land*, 246.

15. Allan Tarshish, "The Charleston Organ Case," *American Jewish Historical Quarterly*, 431.

16. James William Hagy, *This Happy Land*, 248–254.

17. Barnett A. Elzas, *The Jews of South Carolina*, 210.

18. Charles Reznikoff and Uriah Z. Engelman, *The Jews of Charleston: A History of an American Jewish Community*, 124.

19. James William Hagy, *This Happy Land*, 131–132, 144.
20. Robert Liberles, "Conflict Over Reforms in Charleston," in *The American Synagogue: A Sanctuary Transformed*, Jack Wertheimer, ed. (Waltham, MA: Brandeis University Press, 1987).
21. Charles Reznikoff and Uriah Engelman, *The Jews of Charleston*, 129–131.
22. Allan Tarshish, "The Charleston Organ Case," *American Jewish Historical Quarterly*, 412–13.
23. Yitzhak F. Baer, "From the Ancient Faith to a New Historical Consciousness," excerpt from *Galut*, Robert Warshow, trans. (New York: Schocken Books, 1947), republished in Goldin, Judah, ed., *The Jewish Expression* (New Haven and London: Yale University Press, 1976), 390.
24. Lou H. Silberman, "American Impact," B. G. Rudolph Lectures in Judaic Studies, Syracuse University Press.
25. Decision of the Court of Appeals in the Case of the State Ex Relatione A. Ottolengui, vs. G. V. Ancker and Others—Charleston, February 1846. Published in *The Occident and American Jewish Advocate*, vol. III (Adar 5606, March 1846), no. 12.

## FOUR: THE GERMAN IMMIGRANTS

1. Arthur Hertzberg, *The Jews in America*, 106–107.
2. Jonathan Sarna, *American Judaism*, 63.
3. Leon Jick, *Americanization of the Synagogue*, 57.
4. Jonathan Sarna, *American Judaism*, 65.
5. Gary Phillip Zola, *We Called Him Rabbi Abraham—Lincoln and American Jewry, A Documentary History* (Carbondale: Southern Illinois University Press, 2014), 11–25.
6. Hasia R. Diner, *A Time for Gathering*, 64–7.
7. Sydney E. Ahlstrom, *A Religious History of the American People*, 575.
8. Abraham Karp, *Haven and Home*, 53.
9. Stephen Birmingham, *Our Crowd: The Great Jewish Families of New York* (Syracuse, NY: First Syracuse University Press Edition, 1996; originally published 1967), 34, 17–23.
10. Hasia R. Diner, *A Time for Gathering*, 65.
11. Hasia R. Diner, *A Time for Gathering*, 129.
12. Jonathan Sarna *American Judaism*, 23–4.
13. Jonathan Sarna, *American Judaism*, 70.
14. Leon A. Jick, *The Americanization of the Synagogue*, 34–35.

15. Abraham Vossen Goodman, "A Jewish Peddler's Diary," published in *American Jewish Archives*, June 1951.

16. Jonathan Sarna, *American Judaism*, 66.

17. Jonathan Sarna, *American Judaism*, 46.

18. Abraham J. Karp, *Haven and Home*, 23.

19. Hasia R. Diner, *A Time for Gathering*, 113.

20. Hasia R. Diner, *A Time for Gathering*, 108.

21. Leon A. Jick, *The Americanization of the Synagogue*, 103–150.

22. Nathan Glazer, *American Judaism*, 34.

## FIVE: GERMAN RABBIS IN AMERICA

1. Abraham J. Karp, "Overview: The Synagogue in America—A Historical Typology," in Jack Wertheimer, ed., *The American Synagogue: A Sanctuary Transformed* (Hanover and London: Brandeis University Press, 1987, 1995), 7–8.

2. Alan Silverstein, *Alternatives to Assimilation: The Response of Reform Judaism to American Culture 1840–1930* (Hanover and London: Brandeis University Press, 1994), 9–10.

3. Arthur Hertzberg, *The Jews in America*, 33.

4. Gordon S. Wood, "A Different Story of What Shaped America," *New York Review of Books*, July 9, 2015.

5. John M. Blum and Bruce Catton, Edmund S. Morgan, Arthur M. Schlesinger Jr., Kenneth M. Stampp, and C. Vann Woodward, *The National Experience: A History of the United States*, 2d ed. (New York: Harcourt, Brace & World, Inc., 1968), 256–57.

6. Sydney E. Ahlstrom, *A Religious History of the American People*, 379.

7. Sydney E. Ahlstrom, *A Religious History of the American People*, 366.

8. Quoted in John M. Blum et al., *The National Experience: A History of the United States*, 252.

9. Quoted by Arthur Hertzberg, *The Jews in America*, 75.

10. Jonathan D. Sarna, *American Judaism*, 46–47.

11. Leon A. Jick, *The Americanization of the Synagogue*, 71–73.

12. Leon A. Jick, *The Americanization of the Synagogue*, 77.

13. Leon A. Jick, *The Americanization of the Synagogue*, 119–120.

14. Abraham J. Karp, *Haven and Home*, 10.

15. Abraham J. Karp, *Haven and Home*, 59.

16. Michael A. Meyer, *Response to Modernity*, 27–28.

17. Leora Batnitzky, *How Judaism Became a Religion: An Introduction to Modern Jewish Thought* (Princeton, NJ: Princeton University Press, 2011), 13.

18. Simon Schama, *The Story of the Jews*, 91.

19. Michael A. Meyer, *Response to Modernity*, 40–41.

20. Shmuel Ettinger, essays in "The Modern Period" section of *A History of the Jewish People*, H. H. Sasson, ed. (Cambridge: Harvard University Press, 1969, 1976), 834. The preceding section on the Jewish Enlightenment draws from Ettinger's chapters, among other scholarly works, including Michael Meyer's *Response to Modernity*.

21. Quoted in Michael A. Meyer, *Response to Modernity*, 91.

## SIX: THE TURBULENT ISAAC MAYER WISE

1. Isaac Mayer Wise, *Reminiscences,* trans. and ed. by David Philipson, 2d ed., originally published 1901 (New York: Central Synagogue of New York, 1945), 14–17.

2. Meyer, Michael A., *Response to Modernity*, 238.

3. Nathan Glazer, *American Judaism*, 37.

4. Sefton D. Temkin, *Isaac Mayer Wise: Shaping American Judaism* (Oxford, New York: Oxford University Press, 1992), 41–43.

5. Jonathan D. Sarna, *American Judaism*, 92.

6. Michael A. Meyer, *Response to Modernity*, 238.

7. James G. Heller, *Isaac M. Wise: His Life, Work and Thought* (New York: Union of American Hebrew Congregations, 1965), 202.

8. Sefton D. Temkin, *Isaac Mayer Wise*, 43.

9. William Kennedy, *O Albany! Improbable City of Political Wizards, Fearless Ethnics, Spectacular Aristocrats, Splendid Nobodies, and Underrated Scoundrels* (New York: Penguin Books, 1983), 216. Citation is from "The Jews in Albany, NY (1655–1914)," by Louis Silver, *American Jewish Historical Quarterly*.

10. William Kennedy, *O Albany!*, 218 ff.

11. Max B. May, *Isaac Mayer Wise: The Founder of American Judaism, A Biography* (New York: G. P. Putnam's Sons, 1916), 56.

12. Sefton D. Temkin, *Isaac Mayer Wise*, 48.

13. Sefton D. Temkin, *Isaac Mayer Wise*, citing *The Occident* (March 1847), 50.

14. Naphtali J. Rubinger, "Dismissal in Albany," in *American Jewish Archives*, November 1972, 160–183.

15. Sefton D. Temkin, *Isaac Mayer Wise*, 52–53.

16.  Sefton D. Temkin, *Isaac Mayer Wise*, 54.

17.  Max B. May, *Isaac Mayer Wise*, 66.

18.  Sefton D. Temkin, *Isaac Mayer Wise*, 58–60.

## SEVEN: A FISTFIGHT IN ALBANY

1.  James William Hagy, *This Happy Land*, 257, 263

2.  Jonathan D. Sarna, *American Judaism*, 95.

3.  Sefton D. Temkin, *Isaac Mayer Wise*, 64.

4.  Eugene B. Borowitz, "What Do We Expect in the Messianic Age?" *Reform Judaism Magazine*, Spring 1999, 68–86.

5.  Leon Wieseltier, "A Passion for Waiting: Liberal Notes on Messianism and the Jews," in a privately published volume in honor of Daniel Bell. Thanks to the author for providing the text.

6.  Yitzhak F. Baer, "From the Ancient Faith to a New Historical Consciousness," excerpt from *Galut*, Robert Warshow, trans. (New York: Schocken Books, 1947), republished in Judah Goldin, ed., *The Jewish Expression* (New Haven and London: Yale University Press, 1976), 387–396.

7.  See David Biale, "Introduction: Israel Among the Nations," in *The Norton Anthology of World Religions*, vol. 2, Jack Miles, general ed. (New York and London: W. W. Norton & Co., 2015).

8.  Eugene B. Borowitz, "What Do We Expect in the Messianic Age?," 78.

9.  Jacob Katz, "Israel and the Messiah," in *Essential Papers on Messianic Movements and Personalities in Jewish History*, Marc Saperstein, ed. (New York: New York University Press, 1992).

10.  Eugene B. Borowitz, "The Messianic Age: A Reform Perspective," 82.

11.  Isaac M. Wise, *Reminiscences*, 141–152.

12.  James William Hagy, *This Happy Land*, 267–8.

13.  Max B. May, *Isaac Mayer Wise*, 100.

14.  Sefton D. Temkin, *Isaac Mayer Wise*, 68.

15.  Sefton D. Temkin, Isaac Mayer Wise, 71.

16.  Naphtali J. Rubinger, "Dismissal in Albany," 166–167.

17.  Naphtali J. Rubinger, "Dismissal in Albany," 168.

18.  Isaac M. Wise, *Reminiscences*, 161.

19.  Naphtali J. Rubinger, "Dismissal in Albany," 171–172

20.  Naphtali J. Rubinger, "Dismissal in Albany," 176.

21.  David Philipson and Louis Grossmann, eds., *Selected Writings of Isaac M. Wise with a Biography by the Editors* (Cincinnati: Robert Clarke Co., published

under the auspices of the Alumnal Association of the Hebrew Union College, 1900), 38.

22. Naphtali J. Rubinger, "Dismissal in Albany," 178.

23. Isaac M. Wise, *Reminiscences*, 165.

24. Isaac M. Wise, *Reminiscences*, 166–167.

25. Sefton D. Temkin, *Isaac Mayer Wise*, 73.

26. Sefton D. Temkin, *Isaac Mayer Wise*, 74.

## EIGHT: THE "TWO ISAACS"

1. Leon A. Jick, *Americanization of the Synagogue*, 59.

2. Jonathan D. Sarna, *American Judaism*, 102.

3. Marc Lee Raphael, *The Synagogue in America*, 34.

4. Lance J. Sussman, *Isaac Leeser and The Making of American Judaism* (Detroit: Wayne State University Press., 1995), 253.

5. Michael A. Meyer, *Response to Modernity*, 235.

6. Lance J. Sussman, *Isaac Leeser*, 173–176.

7. James G. Heller, *Isaac M. Wise*, 107.

8. Lance J. Sussman, *Isaac Leeser*, 168–169.

9. James G. Heller, *Isaac M. Wise*, 197–199.

10. James G. Heller, *Isaac M. Wise*, 218–20.

11. Michael A. Meyer, *Response to Modernity*, 230–242.

12. Sefton D. Temkin, *Isaac Mayer Wise*, 102.

13. Michael A. Meyer, *Response to Modernity*, 244–245.

14. Sefton D. Temkin, *Isaac Mayer Wise*, 137.

15. Michael A. Meyer, *Response to Modernity*, 248–252.

16. Sefton D. Temkin, Isaac Mayer Wise, 140–141.

17. Sefton D. Temkin, *Isaac Mayer Wise*, 142 (citing *The Occident*, December 1855, 429).

18. Sefton D. Temkin, *Isaac Mayer Wise*, 142–147.

19. Michael A. Meyer, *Response to Modernity*, 255.

20. Stephen Prothero, *American Jesus: How the Son of God Became a National Icon* (New York: Farrar, Straus and Giroux, 2004).

21. Sefton D. Temkin, *Isaac Mayer Wise*, 205.

22. Allan Tarshish, "The Charleston Organ Case," *American Jewish Historical Quarterly*, 446–448.

23. Lee C. Harby, "Penina Moïse: Woman and Writer," American Jewish

Committee Archives; http://www.ajcarchives.org/AJC_DATA/Files/1905 _1906_3_Biographies.pdf (accessed July 21, 2016).

## NINE: JEWS IN THE CIVIL WAR

1.  Eli N. Evans, "Overview: The War Between Jewish Brothers in America," in Jonathan Sarna and Adam Mendelsohn, eds., *Jews and the Civil War: A Reader* (New York and London: New York University Press, 2010), 27. See also Harold Holzer, *Lincoln and the Jews: The Last Best Hope of Earth* (Los Angeles: The Skirball Cultural Center, 2002), 3.

2.  Jonathan D. Sarna, *American Judaism*, 113–114.

3.  Bertram Korn, *American Jewry and the Civil War*, 49.

4.  Jonathan D. Sarna, *American Judaism*, 116–124.

5.  Gary L. Bunker and John J. Appel, "'Shoddy' Antisemitism and the Civil War," in Jonathan D. Sarna and Adam Mendelsohn, eds., *Jews and the Civil War*, 311 ff.

6.  Stephen V. Ash, "Civil War Exodus," in Jonathan D. Sarna and Adam Mendelsohn, eds., *Jews and the Civil War*, 368. See also John Simon, "That Obnoxious Order," Jonathan D. Sarna and Adam Mendelsohn, eds., *Jews and the Civil War*, 353–384.

7.  Jonathan D. Sarna, *American Judaism*, 121.

8.  Eli N. Evans, "Overview: The War Between Jewish Brothers in America," in Jonathan Sarna and Adam Mendelsohn, eds., *Jews and the Civil War*, 44. See also Joakim Isaacs, "Candidate Grant and the Jews," in Jonathan D. Sarna and Adam Mendelsohn, eds., *Jews and the Civil War*, 409.

9.  Bertram Korn, "Jews and Negro Slavery in the Old South, 1789–1865," in Jonathan D. Sarna and Adam Mendelsohn, eds., *Jews and the Civil War*, 117.

10.  Robert N. Rosen, "Jewish Confederates," in Jonathan D. Sarna and Adam Mendelsohn, eds., *Jews and the Civil War*, 232–234.

11.  Harold Holzer, *Lincoln and the Jews*, 4.

12.  Hasia R. Diner, *A Time for Gathering*, 176.

13.  Eli N. Evans, "Overview," Jonathan D. Sarna and Adam Mendelsohn, eds., *Jews and the Civil War*, 37.

14.  Eli N. Evans, *Judah P. Benjamin: The Jewish Confederate* (New York: Free Press, 1988), 32–33.

15.  Eli N. Evans, *Judah P. Benjamin*, xvi–xix.

16. Seymour Drescher, "Jews and New Christians in the Atlantic Slave Trade," in Jonathan D. Sarna and Adam Mendelsohn, *Jews and the Civil War*, 67.

17. Bertram W. Korn, "Revolution and Reform: The Antebellum Jewish Abolitionists," Jonathan D. Sarna and Adam Mendelsohn, *Jews and the Civil War*, 110.

18. Bertram W. Korn, *American Jewry and the Civil War* (New York: Meridian Books; World Publishing Company and Jewish Publication Society of America, new edition 1961), 15.

19. Louis Ruchames, "The Abolitionists and the Jews: Some Further Thoughts," in Jonathan D. Sarna and Adam Mendelsohn, *Jews and the Civil War*, 149.

20. Jonathan D. Sarna, *American Judaism*, 116.

21. Bertram Korn, *American Jewry and the Civil War*, 35–39.

22. Jayme A. Sokolow, "Revolution and Reform: The Antebellum Jewish Abolitionists," Jonathan D. Sarna and Adam Mendelsohn, eds., *Jews and the Civil War*, 135–140.

23. Bertram Korn, *American Jewry and the Civil War*, 41.

24. Bertram Korn, *American Jewry and the Civil War*, 44–46.

25. Howard B. Rock, "Upheaval, Innovation, and Transformation: New York City Jews and the Civil War," *American Jewish Archives Journal*, vol. LXIV (2012). nos. 1 and 2.

26. M.J. Raphall, "The Bible View of Slavery," January 15, 1861, published by Jewish–American Historical Society: http://www.jewish-history.com/civil war/raphall.html.

27. Michael Heilprin, "Michael Heilprin's Anti-Slavery Editorial" Jewish-American History Foundation; http://www.jewish-history.com/civilwar/heilprin.html.

28. David Einhorn, "David Einhorn's Response to 'A Biblical View of Slavery,'" Jewish American History Foundation, trans. from the German, in "Sinai," vol. VI, 2–22, Baltimore, 1861, by Mrs. Kaufmann Kohler; http://www.jewish -history.com/civilwar/einhorn.html (accessed December 16, 2016).

29. Isaac M. Fein, "Baltimore Rabbis During the Civil War," Jonathan D. Sarna and Adam Mendelsohn, eds., *Jews and the Civil War*, 183–189.

30. David Herbert Donald, *Lincoln* (New York: Simon & Schuster, 1995), 565–567.

31. Gary Phillip Zola, ed., *We Called Him Rabbi Abraham: Lincoln and American Jewry—A Documentary History* (Carbondale: Southern Illinois University Press, 2014), 147–226.

32. Eli N. Evans, "Overview: The War Between Jewish Brothers in America," in Jonathan D. Sarna and Adam Mendelsohn, eds., *Jews and the Civil War:*

*A Reader*, 42. See also Bertram W. Korn, *American Jewry and the Civil War* (Meridian Books; World Publishing Company and Jewish Publication Society of America, new edition 1961).

33. Adam Mendelsohn, "Introduction: Before Korn: A Century of Jewish Historical Writing About the Civil War," Jonathan D. Sarna and Adam Mendelsohn, *Jews and the Civil War,* 18.

34. Adam Mendelsohn, "Introduction," Jonathan D. Sarna and Adam Mendelsohn, eds., *Jews and the Civil War,* 8–9.

## TEN: PROSPER AND DIVIDE

1. Leon A. Jick, *Americanization of the Synagogue,* 140–143 and 179.
2. Leon A. Jick, *Americanization of the Synagogue,* 154–155.
3. Abraham J. Karp, *Haven and Home,* 85–86.
4. Hasia R. Diner, *A Time for Gathering,* 117.
5. Leon A. Jick, *Americanization of the Synagogue,* 115.
6. Alan Silverstein, *Alternatives to Assimilation,* 23–24.
7. Jonathan D. Sarna, "The Debate Over Mixed Seating in the American Synagogue," in Jack Wertheimer, ed., *The American Synagogue,* 363–369.
8. Jonathan D. Sarna, "The Debate Over Mixed Seating in the American Synagogue," in Jack Wertheimer, ed., *The American Synagogue,* 363–394. The account and quotations in this section are drawn from this article.
9. Marc Lee Raphael, *The Synagogue in America,* 38–39.
10. Michael A. Meyer, *Response to Modernity,* 226–227.
11. Hasia R. Diner, *A Time for Gathering,* 230.
12. Jonathan D. Sarna, *American Judaism,* 129.
13. Alan Silverstein, *Alternatives to Assimilation,* 20.
14. Michael A. Meyer, *Response to Modernity,* 252.

## ELEVEN: REFORMISTS AND RADICALS

1. Michael A. Meyer, *Response to Modernity,* 243.
2. "Reform Judaism: Declaration of Principles: 1869 Philadelphia Conference," Zionism and Israel Information Center; http://www.zionism-israel.com /hdoc/Philadelphia_Conference_1869.htm.
3. Michael A. Meyer, *Response to Modernity,* 255–258.
4. Sefton D. Temkin, *Isaac Mayer Wise,* 218.
5. Michael A. Meyer, *Response to Modernity,* 259.
6. Sefton D. Temkin, *Isaac Mayer Wise,* 243–245.

7. Michael A. Meyer, *Response to Modernity*, 259.

8. Michael A. Meyer, *Response to Modernity*, 263.

9. Sefton D. Temkin, *Isaac Mayer Wise*, 227.

10. "Illustrated History of 1867 Synagogue," Jewish Historical Society of Greater Washington, "Lillian and Albert Small Jewish Museum," https://www.jhsgw .org/history/synagogue (accessed August 1, 2017).

11. Ralph Waldo Emerson, "Remarks at Organization of Free Religious Association, Boston, May 30, 1867," *The Complete Works*, 1904, vol. XI, Miscellanies, XXVII, http://www.bartleby.com/90/1127.html (accessed August 10, 2017).

12. John Morton Blum et al., *The National Experience*, 251. See also Sydney E. Ahlstrom, *A Religious History of the American People*, 579.

13. Sydney E. Ahlstrom, *A Religious History*, 767.

14. Leon A. Jick, *The Americanization of the Synagogue*, 133.

15. Benny Kraut, *From Reform Judaism to Ethical Culture: The Religious Evolution of Felix Adler* (Cincinnati: Hebrew Union College Press, 1979), 1–168.

16. Benny Kraut, *From Reform Judaism to Ethical Culture*, 18.

17. Benny Kraut, *From Reform Judaism to Ethical Culture*, 56, 74, 78, 85.

18. Michael A. Meyer, *Response to Modernity*, 266.

## TWELVE: THE TREFA BANQUET

1. Lance J. Sussman, "The Myth of the Trefa Banquet: American Culinary Culture and the Radicalization of Food Policy in American Reform Judaism," *American Jewish Archives Journal*, vol. 57 (2005), nos. 1–2, http://american jewisharchives.org/publications/journal/PDF/2005_57_01_02_sussman. pdf (accessed August 9, 2017).

2. John J. Appel, "The Trefa Banquet," *Commentary*, February 1, 1966, https:// www.commentarymagazine.com/articles/the-trefa-banquet/ (accessed August 9, 2017).

3. Matthew LaGrone, "Disagreement and Denominationalism: The Kohut-Kohler Debate of 1885," *Conservative Judaism*, vol. 64 (Summer 2013), no. 4, 71–89.

4. Jonathan D. Sarna, *American Judaism*, 135.

5. Elias Bickerman, "The Maccabean Uprising: An Interpretation," trans. from the German by Krishna Winston (Berlin: Schocken Books, 1937), republished in Judah Goldin, ed., *The Jewish Expression*, 80–81.

6. Jonathan D. Sarna, *American Judaism*, 136.

7.  Jonathan D. Sarna, *American Judaism*, 136.

8.  Isidore Singer, George Alexander, Cyrus Adler "Alexander Kohut," *Jewish Encyclopedia*, 1906 (accessed May 28, 2017; http://www.jewishencyclopedia .com/articles/9436-kohut-alexander).

9.  Jonathan D. Sarna, *American Judaism*, 147.

10. Matthew LaGrone, "Disagreement and Denominationalism: The Kohut-Kohler Debate of 1885," *Conservative Judaism*, vol. 64 (Summer 2013), no. 4, 72.

11. Michael A. Meyer, *Response to Modernity*, 267.

12. Abraham Leon Sachar, *A History of the Jews* (New York: Alfred A. Knopf, 1968), 162 ff.

13. Matthew LaGrone, "Disagreement and Denominationalism: The Kohut-Kohler Debate of 1885," *Conservative Judaism*, 77–79.

14. Cyrus Adler, "Kaufmann Kohler" in *Jewish Encyclopedia*, http://jewishen cyclopedia.com/articles/9419-kohler-kaufmann (accessed February 11, 2017).

15. Jonathan D. Sarna, *American Judaism*, 147.

16. Michael A. Meyer, *Response to Modernity*, 271.

17. Michael A. Meyer, *Response to Modernity*, 273.

18. Sydney E. Ahlstrom, *Religious History of the American People*, 763–765.

19. Matthew LaGrone, "Disagreement and Denominationalism," *Conservative Judaism*, 75–82.

20. Benny Kraut, *From Reform Judaism*, 156, 158, 160.

## THIRTEEN: NEW DIVISIONS

1.  Jonathan D. Sarna, *American Judaism*, 148.

2.  W. Gunther Plaut, "The Pittsburgh Platform in the Light of European Antecedents," in Walter Jacob, ed., *The Pittsburgh Platform in Retrospect* (Pittsburgh: Rodef Shalom Congregation Press, 1985), 18.

3.  Kaufmann Kohler, *Hebrew Union College and Other Addresses* (Cincinnati: Ark Publishing Co., 1916), 67 ff.

4.  Michael A. Meyer, *Response to Modernity*, 245.

5.  Jonathan D. Sarna, *American Judaism*, 148–149.

6.  "The Pittsburgh Platform," in Michael Meyer, *Response to Modernity*, appendix, 387–388.

7.  W. Gunther Plaut, "The Pittsburgh Platform in the Light of European Antecedents," in Walter Jacob, ed., *The Pittsburgh Platform in Retrospect*, 19–21.

8. Samuel E. Karff, "The Theology of the Pittsburgh Platform," in Walter Jacob, ed., *The Pittsburgh Platform in Retrospect*, 76 ff.

9. Sefton D. Temkin, *Isaac Mayer Wise*, 293.

10. Irving Howe, *World of Our Fathers: The Journey of the East European Jews to America and the Life They Found and Made* (New York: Simon & Schuster, 1976), 5.

11. Howard M. Sachar, *A History of the Jews in the Modern World* (New York: Alfred A. Knopf, 2005), 197 ff.

12. Sefton D. Temkin, *Isaac Mayer Wise*, 295–296.

13. Jeffrey S. Gurock, "Resisters and Accommodators: Varieties of Orthodox Rabbis in America, 1886–1983," *American Jewish Archives*, November 1983 (100–187), 105.

14. Abraham J. Karp, *Haven and Home*, 96.

15. Jeffrey S. Gurock, "Resisters and Accommodators," *American Jewish Archives* (November 1983), 108.

16. Quoted in Michael R. Cohen, *The Birth of Conservative Judaism: Solomon Schechter's Disciples and the Creation of an American Religious Movement* (New York: Columbia University Press, 2012), 3.

17. Michael A. Meyer, *Response to Modernity*, 276–287.

18. Nathan Glazer, *American Judaism*, 139.

19. Michael A. Meyer, *Response to Modernity*, 293–295.

20. See "The Guiding Principles of Reform Judaism," "The Columbus Platform" of 1937; Central Conference of American Rabbis, website: https://www.ccarnet.org/rabbis-speak/platforms/guiding-principles-reform-judaism/.

21. "Reform Judaism: A Centenary Perspective; Adopted in San Francisco—1976," https://ccarnet.org/rabbis-speak/platforms/reform-judaism-centenary-perspective/.

22. "A Statement of Principles for Reform Judaism; Adopted at the 1999 Pittsburgh Convention Central Conference of American Rabbis, May 1999," https://ccarnet.org/rabbis-speak/platforms/statement-principles-reform-judaism/.

## EPILOGUE: AN AMERICAN RELIGION

1. Jonathan D. Sarna, *American Judaism*, 66.

2. Hasia R. Diner, *A Time for Gathering*, 122.

3. Hasia R. Diner, *A Time for Gathering*, 178–181. See also Saul Jay Singer,

"Longfellow and the Jewish Cemetery at Newport," in *Jewish Press,* July 21, 2016.

4.  Goldin, Judah. Introductory essay to *The Jewish Expression* (New Haven and London: Yale University Press, 1976), xxi.

5.  Melvin Konner, *Unsettled: An Anthropology of the Jews* (New York: Penguin Group, 2003), 318 ff.

6.  "A Portrait of Jewish Americans," released October 1, 2013, Pew Research Center on Religion and Public Life. The survey was conducted on landlines and cellphones among 3,475 Jews across the country from February 20 to June 13, 2013, with a statistical margin of error for the full Jewish sample of plus or minus 3.0 percentage points: http://www.pewforum.org/2013/10/01/jewish-american-beliefs-attitudes-culture-survey/. Additional material: Alan Cooperman, director of Religion Research, Pew Research Center, "L'Dor Vador: A Generational Perspective on Jewish Life and Broader Trends in American Religion," a presentation to the Jewish leadership of Cincinnati, June 8, 2017. Thanks to Alan Cooperman for sharing PowerPoint presentation.

7.  Quoted in Nathan Glazer, *American Judaism*, 186.

# Illustration Credits

Exhibit at the Museum of the City of New York: 1

Courtesy of Touro Synagogue: 2

Courtesy of Congregation Shearith Israel, New York: 3

Courtesy of Congregation Mickve Israel, Savannah, Georgia: 4

Painting by Solomon N. Carvalho. Courtesy of Special Collections, College of Charleston Libraries: 5

Library of Congress: 6, 10, 15, 17, 19, 22

The Jacob Rader Marcus Center, American Jewish Archives, Hebrew Union College-Jewish Institute of Religion: 7, 9, 12, 14, 16, 20, 26, 27

Jewish Encyclopedia: 8

Everett Collection Inc / Alamy Stock Photo: 11

Painting by Thomas Sully, Courtesy of The Rosenbach of the Free Library of Philadelphia: 13

Attributed to Theodore Sidney Moïse, ca. 1840; Collection of Anita Moïse Rosefield Rosenberg. Courtesy of Special Collections, College of Charleston Libraries: 18

New York Society for Ethical Culture: 21

Wikimedia Commons: 23, 24

Frontispiece of *Semitic Studies in memory of Dr. Alexander Kohut,* Berlin 1897: 25

# Index

INDEX

# About the Author

STEVEN R. WEISMAN, vice president for publications and communications at the Peterson Institute for International Economics (PIIE), previously served as a correspondent based in Washington, D.C.; New Delhi; and Tokyo for *The New York Times*. He was also an editor and editorial writer at that paper. His book *The Great Tax Wars* received the Sidney Hillman Award in 2003.